Latinas on Stage

Latinas on Stage

edited by

Alicia Arrizón
and
Lillian Manzor

Series in Chicana/Latina Studies

Third Woman Press
Berkeley

Manufactured in the United States of America.

Typeset by Berkeley Hills Books, Berkeley, CA.
Printed and bound by McNaughton & Gunn, Saline, MI.

Cover art: Dyan Garza, *Latinas on Stage*

First printing 2000
10 9 8 7 6 5 4 3 2 1

Library of Congress Cataloging-in-Publication Data
Latinas on stage: practice and theory/ edited by Alicia Arrizón and Lillian Manzor.
    p.cm.-- (Series in Chicana/Latina Studies)
  ISBN 0-943219-17-5
    1. American drama--Hispanic American authors--History and criticism. 2. American drama--Women authors
History and criticism. 3. American drama--Hispanic American authors. 4. Hispanic American women in literature. 5. Performance art--United States. 6. Hispanic American women--Drama. 7. American drama--Women authors. I. Arrizón, Alicia. II Manzor, Lillian. III. Series.
PS 153.H56 L38 2000
812.009'9287'08968--dc21   CIP 00-037761

ACKNOWLEDGMENTS

The idea for *Latinas on Stage* originated at a gathering with Norma Alarcón several years ago when she invited us to be co-editors of this book. We need to thank her for bringing us together. For both of us, the completion of this book has been a learning and challenging experience. Our academic interests and our love for the theater arts consolidated our friendship and offered us the opportunity to become friends with other Latina theater practitioners. We also need to thank all the contributors. Clearly, this book would not have been possible without their participation, suggestions, and patience.

We want to express our gratitude to Catherine Watt, copy editor of the galleys, and to the great support of Maria Anna González. Special appreciation is offered to the University of California Humanities Research Institute at the University of California, Irvine, where Lillian Manzor was in residence with Norma Alarcón (1991–1992), the first year of the Minority Discourse Initiative; and to the Chicano Studies Research Center and the Institute of the American Cultures at the University of California, Los Angeles, where Alicia Arrizón was a visiting scholar (1994–1995).

Most importantly, we thank our colleagues and respective institutions, University of California Irvine and Riverside, for their intellectual and financial support. Grants from the Affirmative Action Career Development Award, U.C. Mexus Chicana/Chicano Studies Award, the Ernesto Galarza Public Policy, and Humanities Research Institute (UC Riverside), and the Organized Research Initiative for the Study of Hispanic and Latino Theaters, SCR 43 Chicano/Latino Studies, and Focused Research Initiative on Woman and the Image (UC Irvine), have contributed to the completion of this book, The University of Miami Department of Foreign Languages and Literatures also provided the infrastructure for the coast-to-coast communication during the last stages of the book's production.

Contents

Interviews

Criticism

Introduction

Latinas on Stage is an attempt to define, in practice and theory, a Latina theatrical aesthetics in the United States. Our goal is to construct a space in which Latina playwrights, performance artists, and directors can enter into dialogue with performance theorists and historians. This dialogue is rhetorical as much as it is structural; that is, it frames the organization of our material. The book opens with the plays and performance texts themselves. It closes with critical readings, which present a narrative beginning with a historical grounding of Latinas' work on the U.S. stage. This section continues with comparative readings of contemporary Latina theater and performance art, and concludes with transnational perspectives, which move the Latina subject beyond the borders of the U.S. stage, both theoretically and in practice. The interviews in the middle section serve as articulations where the artists address not only the aesthetic elements of their work but also their views on performance and its vital role for our communities.

Integral to these articulations is a redefinition of Latina identity as a site of cultural and political contestation, and performance's role in that redefinition. In choosing theater and performance, we are not suggesting a one-to-one correspondence between performance and processes of identity formation or between performance and social change, between representation and the real. Performance appropriates mechanisms of cultural mediation, which go beyond the stage. The feminist transformations of La Llorona and Afro-Caribbean religious imagery, the reenactment of internal racism and homophobia between different Latino communities, or the need to address the rising menace of AIDS, for example, are all part and parcel of daily life in Latina/o social and political ensembles as well as the representation of that life in Latina theater. Performance, however, is a cultural production that displays its own organizational ensemble as a style of metarepresentation, as representation about representation. Metarepresentation, as a device, allows us to see and read how representation functions both within performance and within a sociohistorical context. Performance, then, provides the space for "seeing" processes of social change. And talking about performance allows us to address those processes in a keenly theoretical fashion.

While the term *Latina/o* is a much contested one, we use it deliberately, preferring it to *Hispanic*. In principle, both *Latina/o* and *Hispanic* refer to people of Latin American descent living primarily within the United States. As such, neither term is appropriately a racial category. Although some may argue that race and ethnicity are not collapsible categories, in the United States these two usually have been deployed interchangeably.[1] The constructed nature of both race and ethnicity is nowhere more evident than in the legal use of generic racial and ethnic terms on application forms and as census categories after the implementation of the Civil Rights Act of 1964.

Since the reference point for this legislation was the African American community, "race" and "color" were the operable terms of the 1964 Act. Indeed, as LatCrit theorists have studied,[2] Latina/o invisibility and subordination in the U.S. is a result of the Black/White paradigm in U.S. law and culture: "the conception that race in America consists, either exclusively or primarily, of only two constituent racial groups, the Black and the white."[3]

The translation of the white versus black binarism into the "Hispanic" experience gave rise to baffling racial categories such as "Spanish surname," "white not of Spanish descent" and "black not of Spanish descent." These categories not only underscore the confusion and misunderstanding about this heterogeneous group. They also demonstrate that, as a group, we are not "Black enough" for the civil rights model, and we are not "white enough" for the immigration model. Indeed, as Rachel Moran has studied, "Latinas/os are served by neither model for different reasons: the civil rights model was designed to redress the nation's era of institutionalized slavery and its aftermath while the immigration model was designed primarily to assimilate white ethnic arrivals from northern and western Europe."[4]

In spite of the fact that many "Hispanics" do not share racial or ethnic characteristics, they have been racialized in a homogeneous fashion in the United States. In other words, "Hispanic" is a constructed racial category that underscores the racialization of a specific group considered "ethnically" or "racially" differ-

ent *regardless* of its racial composition. For Latinas/os, as we have
begun to suggest, "race," "color," and "ethnicity" are highly problematic. Given that the history of race and ethnicity in Latin
America is much more complex, the resulting racial categories
are more flexible and fluid than in the United States. It seems
that strong United States anti-miscegenation laws and a racial
narrative based on a notion of "racial purity" eventually resulted
in a society in which people are categorized along a white versus nonwhite axis, where nonwhite is almost always coded
"black," as demonstrated by the civil rights legislation and recent LatCrit theory. In Latin America, however, *mestizo* societies are the product of constant miscegenation. The mixture of
white, black, and Indian, and the coexistence of many indigenous languages and cultural practices have resulted in a *mestizaje*
characterized by a cultural heterogeneity that surpasses the narrative of racial purity.

The term *Hispanic*, then, is dismissed because of its bureau-
cratic conventionalism: it is, after all, a label imposed by U.S.
government agencies. It also connotes a cultural heritage that,
by privileging the Spanish or European legacy, censors the
mestizaje of these groups. Moreover, its Spanish equivalent:
Hispano, is the term preferred by a group in the U.S. Southwest
who identifies with the Spanish settlers of the area and not with
the Mexican settlers. Within the politics of naming, *Latino* is a
term that emerges from within the community. Most importantly,
this name has been chosen in Spanish, defying prevalent cultural repression: English-only environment and laws.

It may seem contradictory to resist *Hispanic* because of its
Spanish connection, that is, the legacy of colonization and conquest, and at the same time adopt *Latina/o,* precisely a Spanish
term. This contradiction is a result of our use of the ex-master's
tools, which have now become our own. Most importantly, we
are using them now to try to dismantle the "house" of a new
master.[5] After all, Latinos in the United States are both
postcolonial and neocolonial subjects: post-Spanish colonialism
and neo-U.S. colonialism. Thus Latina/o identity in the United
States is the product of a creative process of understanding the
self in relation to paradoxes and contradictions caused by conquest, annexation, and migration. Finally, *Latino* allows for the
linguistic gender inflection, *Latina.* By using the term *Latina,*

then, we are consciously distinguishing between male and female constructions of racialized group identity. For us, *Latina* invokes the complexities and heterogeneity of identity, a construction which stresses the plural nature of this group.

Latina theater is also a complex and heterogeneous field. It replicates the intersectionality of Latinas as women of color in United States society.[6] As Latinas, we are situated within different hierarchies of social power and discourse. We share a political identity "not because [we] constitute a homogeneous group, but because, as a political construct, [we] represent a shared context of struggle based on [our] individual experiences at the intersection of multiple practices of oppression and identity formation."[7] Latina performance, in turn, is situated between ethnic and Anglo women's performances. Precisely because of this in-between position, its development has not been recognized by scholarly and journalistic studies.

This book is a response to the significant number of Latinas doing theater and performance, and the lack of available documentation. The publication of Latina dramatic works, both by individual artists and in collective anthologies, is minimal, thus making its study, teaching, and dissemination very difficult. Unlike poetry or prose, performance and theater are meant to go beyond the written text. It is a collective endeavor which requires at least a physical space. Until very recently, Latinas have had very little access to this space. Latino community theaters such as Teatro de La Esperanza, Teatro Campesino, Centro su Teatro, Pregones, Puerto Rican Traveling Theater, Teatro Avante, and Prometeo, just to mention a few, provided an alternative to mainstream theatrical institutions. These groups, however, were driven by a cultural nationalism, which also "led to the reinscription of the heterosexual hierarchization of male/female relationships."[8] Women's resistance to this was evident at least as early as 1978, with the establishment of W.I.T. (Women in Theater) by women of TENAZ (Teatro Nacional de Aztlán). This focused group effectively provided a space to question the role of women in the organization and advocated for more women producers, directors, and dramatists and for stronger female characterizations.[9]

While Latina performance is deeply rooted within cultural values and traditions, it critiques the repressive, patriarchal elements of that tradition. Like Gloria Anzaldúa's new mestiza, Latinas take inventory of their history and attempt to break with oppressive traditions of all cultures and religions. Latina theater stages this rupture and communicates this struggle.[10] Among the most representative of Latina dramatists are: Astor del Valle, Denise Chávez, Theresa Chávez, Migdalia Cruz, Evelina Fernández, Amparo García, Lisa Loomer, Josefina López, María Mar, Estela Portillo-Trambley, Dolores Prida, Yvette Ramírez, Carmen Rivera, Yolanda Rodríguez, Milcha Sánchez-Scott, Diana Sáenz, Lynnette Serrano Bonaparte, Ana María Simo, Caridad Svich, Silviana Wood and many others. It must be noted that Laura Esparza, María Irene Fornes, Alicia Mena, Cherríe Moraga, and Edit Villareal have distinguished themselves as both dramatists and directors.

Some of the most recurrent features in these dramatists' work include: 1) the use of oral tradition to tell her story. In these plays, oral tradition does not present the past as nostalgia; rather, it is used to revisit the past while carrying out a feminist critique of culture; 2) the dismantling of stereotypes of womanhood and sexual taboos. This breakdown "denaturalizes" the traditional roles of women by inscribing and subverting the hitherto negative stereotypes of la Llorona, la Malinche, la Chingada, la tortillera, la puta, and la vendida; 3) the use of fragmentation and nonchronological structures in the development of dramatic action; 4) the use of escapism, which distances the female subject from a male-centered world. These features contribute to the creation of an alternative space, open to experimentation, in which traditional constructs of Latina identity are subverted. Most importantly, the Latina characters are placed in the position of subject as they articulate their identity through a process of self-definition and self-determination in both the public and private spheres.[11]

Because of this critique and rearticulation of identity, Latina performance was, almost by default, left out of male-dominated ethnic theatrical circles. Thus Latinas began to explore other staging possibilities. In search of new spaces, Latinas began to be staged in alternative venues which are now well-known locations. These alternative spaces were primarily Anglo-feminist and/or lesbian spaces, such as At the Foot of the Mountain and The Front Room Theater, in which the first two stage readings of *Giving Up the Ghost* were produced in 1984 and 1986, respectively, or the W.O.W. Cafe, which produced Carmelita Tropicana's *Memorias de la revolución* in 1984.

The search for new spaces also contributed to the emergence of other representational strategies, namely, performance art. It is not by chance that Latinas such as Elia Arce, Nao Bustamante, Coatlicue/Las Colorado, Laura Esparza, Coco Fusco, Guadalupe García Vásquez, Marga Gómez, Monica Palacios, Merián Soto, Carmen Tafolla, and Carmelita Tropicana have chosen to work in this genre. Performance art is a hybrid form, insofar as it borrows not only from the fields of visual culture, such as theater, painting, and video art, but also from dance and music. Some situate performance art within the tradition of women's alternative performance practices, from the women mimes of Greece and Rome to the salons of Varnhagen and Barney.[12] It is considered an alternative practice in that it resists a representational system in which the female body is made a spectacle. As Diana Taylor has remarked, performance art "rechaza la institucionalización del teatro e intenta subvertir un sistema de representaciones acusado de ser cómplice de un sistema social represivo" (it rejects the institutionalization of theater and tries to subvert a representational system accused of being an accomplice of a repressive social system).[13] Jeanie Forte sees performance art more specifically as the postmodern genre most capable of radically intervening in "patriarchal culture."[14]

In feminist performance art, the role of the artist is that of the representer of herself, "her body as text, herself as character or costume, her own movement as symbolic of the gestures and rituals of everyday life."[15] Most critics and theorists of performance art rightfully underscore performance's foregrounding of the personal as well as of the role of the body as text. Given this double emphasis, it is surprising that feminist critics have overlooked the work of Latina performance artists as well as the work of other "women of color" in performance art. It is precisely the possibilities that performance art offers the "woman of color" artist to utilize her gendered and racialized body as metaphor, in order to intervene in the system of representation, that make it an attractive medium to her. The "woman of color" performance artist uses her body as script not only "to foreground the genderization of culture," as Jeanie Forte would have it, but, even more, to foreground the racialized genderization of culture.[16] Latina performance artists enter the scene of representation not as an otherwise absent or objectified other but as speaking subject, transgressive and dynamic.

Since the performance artist functions as a representer of herself, the sexual, racial, and class relations that mark the power structures of social performance and shape Latinas' roles are going to be rescripted in performance art. The Latina artist assumes and attacks these roles in a multilayered fashion; for her, gendered and sexualized roles are inseparable from racial and ethnic ones. In so doing, her performance underscores "el proceso mismo de teatralización social... para fines que van más allá de lo estético" (the very process of social theatricality... for aims that go beyond purely aesthetic ones).[17]

The ontology of performance is, of course, the present. It exists insofar as it knows itself to be a representation without reproduction. Peggy Phelan has correctly remarked that "performance's being... becomes itself through disappearance."[18] While Phelan's analysis of the ontology of performance is useful, the analogy to the ontology of subjectivity she proposes—a subjectivity through disappearance via the aims of metonymical representation—is not as generalizable as she would have it. Phelan suggests that "in moving from the grammar of words to the grammar of the body, one moves from the realm of metaphor to the realm of metonymy."[19] Yet the Latina performance artist, for example, cannot move from one grammar to another so easily. Given that words and language carry both literal and figurative accents, which the performance conveys in turn, this grammar forcefully marks a polylingual divided "self," whose "accents" are generally read as a natural sign of "otherness." These signs, when read as the grammar of a body, or an embodied grammar, depict that body as speaking "with an accent." It is precisely the "accents" of that embodied grammar which preclude the easy move from metaphor to metonymy. These "accents" are traces of the fact that in this signifying chain, like in metaphor, meaning surges a priori to the subject while it marks, as in metonymy, the essential function of lack within the signifying chain.

Given that the same system of representation that has constructed woman as spectacle has also constructed people of color, in general, as other, in this system, the woman of color specifically, becomes the ultimate spectacle of otherness. How she sees herself and how she will perform herself on stage is intricately connected to that spectacle, to how others see her and read her. In Latina performance art, then, the body cannot be, as Phelan has proposed, purely "metonymic of self, of character, of voice, of presence."[20] For Latinas, paradoxically, one part of the performer's "self" is always already an "other" for the spectators. Yet if, as Phelan suggests, "in the plenitude of its apparent visibility and availability," the performer actually disappears and represents something else, part of that "something else" for the Latina subject is, again, always already part of the "self."

Partially due to the vexed nature of what could be called polycultural performance, the question of reception and community for Latinas, in both theater and performance art, is a thorny one. While performance art is indeed "marginal" in relation to the theater and art establishments, it is nevertheless marginal *within* the mainstream and given spaces of power. Latinas have performed in spaces in New York City such as the A.I.R. Gallery, Performance Space 122, W.O.W., and the Whitney Museum; in Los Angeles in Highways, Contemporary Exhibitions (LACE), and Beyond Baroque; in San Francisco in Josie's Cabaret and the New Langton Arts Center, as well as in many university galleries and performance spaces which are somehow part of hegemonic Anglo culture. While they are paid little, and their engagements seldom last beyond two weeks, they are still not performing in those ethnic community spaces mentioned earlier. Those other performance spaces in-between the margin and the center echo their own polycultural divided positionality: neither Latin American nor Anglo, Third nor First world, feminist but not quite "American style." As they construct personal and political identities, the aims of metaphor and metonymy permit them to straddle, with oscillation, that unstable border between mainstream and margin.

These comments are not meant to be programmatic. At stake here is not whether we should (if we could) direct Latina/o artists to perform to an audience pre-established as "their community." Rather, the question of audience and venue makes visible the fact that this "community" is no longer stable or fixed along clearly definable national, class, sexual, or ethnic lines.

Consequently, in-between physical spaces might indeed be appropriate for the construction of new theater-going communities and future transformation of the social body. Borrowing from Latino, Third World, and Anglo-European cultural traditions, their works critique concepts of time and space as well as patriarchal, heterosexist, nationalistic, and ethnocentric cultural values held dear by both the Anglo art establishment and by the older Latino community. Most importantly, they rely upon strategies of fragmentation and disruption with tools, images, and references collected from their multiple dis- and re-locations.

This anthology is deeply rooted in the context of cultural studies and feminist criticism. Its interdisciplinary character responds to the nature of the field itself. We hope that this work is only the beginning of a dialogue between academics and community artists as well as among the fields of Ethnic Studies, Women's Studies, American Studies, Performance Studies and Latin American Studies. This book, then, repositions Latina theater, its practice and theory, from the margins to the center of the performing and academic stage.

Alicia Arrizón
Lillian Manzor

Notes

1. For an analysis of the limitations of "race" in the Latina/o context see Juan Perea, "Five Axioms in Search of Equality," *Harvard Latino Law Review* (1997): 230–264. For an analysis of the usefulness of "race" and "ethnicity" in the Latina/o context see Ian F. Haney López, "Retaining Race: LatCrit Theory and Mexican American Identity in Hernandez v. Texas," *Harvard Latino Law Review* (1997): 278–300, and "The Social Construction of Race: Some Observations on Illusion, Fabrication and Choice," *Harvard Civil Rights Civil Liberties Law Review* (1994): 29–40. We thank LatCrit scholar Elizabeth M. Iglesias for bringing these LatCrit articles to our attention.
2. LatCrit theory has heen defined as "the emerging field of legal scholarship that examines critically the social and legal positioning of Latinas/os, especially Latinas/os in the United States, to help rectify the shortcomings of existing social and legal conditions." Francisco Valdés, "Under Construction: LatCrit Consciousness, Community, and Theory,"

California Law Review (1997): 1089. For other LatCrit studies see the following symposia publications: Colloquium, "Representing Latina/o Communities: Critical Race Theory and Practice," *La Raza Law Journal* (1996); Symposium, "LatCrit Theory: Latinas/os and the Law," *California Law Review* (1997); Symposium, "LatCrit Theory: Naming and Launching a New discourse of Critical Legal Scholarship," *Harvard Latino Law Review* (1997).

3. Juan F. Perea, "The Black/White Binary Paradigm of Race: The 'Normal Science' of American Racial Thought," *California Law Review* (1997): 1219.

4. Rachel Moran, "Neither Black nor White," *Harvard Latino Law Review* (1997): 61.

5. Audre Lorde, "The Master's Tools Will Never Dismantle Master's House," *This Bridge Called My Back: Writings by Radical Women of Color* (New York: Kitchen Table, 1981), 98.

6. The term "woman of color" began to be used in the late 1970s. It signaled a coalition between women who had participated in the civil rights, Chicano, gay, and feminist movements, and realized the insensitivity of these movements to issues of gender and racial/ethnic oppression. Moraga and Anzaldúa's collection, *This Bridge Called My Back,* published in 1981, crystalized this coalition and the use of the term. As a matter of fact, although the category "woman of color" seems to privilege the racial axis, it is really "a term which designates a political constituency, not a biological or even sociological one... what seems to constitute a "a woman of color" or "third world women" as a viable oppositional alliance is a common context of struggle rather than color or racial identifications." (Chandra Mohanty. *Third World Women and the Politics of Feminism.* Bloomington: Indiana University Press, 1991, 5–7). We have appropriated this term to underscore a coalition between women who, because of their gender, perceived nonwhiteness, and class have remained on the margins of society and academia, that is, women who, as we are used to reading, "bear the triple burden of oppression."

7. Elizabeth M. Iglesias, "Structures of Subordination: Women of Color at the Intersection of Title VII and the NLRA. Not!" *Harvard Civil Rights Civil Liberties Law Review* 28.2 (Summer 1993): 400.

8. Yvonne Yarbro-Bejarano, "The Female Subject in Chicano Theater: Sexuality, 'Race,' and Class," in *Performing Feminisms: Feminist Critical Theory and Theater,* ed. Sue-Ellen Case (Baltimore: The Johns Hopkins University Press, 1990), 132.

9. Yarbro-Bejarano, 138–139.

10. Gloria Anzaldúa, *Borderlands/La Frontera: The New Mestiza Consciousness* (San Francisco: Aunt Lute, 1987).

11. We thank Alberto Sandoval for allowing us to incorporate some of his ideas in this section. Unpublished manuscript forthcoming in

Ollantay Theater Magazine, a special issue on Latinas.

12. Sue-Ellen Case, *Feminist Theater* (New York: Routledge, 1988), 56–61.

13. Diana Taylor, "Negotiating Performance," *Latin American Theater Review* (Spring 1993): 49. Unless otherwise noted all translations are our own.

14. Jeanie Forte, "Women's Performance Art: Feminism and Postmodernism," in *Performing Feminisms: Feminisms, Critical Theory and Theater,* ed. Sue-Ellen Case (Baltimore: The Johns Hopkins University Press, 1990), 251.

15. Lizbeth Goodman, *Contemporary Feminist Theaters* (London and New York: Routledge, 1993), 182.

16. Forte, 261.

17. Taylor, 50.

18. Peggy Phelan, *Unmarked: The Politics of Performance* (New York: Routledge, 1993), 146.

19. Phelan, 151.

20. Phelan, 150.

21. Phelan, 150.

Play & Performance Texts

Lucy Loves Me

Migdalia Cruz

Bears when first born are shapeless masses of white flesh a little larger than mice, their claws alone being prominent. The mother then licks them gradually into proper shape.
—Pliny the Elder, *Natural History*, Book 7

This play was produced in February 1992 by the Latino Chicago Theater Company in Chicago, Illinois. The director was Juan Ramírez, the designer was Joel Klaff, and the following actors were featured:

Laurie Martinez as COOKIE RODRIGUEZ
Frankie Davila as MILTON AYALA
Elisa Alvarado as LUCY RODRIGUEZ
In the October 1993 encore performance, Laly Torres replaced
   Elisa Alvarado as LUCY.

This play was also produced in February 1991 by the Frank Theatre in Minneapolis, Minnesota, directed by Wendy Knox.

The play is divided into Act One, with six scenes (or seven scenes, including the optional scene*), and Act Two, with four scenes (or five scenes, including the optional scene*).
* The optional scenes are flashbacks which in certain productions were done with slides, voice-overs, and video.

Cast of Characters

COOKIE RODRIGUEZ: *An assimilated Puerto Rican woman, forty-five, who loves all things American. A faded beauty, wanna-be torch singer, almost never leaves the house.*
LUCY RODRIGUEZ: *Her twenty-five year-old daughter. Unaware of her beauty, pragmatic, delivers pizza for a living.*
MILTON AYALA: *A Cuban man in his late twenties. Sells dresses, shy with women in person, but an animal on the phone.*
Setting: *Most of the action takes place in the Rodriguez' one-bedroom apartment in the Bronx. The apartment is decorated in fake Early*

(courtesy of Migdalia Cruz)

*Americana; the furniture is heavy and dark. The walls are light-colored
but seem stained. Three scenes take place in Milton's apartment, a sparsely
furnished studio in Manhattan. One scene occurs in the hall outside the
Rodriguez' apartment; one scene at the Oyster Festival, which is suggested with lights; and another on a commuter train, also suggested by
lights and a train banquette.*
Time: *The present. On and around Halloween night.*
Place: *New York City.*

ACT 1
Scene 1

[In MILTON'S *apartment.* MILTON *is in the bathtub, which is in
the kitchen. A slaughtered rooster is hanging off the side of the tub. He is
singing the Bartok song "Only Tell Me" and washing his feet with a
hand brush.]*
MILTON *[Singing]*
Only tell me, dear one, by which road you lead me.
Tell me and I'll plough it with a golden ploughshare.
I will hoe it also with my golden ploughshare.
I will plough it, I will sow it.
And that road I'll harrow with my golden ploughshare…
[Speaking]
The bathtub's my favorite place. It's the only place where I feel
alive. The warm water tinted green by the bubble bath does
things to me. I'm a horse in this tub. A racer. My thick hair mats
down over my tight muscles and invades those secret places
where I hide things. Big things. Trucks, steamboats. Masculine
things. Warplanes, tanks…, little red sleds, pictures of my father.
There are many folds on my body, and in each fold there's a
pocket. In the pocket is a timepiece. Ancient, worn rocks with
shadows measuring the passage of every second, every minute.
The minutes go to hours, on to days, then to weeks, and weeks
add up. The flaked skin loosened by the heat floats to the surface and I eat it. It contains all my memories. It is the tasteless
wafer of confession. Some days, it doesn't smell so bad, but today it's bad. I can smell my mother bending down to kill a roach
with her thumb. She loved the crunch of it. Roaches were her
breakfast cereals. She snapped them and cracked them, but
couldn't figure how to pop them. My father popped them and
wouldn't show her how. They were collectors. Each had more

than one of everything. Except children. Just one of those. But he had ten toes and ten fingers and two elbows. Just one nose. They were disappointed with the nose. Although it was a big nose and could hold more than its own weight in mucus and bacteria. And milk. And lo mein. Once, I went to a Chinese restaurant and was seized by a fit of laughter while swallowing... some lo mein. Out of my nose it came, but which way to go. To pull or to snort. I was wondering how much damage I was doing to my throat. All this food going down and coming out and returning to that secret inner cavity where I kept my collection. I was afraid they would take away my things, so I swallowed them. I didn't know I was losing them from the other end. I never checked that part. I didn't know I could lose things I loved so much. When I found out, I waited and held it for the bath so I could leaf through it, my body a sieve for my treasures. In the water, all was clean. And I was careful about my soap. Some soap really dried me out. My skin went raw and red like I'd been bitten by a bug. Popped and cracked. Sometimes I squeeze the space between my thumb and forefinger and white juice spurts out. Sometimes it just oozes. If I look at my hand, palm side up, I could follow the ooze through the distance of my life. It ran its course and flowed over love and Mars... No wonder people still live in San Francisco. They all know they're going to die, so why not on a crack. And mud slides are from people thinking too much and too hard about everything. That's why I'm safe in the tub. No room to think. It cleans my soul. My soul is tinted green. If I use a different bubble bath, if it's not green, the green inside makes the water red, and I'm scared of red water. I cut my finger on a razor and held it in the water, and it ran red until I thought I would die. I won't shower because I'm afraid the water will hit my face. Afraid I'll like it too much, and it'll pull me down until I can see the color inside of me. So when I close my eyes, I look in. So when I stop breathing, I'm happy. But it only lasts for ten seconds, because my toes and fingers cry out for me. They want to keep moving. They want to move to a place with trees.

[Long pause]

[Continues]

What will I do tonight? Hello. Hello. I'm only doing this for you. I don't always do this, It's my favorite day. My day of all days. It's Goosey Night Mischief night. Guess what I'm wearing. Yes? Yes? Yes, of course. Of course, the white gold. Not the gold gold. Who would wear that? Who'd be caught dead in such a get-up? I got back early from the store. To have enough time. To have the time to get everything. I stay younger with the blood from a cock in my bath. But it takes time. So much ritual. Everyone names everything. There is a formula. You take out the gizzards after it's sliced through the neck. But the gizzards are at the other end. Why not go in that way? Why not go in through the back door and cut up? Rules. There are rules for everything. Jack the Ripper broke the rules, had consented sex before he killed his women. Better to rape, I think. First give them a little psychological preparation, as it were. A bit of warning. I always wanted to rape a woman, but I never could. I wanted to have that God-like power. Did God love Mary? I wonder. He invaded her. I'm sure of that.

[The doorbell rings]

The pizza boy.

[He gets up and puts on a robe]

Just a minute.

[He opens the door; LUCY stands there holding a pizza]

Ya-you're ne-not a bahbaboy.

LUCY: No. Seven-fifty.

MILTON: Be-Boy! Pizza's getting sss getting so expenssive.

LUCY: Pricks fix.

MILTON: Wa-what?

LUCY: The price of pizza's stabilized, like rent.

MILTON: Oh… yeah… You wah-wanna come in? I ha-have to fe-find my wallet.

LUCY: Okay… but make it snappy. You don't want to make people miserable.

MILTON: No.

LUCY: People don't like cold pizzas. Not at night, anyway. For breakfast, now that's a different story. But we don't deliver breakfast.

MILTON: Oh…

LUCY *[Pointing at the bleeding rooster in the tub]:* Making soup? My mother made chicken soup like that. She'd bleed the bird into the tub. Add some hot water. Throw in the vegetables. Let it soak overnight. And for breakfast we'd have…

MILTON: Sssoup?

LUCY: Pizza Left over from my uncle's store. But we'd put a pot on the stove, sift out the vegetables, put them in the pot with the chicken-head still on, that gives it a full flavor, scoop out maybe four cups of the bloody water, and bingo, just two hours later, soup! And soup in my house, let me tell you. It could last for days.

MILTON: Sshe made a la-lot of it, huh?

LUCY: Yeah... it also tasted like shit. But nobody had the heart to tell her. That's the only thing she liked in life. She thought it cured everything.

[Pause]

When I got raped, she made me douche with it.

MILTON: I-I'm sssorry.

LUCY: That's okay. I mean, he didn't penetrate me or anything. I was nine and he was black, and my mother told me to always try to be nice to black people because you shouldn't be afraid of them even though they look different from you. So I got into the elevator with him. And I smiled at him... I smiled at him and he pulled out a knife. I said, "Don't you understand? I'm not afraid of you." But it was too late by then. By then, I was out on the roof with him, and he pulled down my pants and placed his thing on my stomach. And he shot me in my stomach. It was hot and sticky, like blood. Like I thought he'd shot me, but he didn't.

[Pause]

I was out driving with my father. And he screamed. He thought someone had shot him. But it was only a bird had shit on his arm. He doesn't put his arm out anymore, hanging out the window, when he's driving. All because of that bird. Haven't you found your money yet?

MILTON: Ye-yes. Here.

[Hands her a twenty-dollar bill]

LUCY: I don't have change for this.

MILTON: Tha-that's okay. You cccan keep it.

LUCY: Why? Is it fake or something?

MILTON: Ne-no. It's real ma-money. I got it frrom the ba-bank.

LUCY: Oh... if you got it from the bank it's okay then.

[She smiles]

MILTON: Yeah.

LUCY: You sure you got the right pizza?

MILTON [*Opens the box*]: It la-le-looks right.

LUCY: That's a large. Is that what you wanted? It's awful large for just one… You got a date?

MILTON: Ne-no. I eat a le-lot.

LUCY: Boys do. Boys always do.

[*Pause*]

Okay then. Aloha. Sayonara…

MIlTON: You me-me-must be sssick of pizza.

LUCY: I guess I should be, but I'm not. I have it for every meal. Except my birthday and Thanksgiving.

MILTON: I le-like ta-ta-turkey, too.

LUCY: Nah. We have soup. Mama's soup.

MILTON: Ya-you want to h-have sssome pizza with ma-me?

LUCY: No. I guess not. I've got other deliveries to make. But it was nice talking to you. Funny how you two make soup the same way. It really is a small world, huh? And how many people have told you how small it is? It keeps getting smaller. That's what happens when you get old. Older, I mean.

[*Pause*]

I think I'll stay after all.

MILTON: Ge-good. Ma-maybe I should put sssomething on…

LUCY: Nah. You look fine.

MILTON: Wh-what do you want to dra -drink?

LUCY: You got rye?

MILTON: Crackers?

LUCY: No. Whiskey.

MILTON: Ne-no, but I always wondered about that. Does it tataste le-like rye bread?

LUCY: No. Tastes like scotch. But cheaper. There's something appealing about that.

MIlTON: I have wa-wine.

LUCY: You got Chianti?

MILTON: Ye-yeah. That's my favorite. I la-like the sstraw basket it cccomes in.

LUCY:Can I help you set the table? I'm good with them. I used to be a waitress, but I couldn't afford the shoes. So I started driving the truck.

[*She sets the table*]

MILTON: Wha-what kind of shoes?

LUCY: Any kind.

MILTON: I have some be-beautiful ssshoes. You wanna sssee them?

LUCY: Sure.

[He brings out a pair of silver pumps]

They're gorgeous!

MILTON: Aren't they? I la-love them.

LUCY: Can I try them on?

MILTON: Sssure.

[She tries on the shoes]

They look ge-good on you.

LUCY: Really? Nah! You're kiddig me.

MILTON: Really. They la-look like the-they were ma-made for you.

LUCY: Get out of here!

MILTON: Ye-yeah! Ssseriously. You ssshould keep them.

LUCY: I'll never turn down a pair of shoes. Thank you.

[Pause]

You don't just feel sorry for me? I'm doing okay now. I mean, as you can see, I got shoes. I don't need these.

[She takes off the shoes]

You better not give them to me.

MILTON: But I w-want to. Da-don't you know ha-how to take a pre-present?

LUCY: No. I never did. I used to cry at Christmastime when I got presents, because it only happened once or twice. I thought it was a mistake. I thought somebody would take them away from me, so I gave 'em back. And then I didn't have anything to worry about losing.

MILTON: I wa-woulda kept them. I la-la-love pe-presents.

LUCY: Yeah. That's what I shoulda done. I remember one. It was a doll with a military uniform on. You know the kind, with the big things on the shoulders with fringe. I loved it so much. I rubbed my face on it, and the fringe made my lips tingle. It was like kissing an angel. If I put my tongue out, I could taste the gold chipping off its wings as it flapped at my face.

MILTON: I th-thought about that. About wha-what ge-gold would taste la-like.

LUCY: Yeah? Like what?

MILTON: Like me-milk from a mother's ne-nipple, but drier,

like dust… ba-ba-but then the nipple's really a ge-giant thermometer taking th-the temperature of th-the world. But then it ba-breaks and flu-fluid cccomes out that's the fluid I'm te-talking about the-that it tastes like.

LUCY: I can almost taste it now. Can you taste it?

MILTON: Ye-yeah… I cccan always te-taste it.

LUCY: You're lucky. You're that type. I got no sense of taste.

MILTON: The-that's too be-bad. I like how everything te-tastes.

LUCY: I'd settle for knowing how *anything* tastes. You know that question they ask you at parties: If you could choose either a paradise of sex or a paradise of food, which would you choose? I never know what to say, because with those choices, I don't have a choice. Food's not important and I don't really like sex. It's like being sentenced to purgatory. Why do you think people ask those stupid questions? And then they treat you like you're a nut, if you don't like one or the other. I'm not that.

MILTON: I ne-know. You like garlic powder?

LUCY: Why not? I might as well. It makes me seem stronger if I put everything on my pizza.

MILTON: I de-don't have eh-eh-everything. I just have ga-garlic powder. Ba-because I like it and because my fa-father told meh-me it's ge-good for ma-my heart.

LUCY: You have heart problems?

MILTON: Na-naah. My father did.

LUCY: Oh.

[He takes a bite of pizza]

Good?

MILTON: De-de-le-licious.

LUCY: Why?

MILTON: It has a le-lot of che-cheese. I la-like this ch-cheese.

LUCY: Mozzarella?

MILTON: I know wh-what it is. I just cccan't sssay it.

LUCY: I'm sorry. I didn't mean any thing by that. That's just the way I am.

[She takes a bite]

It feels good. Like the inside of lips but chewy. I like chewing, then I know I'm eating something.

[Pause]

You eat fast.

MILTON: I always we-want more. My fa-father put ma-me in

the be-boy scouts. And I won a bad-a badge for ssswimming. But I wa-wanted two. Ssso I took this be-boy's. He didn't wa-want it, not like I wa-wanted it. He cried and I fa-felt sssorry for him—but what could I do? I ne-needed two.

LUCY: What could you do? You just gotta take what you don't have.

[Pause]

Sometimes. But sometimes you don't got the right to take something and you take it anyway.

MILTON: That ma-man was wra-wrong. He was ta-taking your ba-body. I would ne-never do tha-that. I just wanted a be-badge.

LUCY: I better go.

MILTON: Aren't ye-you ssscared to tra-travel around this te-time of night?

LUCY: I don't have to be afraid of anything anymore. I seen the worse … I don't belong to myself anyway. I belong to the world, and the world does anything it wants to no matter what you do. The more you want it to stop, the more it keeps coming.

MILTON: If I be-believed tha-that, I wa-would ne-never ba-buy ne-new shoes.

LUCY: It's not the easiest way to live.

MILTON: You'll ta-take them, we-won't you? They de-they don't belong with anybody eh-eh-else.

LUCY: Yes, I'll take them. But now I owe you something. Take this.

[She pulls out a little military doll]

It's not the same one I was telling you about, but it reminds me of that one.

MILTON: It's be-be-beautiful.

[Pause]

Ya-you only ha-have one?

LUCY: Yeah.

MILTON: You ssshould ha-have two, so he's ne-not la-lonely.

LUCY: Even if there were two, he'd still be lonely. He's that kind of doll.

[Lights cross to COOKIE *asleep on the sofa in the Rodriguez apartment.]*

Scene 2

[In the Rodriguez apartment, Lucy speaks to COOKIE, *who is asleep*

on the sofa]
LUCY: You always have such bad dreams…maybe you sleep too much. Sleeping makes you sick. I know, because I always have a stomach ache when I sleep too much. The only way to feel good is to never fall asleep, but people can't help it. They always nod off and then what happens? It's all wasted.
[Pause]
When I was real little, I thought you hated me. You never spoke to me. You only screamed when I came near you. When I tried to put my hand in yours as we were crossing a street or walking through a crowd, you pushed me in front of you. "Blaze the trail, Lucy." I was almost always more alone with you than when I was alone.
[Pause]
Why are you only happy when you're asleep? Maybe there's something I could do… But you won't let me. You just won't let me.
[Pause]
Why won't you let me?
[COOKIE stirs in her sleep. She makes a strange sound and rolls over. After a pause, she rolls back, awake and hungry. She tugs at LUCY'S apron. LUCY goes to the kitchen and gets a bowl of soup and a spoon and returns to COOKIE'S side. COOKIE sits up with difficulty, and LUCY tucks a napkin into her blouse. COOKIE blows her nose into it and bunches it up; then she takes a corner of LUCY'S apron and places it under her chin to replace the napkin. LUCY feeds COOKIE in silence. After a few bites, COOKIE refuses to eat anymore.]
LUCY: Finish it.
[She holds a spoonful of food to COOKIE'S mouth]
C'mon. Open wide. Here comes the airplane, open that hangar!
[COOKIE clenches her teeth together]
No go, huh? Okay, I won't force you… I don't believe in force.
[COOKIE whimpers]
Listen, if you ain't gonna eat, then you shouldn't talk either. It's rude. It's horrible. You don't want to be horrible to me.
[COOKIE stares at her own hands in silence]
Are you cold? I can turn up the heat if you are. For me, it's perfect, but others might not think so. But I wouldn't mind turning it up. Not at all. If it's what you want.
[She pours COOKIE'S soup into her own bowl]

So it shouldn't go to waste.

[She eats slowly, slurping each spoonful]

I can't believe you're not hungry. This is such a good meal, too. But now it's too late. All gone.

COOKIE: She was asking for it. I don't care how old she is.

LUCY: Who?

COOKIE: That bitch in the supermarket.

LUCY: You're still upset about that? C'mon, Cooks. She didn't mean nothing by it.

COOKIE: When somebody asks you why you don't buy a bathroom cleaner, they mean something by it!

LUCY: She's a lonely old woman. She just says those things because that's all she ever thinks about. Maybe she just wants to be your friend.

COOKIE: My friend? I'd like to get into her bathroom all right! If you really want to figure someone out, alls you gotta do is go into their bathroom, lock the door, and search. Through everything: the medicine cabinet, the shelves, inside the tank, some people hide jewelry there, in the tub. Smell the used-up soap. You look at the soap extra carefully, so you can figure out where on that person's body that soap last was. Where'd that hair come from? From the head or… other places.

LUCY: What if you found her other-place hairs on that soap? I would scream.

COOKIE: That's the fun of it. You don't know when you might find something you don't want to see. It's the funnest at parties, because you really don't want to scream with all those people out there listening for that kind of stuff, because you know how people are.

LUCY: How?

COOKIE: They listen. All the time. Everybody wants to know if it's number one, number two, or number three. And if it's number three, everybody has a smile on their face when you come out.

LUCY: What's number three?

COOKIE: Don't you know anything?

LUCY: Nope. Want me to read the paper to you?

COOKIE: Diarrhea! Liquid gold! How could a child of mine not know what number three is?!

LUCY: I'm glad you started talking to me again.

COOKIE: Who's talking?!

LUCY: I know what you want, you want to hear your horoscope.

[She picks up the newspaper]

Wait a minute while I find it.

[Leafing through the paper to the horoscopes and reading]

"Giving of yourself brings your lover's attention back to you. A loving and giving attitude is what your loved one truly craves. Aquarius, you can figure and scheme to your heart's delight, but don't expect a heck of a lot to come of it if you don't plan wisely. Persons close to you know exactly what you're up to." Hmmm... What do you think? I don't think people should make any big moves without consulting their horoscopes. Not that I really believe it all, but I don't think you should take any chances... You want a bath now?

[Puts down the newspaper]

I'll bet a nice, hot bath is what you need. I know I could sure use one.

COOKIE: I can't take a bath. No more bubbles.

LUCY: Yes, there are. I just bought us some. They turn your bathwater pink.

COOKIE: Really?!

LUCY: I knew you'd like that. There's probably nothing as nice as a hot bath. But if you think about it... it's kind of disgusting... sitting in your own dirt for a long period of... but there's something comforting about it, too... Would you like to wear your Esther Williams swim cap?

COOKIE: Yeah.

LUCY: I'll get it

[She dries her hands on her apron and moves to the closet that is crammed with stuff some of which tumbles out. Everything in the closet is antique Americana, from old weathervanes to metal thermometers with Philip Morris ads on them. Finally, LUCY finds the swim cap and a "Miss Manhattan" banner.]

Remember this?

[She puts the banner on COOKIE]

COOKIE: How do I look?

LUCY: You musta been a real looker when you were young.

COOKIE: I still am, baby.

[LUCY hums the "Miss America" theme song and dances around]

LUCY: C'mon and dance.

[COOKIE gets up with difficulty; LUCY grabs her hands and swings her around]

LUCY: *[Singing]:* "There she is, Miss America... There she is, your ideal..."

[They twirl each other around until they drop from dizziness]

Awhh... you should a won that. Everything would be different... I guess you wouldn't of had me, though... You know what would be fun? Taking a bath together, just like we used to when I was small enough to fit on top of your belly.

COOKIE: You don't fit there anymore.

LUCY: Don't you ever dream?

[LUCY exits slowly. Lights cross to scene 3]

Scene 3

[COOKIE is alone. She looks at the door as if someone had just gone through it. She makes a path first with her eyes and then with her body, to the mirror. She moves slowly to the mirror and looks at her reflection. She smiles. She touches her face. She moves to a table and picks up her purse. She moves back to the mirror. She touches her face again. Then opens her purse. Looks in it for something but cannot find it. Closes her purse. Looks away. Stares for a moment at the door. Looks back at her purse, opens it, and looks surprised. Pulls out a long, beautiful scarf. Wraps it around her neck. Stares into the mirror. Moves to the lamp and points it toward the mirror. Moves back into the light. Squints at herself in the mirror. Looks into her purse and pulls out a pair of sunglasses. Looks away from the mirror and then looks back coyly. Flirts with the mirror as a young woman would. Stops suddenly and stares. Takes off glasses and stares. Takes off scarf and stares. Opens the front of her dress and stares. Stares at her breasts. Holds one in one hand and pets it with the other, trying to smooth out the gnarled skin. Looks in the mirror. Continues to stare at her reflection, but places her breasts back inside her dress and rebuttons her top. Looks in her purse and pulls out an eyebrow pencil. She draws on eyebrows above her own. Stares. Giggles. Draws two nostril holes above her own. Stares. Draws a beard onto her chin. Stares. Spits at the reflection. Looks away. Turns back. Rests her head on her shoulder and closes her eyes. Runs her tongue along her lips. Drools down her chin. Rubs her face, smearing the makeup. Opens her eyes, nods her head. Stops. Moves to the window, stops and stares out. Turns back. Opens her purse. Pulls out a small American flag and a

*beauty contest banner. She puts the banner on. Then she turns back to
the window and looks out, with one hand in the air waving the flag.
Lights slowly fade.]*

Scene 4

[The next day in MILTON'S *apartment.* LUCY *is pacing in front of*
MILTON.*]*

LUCY: I like my job. Other people might not like it, but I do. I
get a kick out of the kids who come up to me with thirty-six
cents for a slice. "Don't you know what century this is, kid?" I
say. They don't have a clue. So I give it to them anyway. I don't
care. Why should I care? They're just little kids… You know
what else I like? I like it when they turn off the ovens and everybody goes racing home… That's when I whip out a bag of
Twizzlers. I find licorice real relaxing, you know what I mean?
It like gives you time to think, because you gotta chew it so long.
I come to some interesting ideas that way. I'm gonna write a
book about that place someday. One chapter is gonna be just
about Twizzlers and the things it makes you think. Another one's
gonna be about sex. It's something the way people carry on
there. There was this one woman who used to come around all
the time. We called her Blowjob Linda; she used to grab guys
and take 'em into the toilet with her. They'd come out minutes
later with their shirts out and their flies open, looking like something blown in out of a tropical storm. Anyway, that's Linda. I
could write a whole chapter just about her. You know what I
mean? She had style. Not too many people with that. Yeah…you
see all types. I think that's why I like it so much. It's always in-
ter-esting. I think so anyway. I don't know about anybody else.
[Pause]
You know what else? I like talking people into buying things
they don't know they want.. Yeah, that's the best. Pizza with
pineapple and anchovies. Man, some people are soooo stupid,
they'll eat anything.
[Pause]
Some people tell me I'm too old to be delivering pizzas, but isn't
that who you would want delivering your pizza? Somebody older.
Somebody responsible. You know how not getting a pizza you
ordered could ruin your evening. You could be left there with

nothing to eat. And then you would have to go out. That's what I save people from. From the streets. From seeing other people. From having other people see them. I'm a shield.

MILTON: C-c-come into the ke-kitchen. I wah-wanna ssshow you sssomething.

LUCY: What?

MILTON: Ka-ka-c'mon!

LUCY: It's not something scary, is it?

MILTON: Ne-no.

[He takes her hand and leads her into the kitchen]

LUCY: Tell me.

MILTON *[Holding a mouth-shaped cookie mold up to his lips]:* See!

LUCY: Yeah. Ooh! They're so cold.

MILTON: I la-like te-tah keep them fresh.

LUCY: So… You like cookies, huh?

MILTON: Ne-no. You ssee. It's-the-they're ha-her lipsss.

LUCY: Whose lips?

MILTON: My ge-girlfriend. My old ge-girlfriend.

LUCY: She had metal lips?

MILTON: The-they're the sssame sh-shape. I me-made it sp-special.

LUCY: Oh… That was real nice of you.

MILTON: She de-de-idn't think so. She de-de-didn't la-like it She th-thought I wa-was me-me-making fun of her.

LUCY: Were her lips really this big?

MILTON: Ye-yeah… I je-just wanted to ssshow you that I could me-me-make one for you too, if ye-you le-like it.

LUCY: That's a lot of trouble to go through for a stranger.

MILTON: Ye-you're no stranger… We talked a le-lot yesterd-d-day and to-ne-ne-night.

LUCY: You're real easy to talk to.

MILTON: Th-thanks.

LUCY: But I talk to everybody, y'know. I talk too much. That's what people always say to me. My mother told me her face was chapped from all the spit and wind I blew up into her face.

MILTON: I cha-chapped my fah-face once, too.

LUCY: Yeah?

MILTON: Yeah. I wa-went on the fe-ferry without a he-he-hat.

LUCY: I love the ferry, even though it only goes to Staten Island.

MILTON: Ma-me too. Be-but now I ka-carry Vaseline with ma-ma-me.

LUCY: Good thinking! It's funny how much we like the same things.

MILTON: You la-like Vaseline?

LUCY: Oh, yeah. I use it on my lips every day. Ever since I read that girls in beauty contests use it to keep their lips from sticking to their teeth.

MILTON: We-why do their la-lips ssstick to their teeth eh-eh-anyway?

LUCY: Because they're nervous and their mouths get dry. So they put the Vaseline on their teeth and their lips just to be sure.

MILTON: Oh… Me-my mouth's ne-ne-never been the-that dry.

LUCY: You're the relaxed type, I guess. Like me.
[She smiles]
MILTON: Oh…

LUCY*:* I'm joking.
[Pause]
What's your name anyway? I just know your last name, Ayala.

MILTON: My ne-name's Me-Milton. What's yours?

LUCY: I don't like telling people my name. It's a stupid name. I'm gonna go to a judge someday and change it. I wanna change everything about me.

MILTON: You me-mean la-like go on a de-diet? I always fe-feel bab-better when I go on a de-diet.

LUCY: That's because you're thin.

MILTON: I'm ne-ne-not thin. I'm re-re-regular.

LUCY: Regular? Regular's something you are in the bathroom.

MILTON: You're tha-thin, too.

LUCY: No… I'm regular.

MILTON: Are ye-you me-mad now?

LUCY: No… Who's bigger? Mr. Bigger or Mr. Bigger's baby?

MILTON: I de-don't know… Mr. Be-bigger?

LUCY: Nope. Mr. Bigger's baby, because he's a little Bigger!
[Pause]
You're supposed to laugh.

MILTON: I ne-know, but I was je-just th-th-thinking…

LUCY: About what?

MILTON: About Me-me-mister Be-bigger's be-baby. People ma-must mmmake a lot of jokes about him. I fah-feel sssorry for him.

LUCY: There is no Mr. Bigger.

MILTON: Ha-how do you know?

LUCY: I don't know. I just suppose.

MILTON: Be-but if there wah-was one, wouldn't you fah-feel sssorry?

LUCY: Yeah, I would… I'm sorry. I didn't want to make you sad. Jokes aren't supposed to make people sad. That's why I tell them all the time… so people just listen to the joke and then they don't laugh at me.

MILTON: Why wah-would anybody laugh at ye-ye-you?

LUCY: Can you keep a secret?

MILTON: Sssure.

LUCY: I don't think I'm human.

MILTON: How do ye-you mah-mah-mean?

LUCY: I got hair on the knuckles of my feet.

MILTON *[Relieved]*: Oh… Me too.

LUCY: A lot of it. When I walk barefoot, I look like I got mules on.

MILTON: Mmmules?

LUCY: Yeah. You know, those big, furry slipper things.

MILTON *[relieved]*: Oh! Uh huh…

LUCY: That don't bother you?

MILTON: No. I got ha-hair on my ssshoulders.

LUCY: Puppies.

MILTON: No. I can't have pa-pets.

LUCY: No. I mean, puppies on your shoulders… I like that look. It's real… warm looking.

MILTON: Wah-warm all right! I sssweat a la-lot.

LUCY: Do you shave? I do, but then the hair comes back in, hard and spiky like nails, and that proves it.

MILTON: Yeah… Ma-maybe ye-you're ne-ne-not human. Be-be-but ssso what? If you were la-like everybody eh-else, ya-you'd ne-never even talk to mmme.

LUCY: But I still make you nervous.

MILTON: Ne-ne-no. Ne-ne-not at all.

LUCY: But you're still—do you always?

MILTON: In front of weh-weh-women. Essspecially pra-pretty ones.

[He smiles broadly]

LUCY: You got a nice smile.

MILTON: Ge-ge-ge-good teeth. That's wha-what my ge-ge-girl-friend used to sssay.

LUCY: The nape of the neck is my favorite part of a man.

MILTON: Ye-Yeah? I da-don't think ssshe ever la-looked back there…Ssshe was a da-dentist.

LUCY: Let me see.

[He shows her the nape of his neck]

I've never seen a birthmark like that before.

MILTON: It's a tattoo of the United States… We're right here.

[He points]

LUCY: Oh… yeah   But where's Florida?

MILTON: I ta-told them to la-leave it out.

LUCY: Is that where you're from?

MILTON: No. But I was always afraid somebody would send me there.

LUCY: I would never send you to Florida.

MILTON: Tha-thank you.

[They stare at each other in silence for a moment, then the lights cross to the Rodriguez apartment.]

Scene 5

[A few hours later in the Rodriguez apartment. LUCY speaks to COOKIE who is by the window.]

COOKIE: He showed you his what?

LUCY: Cookie molds. He makes them for his women. I think it's sweet. You can make something and eat it and have a part of that person.

COOKIE: Yeah… what kind of cookies?

LUCY: What do you mean? Cookies that you eat, of course. Regular cookies.

COOKIE: That's nice. How tall is he?

LUCY: What do you care?

COOKIE: I care. I don't want my daughter dating a midget. What's his name?

LUCY: Milton.

COOKIE: Milton?! You sure you wanna go out with somebody named Milton? Miltons are always psychos.

LUCY: He's not a psycho! He's nice… He's really cute, too.

COOKIE: Yeah?

LUCY: Yeah. And you better keep away from him.

COOKIE: I don't know what you're talking about.

LUCY: I'm warning you…

COOKIE: You better go to the store before it closes.

LUCY: Why didn't you go?

COOKIE: I was tired.

LUCY: Okay… I'm gonna get something different tonight.

COOKIE: How come?

LUCY: You know what day it is.

COOKIE: Sure I do. It's the day when creepy little children dress up like creepy little things and go around knocking on my door asking for stuff they don't deserve.

[LUCY stares at her for a moment and then exits; insincerely:]

Happy birthday, Lucy!

[COOKIE looks at her fingernails]

My nails are dirty. I want red nails. She won't let me borrow her polish… She should. "It's mine, Mama. Why do you always want everything that's mine?" She should do them for me. Then I can't see the dirt. Don't matter if it's there if I don't see it. That's the kind of hairpin I am.

[She goes to the window and sits on the ledge, spreading her legs; she calls to the people across the way]

Hey, you never saw one like this, did you?!

[She comes back into the room]

They never saw this, that's for sure…

[She picks up a pair of binoculars and scans the room]

There it is.

[She goes to the table, grabs a piece of cheese, and puts it in her mouth]

Still good, too. There's nothing like a good piece of cheese. Men could die for this cheese. I bet cheese could start a war.

[Smiling]

And if it were Swiss cheese, it could be a holey war.

[Laughing raucously]

Oh, dear… I *still* got it. She don't think I got it, but I got it.

[Long pause]

People who got It know they got It, and people who don't, think people who do, don't. But I know. So I got it.

[Pause]

I know she ain't got it. I want cherry red, no, beet red nails. Deep, deep red. Like someone peeled off my fingernails and

the raw, red meat shows through… I'd have to wash my hands more with sores like that.
[Loud music is heard from above; she looks up at the ceiling]
Shut up! Shut up! I can't hear myself think! Stupid kids.
[To the ceiling]
Listen to some real music. Let's hear some Satchmo and Ella!
[She sings to drown it out]
"In your mountain greenery,
where God paints the scenery,
just two crazy people together.
While you love a lover, let blue skies be your cover.
Let…"
Shit! I can't do It anymore. I used to sound just like Ella… sometimes I sounded like Billie, too.
[Singing]
"My funny valentine… sweet funny valentine. Mmmmmhmmmmhnnn… Is your figure less than Greek? Is your mouth a little weak? When you open it to speak, are you smart? Don't change a hair for me. Not if you care for me…"
[She continues to sing louder and louder as pounding begins from above and below]
Stay, pretty Valentine… Stay!
Shut up! Shut up! I can too sing! I'm a professional!
[All the noise stops]
I'm a professional.
[She goes to the table, gets her hat, puts it on her head, puts her purse over her arm and moves to the center of the room]
I can't stand it here. No one could. I hate her and I hate this room and I hate my… I don't know why I called her Lucy. That's my name. Everyone thought it would be cute. Only boys are juniors, I said. I said it would be dumb. I said it was too pretty a name for such an ugly baby. And it was ugly. I'm not just saying that. Believe me. I was there. She didn't have any hair on her head until she was five. Ugly. Ugly, I tell you. Plain ugly. That's when I changed my name to Cookie. Who does she think she is anyway? I'll tell you what she is. She's an ugly little girl who's bad to her mother. She doesn't care if our home smells like the monkey house in the zoo… I haven't been there in a long time. I don't go anywhere. I don't remember what the Atlantic Ocean looks like… It probably hasn't changed, though. But I'd like to

see it again anyway... She likes the way it smells. She likes everything rotten. Her food tastes rotten. I can't even get a decent piece of cheese around here. One side or the other always has something green on it. She just cuts it off, but me, I can't do that, that's the kind of hairpin I am.

[A bang from below]

I think he robs banks.

[Pause]

Mr. 5K robs banks. Small ones and he keeps the loot stashed in his ceiling under a drop tile. I wonder if he'd murder me if he knew I knew his secret. I won't tell anyone, though, Mr. 5K. I don't snitch. There's honor here. And I'm full of it. Look.

[Reaches into her purse and pulls out a small American flag]

You see.

[Singing]

Oh, beautiful, for spacious skies..."

[Loud bang from below]

He loves it when I... Hey, Mr. 5K do you play on your piccolo when I sing? I bet you do. I bet you beat your tom-tom for Cookie-Lucy... I coulda done it professionally, know what I mean? I used to always go around singing to myself and people, people I didn't even know, would come up to me and ask if I was a pro. It's something the way people pick up on the truth like that. I mean, I wasn't a singer, but that's what I always wanted to be. And people just pick that stuff right up, just like that...It's funny, isn't it? I mean, you never know, people always surprise you.

[Long pause; she moves to the window and puts the binoculars to her eyes; the telephone rings, she points her binoculars at it; she slowly moves toward the phone like a hunter stalking some elusive prey and suddenly she pounces on it.]

Hello?

[Blackout]

Scene 6

[MILTON'S apartment. Overlapping in time with the previous scene. MILTON is seated by the telephone—a blanket covers his body. Only his head and arms are exposed.]

MILTON: Her face torments me. She reminds me of another. One I couldn't have. I used to dream about putting her in a freezer so if I wanted to look at her face, I could just open the door and there she'd be, staring at me, eyes only for me. I remember the pain flooding her eyes as I entered her, and I wonder why love and pain always come together. You fight love...but it's stronger than rope.

[He picks up the phone and dials; then he listens for a moment in silence]

At the tone...the time will be...1:32 and 13 seconds...At the tone... the time will be...1:33 exactly... At the tone the time will be... 1:33 and 13 seconds... You have such a beautilul voice. I bet that's why you do this. Isn't that why you do this?

[Listens; hangs up the phone abruptly]

Can't even get a full minute of their time...

[He looks slowly around his apartment moving from one possession to the next like a buyer at an auction; his gaze finally rests on a photograph of Lucille Ball]

[Sings]

"I love Lucy and she loves me. We're as happy as two can be..."

[Continues humming the rest of the I Love Lucy *theme song as he strokes his hair like a woman would and takes a bright red lipstick from a makeup bag which rests on the telephone table, and puts some on while staring at the photograph; he then picks up a phone book and thumbs through it, stopping at a certain page and dials a number from it.]*

Hello? Lucy Davis?

[Pause]

How are you today?

[Pause]

I'm not with anybody... I just called to say hello. Don't hang up, Lucy.

[Pause]

Because I want to speak with you. I want to... Lucy? Lucy?! Lucy!

[He hangs up quietly]

Bitch.

[He opens a small mirrored compact and reapplies the lipstick, making his lips even more pronounced]

There. Now...

[He opens the phone book and picks out a number and dials]

Is Lucy Miller at home?

[Pause]
Oh. Oh, she's not. Now which lovely Miller am I talking to now?
[Pause]
Oh, I've been wanting to talk to you for a long time... Lucy's told me so much about you. You wear size ten dresses, don't you?
[Pause]
It's not my business. But that's the business I'm in. I sell dresses. Do you like dresses, Mrs. Miller?
[Pause]
I'm glad.
[Pause]
It's not my business, I know. But you say you're a size twelve?
[Pause]
Even better. where do your dresses fit you the tightest? I mean, Lucy told me you had trouble buying dresses because they were tight in odd places...sometimes.
[Pause]
The hips. Oh, dear. The hips are a tough spot to fit, it's true. Maybe you should come over. And try some of my dresses on, Mrs. Miller. I'm sure we'll find something that suits you.
[Pause]
I'm always open. Come anytime, Mrs. Miller. Just call me and let me know you're coming.
[Long pause]
Yes, of course. We went to school together. My name's Milton. Milton Ayala.
[Pause]
We went to high school together.
[Pause]
Why would I lie?
[Pause]
Mrs. Miller?...
[He hangs up loudly]
Some people are so paranoid.
[He goes through the phone book furiously, finds a number, and dials; takes a tissue and blots his lipstick against it; lets the phone continue to ring. Finally someone answers; lights come up on COOKIE.]
May I speak to Lucy Rodriguez, please?
COOKIE: Her name is...Ana.

MILTON: Her name's Lucy, of course it is. It says, uhm, she told me her name was Lucy.

COOKIE: I tell you, her name is Ana, I don't care what the phone book says. Do you understand?

MILTON: But I want to speak to her.

COOKIE: I know you want Lucy. But no Lucys live here. Somebody gave you the wrong number.

MILTON: Is this 750-2537?

COOKIE: Yes, that's our number.

MILTON: But there's no Lucy there? Huh. That's funny. Do you live there alone?

COOKIE: Not alone. With my daughter. And her name is Ana.

MILTON: Ana's a pretty name, too; but is it really Ana and not Lucy?

COOKIE: Maybe...

MILTON: What's your name?

COOKIE: It's Ana, too.

MILTON: You're kidding! Two Anas?! That's incredible. Two Anas and no Lucys.

COOKIE: No, I'm not kidding you. It's true. We're both Anas. Two Anas, no Lucys.

MILTON: I see.

COOKIE: I'm glad you understand.

MILTON: I see very well.

COOKIE: I'm very glad.

MILTON: I don't mean to bother you. Am I bothering you?

COOKIE: No. It's all right.

[She puts on some lipstick that she takes out of her purse; he puts on some lipstick as he speaks]

MILTON: That's good, because I like talking to people. I get so lonely in my apartment. Cities do that to you.

COOKIE: Lots of people are lonely.

MILTON: I know, but I'm lonelier than most. Can you come visit me? You have a friendly voice.

COOKIE: I'm sorry. No.

MILTON: Why not? I bet you're beautiful. A beautiful woman shouldn't spend any time alone. Are you beautiful?

COOKIE: Nooo...

MILTON: I don't believe that. I bet you're great in bed. We can go to bed together.

COOKIE: I'm sorry. I couldn't do that even if I wanted to.

MILTON: Or I could just hold you. Couldn't I just hold you?

COOKIE: Wellll… ummmm, no. No. Impossible.

MILTON: Why don't you let me come over, Ana? Are you afraid of your daughter?

COOKIE: Are you kidding?! Maybe she would enjoy seeing a new face.

MILTON: Tell her I'm a surprise dinner guest. She doesn't have to know how we met.

COOKIE: Uh-huh. I'll tell her. Do you know where we live?

MILTON: 1827 Washington.

COOKIE: That's right… Is that where Lucy lives, too?

MILTON: Are you sure there are no Lucys at this number? I feel Lucys.

COOKIE: Nope. So we'll surprise her, then?

MILTON: Yes. You know how daughters are.

COOKIE: Amen. I won't say a word.

MILTON: See you soon.

[COOKIE *blows him a kiss*]

Good-bye.

[They hang up. He takes off the blanket; he is naked, covered by sweat. Slowly, he kisses his arms, covering them with lipstick marks]

She'll be so surprised. Birthdays are good days for surprises.

[Lights quickly fade]

ACT 2
Scene 1

[The hall in front of the Rodriguez door. MILTON stands there, holding a bunch of flowers and a box of candy.]

MILTON: I have a hard time climbing stairs. I run out of breath real fast. I don't mind, though. I don't mind breathing hard. I like the urgent sound of my own breath beating against my lips.

[Pause]

I've gotten to where I'm going. The flowers are swaying in my hand. Is the valentine too big? Women like them big, though. They consume large amounts of candy on days like today. But the plastic flowers on the box are so…plastic. They make candy boxes with velvet bows and flowers, but I can't afford them, so I went to the five and ten and got the biggest. I hope she likes chocolate. I hope she'll be there. I don't like to be lied to. I don't like liars, though liars can be pretty. Some of the prettiest are liars. I wonder if being pretty makes you one. Women make me nervous. I walk up these stairs nervously. I never dated before. I wish I knew how to talk to the ladies.

[He rings the doorbell; lights up on the Rodriguez apartment. COOKIE, dressed for a hot date and sitting on the couch, turns sharply at the sound of the doorbell and smiles. LUCY is cooking.]

LUCY: What do you look so happy for? Somebody must be lost.

[Goes to the door and speaks through it]

Who is it?

MILTON: It's me.

LUCY: Me, who?

MILTON: Me. Milton. Milton Ayala.

[Pause as LUCY checks her appearance before opening the door]

I spoke to you on the phone today. You said I could hold you.

LUCY *[Throws open the door]:* Milton! How did you find me?

MILTON: I-I de-don't know… I bra-brought you these.

[He hands her the flowers and candy]

COOKIE: Didn't you bring me anything?

[He takes a black silk teddy out of his pocket]

MILTON: I was sssaving this for a spa-special occasion.

[He hands the teddy to COOKIE]

COOKIE: Why, Milton! It's just so…me. I love it!

[She puts it on over her clothes]

LUCY: Mama.

COOKIE: What?! I was the one who invited him.

LUCY: What are you talking about?

COOKIE: He called me. Asked me if he could come over.

LUCY: You called… I never gave you the number.

MILTON: Ya-you de-de-didn't have to. Ye-you left your la-lip-stick mmmarks on mmmy refrigerator. I wah-was bound to find ye-you.

COOKIE: He got it from the phone book.

MILTON: You de-de-didn't tell me your ma-ma-mother was ssso young.

LUCY: She's not. She just thinks she is.

COOKIE: Sit down, Milton. Sit over here, by me.

MILTON: O-ke-kay.

[to COOKIE]

Da-do you take bla-blood baths?

[Pause]

COOKIE: Maybe you should go help with dinner, dear.

LUCY: It's good for your skin, Cooks. You should try it. All those lines around your eyes and mouth, they'd just vanish...

MILTON: What's for dinner?

LUCY: Lamb chops.

MILTON *[Moving to LUCY'S side]:* I la-love lamb. I la-like their fu-fu–their wool.

LUCY: Yeah, I try not to think about that too much. I mean; I'd have a real hard time eating something that cute, you know. They're such innocent little things, so it's better if I don't think.

MILTON: Yeah, I ne-know. Thinking too m-m-much is ba-bad for you.

[Looking out the window]

You've got a ne-ne-nice view of the ska-ska-

LUCY: It's a pretty sky tonight. Real clear. Even Mars is out. Look, I'll show you.

[She goes over to the window and stands next to MILTON; COOKIE moves to his other side]

That red sparkly guy is Mars.

MILTON: I always th-thought that was Ve-Venus.

LUCY: No. Uh-uhn. Mars. The planet of war. Red, right?

MILTON: I ge-ge-guess... Ve-Venus c-could be red, 'cause it's the p-planet of la-love.

LUCY: Maybe... No, it's definitely Mars. I read that somewhere.

[COOKIE spits]

LUCY *[to MILTON]*: You have to forgive her. Old people spit a lot.

MILTON: I d-don't mind. I like to sp-spit, too. I mean, not i-i-indoors, of course. Ba-ba-but outside...essspecially into the ocean.

LUCY *[Looks at MILTON in silence for a moment]:* Which ocean?

MILTON: Wh-what are the p-packages for? Is it somebody's birthday?

LUCY: Yeah. Mine.

MILTON: Ssso ma-many presssents...

[to COOKIE]

You ma-must love her. Does your fe-face burn when you le-look at her?

COOKIE: Are you kidding?! She bought 'em herself. She won't take presents from me anymore.

LUCY: That's because you only give me things you like, so I'll give 'em back to you.

[to MILTON*]*

Clean the mushrooms, okay?

MILTON: Do you have a br-brush?

LUCY: Your hair looks okay.

MILTON: Ne-no. For the mushrooms.

LUCY: You use a brush? I'll be damned. I just wash 'em in cold water. What kind of brush? I never heard of that.

MILTON: Yeah, it's gre-great. Then the mah-mah-

LUCY: Yeah?

MILTON: They d-don't get sssoft and mmmushy.

LUCY: Mine never get that way. That's the kind of hairpin I am.

MILTON: Ye-yeah. You-You're a lucky person.

LUCY: Humph! If I'm so lucky, why do I keep getting older?

MILTON: Ye-you don't.

LUCY: I was just kidding.

MILTON: Ha-How old are you?

LUCY: How old do I look?

MILTON: I d-don't know… Thirty-five?

LUCY: I'm twenty-five, but I might as well be thirty-five, cause nothing's gonna change in ten years.

*[*COOKIE *is draping herself in several brightly colored scarves that she takes from her purse. She poses and flirts with an imaginary suitor as the conversation between* LUCY *and* MILTON *progresses.]*

LUCY: Do you ever think about God?

MILTON: No.

LUCY: Why not?

MILTON: Be-because I think he ssstopped thinking about me.

LUCY: Yeah, I know. Sometimes I feel like this is just a test. Like someday I'll wake up, and it'll be just like I had a long, bad dream and the world is really different. It's really wonderful. Do you ever feel that way?

MILTON: Sssometimes. But sssometimes I think about what they say, that God cre-created us in his mirror… But I don't know.

LUCY: What?

MILTON: I-I mean, how do we know what kind of m-mirror he was looking into? H-how do we know it wasn't a funhouse mirror and Ge-Ge-God isn't really this funny-shaped ge-ge-guy laughing at us 'cause he thinks we're funny. You know, how do we know?

LUCY: I don't know. We don't know, I guess.

MILTON: You-you're very smart to think of those things... I mean, Ge-Ge-God and all.

LUCY: Yeah? I feel stupid today. I can't understand what people say if I don't watch their lips when they talk. Not that I hear the words then. But I can tell what they're saying by the expressions on their face. I hate that feeling. Do you ever feel that way?

MILTON: Sssure. Ma-Most of the time.

LUCY: Does your life change as you get older?

MILTON: Mine pppersonally?

LUCY: Yeah.

MILTON: Sssometimes I think so.

LUCY: How?

MILTON: I d-don't know, I got-I got ta-ta-taller, for one.

LUCY: How tall are you?

MILTON: About sssix, I think.

LUCY: I always wanted to be tall.

MILTON: You did? Wa-why? It's terrible.

LUCY: I don't believe that.

MILTON: You ge-go into bars and things and eh-everybody is shhhorter than you. You feel like a mmmmonster.

LUCY: That sounds great. Then nobody fucks with you. I hate when people fuck with you when you want to be left alone.
[Looking at MILTON]
What's wrong?

MILTON: Nothing... I just never heard a wo-woman curse.

LUCY: Does it bother you?

MILTON: Ne-no. It sssounds la-like sssinging. Like I could fa-fall asssleep listening to that.

LUCY: I always curse before I go to sleep.

MILTON: Ge-good.

LUCY: Good... Do you like goldfish?

MILTON: They're okay.

LUCY: We got some. You want some?

MILTON: I de-don't have anywhere to keep 'em.

LUCY: I'll give you a plate.
[Opens the kitchen cabinet and pulls out a box of cheddar cheese goldfish crackers]
These are the best.
MILTON *[Embarrassed]*: Oh… Oh, Ca-crackers. Yeah, I like crackers.
LUCY: Me, too. What else do you like?
MILTON: Wh-what do you mean?
LUCY: Like who's your favorite person?
MILTON: I d-don't know. I d-don't know anybody…anymore.
LUCY: You know me. And you know Mama.
COOKIE: Don't call me that.
MILTON: I ge-guess you're it th-then. Who's yours?
LUCY: Mom, Cookie…maybe. I said that without thinking.
MILTON: It mmmust be true, then.
LUCY: I don't know.
[to COOKIE]
Who's your favorite?
[COOKIE smiles and points out the window]
LUCY *[With a nod of acceptance]*: She likes the stars. But I don't know if it's one particular one or the whole mess of them up there.
[Pause]
Guess it doesn't matter.
COOKIE: Stupid. It's the people next door I like. The ones with the red eyes.
LUCY: Oh.
[They finish preparing the salad in silence]
You like broiled chops?
MILTON: Sssure.
LUCY: I'll just pop 'em in when we're ready to eat. Broiling takes hardly any time.
MILTON: Yeah, it's fe-fe-fast.
LUCY: Yep. You wanna glass of wine or something?
MILTON: Sure.
LUCY *[Fills a tumbler with wine and hands it to him]*: It's the only kind of glasses we got. I hope you don't mind.
MILTON: Fine…
[Takes a sip]
Fruity.

LUCY: Yet innocent?

MILTON *[Seriously]:* Tha-that's how I like it.

[With a smile]

Isn't this sssupposed to be a pa-party?

LUCY: I...

MILTON: Where's the mah-music, then? And the d-d-dancing girls?

LUCY: No dancing girls, but the phonograph's over there.

MILTON: Okay.

[Goes to the stereo and picks an album]

Tha-this is an old one.

LUCY: Yeah. I bought it because it reminded me of my father.

MILTON: He liked music?

COOKIE: He liked himself.

LUCY: He loved music. He used to dance around the house, singing songs. He'd pull me up into the air and stomp his feet and hoot just like a wild Indian brave.

COOKIE: He was a piss-poor Indian.

LUCY: He was not. You're just jealous!

COOKIE: Jealous?! I'm not jealous of him. I never was. And if he was such a big shot, why couldn't he make me a wigwam? That's all I asked for. Do one Indian thing, so I know you're on the level. Make some firewater, for instance. Nothing. He didn't know the first thing about being an Indian.

LUCY: He didn't have to prove himself to you.

COOKIE: But I had to prove myself to him all right. I did everything he told me to do.

[Looking at LUCY]

Everything.

LUCY: He was real tall, wasn't he, Cooks?

COOKIE: That's what you remember.

LUCY *[to MILTON]:* He was about as tall as you, maybe taller.

MILTON: Th-that's real tall.

LUCY: Put side one on. That's my favorite.

COOKIE *[to MILTON]:* Get me some wine, baby.

LUCY: Cookie!

COOKIE: I wasn't talking to you. I was talking to Milton.

[to MILTON]

You want me to have some fun too, don't you?

MILTON: She-sure. Why ne-not?

[He gets up and goes for the bottle of wine]
A le-little wa-won't hurt.
LUCY: She'll throw up, she likes to.
[He pours COOKIE a glass of wine and hands it to her]
MILTON: I'll clean it if ssshe does. I de-don't mind cleaning.
[COOKIE *grabs his hand as he hands her the glass]*
COOKIE: You have such smooth hands.
MILTON: Th-thank you. And yours are…
COOKIE: Experienced. I have trained hands. They know just
what to do before I even tell them…before I even know what
I'm going to do.
[She lets her hand travel up his arm]
Call me Cookie.
LUCY: Where's that music?
MILTON: Oh, ye-yeah…
[He pulls himself away from COOKIE and moves to the stereo.
COOKIE *smiles at LUCY who frowns at COOKIE. The record
comes on loudly. It's the song 'Witchi-tai-tai' sung by Brewer & Shipley.*
COOKIE *and LUCY move to the rhythm of the music. LUCY sings
with the first part and COOKIE with the second.]*
What a spirit Spring is bringing round my head
makes me feel glad that I'm not dead.
Witchi-tai-tai kimbawah,
ooh, wah nicka, ooh, wah nicka, Hey neh, hey neh, noh wah…
MILTON: Th-that was great. You're ge-great sssingers. And danc-
ers too.
LUCY: We do okay, right, Mom?
*[COOKIE goes back to playing with her scarves, but keeps moving to
the music]*
Music's the only thing she likes anymore.
MILTON: I can unda-da-derstand that.
LUCY: I guess I can, too.
*[COOKIE goes to the closet and takes out a box with a big number
eight on it, and brings it to LUCY and MILTON]*
LUCY: Oh… I forgot *all* about that.
COOKIE: I thought you did.
MILTON: Wa-what is it?
LUCY: It's got all the stuff from my eighth birthday in it. It was
my first party. Firsts are important.
MILTON: I know…they really are.

LUCY *[Moves to the stove; referring to the chops]:* Better pop these babies in.

[Indicating the box]

Go ahead. Open it

MILTON: Okay.

[COOKIE opens it before MILTON can, pulls out a birthday hat and puts it on MILTON]

Thanks.

COOKIE: Anytime.

[COOKIE continues rummaging through the box until she finds a pink birthday crown and places it on LUCY'S head]

LUCY: How's it look?

MILTON: Bah-beautiful. You're beautiful.

[COOKIE puts on a hat]

Ye-ye-you're bah-beautiful too.

LUCY: Cookie was a beauty queen.

COOKIE: Yeah…that was a long time ago.

MILTON: I be-be-bet you could win a ne-ne-nother one.

COOKIE: Naah…

LUCY: Naah.

MILTON: Be-both of you, I ma-ma-mean.

LUCY: Yeah?

MILTON: I tha-think ssso…

COOKIE: I don't think so.

[Pointing at LUCY]

She's too shy.

LUCY: No. I'm not.

MILTON: You ssshould go to the Oyster Fe-fe-festival. They gege-got a bab-beauty contest. I be-be-bet you'd win.

COOKIE: Where is this festival? I never heard of it.

MILTON: In Ne-ne-norwalk. In Conn-ne-necticut.

LUCY: I don't think we could win. They got a lot of pretty girls in Connecticut.

COOKIE: They're not pretty. They're just rich enough to seem pretty.

LUCY: They're blonde. Judges always like blondes the best.

MILTON: Ne-no. Last ye-year a brun-ne-ne-nette won.

LUCY: Hmmm…

MILTON: You ge-ge-gotta have a ta-talent, though.

COOKIE: I can sing.

LUCY: I can't do anything.

COOKIE: Sure. You can play your clarinet.

LUCY: I haven't played it in years.

COOKIE: It'll come right back to you.

LUCY: You really want to do this?

COOKIE: You don't?

MILTON: You ge-ge-got to. You'll be ga-ga-great.

LUCY: When is it?

MILTON: Tonight.

LUCY: That's too soon.

COOKIE: I'll go.

LUCY: But don't you think that's too soon?

COOKIE: You gotta be ready for things when they come. They don't come all the time.

LUCY: I know. Do you gotta show your belly?

MILTON: No, I de-don't think ssso…

LUCY: Okay, then.

MILTON: Ge-ge-good. We de-don't have te-time for de-dinner, then. Je-just pack up sssome clothes. A ne-nice dress and a be-be-bathing sssuit is all you ne-need.

COOKIE: And your clarinet, baby.

LUCY: Yeah. Yeah! This is gonna be fun, right?

MILTON and COOKIE: Yeah!

COOKIE: Is there gonnabe people from all over the world there?

MILTON: Sssure.

COOKIE: Maybe my Uncle Manny from Bridgeport will be there. He has a cuchifrito stand right next to the circus museum, I liked him because he had a '64 Rambler with my name on the license plate.

LUCY: It said *kook,* not *cook.*

COOKIE: How would you know?

LUCY: Because I know.

MILTON: Were ya-you in je-je-jail? The only pe-people I know who ne-know about le-le-license plates are from je-je-jail.

LUCY: No. I just know.

MILTON: Ye-you're gonna le-le-love this fe-feh-festival. Th-th-they got oooysters and clle-clams and shrimps and pe-people dressed la-like oooysters and cl-cl-clams and shrimps. And the we-we-winner of the be-beauty ke-ke-contest gets to be Ma-Miss

Oooyster Festival and they ga-give her a crown me-me-made of oooyster ssshells and her pa-picture's in all the pa-papers... and they get two fat girls to carry her train.

COOKIE: Is it made out of fur?

MILTON: I tha-think so.

COOKIE: I'd kill somebody to wear one of those...

LUCY: I'd kill for one of those houses everybody in Connecticut has. I always wanted a house.

MILTON: What ke-kind of ha-house?

LUCY: Big. Blue. Blue with gray trim. And a dark blue door. That keeps out the evil spirits.

MILTON: De-Don't they ke-ke-come in through the we-windows then?

LUCY: Sometimes.

COOKIE: That's why people put up gates. We used to have 'em until they fell off. But that's better for me. I like to sit on the ledge.

MILTON: Isn't the-that de-de-dangerous?

COOKIE: Not yet.

[Blackout]

Scene 2

[At the Oyster Festival, MILTON, LUCY *and* COOKIE *stand on the apron of the stage. When one person speaks, their spotlight comes on and, once on, it only dims when another speaks.]*

MILTON *[Recites the first stanza of Wordsworth's "Lucy: She Dwell Among the Untrodden Ways"]*

She dwelt among the untrodden ways.

Beside the springs of Dove,

A maid whom there were none to praise

And very few to love.

LUCY: Thank you. My name is Lucy and I play the clarinet. I mean, I used to play. The clarinet. But now I'm playing it again. For the first time in eight years. And, well, I should warn you. I mean, it's probably okay. I mean, I'll be okay, the playing, that is. Because when I stick my fingers on the holes of my licorice stick, I forget where I am.

[COOKIE crosses her eyes and knees. She bends to the floor and licks the stage at the edge of the spot in a semicircle in front of her. She then gathers the circle of light into a small spot in her palms.]

Who needs food?

MILTON *[Reads from a book: Les Brown's* New York Times Encyclopedia of Television, *page 30]:* Miss Ball portrayed a beautiful, well-meaning schemer who seemingly never lived a day on Earth without becoming involved in an outlandish predicament. The situations gave full range to her talents for sight comedy, but remarkably, through all the absurd disguises and broad physical antics, she was able to preserve a ladylike persona."
[Making the sign of the cross]
Amen.

LUCY *[Makes the sign of the cross and brings the clarinet to her mouth, pulls the clarinet away from her mouth]:* I'm going to explode. My blood will pump fast up to the top of my head, and I'll spill my brain custard all over this pretty green dress. I made custard once. It takes a lot of eggs. If those eggs were chickens, I could never eat them all up. Like I did.

COOKIE: You're in for a treat. I don't do this for everybody… but you, you're special.
[To an imaginary band]
You guys know "God Bless America?"
[To audience]
Didn't you just love her?! Kate Smith was a goddess. Big, beautiful, righteous. Everything you wanted in a songbird. And the voice. Lawsy! Lord! Is a pig pink?!
[She establishes a jazzy rhythm snapping her fingers]
Put it right in here, boys…

MILTON *[Recites the second stanza of "Lucy…" by Wordsworth]:*
A violet by a mossy stone
Half hidden from the eye!
Fair as a star, when only one
Is shining in the sky.

COOKIE *[Sings]:*
God bless America. Yeah. Yeah.
Land that I love. Ho, Ho, Ho.
Stand beside me and guide little ole me, Ho!
Through the night with a light from the man above!
[Speaks]
What do you get when you cross a donkey with an onion? A piece of ass so good, it makes you cry! Pa-rum-pum!

LUCY: How do you like this dress? I'm going to keep it forever.

When Mama gave it to me, she said it was her wedding dress, but I remember when she bought it, because I put my hand on it, all covered with popcorn butter, and it left a little mark. You see?

[Raises the hem of her skirt and shows it]

Right here.

[Measures her hand against the hand mark on the dress]

It's much bigger now.

[She plays "Mary Had a Little Lamb" on the clarinet, very well]

MILTON *[Recites the third and last stanza of Wordsworth's "Lucy"]*:

She lived unknown, and few could know

When Lucy ceased to be;

But she is in her grave, and oh,

The difference to me!

[He smiles and nods appreciatively]

LUCY: I thought I was gonna die up here. But you love me…

[She throws kisses out to the audience. Lights up on COOKIE, who is also throwing kisses, but she catches a few of them and playfully plants them on her own cheek. Lights up on MILTON, who is sitting on the floor eating popcorn.]

COOKIE and LUCY: Thank you! Thank you!

[Popcorn pours on them like confetti from above]

Thank you.

LUCY: They love me.

COOKIE: You love me, don't you?!

MILTON: I love you.

[Lights slowly cross to the commuter train]

Scene 3

[On the commuter train to New York. The women are still in their gowns. COOKIE is fuming, LUCY is crying. MILTON is trying to be comforting.]

MILTON: I da-don't unda-da-derstand. You were ssso ge-good. Ne-nobody was be-better than you.

COOKIE: It's simple, Milton. We were *too* good, too beautiful.

[She slaps LUCY on the arm]

Stop crying, will you?!

LUCY: No!

COOKIE: You're driving everybody away. Look! Look. You got them running like trout.

MILTON: Mab-maybe there's sssomething going on in another car. I'll go la-look. These tra-trains are ssso fun.
[He exits]
LUCY: Fuck them!
COOKIE: I would if I could, but I can't so I won't.
LUCY: Jesus! Is that all you ever think about?!
COOKIE: Let's see… Yes. That's it. That and my voice.
LUCY: You sang good tonight.
COOKIE: Thanks. You were okay too.
LUCY *[Starts to cry again]:* Ba-but I didn't win.
[COOKIE hits her again]
Stop it!
COOKIE: You stop it! Stop feeling sorry for yourself.
[Raises her hand again as if to strike]
Stop now or I'll bash your pie.
[LUCY pulls COOKIE'S hand down]
LUCY: But I wasn't just crying for me.
[Pause. They both start crying. MILTON returns. He carries a red leather purse, shaped like a chicken .]
MILTON: La-Look what I fe-found!!
[They ignore him and keep crying]
Look! It's red! It was just sssitting there. It ah-asked me to pick it up because ne-nobody else wah-wanted it and it's ssso pretty, I ka-couldn't sssay ne-no. You wah-want it?
[He holds it out, first to LUCY, then to COOKIE, who takes it, opens it, and throws it back to him, still crying]
COOKIE *[imitating MILTON]:* Ne-no me-money.
MILTON: Tha-that's okay. It de-doesn't ne-need mah-ney to be beautiful. I'll fe-find a ge-good home for it Mah-maybe my closet will ta-take it in and bah-be ne-nice to it. It looks ssso ne-nice on my…
[He puts it on top of his arm]
See?
[COOKIE karate kicks it off his arm]
Ye-you're a fe-funny he-hairpin, Ka-Cookie.
LUCY: When do we get off this stupid train?
MILTON: When it ssstops mah-moving.
LUCY: Stop!
[Blackout]

Scene 4

[Lights up on the Rodriguez apartment. LUCY *and* COOKIE *are seated on the couch.* LUCY *is trying to stop crying.* MILTON *stands over her, holding two ice cream cones.* COOKIE *is eating an ice cream cone of her own. The women are still dressed in evening gowns, and they have oyster shell crowns on their heads.]*

MILTON: If you eat ye-your ice cream, I'll beh-bet you feel be-better.

[No response]

You know you'll always bah-be mah-my Miss...

[LUCY *cries harder]*

COOKIE: Nothing makes her feel better, Milty. She likes to cry.

Red lights make her cry... Nighttime, too.

LUCY: They do not! I don't!

COOKIE: Come over here and I'll show you how a real woman eats ice cream.

[She rolls her tongue sensuously over the ice cream, the cone, and her finger]

Tongues are so important, aren't they?

MILTON: Yeah... Otherwise you couldn't hold de-down ther-mometers when you've ge-ge-got a fever. And you couldn't sssend any letters to anybe-body, or put stamps on postcards. I like sssending postcards.

COOKIE: I like getting them. Do you travel?

LUCY: Give me that!

[She takes the ice cream from MILTON's *hand and bites it viciously]*

MILTON *[to* LUCY*]:* Jeess! You ma-ma-must love ice ke-ke-cream.

LUCY: Any flavor but vanilla. Especially the kind with brown specks. If I have to eat vanilla, I like the artificially flavored kind. That's something how people think that natural is better. It's not, it's just natural.

COOKIE *[to* LUCY*]:* You're not supposed to do that.

LUCY: What?

COOKIE: You're not supposed to bite ice cream. It means you're impotent.

LUCY: Women don't get that.

COOKIE: It means something, though. It means you're not sen-suous, like me. I lick my ice cream all the way around. I start at the top and slowly turn the cone. Just the tip of my tongue touches the ice cream.

LUCY: That takes too long. I like to fill up my mouth fast. Bite, swallow. Bite, swallow. This way I get two or three whole cones while people like you are still on the first one.

MILTON: I de-do be-be-both.

COOKIE: I like you, Milton.

MILTON: I la-like you, too. Be-both of ye-you.

COOKIE: But who do you like the best? Huh?

LUCY: Stop it, Mama.

COOKIE: Bad milk.

LUCY: What?

COOKIE: That's what you are: spoiled!

LUCY: In more ways than one.

COOKIE [*to* MILTON]: She's crazy. You can't listen to anything she says.

LUCY: You think I don't remember, but I do.

COOKIE: I don't know what you mean.

LUCY: I mean!

COOKIE: You don't know what you mean. Why don't you play the clarinet for us?

[*She puts her arm around* MILTON]

For me and *this* handsome boy?

[*She touches his face*]

LUCY: Don't touch him.

[COOKIE *puts her other arm around* Lucy, *who pushes her away*]

What are you trying to do?!

COOKIE: I was trying to show you how I feel about you.

LUCY: You don't feel nothing for me.

COOKIE: I didn't kill you, did I? I didn't kill you when I could have. When you were a little tiny thing. When I could've picked you up and thrown you against the wall. I could've done that but I didn't. I let you sit on my belly instead. And I combed your long, beautiful hair. Pulled out all the knots. Let you stay home with me if you wanted, if you didn't want to go to school. I watched you run into the wall to make your nose bleed so you wouldn't have to go to school. I cleaned you up and let you sit on my bed.

LUCY: You hit me.

COOKIE: Not all the time.

MILTON: I hit things sssometimes.

COOKIE: I didn't hit you all the time.

LUCY: Yeah. Sometimes you hit my dolls instead,

COOKIE: You see. It wasn't always you.

MILTON: I be-bit mah-my cheeks ah-ah lot be-because they fe-fall asleep. That's the only way to wah-wah-wake 'em.

COOKIE: You got me back…

LUCY: Only once.

COOKIE: You almost killed me.

MILTON: We ssshould ba-be ce-celebrating. I ge-got the two rurunners-up of the Ma-Ma-Miss Oooyster Fe-festival with mame to-ne-ne-night!

LUCY: Almost doesn't count.

COOKIE: How many daughters does it take to change a light bulb?

MILTON: How mmmany?

COOKIE: None.

[MILTON laughs and then puts on some slow dance music]

MILTON: Who we-wants to de-de-dance?

LUCY and COOKIE: Me!

LUCY: No, you don't. Don't you fucking touch him!

COOKIE: We can all dance. All together.

LUCY: I don't wanna dance all together.

[MILTON and COOKIE begin to slow dance; Lucy takes off her crown and slashes her fingers with the shells; COOKIE and MILTON take her hands and make her dance with them]

LUCY: I'm gonna bleed to death.

MILTON: I de-don't think ssso… blood fffeels ssso ge-good, doesn't it?

COOKIE: Yeah. It's good for your complexion, too.

[She draws warpaint lines on her face with LUCY'S bloody fingers]
I look like your father now.

[They dance to the end of the dance in silence]

LUCY *[Looking at her fingers]:* They already stopped.

MILTON: Ne-ne-nobody bleeds fe-fo-forever.

COOKIE: Most people die first.

LUCY: I'm ugly, aren't I? Why'd you let me go there? To that contest? They weren't laughing at my clarinet playing, were they? I've got a fucking ugly face.

COOKIE: It's not that bad.

LUCY *[Going to a mirror]:* Yes it is. I'm a pizza face. That's why they like me at my job. People can look at me, and they know right away that I'm the pizza girl. It's like free advertising! People see me and they think anchovy, mushroom!

COOKIE: Eggplant, sausage…

[LUCY breaks the mirror]

MILTON: You ssshouldn't've d-d-done th-that. You always pe-pe-pay when you do the-those th-things. I de-did sssomething la-like that, be-but it was all right bebe-because I la-la-loved her… When you la-love sssomebody, it's all right.

LUCY *[to COOKIE]:* Why do you take everything away from me?

COOKIE: Why do you let me?

MILTON: Ke-ke-Can I use ye-your be-be-bathroom?

LUCY and COOKIE: Yes.

[MILTON exits to bathroom. Pause]

COOKIE: You really like him?

LUCY: Yeah. So why do you have to like him too?

COOKIE: He's my date, baby.

LUCY: I saw him first.

MILTON *[Re-enters, holding his hands to his nose]:* Ye-you have ne-ne-nice sssoap. It tah-turns your hands into fl-flowers.

[They stare at him blankly]

That's what the commercial says…

COOKIE: Let me see your hands.

[He holds them out to COOKIE]

MILTON: Do you read pe-palms?

COOKIE: I just wanted to see your knuckles. They look so old.

[MILTON pulls his hands away]

MILTON: Th-they've always la-la-looked th-that way.

LUCY *[Taking MILTON's hand]:* I think your hands are pretty.

MILTON: How c-c-could th-they ba-b-be? Th-they have ssso ma-many veins.

COOKIE: They look like oysters.

LUCY *[She turns his hands so she's looking into his palms]:* It says you better watch out for people named Cookie.

COOKIE: You're the one to watch, baby girl.

LUCY: She'll take you by the neck.

COOKIE: Baby, baby.

LUCY: She'll take you by the neck and cut off your head. She'll hold you by your feet and make all the liquid!

COOKIE: God, Lucy! We didn't even do the cake yet. We gotta do the cake.

LUCY *[dropping his hands]:* No cake.

MILTON: It's c-c-cold in ha-here, Lucy. Why de-don't we ga-go to mah-my house? I gege-got a lot of heat.

LUCY *[to* COOKIE*]:* Do you know what I want?

COOKIE: What?

MILTON: What?

LUCY: I want someone to kiss. I wanna feel lips on my lips. I'm tired of kissing my pillow. I'm tired of sleeping with my pillow tucked up between my legs, I don't want to end up like you.

COOKIE: You always scared the shit out of me, even as a baby. The first time I called your name, you looked right at me, into my eyes and through my head. I felt like the back of my head was on a hook and your eyes kept me hanging there. You were too small to know that much.

LUCY: You always thought I knew something... I didn't. There was nothing to know. I only know what you taught me, that's why I'm like you.

MILTON: De-doesn't anybe-be-body wanna ge-go for a walk? It's a new mah-moon.

LUCY: That means there's nothing to see, Milton.

MILTON *[to* LUCY*]:* Ye-you have a le-le-lovely voice. Ye-you should bah-be on TV.

*[*LUCY *kisses* MILTON*]*

Th-thank ye-you.

[He kisses LUCY *roughly and she pulls away. He grabs her again; he kisses her roughly, biting her lips until she bleeds, then he licks her lips.]*

There. Quiet.

[He kisses her eyes softly]

There.

[He strokes her stomach]

I love red lipstick.

COOKIE: I told you, you wouldn't like it

LUCY: I loved it, Mama. I like red lipstick too.

*[*LUCY *kisses* MILTON *biting his lips till they bleed; then she licks his face in a semicircle and holds it in her hands.]*

MILTON: Let mah-me take you to mah-my house. I c-c-can take ke-care of ye-you there. We ke-can mah-make sssoup.

LUCY: Nobody has to take care of me.

COOKIE: She won't go anywhere. She can't leave me.

MILTON: Ye-you can c-c-come, too.

COOKIE: He called me up, Lucy. He didn't even know who I was. He wanted to come see me because he doesn't have anybody else. A man like that's no good for you. But me, I'm used to men like that. I know what they need. You'll just disappoint him, baby.

LUCY *[to* MILTON*]*: Let's go.

COOKIE *[blocking* the *door]:* You won't be there very long. He'll kick you out. And don't expect me to let you back in here.

LUCY: I don't expect nothing from you!

*[*COOKIE *slaps* LUCY. LUCY *jumps on* COOKIE *and hits her savagely.* MILTON *pulls* them apart.*]*

MILTON *[holding on to* LUCY*]*: Save that for later, baby. For us. I'll show you a better time. You can hit me longer than her, you can hit me forever.

*[*LUCY *turns on* MILTON *and pummels him]*

Yes. C'mon now. Keep doing it. Harder.

[She continues to punch him]

Feel my bones on the back of your hands…

[He kneels in front of her. She kicks him.]

Yes. That's nice. That's real nice.

COOKIE: She'll kill you.

*[*MILTON *smiles and curls into a fetal position.* LUCY *sits on him and pounds on his chest.]*

MILTON: Thank you.

*[*LUCY *suddenly gets up]*

LUCY: No.

MILTON: You really love me.

LUCY: God, you looked like me lying there. You looked like me.

*[*LUCY *goes to* the closet, grabs her clarinet and exits. MILTON *goes to* COOKIE *and helps her up.]*

COOKIE: She's never getting back in.

MILTON: You ka-come with mah-me.

COOKIE: No way, loser.

MILTON: Please…

COOKIE: Call me. You're cuter on the telephone.

MILTON: I ke-can ge-go home right ne-ne-now and ke-call you.

COOKIE: You just do that.

MILTON: The fe-phone's my fah-favorite instrument.

[MILTON exits. COOKIE *begins stacking furniture against the door. When all the furniture is stacked, she looks around, and wipes her bloody face on her dress.]*

COOKIE: You never notice how much dust there is until you move something.

[She gets a broom from the closet and starts to sweep, humming the song "Witchi-tai-tai" as the lights fade to black.]

END OF PLAY

Optional Scene for Act 1, between Scenes 3 and 4

[In the past COOKIE *is thirty-two and* LUCY *is twelve.* LUCY *is sleeping on the sofa.* COOKIE *wakes her.]*

COOKIE *[Holds out an object wrapped in a flag]:* Look, Lucy. Lucy.

[Startled]: No, Ma! What?! Ma!

COOKIE: It's okay, baby. 'Cause you know what happened? Louis was chasing a girl-cat and just didn't make it over the fence. But that's okay...

[LUCY begins to cry]

Because he died for love, and there's no better reason for dying, Lucy. Isn't that true? Baby? Look at me.

[She takes LUCY'S head in her hands]

Isn't that true?

[She squeezes LUCY'S face]

LUCY: Ouch! Stop it! Mama!

COOKIE: Say it's true.

LUCY: It's true, Mommy.

[She pulls away from COOKIE]

COOKIE: Alls he thought about was her... That's what got him into trouble. Love always gets you into trouble.

LUCY: Yeah...

[She picks up the dead cat and cradles it]

COOKIE: It's lucky for you I found him. He was pierced right through the middle—just like Christ or something. It would've upset you, baby.

LUCY: We gotta bury him.

COOKIE: Yeah... He'll start to smell soon.

LUCY: I don't got nothing to put him in.

COOKIE: Oh… Well, we'll just use my jewelry box.

LUCY: But that's so beautiful. Why would you give it to him? It smells like roses and everything.

COOKIE: I'm not using it much lately. And if I need it, I'll know where to find it… And he died so romantically, Lucy. I guess that's really it. I'm just romantic.

[She takes the cat from LUCY *and puts him in the box]*

LUCY: We should say a prayer for him, huh?

COOKIE: I am, baby.

*[*COOKIE *starts to hum "Isn't It Romantic?" and dance with the box. She takes* LUCY's *hand and makes her dance, too]*

I'm in love… Isn't it romantic?

[She keeps humming and they keep dancing as lights cross to MILTON's *apartment in scene 4]*

Optional Scene for Act 2 between Scenes 1 and 2

[Lights up on young LUCY *and* COOKIE. COOKIE *is teaching* LUCY *a song and dance routine to "Over the Rainbow." COOKIE has a hand motion for almost every word.]*

COOKIE *[demonstrating]* Birds fly

[She flaps]

high in the

[Points]

sky.

[Makes a circle with her finger]

Oh,

[Draws an imaginary question mark]

why, then,

[Makes a circle]

oh,

[Draws a question mark]

why, can't I?

[Shakes head no and points at herself]

When every little bluebird!

[Speaks]

Flap! Flap on, bluebird!

[Sings again]

When every little bluebird flies around the rainbow!

[Speaks]

Now I'm the rainbow.
[She bends over. Sings, repeating all the hand motions above.]
Why, oh why, can't I?
[Speaks]
Okay. Let's take it from the top.
*[She bends over LUCY, who is the rainbow in the first part. LUCY
gets most of the hand motions right.]*
Somewhere over the rainbow. Bluebirds fly.
Birds fly high in the sky.
Oh, why, then, oh, why can't I?
[Speaks]
Point at yourself, goddamn it!
[She slaps LUCY. LUCY cries.]
Don't you ever wanna be something?!
[Singing]
Why then? Oh, why can't I?
[LUCY continues to cry quietly, but does the routine perfectly.]
When every little bluebird flies around the rainbow!
[Speaks]
Now you sing, too.
LUCY and COOKIE *[Singing]:* Why, oh, why can't I?
[As LUCY continues to cry softly, lights slowly cross to the Oyster Festival, scene 2]

I DisMember the Alamo:
A Long Poem for Performance

Laura Esparza

Thanks to: Los Norteños Writing Group and Larry Pisoni

First performed by Laura Esparza at the Centro Cultural de la Raza, San Diego, California, in 1991; and at the University of California, Irvine, October 30, 1992.

> *The theme music from John Wayne's movie* The Alamo *plays in the pre-show ritual. The stage is delineated on three sides by a low, straight row of sandbags. A small table upright serves as an altar and a podium. A stool sits down left.*
>
> *I am sitting behind a white rectangular screen, or in a white tent, or better yet a white 1950's refrigerator with two white wings, somewhat resembling the Alamo facade. A rectangular hole is cut in the center surface to expose only my eyes. Left and right, out of holes in the screen/ tent/refrigerator, my legs appear, spread-eagle, in black fishnet stockings.*
>
> *With the Alamo theme playing in the background, slides of my ancestors who lived in San Antonio near the time of the Alamo are projected over my eyes, as seen through the white screen/tent/refrigerator. In a much larger production, there would also be another very large screen looming over the screen/tent/refrigerator with a second set of projections.*

[I sing]
Y volver, volver, volver,
a sus brazos otra vez,
Llegaré hasta donde estés,
yo se perder, yo se perder,
quiero volver, volver, volver. *[As music fades]*

We have a family story,
A little familial history,
A ritual secret of sorts. We tell it to each other,

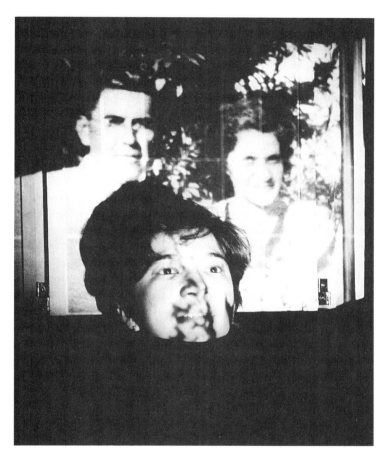

(courtesy of Laura Esparza)

The family secret,
Our creation story
of how we discovered
—ourselves.

We were telling this story—
a little familial performance art—
long before I ever got here.
I'm sure each of us tells it differently—
it's hard to get all the facts straight
about something that happened 150 years ago
but it's not about facts—
it's about family.

That's how I have this story to tell you now
because it was never found in history books.
It was part of being my name, part of my body,
my locus,
mi tierra,
family rooted in story.

In the family mantra
We have a grandfather
Actually, he's not my grandfather but
My great great great grandfather
or is it my great great great great grandfather
I can never get it straight.
Maybe only three greats for
old Gregorio Esparza.
Anyway, he's the star of the story

Greg, greg, greg, greg, Gregorio.
[Sung as a Gregorian chant]

He was married to a woman named Ana,
and they lived in San Antonio in 1836,
not a great year, but not far from where my family lives today.
Great, great, great Ana.
She's the real story.
They had three, no, four, no, maybe it was only three children,

it was a long time ago,
and the oldest was named Enrique.
They lived in an adobe house
or maybe it was a shack, but it might have been a lean-to
near the walls of the Alamo mission,
not far from how my family lives today.

Gregorio had a friend named William Smith,
who,
the story goes, fished Enrique
out of the San Antonio River
when Enrique fell in during a
boyish prank, quite probably—
likely so, anyway.

William Smith was a good friend to Gregorio.
He was married to a Mexicana, and
they probably called each other compadre,
brothers under the skin and all that shit.
They both believed in the revolution.
Nationhood for Texas was at stake.
Nevertheless,
William had commissioned a cart to carry their families away
from San Antonio before General Santa Ana arrived
with his four thousand.
A battle was about to occur at the Alamo.
But the cart never came,
or the driver was scared,
or Santa Ana was early,
you know how these things never work out.
So, William, *el compadre,* asked Gregorio for a really big favor.
Well, the rest you'll never see in the movies.

[Slides from various Alamo movies are projected on the screen/tent with
The Alamo *theme music only. Spoken word amplified.]*

Enrique was among the boys that first saw the horses
of the Mexican soldiers arrive.
Heart beating.
Hooves pounding.

Feet in red dust
Run for cover. "The man, the man
on the big horse."

William Smith asks Gregorio to stay on inside the Alamo.
Gregorio makes the choice, saying,
"I will stay and die fighting."
Ana made her choice, too. "I will stay by your side.
And, with our children, die, too.
They will soon kill us, but
We will not linger in pain."

John Wayne never had it so good. My grandfather and my grandmother crossed that famous Travis line and fought the battle of
the Alamo. Yes, John, there were Mexicans in the Alamo.

See, all he had in his movie version were "heroes" who were
white. Nothing so complicated as interracial marriages and
friendships between Anglos and Mexicans.

The message was simple but clear: Kill the savage Mexicans.
Save Texas, Western civilization, from the heathens. Hollywood
formula made history.

They lived inside the belly of the beast,
in the central chapel of the Alamo,
for thirteen days and thirteen nights. Oh, holy war.
My grandfather shot a cannon from a high scaffold stuck in a
window with a patch of sky that turned blue and then black,
blue, black, blue, black.
Oh, holy night.

Down below, Ana waited, the stench of death and the sound of
dying all around her.
Three frightened children and a baby stuck at her breast.
She waited.
She waited for that last day, when Gregorio shot his cannon and
a cannon shot right back.
He caught a cannonball with his sternum and fell from the sky
into Ana's waiting arms.

End of my movie. Credits roll.
Oh, but the story doesn't end there.

[Music stops. Image freezes on movie images of Santa Ana.]

Generalíssimo Santa Ana won the battle,
and ordered all survivors,
women and children, out of the Alamo.
On a gray morning
my great, great, great grandmother,
began her own battle:
Ana taking on Santa Ana, no relation, face-to-face.
No relation, except both were warriors;
no relation, except they spoke the same language;
no relation, except they both had this land in their blood.

Whether Ana was party to the sentiment of revolution in 1836,
I'll never know.
Who will know the thoughts of a mestiza woman 150 years ago.
There were charges of unfair taxation,
but also numbers of Americans
making claims on land,
wanting Texas as their own country
wanting gold, wanting slaves.
If history is made of the desires of men,
who would listen to Ana and her four hungry children?
My grandfather had a brother named Francisco,
who lived in San Antonio, too, but
who served in Santa Ana's army.
Brother against brother.
After the fall
he stepped forward,
begging Santa Ana for custody of Ana and her children.
They returned to the Alamo
to the stench of body rot,
to the maggot-ridden graveyard,
to the birthplace of our assimilation,
and countless colonizations.
Lit by the pyre that burned men's bodies
They dragged my grandfather's to bury in hallowed ground like

a couple of Antigones in the night.
Oh, holy light.

[Slide of Francisco carrying out Gregorio from the movie The Price of Freedom*]*

This scene was cut from the movie.

[Slide up of small girl with an older girl and a cat]
Oh, this is me and my sister. The cat wasn't ours.

I was born across the street from that graveyard in 1958.
I suckled on the tit of history. I guess you could say I remember the Alamo.

*[*The Alamo *soundtrack begins, and a high wailing is heard from behind the screen. Theme from* The Alamo *on. Up left a small stand of upright paper dolls of Alamo heroes, with two paper dolls that resemble a Mexican couple, are lit.*
    Enter, dressed in a sexy Texas showgirl leotard with fishnet stockings and pointy high heels. Speaking in a thick Texan accent, applying ruby red lipstick with a mirror.
    Slides of funny scenes from Alamo movies. Then sexy Mexican actress with John Wayne.]

It's a crock of shit. This Texas history lesson is a crock of shit. What do you remember about the Alamo, huh? Viva Max? John Wayne? It's all a pack of lies. Epics. Sagas! Truth and lies all done up to make each other look good. But I love a good story, don't you? You see, a good lie can be kind of sexy. You know what I mean? Pow—instant intrigue. You can make any story a better one. And here I am, telling you my version, but there's another and another. Remember the Alamo.
Remember Cortés?
Hernán Cortés?
When the Spanish sonuvabitch set out to conquer Mexico,
what kind of promises did he make
to promise a people's revolution
against the despot dictators: the Aztecs?
When Cortés set the Toltecs and the other Indian nations against

(courtesy of Laura Esparza)

the Aztecs,
who came out the winner?
Cortés.

[Slide of Jim Bowie]

There are some who say that Jim Bowie, hero of the Alamo, was
protecting a hoard of gold he stole from the Apaches and hid in
a well at the Alamo. Westward expansion, slaves, there was something for everyone, besides "freedom." And freedom for whom?
Did Gregorio know what he was fighting for?

The history of Texas, to me, is a neighborhood I know by heart.
The history of Texas is located here *in* my heart, in my blood.
[Lipstick X applied over heart]
The history of Texas is never like a book or a movie. You can't
put your hand on it. What happened can only be described one
mirror at a time.

You know this Texas history lesson is a crock of shit because no
one ever tells the story of Ana. You never see her story in the
history books. I was flying back to Texas one day, and I opened
a Southwest Airlines magazine and there, there, a story on my
grandfather; he got all the press. But never a word about Ana.

My mother's family has a story, too, but never mind that.
[To audience member]
We have better things to think about, don't we? Like bowling
for glory.
[Slide up of smiling man covered in blood]
[Taking a bowling ball out of a sandbag, bowls dolls over]
Huh, caught you! Making up history inside your head.
A girl's gotta take care of her looks.
History's sexy if you gonna sell books!
Ever lie on your taxes?
Ever sign a fake name at a motel?
Do you really believe a homeless person's story?
When anyone asks me if I speak Spanish, I say, "Oh, sure."
It's a nation of cynics.

[Slide of Enrique Esparza]
No one ever believed the story Enrique told until he was a very old man. Even then, when Enrique told his story to the *San Antonio Express and News* in 1907, he was interviewed by a white reporter, who made his story sound like a lie. They even mentioned that he spoke English pretty good, for a Mexican.

He said, "You ask me, do I remember it. I tell you, yes. It is burned into my brain and indelibly seared there. Neither age nor infirmity could make me forget, for the scene was one of such horror that it could never be forgotten by anyone who witnessed its incidents."

[Exploring Enrique's face with my fingertips, trying to fit myself into his image, rolling into a tight little ball before the screen.]

This is me against the backdrop of Texas history.

[Enlargement of Enrique's image, then blackout. Singing "Y volver, volver, volver..." I light a candle over the fallen effigies of my ancestors. Slides of movie images of women and children at the Alamo. Then slide of older Mexicana woman wrapped in a rebozo. I enter with a rebozo wrapped around my head. Standing in front of screen.
During this text, a voice-over repeats the following in Spanish.]

I am Ana of San Antonio. I was living here in 1836 with my husband and my children, Enrique. Francisco, Manuel, and Maria, my little one. When this crazy war broke out, I had no choice but to try to assure the lives of my children. But I chose to die if need be. We chose to die together as a family, and I think we did, in a way. Buried in the darkness, and the blood.

After Santa Ana took us out—how I hated to leave Gregorio—we were placed under guard in the house of my compadre, Señor Musquiz. The children were hungry. So I went into the kitchen, I knew my way around, the pantry, the larder. Señor Musquiz comes in. Huh, he made me jump. "What are you doing here?" he says. "Don't you know it is dangerous to leave the room that was put under guard?" I don't care whether I am under guard or not, I said. I am going to have something to eat for myself, for my children, and for my compadres if Santa Ana does not feed his prisoners. Well, Señor Musquiz found us some food.

But the journey back from death was hard. I pulled my children in a cart sixty miles–sixty miles with no mule but my back–till we came to this red dirt land. There we built a home, a simple cabin. Later a chapel and then a school. We started with nothing and helped ourselves the best we could.
[Tape ends]

[Removing rebozo, I light a candle on the altar stage right for Ana. Sifting a steady stream of red dirt into a clear dish lit by a candle.]

For thirteen days and thirteen nights, she was Death's midwife. She waited through the endless night until her husband fell from the sky like Icarus, a cannonball stuck in his sternum. Four babies and a bloody corpse. Four babies and a bloody corpse. *Hero* is too big a word to waste on the dead.

1,920 acres of land she could not claim by her rights as a hero of the Alamo.

1,920 acres she could have tilled to feed her family.
She fed her babies buggy meal to keep them alive.

1,920 acres she could not claim because her last name was Esparza,
Mexicana like the land she stood on.
An exile in her own land.
Her cells are my cells.
Her grit is mine.
She lived past the glory
the hype of history,
And I am here
simply because she survived.

[Guitar]

[Exit]

[Slide up says "My Private Alamo." Enter rolling in with a bowling ball.]

When I was a kid, I used to hide behind the refrigerator, or underneath the couch, or in the back of the closet, where it was cool. Underneath the blankets I was very, very shy, but, more than that, I was scared of the gunshots in the night, scared of fireworks and explosions that sounded like cannonballs roaring past. Scared of all the people speaking Spanish.

My sister, my favorite person in the whole world, dodged the draft for the Vietnam war with her husband in 1971. When she moved to Ontario, she was the first to ever leave Texas for good. I think Ana might have done the same if she had had a choice. I think she too might have said no to any kind of senseless killing. She might have liked Canada, with its cool, crafted landscapes, might have forgotten for a moment the burden of identity, the multiple colonizations of her land.

[I roll the bowling ball, chasing it around the stage, falling over it or running in its path]

When I was sixteen my father asked me to join the Daughters of the Republic of Texas. Every year, he dressed up as Gregorio and marched in the Fiesta Day parade, the one where the Fiesta Queen was never Mexican.

I went to one meeting. The garden of the Alamo was filled with bobbing white heads like a float made of white chrysanthemums. I collected the application–I was the only brown face besides the waiter. The application said that the DRT, Drat for short, was open to descendants of residents of Texas prior to 1836– that checked out with the pedigree. That I needed to be sixteen–I was just–and that I should be white.
[Gulp]
What am I? I couldn't do it. I couldn't meet them in the eyes. Not even sure who I was, I couldn't, even when my father begged me; to infiltrate enemy ranks and perhaps fire the first cannonball into the safety of their garden.

[I bowl for glory]

The other day, I was talking to a friend of mine, a prominent Chicana activist, and we agreed that things would probably not significantly change in our lifetimes. That racism may be eternalized as well as internalized. And some days, wouldn't it be nice to just forget the whole battle. Wouldn't it be nice to move someplace cool, like Nova Scotia, where you could forget the whole Chicano thing, never see another soul, and put the culture on ice.

[Bowl again]

The other day, I was talking to a friend of mine, a prominent Chicana performance artist, and I told her that even though my father didn't like the word, there might be some honor in calling myself a pocha. And she said, "A what?" and I said, "A pocha." And she said, "A what?" and I said, "A pocha." And she said, "Oh, that's funny. I thought you said 'a pork chop.' "

[I throw the cannonball in the air and catch it two times, each time rolling it deeper into my stomach, letting it drop the third time.]

Shot from a cannon of history,
a ball of confusion
into the gaping mouth of the sky,
a wayward seed in diaspora
in a world of places
I didn't belong.
Chicanitas, firmly rooted,
planted by the sun,
know the meaning of mi tierra.
But skyward cannonballs run in my family.

My sister and I broke tradition,
we broke into a run,
the day they let us out of the Alamo.
Shot from a cannon in a flash,
history is circumstance merely,
lost to the touch.

Soaring through the sky,
always feeling like a spy,
I lose touch,
I lose touch.

[I roll with the bowling ball. Then, lying on my back, I place it on my belly. I pour the rest of the red dirt over the ball. Lights out.]
[Exit]

[Lights out. Slide of one of my elderly male ancestors. Enter as Francisco.]
How I remember him
I remember him
as another me
Not identical but a reminder
there is always someone
other than a me.
He was a brother as I was a brother,
We were little brown feet in a red dirt road.
What short years of childhood we shared.
When my mother wore me
like a muff,
I was there in her love for Gregorio,
sharing the language of her blood,

My name is Francisco.
Oh, that my name were somebody else,
because I did not want to be the one
in that terrible war;
the spirit of Death
walking behind me.

I was not at the battle,
but some miles away,
in the battalion of sheep,
more for the slaughter.
We heard the cry of the lambs,
days and nights of thunder,
no, not thunder,
because thunder brings rain,

fruit and bounty,
and these were sounds of
mouths parched with fear
desiccated by death
and pounded into the dust of our land.
We were in the molcajete of death, cabrón.
And who knew which one of us chile petins
was gonna make it.
I was praying like I have never prayed again,
for me, for my compadres,
that someone would come to their senses,
for Gregorio and Ana,
who, I knew, were living in San Antonio.
Gregorio was not a stupid man.
Ana had cojones of her own.
I'd only hoped that they had had enough warning–
I could do nothing.

I was fighting for our country, wasn't I?
This land is, will always be, the great
the very great,
the great, great, great
Mexico.

I can't tell you what I saw when I got there.
Goddamn... me,
[Sign of the cross, twice]
I had no idea.
What spectre came into the heads of men,
which conquest gave us the legacy
of this slaughter?

And then I saw Ana,
[He calls her]
"Ana"
led from the Alamo with a convent of souls,
baptized in blood they wore for cloaks.
Women of blood,
carrying children and bodies of children,
carrying last words, last sight, last love,

of the men that followed them in spirit.

Like a pane of glass
that sliced my head in two,
I heard Gregorio tell me,
Take care of my children.

I had no choice but to approach
Generalíssimo Santa Ana
for the custody of Ana,
Enrique, Maria, Manuel,
Francisco, and little Gregorio.

[Slide out, exit behind the screen]

*[Slide up: "Con Safos" With minor adjustments of bandanna and cigs
rolled in the sleeve of a shirt, re-enter as El Cholo.]*

Hey, hey, hey, hey, orale.
I grew up on the westside of San Antonio speaking English only,
and I lived to tell about it.
You have a story like this one. Our parents were
Mexicano, Salvadoreño, Guatemalteco
or they were Czech or German or Russian.
Real nice people,
the sort of people who say,
"Be nice, it fights racial discrimination,"
or "Speak English, you're American now."
You have a story just like this one.

Well, my folks were poor, and Spanish was their world.
But they lived through some of the big bummers of the twenti-
eth century, like the Depression and World War II.
And they thought it was all their fault!
Well, they could see the writing on the wall:
"Speak English or get screwed, con safos!"
They weren't pendejos.
They were doing what was right by the times,
according to their experience–the Depression and World War
II–mere circumstance, history, really, and who's to blame them

but the '60s and me, because for the rest of my pinche life, people
are asking me,
"What, you don't speak Spanish?"
C'mon, you've said it, too.
"What, you don't speak Spanish?"
You can say it.

*[One by one, I urge each audience member to repeat the refrain after me.
Using the rhythm with which the audience chants "You don't speak
Spanish?," I pull two pork chops from a sandbag and flail myself into
laughter, tongue (la lengua) hanging out, exposing a psychic hole. Exit.]*

[A DisMembered version of the Alamo *theme song returns. Slides of the
Alamo, my body, and of dismemberment, while stage is bathed in red
light. Through the hole in the screen, mouth only appears: music stops.
Spoken amplified or recorded with reverb.]*

Language is not language,
when it's a culture filled with holes.

*[Calliope music. Reappearing with an absurd sombrero, sunglasses, and
big bag of popcorn.]*

My father's passion paid off when he got a role in the IMAX
movie of the battle of the Alamo that plays across the street, in
perpetual homage to the heroes, seven shows a day.
[Slides of the IMAX movie The Price of Freedom*]*
My father in the IMAX movie has become a family ritual we
replay once a year or whenever relatives come to town. We buy
our tickets even though we don't feel we should have to and buy
the biggest tub of popcorn there is. We take up a full row in the
movie theater and put our feet up like we owned the place. Then
we put on our funny glasses and we wait–through the bad acting and the fake gunpowder, our eyes filled with 90 millimeters
of bloody battle, it's almost like being there. The cannons always make me jump. The story of Gregorio and his brother is
the only subplot in the movie. Is that how he died?– Ooh. In the
movie version, they have a shot of Francisco praying for his
brother as he is about to march into the battle of the Alamo.
Huh, lies. But the moment comes when Travis calls on all the

faithful to cross over that famous line, and there's my father, sixty-seven years old, in a red bandanna, waving his arm and smiling that long-toothed grin right into the camera. For all perpetuity, or as long as IMAX can hold this tourist trap together, waving, waving, waving into the camera.

[Black slide. Then slide of my mother. I light a candle for my father and begin to assemble an altar of photos and candles over the stage.]

My mother remembers her childhood as a red dust road on a sharecropper's farm. Stories of her illustrious ancestors were traded in the meager currency of words. She grew up with stories of her ancestor Francisco Ruiz, who was the mayor of San Antonio at the time of the Alamo. He signed the Texas Declaration of Independence; a direct vindication of Gregorio's death. How did our heroes become farmworkers... and our farmworkers become heroes? Colonization transformed our acts of bravery.

[I light a candle for my mother]

[Slides of family members of recent generations]
There's my grandmother and my great-aunt. My aunt with my mother. I grew up in an army of brothers; that's them in our '56 Ford Ranch wagon. I was their cannonball. Oh, and there is my grandfather Manuel, son of Manuel, son of Manuel. All survived the Alamo. We are all here because of Gregorio and Ana.

[More candles lit. Slide of my sister]
My sister also tilled the soil, raised her children well, and died in exile. She died in my arms, a cannonball stuck in my memory. And I am here only because her soul survives in me.

[Slides off. Stars cover the stage. I light candles in all four directions to pre-Columbian flute music.]

This is my story, my story, mystery, mystery. My body is the battlefield of
the colonized self.

The land where conquests of
Spanish, and Mexican, and American
have occupied my cells.

The battle of the Alamo
will be staged inside my sternum
As long as I remain I
under the lie
of conquest.

I will be the battlefield
in the war, the profane war
of lies.

The Indian in me will battle my Spaniard.
My Spaniard will battle my Mexican and
my American will have its own internal Alamo with my Chicana.
My family changed nationalities four times
without ever leaving the neighborhood.
Repeated colonization was the gang-rape of my language.

Borders leapt over us like comets,
and we die a slow death
in the battle of the Alamo.

*[Using lipstick on my naked chest, a rebozo wrapped around my waist,
I diagram my body like a side of beef, to describe the following]*

I am this:
an india
inside a mestiza
inside a gringa
inside a chicana.
I am all of these
and my psyche is like a road map of Texas
traversed by borders
with never any peace at these borders.
I am this:
part india
part mexicana

part spanish
part comanche
part cherokee
part tejana
part english
part french
part Ana
part Gregorio
part Manuel
part Nora
part Reynaldo
part you.

Please join me in homage to our ancestors and to los indios who are buried on sacred ground at the Alamo.

[I light the last candle and perform a ritual to the ancestors as lights fade to black]

Finito

Latin Lezbo Comic:
A Performance about Happiness, Challenges, and Tacos

Monica Palacios

Black stage.
General lights up.
A black platform (8 feet wide x 4 feet deep x 2 feet high), is up stage right. A microphone on a mike stand is on the platform's right corner. Monica is downstage left in muscle-man pose.

MONICA: In the eighth grade, I was this jock!
[Emphasizes present pose, exaggerates two more poses and stops]
I loved getting sweaty with a bunch of girls–but I didn't know why! I felt frightened–yet HORNY!
I was a good basketball player, and that year we got a new coach. She was tough but it paid off; because we won the championship.
CHEERLEADER: Beat 'em at the jump ball, goooooooooooo!
Sink it,
[Sensuously bends her knees down]
Monica.
[Slowly stands up, thrusting out her pelvis and breasts]
Sink it!
[With breasts out, she slowly sticks her tongue out, then blows kisses]
MONICA: I loved that! Anyway, this coach–she was a Chicana, she was a tomboy, she was attractive, she had girlie long hair, and she was funny! So, of course, the cool people got chummy with her and we would hang out. Go to the movies, get a pizza– you know, she had a car.
But then one day, my mom and my sister stepped in and said a woman her age, which was about twentyish, shouldn't be hanging out with kids and maybe she even likes girls. Heaven forbid! "Mother!" I would say in my Samantha Stevens kind of way, "You are so unfair to teenagers!" Then I'd storm upstairs to my room. Forgetting we lived in a one-story house. I agreed she was hanging out with us too much, but it never tripped me out to think she could possibly be a–LESBIAN! I've noticed the word

(Photo by Becky Villaseñor)

LESBIAN makes some people cringe. And I think this is happening because the word LESBIAN makes people think of some yucky sexual activity that has to do with a TRACTOR!
[Mimes driving a tractor, then raises right hand and waves]
And that's silly! But I used to call myself a "gay woman" because the word LESBIAN was soooo upsetting to me!
YOUNG COLLEGE COED: I mean, like, why do we have to use that word?! It's sooo gross! Why can't there be a different word, like–PRECIOUS! If men are GAY, I WANT TO BE PRECIOUS!
MONICA: I'm so glad I've matured. And as I became more involved in the gay and lesbian community, I started using the word more. And one day, I said the word a bunch of times,
[Repeats the word LESBIAN seven times]
AND I GOT OVER IT!
Because, folks, it's just a word. I was making a big deal out of nothing. It seems to be the American thing to do!
I was pleased to find out that the producers of this show went out of their way to attract a good amount of lesbians to this event. As I want to ATTRACT a good amount of lesbians. It's kind of a hobby of mine. Okay, it's an obsession–all right, I'm seeing a counselor for it!
So they put billboards along Interstate 10:
"Entertainment, comedy, lesbians–5 miles. Hungry? Burgers, fries, lesbians–2 more miles. Cold drinks–hot lesbians–1 more mile!"
[Mimes driving a tractor, raises right hand, waves]
[Runs to the front center of stage]
Hey, I remember when I was little and I stole a pack of gum, and my mom found out and she made me go back and steal–A ROAST?
I love those Kodak moments.
I hung out with my little brother Greg. An adorable stubborn brat, but we got along because we did and because I was the boss of him.
Our favorite times were pretending to be James Brown, cap and all, and the BEATLES.
[The song "Girl" starts. After the first line, "Isn't anybody going to listen to my story?" music becomes background]
I was Paul. He was Ringo. I was cute. He was not.

I would play the tennis racket left-handed, and Greg would play the drums by using empty coffee cans. Ohhhh, we were poor but–crafty!

Our favorite jam was

[Sings]

Well, my heart went boom when I crossed that room and I held her hand in Hawaii!!!!!

[Stops singing]

No, it's not *Hawaii!* It's held her hand in *mine!* Not *Hawaii.* So stupid, but–crafty!

[Music fades out]

We had this "music thing" because my dad, Guadalupe–Lupe to his friends. My mom calls him Pal, it's short for Palacios. Now everybody calls him Pal. He played several instruments and he sang. And my older brother Art was in a band. Totally cool, man!

I always thought my dad was this pseudo-mariachi guy, because he had the guitar but he didn't–have the outfit. On Sundays, Pal was part of a band for the Spanish-speaking masses. Four guys with gypsy guitars dressed in quasi-decorative outfits that their wives had picked out.

Now, everybody in the parish would come to these special masses, because the music was–I hate to use this word but–FESTIVE!

RICH WHITE WOMAN: These Mexican people are soooo festive–pass me a sombrero!

[Strikes a pose with hands up in the air like a showgirl]

MONICA: This happy music silenced all that stuff about "You're a sinner! Don't use birth control! Homosexuality is wrong!" Nobody wanted to admit it, but this was a cultural, musical cleanse.

For special events, like the time Bobby Kennedy came to our church. Yeah, we have this day on our home movies. Jealous? I think so. For these special times, real mariachis would perform. I was in MARIACHI MILIEU.

Because I loved watching mariachis! And their outfits–this tomboy definitely wanted one. Plus, they had all those horns and guitars.

And every song ended the same way–TAN! TAN! Every now and then, my parents would invite friends, relatives, compadres to the house, and these people would bring instruments, voices, and beer! And they would jam, creating great Mexican music. Everyone loved when my parents did duets, because they thought they were Steve and Eydie.

[Singing]

STEVE AND EYDIE: Cuando calienta el sol.

[Stops singing]

Hey, how ya doin'? Where ya from?

MONICA: But the highlight was, my parents knew these two comadres, Lala and Trini, who sang together professionally–sort of. They would sing, they would rock the house. My favorite song of theirs was "CU CU RU CU CU PALO MA"–I'm sure it's a favorite here.

They would get to that one point where they would be really close together, looking into each other's eyes,

[Mimes their activity]

like only Mexican women can who sing together.

Just comadres? I don't think so.

Comadre Lala would sing: Cu cu ru cu cu

Comadre Trini would sing: Cu cu ru cu cu

Comadre Lala would sing: Cu cu ru cu cu

And then they would both sing: Palomaaaaaaaaaaaaaaa

Holding it on that one note: Aaaaaaaaaaaaaaaaaaaaaaaa

Because this is what you do with these rancheras:

Aaaaaaaaaaaaaaaaaa

And then, dramatically and full of passion, they would sing:

NO LLORES!

And their lips would be really close together–quivering like this.

[Quivers lips]

Full of passion and ruby red lipstick. Filling the air with music, culture, MAKEUP, woman sweat, woman breath, AND BEER!

[Cross-fade to dreamy lights: blues, reds, purples. And the song "CU CU RU CUCU PALOMA" plays the exact part the comadres did, as MONICA overdramatically lip synchs.

Song ends.

Holds pose. Fade to black.

General lights up.]

The comadres, the mariachis, the history, the passion, the pride, the family, even the menudo–all of it made me feel proud to be MEXICAN, and I thought it showed.

But growing up, people could never figure out my nationality. My family was often asked, "What part of Spain are you from?" They would ask, trying to be so international. And we would tell them, "California." They would ask if we were Spanish because they thought they would be insulting if they asked if we were Mexican. And when I'd tell these people I was Mexican-American, they would respond: "But you don't look Mexican." "You don't have an accent." "How come you don't speak Spanish?" "No, you're not really Mexican." I guess I didn't fit their stereotypical image. Because to these people, Mexicans were either ignored or hired! *[Cross-fade to flashing lights as kooky sax music swells.* MONICA *runs to center of stage with mike in hand.]* Hey, folks, it's time once again for MEXICAN DENIAL! *[Flashing lights cross fade to general. Music fades out.]* I'm your host, Hope Crane. I used to be Esperanza Garza, but the United States has me in MEXICAN DENIAL. As you know, I'll give you the answers, and you'll give me the questions. So let's play MEXICAN DENIAL. Answer: Rodeo, Canon, Moreno. Question: Name three streets in Beverly Hills that have Mexican influence but nobody knows or really cares. Better luck next time. Answer: It refuses to embrace the Mexican culture. Question: Name one reason why LA. is a plastic city. Get ready for this. Answer: Good food, colorful people, cheap labor. Question: What do some people think of Mexicans? *[Package of tortillas is thrown on stage and–lands by her feet. Picks up package. Shows the audience.]* Hey, it's the DAILY TORTILLA! *[Kooky sax music up fades out]* This is where MEXICAN DENIAL gives a chance to a Mexican family to live in California. The lucky winners tonight are *[Reads name from package]*

Mr, and Mrs. Ramirez, you and your family have been chosen to fly to FRESNO!
[Kooky sax music up for three seconds, then fades to background]
There you'll stay in the lovely grape fields. Working long hours in the hot sun. Getting paid below minimum wage. Inhaling those nasty pesticides. Receiving unnecessary harassment from Americans—but hey, you'll get to enjoy the land that was once yours!
All courtesy of MEXICAN DENIAL!
[Music fades out]
But don't worry, folks, because you're going home with prizes, too! Johnnie, tell them what they're taking home.
JOHNNIE: Weeelllll, you've each won a block of government cheese. Government cheese, because it's free and it's great for insulating your home!
And a hairbrush. A hairbrush, because everybody has to brush their hair!
And Spam! Yummmmmm, Spam, because you would never buy it for yourself.
[Kooky sax music up for three seconds, then low for background]
 Hey, that's all the time we have. I've been your host, Hope Crane. I used to be Esperanza Garza. If this show has made you uncomfortable and nervous—it worked! Goodnight, everybody!
[Music comes back up for five seconds as special lights flicker. Music fades out.
Special lights cross-fade to general.
Places mike back on stand, then kneels down on stage left. She attempts to make the "sign of the cross" three times, but seems to be confused and impatient. Finally, she quickly completes her task and then nervously blurts out:]
Hail, Mary, full…of—gravy. Blessed be the—taxpayers. He turned water into wine. They ate baguettes and fondue—thank you very much. Can I go, Sister?
I went to an all-girls Catholic high school.
[Big smirk comes over her face]
This is where I got my training. Thanks, Mom and Dad.
[Stands]
Actually, I didn't know I was a lesbian at this time. I just knew certain women made my uniform feel tight.
[Wiggles out of tight uniform]

With no boys around, I was on top of the world. I made women laugh. I made them read my short stories, and I was their basketball hero—varsity—four years. Go ahead—touch my hand.
[Makes an audience member in the front row touch her hand]
You'll like this.
Once, during practice, this woman who we labeled as DYKE was being very chummy with me. Chummy, chummy, chummy. At the end of practice, we hung out and shot baskets, because we're jocks. I got tired so I sat on the floor. She walked over, squatted on top of me.
[Walks across the stage and pretends to straddle the woman, then shifts into a squat]
And gave me a very cute smirk. Many thoughts ran through my confused head as I looked up at her sweaty body.
[Slowly stands, thinks out loud, looking at woman]
I should tell her to get off of me. I'm not supposed to like this.
[Speaks to the audience]
Eeewww—tractor!
[Does a tip-toe escape from the woman across the stage]
After seconds that seemed like FOREVER, I told her,
[Hysterically]
"GET OFF OF ME!"
I should have told her to get off—on me.
[Slowly wipes hands across chest]
Get off—with me.
[Presses fists together—knuckle to knuckle]
Get me off, baby.
[Points with right hand, arm is bent]
I regret that moment. It would have saved me many awkward, frustrating dates with men. Because I didn't know. Somebody should have told me. A letter would have been fine.
[Mimes writing a letter]
To whom it may concern:
[Looks up]
YOU'RE A LESBIAN!!!!! FIGURE IT OUT!!!!!!!!
Toward the end of high school, a microphone appeared to me. I thought it was the Virgin Mary granting me a miracle, but it was a microphone. Did some "stand-up" for class assembly and I was hooked. After high school, I knew I had to do two things: come out as a lesbian and come out as a comedian. So I headed

for the girl bars, and I headed for the stage. And a star was born.
[Walks to platform to do stand-up.
Central lights cross-fade to special spot on platform.]
Well, in my own mind. I can dream. Can't I?!
[Does stand-up for five minutes. Material varies.
Ends stand-up and walks off platform. Special spot cross-fades to general.]
After several years as a successful comedian in San Francisco and beyond, I needed a drastic change. I decided I was going to do my graduate studies at NYU. Get into the Film Department because,
[Uses fake French accent]
cinema is my genre.
So I moved to New York. I hadn't been accepted yet–but I moved there.
I applied and a month later I received a letter stating, "DEAR APPLICANT–LIKE I'M REALLY SURE!"
ALL OF MY HOPES, MY POSITIVE THINKING, MY WILL TO LIVE–VANISHED!
[Cups hands over mouth and yells]
LIFE SUCKED!
[Wanders aimlessly]
But underneath all the DISAPPOINTMENT,
[Gets weak in the knees]
FRUSTRATION,
[Doubles over]
UNHAPPINESS,
[Spastically walks over to platform and loosely sits]
DRY SKIN,
[Holds stomach]
AND DEBT,
[Plops backwards and is laid out flat on back on the platform]
I HATE NEW YORK!
I knew that I wanted to continue with comedy and become more of a writer.
Where was I to go? I immediately thought of TIJUANA! But I wanted to be bothered with my environment, so I–moved to LA.
[Sits up and sings]
California, here I come. Right back where I started from.

[Stops singing]
WHAT A BURN!
[Stands and walks around]
Actually, I wasn't living in LA, really. I was living in Glendale!
Do you know where Glendale is located? It's between Burbank
and Purgatory!
Hey, remember that commercial a few years ago with this tune:
[Sings]
Get a little Glendale going,
you're gonna be all right...
[Stops singing]
Dinah Shore sang that. Dinah Shore–
[Under her breath]
LESBIAN!
I found Glendale very rich, white–conservative. Actually, I found
much of Southern California very rich, white–conservative. And,
as a matter of fact, the first thing I noticed about this area was
the racism and the discrimination toward Mexicans! But more
on that later.
[Does goofy laugh with hands on hips]
So here I was, this confused, broke, depressed thing trying to
live, trying to blend in, and I did not want to tell my family
about my return to California. But I told them and their re-
sponse–
MY FAMILY: Monica, why can't you get a real job?
MONICA: And my mom's response–
MY MOM: AAAYYYYY, MONICA!
MONICA: And my response to my family:
[Firmly]
"Family, I am an independent woman with goals and needs."
[Slouches–holds hand out–humbly]
"Can I borrow a thousand dollars?"
So after I accepted the fact that I was a loser, I set out to find a
job. And it was really nauseating.
One day I got desperate, I walked into,
[Walks down center to edge of stage]
a temp agency and said, "Look, I have absolutely no office skills–
can you help me?"
And they said–
TEMP AGENCY: No, really, absolutely no office skills?

MONICA: And I said, "Yes, absolutely no office skills. Is there something wrong with your hearing?"

And they said—

TEMP AGENCY: No, it's just that we always answer with a question. Do you understand?

MONICA: And I said, "What do you mean by understand?" So they eventually got me work and…

[Cups hands over mouth and shouts]

MISERABLE!

I always dressed in black. I was in mourning. I had moved again. I wanted to die! But no, oh, no. I got a job with Happy Temp Agency: People helping people who can't hold down a real job. But within a few weeks, I became a waitress because,

[Mimes holding tray over head. Stands in a suggestive pose.]

I was born to serve you.

I got a job at a traditional family steak house—that should have been the tip off, right there.

Home of the world famous garlic bread—I'll be the judge of that. For the first month, I was this new girl, a mystery, a lezbo in fear—

[Strikes lezbo-in-fear pose]

Because all of my former restaurant jobs were with fellow homosexuals. Not this place. This was the heterosexual capital of the world. A loaf of garlic bread under each arm. Every day was an inner struggle with, "Should I come out to them so I can get rid of this big stressball in my gut? Or do I stay in the closet and be miserable?" I pondered. I contemplated. I cudgeled my brains. And then I figured, "I like living in constant fear. I'll stay in the closet and be miserable."

[Does goofy laugh with hands on hips]

Of course, every staff member had to ask—

STAFF MEMBER: Monica, are you married?

MONICA: And I would tell them, "No, are you?!"

Because I had learned that from the temp agency.

I should have told them I was married, so they would,

[Cups hands over mouth and shouts.]

LEAVE ME ALONE!

Instead, I told them I had a BOYFRIEND! Well, mostly to the guys, because they kept hounding me. Every day, up in my face, it was—"Monica, I love you." "Monica, come home with me."

"Monica, I'll give you extra garlic bread," One day, this guy asked—
GUY: Monica, why won't you go out with me? Is it because you don't like men?
MONICA: Oooooooooh! My paranoid self wanted to respond,
[Hysterical]
"Who else knows?"
[Strikes lezbo-in-fear pose]
But my cool self responded, "What are you talking about?" And I shook my head like this.
[Shakes head]
"I have a man!"
And I turned and walked
[Turns and walks up stage]
down that path so many homosexuals do.
[Stops, pivots, faces the audience]
I know you're disappointed in me. I should have come out to him. This would have been the perfect opportunity. I would have educated him. He would have told others, and I would have felt better about myself!
But I didn't! I had to tell this guy for the umpteenth time that yes, I had a boyfriend, because I was scared!
You probably think less of me now. You're looking at me like an amoeba with hair!
[Holds up strand of hair]
But I don't care. I don't give a shit! I didn't feel safe. I thought he was going to come at me with the—DESSERT TRAY!
[Hysterical]
"NO, NOT THE DESSERT TRAY!"
[Strikes lezbo-in -fear pose]
I was always ready to quit—but—I needed the garlic bread! Basically, I wanted to work, make money, and leave. I was unhappy. NEW YORK HAD REJECTED ME! MY EGO WAS SQUISHED! I WASN'T BEING CREATIVE! I WAS BROKE!
[Drops down to knees]
I DIDN'T EVEN HAVE A CAR!
[Gets on all fours]
PLEASE FEEL SORRY FOR ME!
[Crawls toward audience, holding out hand]
Thank you.

[Stands]
So I got a bicycle, and it changed my life. I no longer have female parts, but hey, I am in shape.
And after six months of steady income and believing in myself,
[Clenches fists over chest]
my soul,
[Places hands in front of face and slides them down over body]
my spirit—
[Rubs right hand over heart]
like I always have—things got better. And I began to understand that these work people were good people—some became very dear to me. But the majority believed women should be passive and men should be in charge. It felt like the restaurant time forgot! Even the customers acted this way. I hated when men would order for women!
[Cross-fade to special spot, center stage. She is standing in this.]
WAITRESS: Good afternoon. My name is Monica, what can I get for you?
MAN: Well, my wife will have—honey, what did you want again?
WIFE: I would tell you, but she's looking at me. Help! I can't speak!
MONICA: I felt very sorry for these women, but I will say this, things started to change drastically in my section of the restaurant.
WAITRESS: Good afternoon. My name is Monica, what can I get for you?
MAN: Well, the little lady—
WAITRESS: Sir, the little lady has a mind of her own, and she will order for herself. Ma'am, what can I get you?
WIFE: Hi—um, I'll have… I'll have a-a-a steak!
WAITRESS: Okay, a steak. A little hesitant but that was good. Keep it coming!
WIFE: And ah, ah, ah baked potato!
WAITRESS: Okay, a baked potato. Much more assertive. Let it out. Let it out!
WIFE: And a salad!
WAITRESS: Okay, a salad. You were fantastic!
[To man]
Wasn't she great?
[To wife]
Don't you feel much better? Now turn to your husband and de-

mand ORAL SEX!

[Blackout]

[General lights up–standing on platform.]

MONICA: Did I tell you I escaped from Glendale? Yeah. I found a bungalow in North Hollywood. I really wanted to live in West Hollywood, so I could be a hip-happening-homo, but I didn't want to devote my life to–pastels.

Finally, a place of my own. Everything in my name. I was sitting pretty. My house was a part of me. I turned it into a GIRL TRAP! A flick of a switch dimmed the lights–

[Lights dim. Nightclub look, smokey blue.
Takes mike out of stand.]

poured the wine, made them get–naked. I was grateful. GIRL TRAP.

[Girl-trap music starts and she sings with the music]

Hey, you over there.

[Jumps off stage]

You with that nostril flare.

Follow me home tonight.

And I'll give you my '49er cap.

Then I'll get you into my GIRL TRAP.

GIRL TRAP is a neat place to be.

Just wait and see.

Please stay at least for 30 minutes!

When all is said and done

You're gonna say you had–FUN, FUN, FUN!

You could have been with some other chick.

But you chose this little sap.

And so I got you inside of my GIRL TRAP!

[Strikes girl-trap pose and ends with a snap. Music stops.
Smoky lights cross-fade to general. Places mike back on stand.]

Yeah, I was trapping all kinds of chicks. Here a chick. There a chick. Everywhere a chick, chick.

I was going out to many clubs, and I always got lucky. I always found–money on the floor.

[General cross-fade to special rich blue spot down stage left. Henry Mancini "love music"swells.
Walks into blue spot and delivers most of the monologue looking up into the light.
Music lowers to become background.]

But the most interesting woman that I dated was a babe I met at a club in Provincetown, Massachusetts. She was a young–pilgrim woman.

There she was in the middle of the dance floor, making–a quilt. And I don't know if it was her alluring beauty, her bonnet, the needle and thread, or her BIG, BULKY, BUCKLE SHOES– but I had to meet her.

As I slowly walked up to her,

[Walks in place. Stops.]

I could feel the tug of her sexy seamstress energy.

I remembered I was wearing shorts I had hemmed with masking tape.

[Gives a surprised look–covers mouth]

So I was hoping she wasn't going to find out.

Her eyes invited me closer as she pulled the needle and thread up, up-up, up,

[Mimes thread up]

trying to figure me out–but knowing I carried a traveler's sewing kit with me–always.

"What's your name, sweetie?" I asked. "Manifest Destiny," she said.

"I think I read about you in my history books," I said.

And she said, "Well, I don't want to brag, but I was responsible for the Treaty of Lesbos."

"Right," I said.

And she definitely looked like a leader, capable of making things better for the people. She had power from her passionate brown eyes, her strong, high cheekbones, a sensual colonial mouth that I wanted to touch, but I didn't want to seem too forward. So I– patted her–BONNET.

[Sticks hand straight out to pat bonnet twice]

She smiled and gave me a horn of plenty. I shivered–it made me plenty horny!

"Do you want to go to my cottage and watch me churn butter?" she asked.

I didn't know how to respond. I mean, I wanted to watch her churn, and maybe she was going to teach me. But I was hesitant with an answer–because-well…I just was. "Look, Manifest Destiny–may I call you Destiny?" She nodded, smiled, and stitched.

[Mimes the entire line]

"Destiny, I'm truly intrigued with you, and I can't figure out why. Oh, sure, you're beautiful and I want to get you into the sack, but there is something so hauntingly historical about you, and I can't put my finger on it!"

She snickered, opened her arms to me, and said, "Come here, you, my New World!"

We spent the next two days in bed, making love, talking about quilts, her loom–Puritans.

It felt so good snuggling up to her–feeling her warmth, her tenderness–her jugs.

Dating–it's soooooooo...MULTICULTURAL!

[Walks out of blue spot.

Music fades out.

Empty blue spot is held for four seconds, then cross-fade to general.]

Once, on my way to pick up a date, I stopped and got some roses. The florist figured out it was a date and said, "Men appreciate flowers from women."

I told him it wasn't for a MAN!

He gave me that familar pause and then asked that annoying question.

ANNOYING FLORIST: How–ah, do you...how do you guys... I want to be sensitive. How do you guys–DO IT?

MONICA: You see, people are stumped with lesbian sex and truly misinformed with lesbian sex scenes.

[Stagehand delivers two diagrams on easel]

Society cannot fathom two women having sex, because there is no man.

The rule is insert item A into slot B.

[Shows first diagram of mechanical drawing of nut and screw]

This is the universal language.

[Points to nut]

See this right here? I posed for that.

[Places diagram down]

Other pesty questions often asked lesbians:

"Who's the man?"

"Who's the woman?"

"And who wears that fake thing right about here?"

[Places hands, which are shaped in a triangle, over crotch]

Statistics show lesbians do not have sex. Lesbians reach orgasms through–GIGGLING!

[Shows second diagram of two funny-looking bee-hive women giggling]
BEE-HIVE WOMEN: Oh, Hilary! Oh, Claire! Oh, Hilary! Oh, Claire!
[Giggles and smokes a cigarette. Stagehand strikes diagrams and easel.]
MONICA: And lesbian sex scenes–in videos and films–are so misrepresented. It's not sex. It's more like a folk song!
[Sings]
How about an orgasm, lesbian woman.
[Stops singing]
First of all, you have straight actresses playing lesbians, because why use real lesbians to play lesbians!
The scene usually starts off with two women–engaging in–TEA! The drink of all lesbians.
One says, "More tea?"
The other, "Yes...more!"
Coincidentally, their favorite woman ballad comes on.
[Sings the woman ballad by repeating the word woman five times.]
And a slow dance is in order.
[Sings the woman ballad]
Is it hot in here or is it just them?
[Sings ballad]
They get themselves all worked up, and I want them to go at each other like wild animals. GROWL!
But they start doing that artsy interpretive dance move stuff.
Swaying and swaying.
[Sways]
Twirling and twirling.
[Twirls]
Becoming one with their womanhood.
[Sings ballad]
What is going on here? "Honey, I'm horny. Get the leotards." NO!
If I'm watching lesbian sex scenes, I want to see these gals SUCK FACE!
I want to see them bump, grind, insert–to name a few verbs! I want to get so hot and bothered, I have to get up and pour myself some TEA!
And now there are safer sex lesbian videos–which I think is a very good idea. But you get swaying women wearing condoms–ON THEIR HEADS!

FOLKS, REMEMBER WHEN SAFER SEX FOR LESBIANS WAS JUST KEEPING YOUR FINGERNAILS SHORT!
I was loving my life. I adored my GIRL TRAP. Drama still continued at the restaurant, but I managed to remain sane by performing and writing comedy. I did shows here and there, performing mostly for homo audiences, because I could be myself. "Take my lesbian–please!"
But I figured since I was living in L.A., I should attempt the mainstream clubs, because some bigwig could discover me, give me a TV series and enough money to pay off my student loan. So I went to these clubs and I hated it! I was so uptight. No one was to find out I was a LEZBO-DYKE-QUEER-HOMO-*BUTCH-MUFFDIVER!*
[The instrumental surfer song "Wipe Out" blares as MONICA *does the Swim.*
Music stops abruptly when she does the second backstroke.]
And everybody I met was either homophobic, racist, or sexist–usually, all three.
But I had to give the biz a good shot. I was a fighter–sort of.
I tried my darndest to act like a generic comic: straight, white, male–always on, cruising chicks–talking fast, always networking–always. But it just wasn't me.
And every time I'd tell male comics I was from San Francisco, they would respond with a stupid homophobic comment. I wanted to smack them in their abdomens with an oar!
Instead, I walked away angry, confused, my tummy ached. So you can imagine how I felt on stage.
[Heads for platform as general cross-fades to special platform spot. Continues monologue–no mike.]
I did okay but my confidence was low, so my punch was weak. And sometimes I really sucked, because I couldn't be myself and l couldn't relate to the audience. You try following some jerk doing material on beaners, bitches, AIDS–of course he's grabbing
[Grabs crotch like a man]
himself the whole time. The sad part was, the audience laughed.
I just hated how comedy was and still is a boy's game.
Club owners don't like to book women because, quote, "They talk about women things and their periods." End of quote.
Yet guys would get on stage, grab their dicks, talk about shit, talk

about farts, and the audience was on the floor! I wanted to make them stick their tongues on ice trays!

Bitter?! I'm not bitter. I'M A WAITRESS!

My true frustration was that many of these comics were not funny, yet they had gigs. Here I was this comic with an impressive resume, but I couldn't boast about it. Performing for gay and lesbian events didn't count!

[Walks out of spot. Spot is empty for five seconds. Then returns with a happy face.]

But hey, life wasn't that gloomy! Because the commercial world of comedy led me to TV auditions. For Consuelo–THE MAID! Maria–THE MAID! Anita–THE MAID!

Believe me, folks, I did not want to go, but I figured this was how every great Latino actor got their start–a foot in the back door.

On my last and final audition, I waited with a bubbly, blonde, blue-eyed woman, who asked–

BBB EYED WOMAN: Are you here for the role of Tracy?

MONICA: I could only shake my head no, because I was too embarrassed to tell her I was here once again auditioning for the maid. I... was... too... embarrassed.

[Looks down–pauses–slowly walks off platform.
Empty spot held for five seconds, then cross fade to general.]

After all these run-ins with a cruel world, I had to sit down and take off my bra–THUMP, THUMP!

I had a chat with my creative guru–you know, my higher self. And after a pack of M&Ms and a wheel of brie, I decided, FUCK THIS SHIT, MAN! I HAVE TO BE WHAT I'M ABOUT!

Wow! I am so profound!

I stopped going to these clubs and those stupid auditions! I couldn't put my LATIN LEZBO COMIC self into those Hollywood molds.

I figured it out. I now only did shows and got involved with projects that had to do with me: gays and lesbians, Chicanos, Latinos, women, politics–PANTY FASHION SHOWS!

As I was promoting myself as a lesbian comedian, I was always doing shows for Latinos. Because I am proud of who I am. I want to show this family-oriented culture, with its deep roots in the church, that they still can achieve greatness even when stepping out of their traditional roles.

And yes, I have been a role model. But I have had to deal with one problem: HOMOPHOBIA.

I'll be with relatives and we're bonding. We're working on a takeover plan of the world! And then someone makes a really stupid homo joke and I feel so paralyzed. But I want to change that.

Being around those cousins reminds me of when I worked at a Mexican restaurant in San Francisco. There were three gay men. We became friends and we were "out." Every time the cooks would refer to me, they would shake their heads in disbelief.

One time I was picking up my scalding hot combination plates, with my asbestos hands, and the cook tells me—

COOK [*Thick Mexican accent*]: I know why you are the way you are. It is because you have not been with a real man. UN HOMBRE!

MONICA: I put the plates down—too hot to handle—and I said, "Chuy, I have been with a real man, and that's why I am queer! GRACIAS!"

Look, folks, I didn't come all the way from LA to trash my people. It's just that I am walking a very fine line. And what has troubled me for so many years is that Latinos and gays and lesbians are very oppressed groups. Why can't we come together, discuss our similar problems, go forth, AND KICK ASS! And then—go get a beer.

But as I struggle with Latino homophobia, I see so much discrimination and racism get thrust into Latino faces. Especially Mexicans—especially in Southern California.

ARE WE INVISIBLE?!

[Blackout
Speaks in the dark.]

OK, all right.

[Pause]

Do I sound angry? Are you sitting there thinking, "Oh, brother, we came here for comedy, but she is just another angry Latina lesbian! STOP TRIPPING AND MAKE US LAUGH, BITCH!"

[Cross-fade to *special on platform.*
Stands with mike in hand.]

I loved going to my grandmother's house, because there I could watch the *Beverly Hillbillies* in Spanish.

[Sings theme song in Spanish]

voy a contarles de un hombre llamado Jed
un pobrecito que ni si quiera tenía para dar de comer a su fa-
milia
Y un día estaba muy desesperado
Y de la tierra apareció aceite espumoso
Aceite, como no
Oro negro
Te de Texas
Y ahora Jed es un millonario
Sus vecinos le dijeron, "Jed–sal de aquí!"
Dijeron, "California es el lugar que quieres."
Y llenaron el camión y se movieron a Beverly
Lomas, como no
[Cross-fade to general.
Places mike back and walks off platform.]
As I was dealing with social/political ethics, racism, homopho-
bia, the restaurant that time forgot, and HEAT RASH–I was
getting into relationships and I was getting out of them. Finally,
I reached a point in my life where I declared, "No more com-
mitments! No more compromises! Couples are stupid! I just want
to be a DON JUANITA!"
DON JUANITA: Hey, mamacita, let me touch those chi-chis!
[Mimes pinching nipples]
MONICA: And just when I was about to conquer las mujeres,
the babes, those little gazelles–I met a woman at a party. There
were people all around. Breasts everywhere.
[Grabs breasts everywhere]
But when I shook her hand, it felt like *we* were the *only ones* in
that room.
[Sings the first verse of theme song from A Man and a Woman, *and
says]*
Hi, my name *is* Monica Palacios.
[Sings next verse]
I make a decent amount of money.
[Sings next verse]
I'd like to have sex with you–PLEASE!
And within a month, we were married. It just happened. No
invitations were sent out. No one told us to kiss the bride. I just
knew she was the woman I wanted to spend the rest of my life
with.

[Instrumental "love music" starts as cross-fade to soft spot.
Sings with mike.]
Hey, girl
There comes a time in every woman's life
When she needs another woman to love, to commit to, to share—
a checking account
But, girl, I don't mean to get into your business, now
I don't want you to change for me
I want you to maintain your individuality.
'Cuz, girl, I need you
And, girl, I want you
And, girl, get off my foot!
But, girl, people are going to talk about us
But we must be strong
'Cuz two women in love—that ain't wrong
Our society thinks we should not be affectionate at Disneyland,
the mall
We can't get legally married
I can't put you on my insurance plan!
Does anybody know what I'm really talking about, baby?!
Shucks, girl, come over here and shake that booty on down
Lower—lower still—oooh, yeah, right there
Be careful with those teeth, now
Please, baby, please. Please, baby, PLEASE!
[Music fades to stop.
Places mike back.
Cross-fade to general.]
I love my wife—the Mrs.—the little woman. We even do typical
married things.
When we go to restaurants, I have to ask her for guidance.
"HONEY, WHAT DO I LIKE? WHAT'S MY NAME?
WHERE DO I LIVE?"
My marriage is great, because it's happiness, pleasure, creativ-
ity, love, hopefulness, passion, smiles, communication, Mexi-
can food, everything good and great sex! What a marriage should
be! SO LET'S MAKE IT LEGAL!
It became time for my wife to meet my family, because I love
them very much and, this way, I thought I could do my laundry.
We all decided on a Sunday dinner, but we stumped everybody
about what to make for dinner, because we are vegetarians. My

family was confused.

FAMILY: WHAT? You don't eat chicken, fish, or cheese?! Well, then, what do you eat? What do you eat?!!!!!

MONICA: Finally, after many phone calls and much, much research, we all decided on–Mexican food.

Ooooh, that was tough.

The day arrives and they are all excited to meet her. The nieces and nephews all run up to me.

NIECES AND NEPHEWS: Auntie, Auntie Monica, we've missed you. You don't eat chicken, fish, or cheese? What do you eat? Of course, my precocious niece starts in on me.

PRECOCIOUS NIECE (SMART ALEC): Auntie Monica, why don't you have a husband? Why are you a vegetarian? Why are you and YOUR FRIEND wearing the SAME RINGS!? So I just kind of pushed her out of the way and KICKED HER!

[Mimes kicking a field goal]

My dad was playing the piano and singing away.

DAD SINGING: You are my sunshine, my only sunshine. You don't eat chicken, fish, or cheese.

MONICA: My mom was great. She warmly welcomed my wife–very sincere. Then she tried to get the kids to eat before the adults, but they were not cooperating, so she had to resort to her Mexican mom sound effects and her chin.

[Does mom making sound effects and points with her chin]

Halfway through dinner, my mom became cranky and started doing that motherly martyr thing.

MOM: No, no, that's okay, I'll eat the BURNT TORTILLA!

MONICA: Finally, the time was right. Everybody was around the room and I said, "My family–mi familia, THIS IS MY WIFE!"

Everybody stopped talking. After a moment of thick, intense silence, my mom says–

MOM: Come on, everybody, let's eat. Food is getting cold. C'mon, *andale*. C'mon, get the baby. Where's the baby?

MONICA: YOU SEE, THEY KNOW, BUT THEY DON'T WANT TO TALK ABOUT IT. WHAT FOR? WHY RUIN A GOOD MEAL?!

[Blackout.

Speaks in the dark.]

Family thoughts around the dinner table. My mom:

[Special spot around head and shoulders]
MOM: We know that you are, but we don't want to know again!
Pass the butter!
[Points with chin. Blackout]
MONICA: My dad–
[Special spot around head and shoulders]
DAD: She's not married. She brings a woman to family functions.
[Sings]
Qué será, será, whatever will be, will be.
[Blackout]
MONICA: My older sister–
[Special spot around head and shoulders]
OLDER SISTER: Well, I don't approve of it. But she *is* my baby sister. Her girlfriend *is* pretty–THANK GOD!
[Blackout]
MONICA: My older brother´–
[Special spot around head and shoulder]
OLDER BROTHER: I guess she knows what she's doing. We don't talk about it. She better not try to hit on my wife!
[Blackout]
MONICA: My other older sister–
[Special spot around head and shoulders]
OTHER OLDER SISTER: I'm not sure I understand it. Her girlfriend is nice–I GUESS THAT'S WHAT SHE CALLS HER! HER WOMAN? HER LOVER-PERSON?!
[Blackout]
MONICA: My little brother–
[Special spot around head and shoulders]
LITTLE BROTHER: Hey, man, she can do what she wants. It's her business. She seems happy. OH, MY GOD! MY WIFE IS FLIRTING WITH HER GIRLFRIEND!
[Blackout]
MONICA: My precocious niece–
[Special spot around head and shoulders]
PRECOCIOUS NIECE: LEZBO!!!!!!!!!!!!
[Blackout.
Lights up general]
MONICA: But what a big burn on my family, because my other older sister is also a LESBIAN! You know, my family thinks–

FAMILY: Did you guys eat the same thing? How does this happen?

FILM ANNOUNCER *[Commercial voice]:* Just when the Mexican Catholic family thought they had one lesbian daughter, they actually have two! Experience their confusion in DOUBLE DYKE FAMILIA!

Every year, the familia had that same holiday wish: "Por favor, let them bring home men to dinner. We don't want to march in that gay parade!"

DOUBLE DYKE FAMILIA!

MONICA: Having a lesbian sister has made my life peaceful. Believe me. She has always been a great role model.

And about our family, the kooky Mexicans, we could never take them to a movie called *Rodeo Girls in Bondage and Birkenstocks.* But we remain connected and that's important to me.

It's the relatives who make me crazy. You know, the ones that never encourage their daughters to say hello to me, because they think I'm going to hypnotize them!

[Mimes hypnotizing the girls with hand and eyebrow movements, then quickly pops into lesbian driving a tractor, waves, and quickly pops back to hypnotizing.]

You are getting sleepy but you will soon want the love of another woman.

[Makes the shape of a woman with hands]

You will also want—A MEATLESS DISH!

[Stops hypnotizing]

And these people know I'm a lesbian, but they still ask me those stupid questions!

RELATIVES: So, Monica, where did you meet your friend?

MONICA: We met at a party. Now we live together.

RELATIVES: Are either one of you—MARRIED?

MONICA: Yes—not legally!

RELATIVES: Mmmmmmm, are your husbands on the road?

MONICA: And I want to tell these people—but I don't, because of my own homophobia from my culture and society. Thank you very much, but I would love to tell them,

YES, I'M MARRIED TO THIS WOMAN. WE ARE EXTREMELY HAPPY! FAR HAPPIER THAN ANY COUPLE HERE!

RELATIVES: Are you two sisters?

[Cross-fade to special spot around head and shoulders which she is standing in.
Instrumental "Sabre Dance" plays, then goes lower background.]
MY MOM: C'mon, everybody, dessert. Ice cream is melting.
C'mon. Get the baby. Close the refrigerator. Did you wash your
hands? Go wash your hands.
[Points with chin]
Where's your father? You don't eat chicken, fish or cheese?
[Lights fade to black.
Music up, then fade out. Lights up to general.]
MONICA: Just to let you know, I finally quit the restaurant,
because life is too short. And I didn't want to limit myself to—
garlic bread!
Because I believe in happiness, self-love, self-worth, self-PARK-
ING.
You see, I figure artists are going to save this planet. So I must
continue with my plan. Weaving the lesbian side of me with the
Mexican side of me. And writing about it. And talking about it.
And pushing for and demanding change! BECAUSE, HEY
FOLKS, IT'S TIME!
Well, I gotta go.
[Heads for the platform.
Gross fade to special spot.
On platform with mike in hand.]
My carpool is here.
But I'd like to leave you with this special song, and I want to
dedicate it to my parents for going all the way.
[Sings the vagina medley]
Women gather 'round women
we must laugh, we must laugh
[Does goofy laugh with hands on hips]
We must learn to be less uptight, so we can relax our vaginal
muscles.
[Speaks]
You know, folks, we haven't heard enough about that great word
vagina.
[Sings to the tune of "Lullaby of Broadway"]
C'mon along and listen to
My lullaby of Vagina.
The hit parade and belly-hoo,

My lullaby of Vagina.
[Sings the next lines like a traditional medley, but replaces the key word with vagina]
I left my vagina in San Francisco...
Vagina Cathedral...
The days of wine and vagina...
I want to hold your vagina...
I'm a little vagina, short and stout. Here is my handle. Here is my spout...
The shadow of your vagina...
La panocha. La panocha.
One less vagina to answer. One less vagina to fry...
Put your vagina in. Take your vagina out. Put your vagina in and shake it all about...
I'm gonna wash that vagina right out of my hair...
[Sings next line to the tune of "Lullaby of Broadway"]
So you've listened to my melody of ooollllddd, vaaa-giiii-naaaahh!
[Sings the last line exactly like the last line from the Bobby Darin classic "Mack the Knife"]
Look out old vagina is back!
[Blackout—hold for thunderous applause.
Lights up.
Takes bow.
Blackout.]

Milk of Amnesia
Leche de amnesia

Carmelita Tropicana

Setting: *Stage has a minimal look. It is divided into two halves. The left is the writer's space and is dimly lit. It has a music stand with makeup, costumes, hats. The right side is painted white, resembling a white cube. There is a mike and mike stand, and a chair that gets placed there, depending on the scene.*

Piece begins with a blue light bathing the chair inside the white cube as an audiotape with the voice of the writer is heard.

Years ago, when I wasn't yet American, I had a green card.
[Darkness]
On my first trip abroad, the customs official stamped on my papers "Stateless."
When I became a citizen, I had to throw my green card into a bin along with everybody else's green cards. I didn't want to. I was born in an island. I came here when I was seven. I didn't like it here at first. Everything was so different I had to change. Acquire a taste for peanut butter and jelly. It was hard. I liked tuna fish and jelly.
I used to play a game in bed. About remembering. I would lie awake in my bed before going to sleep and remember. I'd remember the way to my best friend's house. I'd start at the front door of my house, cross the porch. Jump off three steps onto the sidewalk. The first house on the right looked just like my house, except it had only one balcony. The third house was great. You couldn't see it. It was hidden by a wall and trees and shrubs. Whenever I'd look in, the German shepherd sniffed me and barked me out of his turf. I'd continue walking, crossing three streets, walking two blocks until I came to my best friend's house. I did this repeatedly, so I wouldn't forget. I would remember. But then one day, I forgot to remember. I don't know what happened. Some time passed and I couldn't remember the third block, then the second. Now I can only walk to the third house.

(Photo by Paula Court)

I've forgotten. I had a dream when I was a kid.
[Sound of steps running]
I guess because we were refugees. Me and my cousin were fugitives running away from the police. We had to escape. We were running through the streets. We saw a manhole cover and it opened up.
[Sound of metal door shutting]
We went down. We were in a sewer.
[Sound of dripping water, echo]
We were safe. But it started to get hot. Stifling hot. And as it happens in dreams, one minute my cousin was my cousin and the next, she was a peanut butter and jelly sandwich. The heat was making her melt. I held her in my hands. She was oozing down. I was crying: Don't melt, Pat. Please don't melt. I woke up in a sweat.
[Sound of alarm clock]
In the morning, I went to school. Our Lady Queen of Martyrs. That's when it happened. In the lunchroom. I never drank my milk. I always threw it out. Except this time when I went to throw it out, the container fell and spilled on the floor. The nun came over. Looked at me and the milk. Her beady eyes screamed: You didn't drink your milk, Grade A pasteurized, homogenized, you Cuban refugee.

After that day, I changed. I knew from my science class that all senses acted together. If I took off my glasses, I couldn't hear as well. Same thing happened with my taste buds. If I closed my eyes and held my breath, I could suppress a lot of the flavor I didn't like. This is how I learned to drink milk. It was my resolve to embrace America as I chewed on my peanut butter and jelly sandwich and gulped down my milk. This new milk that had replaced the sweet condensed milk of Cuba. My amnesia had begun.

[PINGALITO, a cigar-chomping Cuban man, enters as a tape of a mambo plays. He greets the audience. He is on the cube, brightly lit.]
PINGALITO: Welcome, ladies and gentlemen, to the show de jour, *Milk of Amnesia.* I am your host, Pingalito Betancourt, the Cuban Alistair Cooke. For those of you who are from Cuba, you may recognize my face. I was the conductor in 1955 of the M15 bus route, the route that goes from La Habana Vieja to El

Vedado. And it was in that bus that I meet Carmelita. There is *A Streetcar Named Desire* for Stanley Kowalski. For Pingalito, this was *Destiny on the M15 Bus Route*.

When I heard of Carmelita's tragic accident, I rush right over, hoping a familiar face can trigger something in the deep, recessed cavities of her cerebro, cerebellum, and medulla oblongata. You see, people, the doctors have their methodologies for curing amnesia, and I have mine.

I make my way through the hospital corridors, saying hello to all the nice Filipino nurses, and I enter her room. She is asleep, looking like an angel, mouth open, pillow wet, making puttering sounds of a car engine. And I think of a childhood memory she used to tell me about. Her grandfather, who smoked a cigar, would take her for a drive in his Chevrolet, driving with a foot on the brake, stopping and starting, stopping and starting. She would get so carsick. So I decide to simulate this memory. By blowing smoke in her face, playing with the controls of the hospital bed, making the legs go up, the head go down, up and down. I am playing her like a big accordion when a doctor comes in and says I gotta go. Something about my cigar and an oxygen tank.

But I don't give up. I return the next day. I think, What above all, is Carmelita? I tell you. Cuban. Cubanita. 150 percent. So I decide to tell her some facts about Cuba. See if it jiggles something.

[Shows a map of Cuba to audience]

I have here audiovisual aid number one, a placemat I pick up in Las Lilas restaurant of Miami titled "Facts about Cuba." How many of you know Cuba is known as the Pearl of the Antilles, because of its natural wealth and beauty? And the first thing we learn as little children is that when Christopher Columbus landed in our island, kneeling down, he said: Esta es la tierra más hermosa que ojos humanos han visto. This is the most beautiful land that human eyes have seen. The majestic mountains of la Sierra Maestra. Our mountains, not too tall. We don't need high. If we get high, we get snow, then we gotta buy winter coat. And the beaches of Varadero. But, ladies and gentlemen, none can compare with the beauty of the human landscape. Oyeme mano. Esas coristas de Tropicana. With the big breasts, thick legs. In Cuba, we call girls carros, and we mean your big American cars.

Your Cadillac, no Toyota or Honda. like the dancer Tongolele. I swear to you, people, or my name is not Pingalito Betancourt, you could put a tray of daiquiris on Tongolele's behind, and she could walk across the floor without spilling a single drop. That, ladies and gentlemen, is landscape. For that, you give me a gun, and I fight for that landscape. Priorities.

Fact two: Spanish is the official language of Cuba, and it's a beautiful language. You talk with your hands, you talk with your mouth. My favorite expression when you want to find out the color of someone, you say, Oyeme mano ¿y dónde está tu abuela? Tell me, brother, where is your grandmother? Which brings us to fact three.

Three-fourths of all Cubans are white, of Spanish descent, and a lot of these three-fourths have a very dark suntan all year round. When they ask me, Pingalito, and where is your grandmother?, I say, Mulata y a mucha honra. Dark and proud. Well, I look at Carmelita and she is not blinking, and I have fifteen more facts to go. So I decide to change my route. If the M15 bus doesn't take you there, maybe the M21 does. So I ask you, people, what is Carmelita above all? Eh? Above all, she is an artist. 150 percent. So maybe a song, a poem will do the trick. Poetry is something we all have in our souls. It is our tradition. I don't know how many of you know that our liberator Jose Martí, our George Washington, is also the Emily Dickinson of Cuba. So I recite for Carmelita, "Ode to the Cuban Man."

[PINGALITO recites]

Spielberg, forget your Assic Park
Some say the Cuban Man is disappearing
Like the dinosaur
I say, que no
The Cuban Man
This specimen
Will never go away
We are here to stay.

Like the Cuban crocodile
One of a kind in genus and species

You find us in the Bronx Zoo

The swamps of Zapata
Calm in the water but also volatile
So don't bother the crocodile
Because we got big mouths
We open up and swallow a horse and a cow
That's why we have the Cuban expression
Te la comiste, mi hermano
You ate it, bro.

The Cuban Man is persistent, stubborn
Like the mosquito, always buzzing around
Why you think Yellow Fever was so popular?

The Cuban Man is the apple of his mother's eye
Even when he is a little dim of wit
To his mami he is still the favorite
And at eighty she still calls him el baby.

The Cuban Man has no spare parts
Nature did not create any excess waste
She made him compact
Not tall in height, but what street smarts!
Suave, sharp, slippery, and shy
Like yuca enchumbra in mojo greasy pig lard
Or like the Yankee from New England, say
Slicker than deer guts on a doorknob.

The Cuban Man has a head for business
He combines boobulah with the babalu
That's why they call him the Caribbean Jew.

Above all, the Cuban Man is sensitive, sentimental
With sex appeal for days
And this is where our problem comes
Our hubris, our Achilles tendon
It is our passionate and romantic side
We love women too much
Too many women, too many kids.

But when you tally up

The good, the bad
You too will decide
He is like a fine Havana cigar.
You gotta have
After a big heavy meal with an after dinner drink and
Coffee on the side
The one that truly satisfies.

[PINGALITO exits. An audiotape with the writer's voice comes on.]
In high school I was asked to write an essay on the American character. I thought of fruits. Americans were apples: healthy, neat, easy to eat, not too sweet, not too juicy. Cubans were mangoes: juicy, real sweet, but messy. You had to wash your hands and face and do a lot of flossing. I stood in front of a mirror and thought, I should be more like an apple. A shadow appeared and whispered, mango stains never come off.

I didn't write about fruits in my essay. I didn't want them thinking I wasn't normal.

In the '80s, that's when my amnesia started to show cracks. As I joined the ranks of Tchaikovsky and Quentin Crisp–I became a civil servant. And a thespian on the side.

As a teen, I had gone to the Circle in the Square Theatre, but my thespianism had been squelched the day the teacher announced the Puerto Rican Traveling Co. was holding auditions and needed actors. When she said "the Puerto Rican Traveling Co." everyone started to laugh. As if it was a joke, like a Polish joke, only a Puerto Rican one. I was the same as a Puerto Rican. Maybe the island was bigger, but same difference. I guessed I wouldn't do theater.

Until I came to the WOW Theatre and got cast in Holly Hughes's play *The Well of Horniness*. We were asked to do it on the radio. I had a dilemma. Would my career as a civil servant be stymied if people knew I was the one who screamed every time the word *horniness* was mentioned, or that I was playing Georgette, Vicky's lover, or Al Dente, chief of police? Maybe I needed a new name.

As if by accident, the pieces were falling into place when I entered the WOW Theatre and a comedy workshop was to take place. The teacher would not give it unless four people took it. There were three signed up for it, and, with me, the body count was four. I said no. No. No. But the teacher, she was cute. So I took it.

But it wasn't me. I couldn't stand in front of an audience, wear sequined gowns, tell jokes. But she could. She who penciled in her beauty mark, she who was baptized in the fountain of America's most popular orange juice, in the name of Havana's legendary nightclub, the Tropicana, she could. She was a fruit and wasn't afraid to admit it. She was the past I'd left behind. She was Cuba. Mi Cuba querida, El Son Montuno…

[CARMELITA is sitting on a chair inside the cube, wearing a hat made of helium balloons. A spotlight is on her face. As the scene proceeds, more light bathes the stage.]

CARMELITA: The doctor said hypnosis might help. I said, anything, Doctor, anything for a cure. So he started to hypnotize me, but he said I had to count backward. And I got this sharp pain in my throat and I felt these blood clots in my mouth and I said, No, Doctor, I can't count backward. Don't make me. Count backward! Never count backward. Never. I don't like it. So he writes on his chart, subject is mathematically impaired. They wanted to know what other impairments I got. So they connected these wires to my brain, my computer, my mango Macintosh. The doctors, they monitor my every move.

[Pointing to deflated balloon]

This is connected to my organizational skills, musical memory, and housecleaning ability. This is linked to my libido. When I think of Soraya, my nurse, giving me a sponge bath or rubbing Keri lotion on my chest, it pops uncontrollably.

[Pops balloon]

And this one is for languages. Schpeiglein Schpeglein on der vand. Wer is di schonste in ganzen land… What language is dis? Is this the language of Jung und Freud? Oh, Herren and Herrleins, pierce me with your key. Let me not be a question mark anymore.

The doctors, they tell me my name is Carmelita. I've had a terrible accident. I hurt my head when I was chocolate pudding wrestling. I don't remember a thing. Remember walking in the sand, remember her smile was so inviting, remember.

I don't remember the lyrics to this song. So much flotsam and jetsam inside my head. And I want to remember so much I get these false attacks. In desperation, I appropriate others' memories.

The doctors try to control these attacks by surrounding me with familiar things.
[Shows outfit]
Clothes pretty but... And these shoes–I must have been a tall girl. Then they tell me to eat the food they bring, because the French philosopher Proust ate one madeleine cookie, and all his childbood memories came rushing back to him.
[Picking up a can of goya beans]
Goya?
[Picking up a yuca]
Is this a yuca or a yuucka? Do I eat it or do I beat it? Oh, yuca yucka, to be or not to be. But who, that is the question.
That short guy with the cigar–what was his name? Pingalito. He tells me I'm from Cuba.
Maybe there is only one way to find out. To go back to the place I was born in. My homeland, the place that suckled me as a newborn babe. In the distance, I hear the clink, clink, clink of a metal spoon against glass. It is my mami stirring condensed milk with water. She holds a glass. The milk beckons me to her.
[Takes off balloon hat. Lights change, she speaks into the microphone.]
My journey begins at 5:10 a.m. at the Miami airport. I am so sleepy. Crazy to be at the airport at 5:00 a.m. I don't know where I am going. I hear "Follow the Maalox, follow the Maalox," and then I spot a multitude. A Cuban diaspora that's going back, holding onto plastic bags with medicines and the most magnificent hats. I am so underdressed. These people are so dressed: skirts on top of pants on top of skirts. The gentleman in front of me, an octogenarian, has his head down. I don't know if it's age or the weight of his three hats. I discover my people are a smart people. They can weigh your luggage and limit you to forty-four pounds, but they cannot weigh your body. The layered look is in.
The excitement mounts when I enter the plane. The doctors told me to be careful. Too much, too soon can cause attacks. In only forty-five minutes, I will cross an ocean of years.
When we land, it is scorching hot outside. People desperately rip off the layers on the tarmac. I see a field in the distance. Palm trees, two peasants, and an ox. It reminds me of Southeast Asia, Vietnam. I never been there. But who knows where memories come from: movies, books, magazines.

I go to the counter in the airport, holding onto my Cuban passport, my American passport, and a fax saying my visa is waiting for me here. Names are called for people with visas, but mine is not one. The immigration guy says I gotta go back. Say what? You know who I am. He says, "Who?" Yo soy Cecilia Valdes... Oh, my god. I started to sing an operetta, a zarzuela. The guy thinks I am making fun of him. I say no. I'm sorry. I say I hurt my head, and it has affected my vocal cords. He don't care. I am returned. Back to El Norte. But I have my determination. I go back, especially now that I know how to dress. I go in style. I make myself a magnificent hat. Check it out.

[She models a hat]

Soy una tienda ambulante. I've my Easter bonnet with toilet paper on it I'm a walking Cuban department store. Tampons and pearls, toilet paper, stationery supplies. What a delight. When I go now, the immigration people are so friendly. "Back so soon? I like your hat."

I take a taxi to the Hotel Capri. I tell my driver, Francisco, I want to see, touch, feel, hear, taste Cuba. All my orifices are open. Francisco says, No es fácil. It's not easy. I have come during the Special Period. The Special Period—that's what the government calls it. No gas, no electricity, no food. I look out the window. Cubans are all on bicycles: They look like skinny models. Francisco says when there is no gasoline and the buses are not running, he fills his body with water, with sugar. Water with sugar. The great Cuban energizer. Agua con azúcar and then he can walk for miles.

When I arrive at the Hotel Capri, I go in the dining room of the hotel. I can tell who the Cubans are with relatives here. They are the ones wrapping up food. I meet Maria Elena, who is here for a conference and is wrapping chicken, breads, cheese. I ask her, What about eggs? Don't forget the eggs. She says, "Eggs. Qué va; Yesterday I had to give a lecture on the poet Julian del Casal, and when I took the paper out of my briefcase, there was egg yolk all over. Egg yolk all over. No es fácil. It is not easy."

[The taped voice of the writer plays]

WRITER: Sometimes New York is too much. So is Havana. I toured the colonial part of the city. Kids flocked to me for candy, gum. Two decrepit, mangy dogs limped along the cobblestones. Two guys tried to sell me a potent drug, PPG. Makes the man potent, satisfies his woman. A girl about fourteen asks me for my pinta labios. I part with my Revlon #44 "Love That Red" lipstick. I eat at La Bodeguita with two Cuban artists, a meal of fried yuca, fried pork, fried bananas. Cholesterol is not a problem. I take a ride to my hotel in a private vintage Chevrolet, circa 1955, rumbling as it plods through the darkened streets, except for a building blindingly bright, a beacon of light, the Spanish embassy. And the new currency is the dollar. Five dollars for the ride, five dollars for the beer at the hotel lobby. And who do I see coming in? Pinta labios, Revlon #44 looking good with a man. What is she doing with that man and my lipstick? She looks down when she sees me. I'm pissed, but with a swig of beer, reconsider: maybe the lipstick got her a steak dinner. And I go to my room, place a call to New York, and put the TV on. CNN news. And the call comes through, and I switch channels. A movie is beginning: *The Green Berets.* I am in Cuba watching *The Green Berets.*

[CARMELITA goes to the cemetery. A son is playing when CARMELITA enters the white space.]

CARMELITA: I have been in Havana for three days, and I don't have any flashbacks, not even an attack. I decide to go visit my relatives, the dead ones at the cemetery. Maybe they'll talk to me from the grave. El Cementerio de Colón is a beautiful cemetery with big trees that give shade and lots of statues and mausoleums. I start to look for the Tropicanas, but find Menocales, Menéndez instead. Menéndez? I see four senior citizens hanging out by the tombstones. They look like they're in their seventies–two men and a couple. I go ask if they know the Tropicanas. They don't but they are very curious about me and start to ask me my name, what I do, where I live. When I say New York, they all say "Nueva York!" The woman, Consuelo, looks at my nose

CONSUELO: José, mira que se parece a Luisita. De la nariz pa abajo. Exactica. You look like my niece Luisita. She's a very smart girl, a painter. She went to New York last year. Went to all the museums. ¡Quedó facinada! She was fascinated, fascinated. All those restaurants you have! Japanese, Chinese, hasta Filipino! She said the food, that was the real art. She came back twenty pounds heavier and her work changed. She went from abstract to realism. I have a new painting hanging in my living

room. It's a triptych of desserts. There's a strawberry cheese-cake, crème brulée, y cake de chocolate. Está lindo, lindo.
JOSÉ: Carmencita, you don't know this, but Consuelito here used to be obese. Obese. A diabetic with a sweet tooth. ¡Imagínate! Now in nine months of the Special Period, she has lost ninety pounds. No es fácil. No es fácil.
[Getting excited]
CONSUELO: José, your blood pressure y el Stress.
JOSÉ: Déjame hablar. How am I going to get rid of el Stress unless I talk? Mira, Carmencita, people here are doing every-thing to survive. They are keeping roosters, chickens. Animals right here in Havana. ¡Animales! Pa que contar...
[Sound of crackling smoke]
CARMELITA: What's that smoke? Who's that tied to a tree?
[Stampede sound, neighing on tape]
I see... I was born in Badajoz, España. Todo era tranquilidad. Un sueño dulce. The sky clear, not a cloud in the sky for miles except for the clouds of dust me and Dulcinea made as we gal-loped across the dry fields. The sun was strong. One day, it rained and the mud spattered from our pasterns to our forearms. When I turned two, my master told me I had been sold to a conquista-dor. A conquistador, what a strange and exciting sound. The day came when I had to leave Spain and become a stallion. The stallion of a conquistador. But I was too excited that night to sleep.
[Whinnies]
We horses are a bit high-strung. I stayed up with my mother, counting stars. At daybreak, she gave me her bendición. "Arriero, from now on, you will be counting stars in the New World."
I was one of the first horses to set hoof in the New World. And I should have known from the voyage from Spain to Cuba what was to happen. All of us animals herded into a tiny ship. The roosters that climbed on my back, the rats I had to stomp on. But the worst was the boredom. Nowhere to go. Always fed the same thing, hay and oats, hay and oats; for variety, I ate my own dung. I thought the voyage would never end. I started counting the days. Uno, dos, tres, cuatro. I gave up. I fell into such a depression, and there was no Prozac in those days.
[Singing]
Quiero escribir los versos, más tristes esta noche...

Then somebody yelled, Land! Land! It was the island of Cuba.
I couldn't believe my 180-degree peripheral vision. Grass everywhere. And trees with fruit: guanábanas, mangoes, mameys.
And the natives were so friendly, they walked around smoking,
offering us cigars: Partagás, Panetela. Tiparillo. No, thank you. I
don't smoke. What smells. But the best was the yuca barbecue.
My favorite. I hated the guinea pig. I'm a vegetarian.
Havana in those days was teeming with life, especially the mosquito kind. I couldn't swat them fast enough with my tail, which
is why I hated Gonzaga the priest, who kept plucking the hairs
out of my tail to make hair shirts, hair shirts to give to the natives as gifts. Gonzaga was not my master, it's just that I was
given to him for a little while. I was on loan because of my
name, Arriero: the one who can carry much weight. And joder,
that priest was fat! It took three men to put him on my back.
That day we were delivering the hair shirts is when we saw the
Indian Hatuey. There was smoke in the distance. I didn't want
to go, because I know where there's smoke, there's fire, but
Gonzaga saw some of his fellow priests and we had to go. There
was a crowd gathered, so much commotion we couldn't hear,
but I rotated my left ear and heard a priest say to Hatuey, "Repent, repent, and if you will, you will go to heaven. If not, hell."
Hatuey looked at the priest and said, "If heaven is where the
Spanish Christians go, I'll take hell." And the flames took Hatuey
away. Right there. I saw it. And so much more. I saw so many
Indians die, so many. So many dead Indians from disease and
overwork. I thought of my mother's farewell words, "Arriero,
from now on, you will be counting stars in the New World." No,
Mother, not stars.
CARMELITA: Ai, my head. I must have fallen into a CUMAA.
A Collective Unconscious Memory Appropriation Attack. I need
an aspirin. When I take out the Bayer aspirins, the four senior
citizens yell, "Bayer!" Like they have never seen an aspirin. So
we decide to divide the 135 aspirins into 4 senior citizens. Some
fall on the ground. It is too much, so the men take the ones that
fell on the ground and Consuelo takes the bottle. As I am leaving José Miguel says,
JOSÉ MIGUEL: Do you pray? Do you believe? I do. Every
day. If I didn't, I'd be dead.
[An audiotape is heard with a joke]
Did you hear the one about the eggs and the fried steak? There

are these eggs running through the Malecón Boulevard in Havana. And they're running because they are being chased by a million hungry Cubans. And these eggs are running and the Cubans are after them. And as the eggs are running, they pass in front of a fried steak that is sitting on the wall of the Malecón, very relaxed. And the eggs yell at the steak, "The Cubans are coming, the Cubans are coming. Aren't you afraid they'll come get you?" The steak says, "No way, these Cubans don't know what a steak looks like."

[Stage is dark as slides are projected onto a wall. The writer reads into the mike, and when the slide of her house comes on, she stops reading and speaks into the mike, pointing to the different parts of the house.]

WRITER: As I go sightseeing, I try to strike up a conversation with everyone I meet. But when people ask me where I'm from, I have a certain trepidation. How will I be received? I lie. I begin by telling them my father is Puerto Rican. After five minutes, I feel comfortable enough to tell them I was born here, but don't remember much.

I am like a tourist in my own country. Everything is new. I walk everywhere, hoping I will recall something. Anything. I have this urge to recognize and be recognized. To fling my arms around one of those ceiba trees and say, I remember you from the park when I went with Cristobalina, my nanny who had Chinese eyes, kinky hair, and used to sing, "Reloj, no marques las horas." I want a crack on the sidewalk to open up and say, yes, I saw you when you jumped over in your patent leather shoes, holding onto your grandfather's index finger. But it doesn't happen. There is no recognition from either the tree or the sidewalk. So I do what Ronald Coleman did in the movie when he had amnesia, and what Cubans do when they go back. I visit the house I was born in...

[Four slides go on as writer speaks in the dark.
Slide of plaza with flag. Slide of countryside.]

So I do what most Cubans do when they go back. I go back to the house I was born in.

[Slide of aerial view]

319 de la calle 8 entre 5ta y 3ra. The address pops out as if I'd been there yesterday.

[Slide of Centro Gallego]

I'm nervous. Why? It's just a house.

[Slide of house]
Oh, my God. There it is. The house I was born in.
[Pointing to different parts of the house]
There was a patch of dirt here, and in this corner, there was a
slug. I used to poke him with a stick.
The slug, he's gone. And on this side, I planted my mango tree.
We had invented a new game, "agrarian reform," and had to
cultivate the land. It was by the mango tree that I had an
epiphany. I was poking at the ground to see how my mango tree
was doing when I heard her footsteps. She had long hair tied
into a ponytail, red lips, and dreamy eyes like a cow. I ran to her
and jumped on her and kissed her creamy cheeks. "Okay, okay,"
she said, putting me down. We looked at each other for an instant. I ran and hid by my mango tree. My heart was beating
fast, I was sweating. I knew then that that was no ordinary kiss.
And it was on this balcony that we played with our live Easter
chicks. Live chicks dyed purple, pink, and green. We left my
cousin Teresa with the chicks while we went to make skirts for
them from plastic ruffled cookie wrappers, and when we came
back, Teresa was throwing the last chick from the balcony to its
death. And on this porch, we used to play Tarzan and Jane. I
begged for a human part, but I was told I had to play Cheetah or
the elephant. I was playing Cheetah when my father came. I
called him the stranger, because he had been away fighting in
the revolution. He gave me and my sister gold bullet shells.
[Slide of stairs]
I couldn't wait to go inside. Those are the stairs, the stairs I fell
from when I was six months old. I bolted upstairs to my bedroom.
[Slide of water by door]
Two men are in the middle of a business meeting. I interrupt.
I'm sorry. I used to sleep here. The woman who has been following me, the secretary, tells me I can't just barge in as if it's my
house. You don't understand, I say, this was my house. She opens
the door to the bathroom.
[Slide of bathroom]
Oh my bidet, my toilet. She says, "Hey, you're not one of those
Cubans who plans to come back and take over their house." I
say, "Oh no, we only rented." The moment I say this, I feel like
I'm not like one of those Cubans who left–who never would

have said they rented. Are you kidding me? We owned the whole block.

[Slide of construction]

My house is now a construction company. Privatization entering Cuba right through this, my house.

[CARMELITA enters the white cube as recorded salsa song plays]

CARMELITA: It's the middle of the afternoon. There's salsa music playing. From the window I see the Hotel Nacional as it sits on a rock and overlooks all of Havana Bay. I think of having a mojito, the favorite drink of Papa Hemingway. It could also be mine, since I don't remember what it tastes like. I walk to the renovated, four-star Hotel Nacional, smelling the delicious grass. The sun is trying to come out. It just rained. I walk to the entrance of the hotel. The doorman winks. I say, "Buenas tardes." Inside, it is cool and beautiful. There are potted palm trees, Spanish leather chairs, and blue tile. Blue tile. How I hate blue tile, especially with yellow squiggles. It doesn't go with anything. Bad decorating choice. A hotel employee looks at me. The blue tiles are making me sick. I'm holding tight to the potted palm frond.

DOCTOR: Carmelita, suéltala. Let go. Let go of your mother's hand. You have to be brave. Hay que tener coraje, mucho coraje en la vida.

CARMELITA: No. Mami. No, mamita. Please don't let go of me. I'm your child. No dejes que me lleven. I want to be with you, Mami. I don't want to go with the green man.

MOTHER: Carmelita, it's just a green uniform. Mi hijita. Don't be afraid. It will be over soon.

HOTEL EMPLOYEE: Ahora, Señorita, if you don't let go of the palm frond, I'm going to have to call security.

CARMELITA: I'm sorry. Yes. I don't feel well. I need to eat. I'm hungry. I have to sit down in the dining room and eat. I go into the dining room like a somnambulist following the song "Lágrimas Negras" played by a trio. Where have I heard Lágrimas Negras" played by a trio like this?–Oh yes, last week in a Miami restaurant. At least the short-term memory works. I should try to remember a lot. The more I remember, the more I will remember. Let's see, what did I learn today? Ochún is the goddess of the sea. No, that's Yemayá. Ochún is like the Caridad del Cobre, and if you want to get the love of your life, you have to leave honey under your bed for five days. You get the love you want and the cucarachas you don't. And the slang word for dyke is *bombera*, "firefighter." So maybe if I yell, fire, *fuego,* would all the dykes come out now? I feel much better. So much better I order a mojito and pork sandwich. "La Ultima Noche que Pasé Contigo" is playing. The waiter brings me the sandwich. He has a green jacket on. I try not to look at his green uniform. Trembling, I pick up the sandwich. A slice falls, no, it jumps.

[A pig flies in and hangs above Carmelita's head]

PIG *[Snort, snort]:* The horse thought it was bad in colonial times, he should talk. I was a pig in the Special Period. Cochinito Mamón. I was just two weeks old, lying under my mother's belly, sucking her sweet milk with my brothers and sisters, when I was yanked off her tit by a man who put a blanket over my head and took me from my farm in Santiago to live in an apartment in Havana. It was so quick, I couldn't even say goodbye to my family. The apartment was on the second floor. My legs were too short. I couldn't go up the stairs. Señor, I am no goat. I went into the apartment. I looked for mud but everything was so clean. The woman in the apartment, the wife, cradled me in her arms, calling me Nene. She fed me milk in the bottle. Hey, lady, I'm not into rubber. I want real nipples. The man complained about my smell, so every day she had to give me a bath in the tub.

WOMAN: Nene, sit still, Nene, don't splash, Nene, let me wipe your nose.

PIG: I'm not a boy, I'm a pig, I'm a pig! One day, the man came in, walking funny. He had been drinking with his brother, who worked at the Hotel Nacional. He smacked the wife on the rump and made her get the tape measure from her sewing kit. He put it around my belly.

MAN: ¡Coño, que gordo está este puerco!

PIG: I could smell the rum on his breath. She should give him a bath. The phone rang. It was long distance, the relatives from the United States. The man said something about showing me to them. The next day was Sunday. I didn't know what was happening. The woman put a hat on my head. It was a gift from a cousin in New York. A baseball cap. It kept falling off, so she tied it with another gift she got from New York: a bungee cord. The cord was tight around my neck. She was holding me on her lap, lifting my head to look up. The man quickly got behind us when a flash went off. I got scared. I didn't know it was a family portrait. I jumped down. My hoof ripped her pantyhose. I tried to run but I had put on some weight. I slid behind a table and knocked over a lamp. It broke. The man went after me. He was screaming.

MAN: ¡Puerco, puerco de mierda!

PIG: She was screaming.

WOMAN: ¡Nene!

PIG: I was squealing, ¡Mami! With all the noise, the neighbors were knocking on the door.

NEIGHBORS: ¿Qué pasa? ¿Qué pasa?

PIG: The man flew across the room and tackled me. He whispered in my ear.

MAN: Coño, puerco de mierda. You are going to be roast pork, but before that, we are going to cut your vocal cords, so you don't squeal and disturb the neighbors anymore.

PIG: The next day, I was put in a box. The woman was crying as she punched holes in the box so I could see. We got to the place. I could see blue tiles.

DOCTOR: Carmelita, relájate. Estamos en la sala. I'm going to put this on, so you can breathe deep. Respira profundo.

CARMELITA: No. I don't want to breathe.

DOCTOR: Déjate de tonterías, niña. Carmelita, quiero que cuentes. Count backward: 100, 99, 98...

PIG: When I got out of the box, I saw a man in green. He had a shiny knife. I squealed, Mami! Mami!

[Silent. She pulls a string from the pig's neck, and red glitter gushes down, spilling onto the white linoleum.]

CARMELITA: My vocal cords, my tonsils. The pig and I, we had our operations at the same clinic. The clinic with blue tiles. I remember. We are all connected, not through AT&T, e-mail, Internet, or the information superhighway, but through memory, history, herstory, horsetory.

[She shadow boxes as she recites the poem]

I remember

Que soy de allá

[She exits singing and dancing]

Cochinito mamón

Sandwich de lechón

Cochinito mamón

Sandwich de lechón
[Lights fade down. Audiotape with writer's voice comes on.]
WRITER: September 1993. I met an American lawyer who is
here in Cuba to witness a period of "transition." It seems in
1993, anything can happen. In the theater festival, there were
plays that were critical of the system and played to packed houses.
I thought by coming to Cuba, I would have answers. Instead, I
have more questions.

These are *Star Trek* glasses. They form rainbows around every
thing you look at. Am I looking at Cuba from an American
perspective? No es fácil. It's not easy to have clear vision. In
seven days, I can only get sound bytes. Cuba is a land of contradictions.

No one is homeless in Cuba, although homes are falling apart.
Everyone gets health care, but there is no medicine. There is
only one newspaper, but everyone is educated. No conspicuous
consumerism. The dollar is legal, but there's the U.S. embargo.
Que soy de aquí
Un pie en New York (A foot in New York)
Un pie en La Habana (A foot in Havana)
And when I put a foot in Berlin (Cuando pongo pata en Berlin)
I am called
A lesbische Cubanerin
A woman of color (Aquí)
Culturally fragmented
Sexually intersected
But I don't esplit
I am fluid and interconnected
Like tie-dye colors I bleed
A blue blue sky into a halloween pumpkin orange
Que soy de allá
Que soy de aquí
[Lights up bright]
Hello, people, you know me. I know you. I don't need no Ameri-
can Express card. I am Carmelita Tropicana, famous nightclub
entertainer, superintendent, performance artist. And I am so
happy to be here with you today, because ever since I was a
little girl, I ask my mami, When can I do a show called *Milk of
Amnesia* at P.S. 122? And here I am. I am so lucky. Lucky I can
dance un danzón, cantar un son, tener tremendo vacilón. Thanks

to El Cochinito Mamón, sandwich de lechón. I got to exit with a song, sabrosón like the sandwich de lechón. The clothes are threadbare; vivid colors now turned pastels. So much food for the soul, none for the belly.

I don't want to keep score. It's not a competition. Cuba vs. the U.S. When the Olympics are on I'm at a loss as to who to root for... No, not really. I root for Cuba. Why? Is it that I'm for the underdog and that if I'm in the U.S., I am more Cuban and if I'm in Cuba, I'm more American? Is Cuba my wife and America my lover or the other way around, or is Cuba my biological mami and the U.S. my adopted mom?

[Lights go up bright]

CARMELITA: My journey is complete. My amnesia is gone. After so many years in America, I can drink two kinds of milk. The sweet condensed milk of Cuba, and the pasteurized homo kind from America.

My last day in Cuba, I spend at an artist's house. We sit, ten of us, in a circle, all sipping our one bottle of rum. I turn to the man next to me and tell him I have one regret. I didn't hear any Cuban music and, to me, Cuba is music. He smiles. He is Pedro Luis Ferrer, famous composer, musician. He will play me his songs, but first he tells me, "The embargo is killing us." He wanted me to tell you, so I tell you with Pedro Luis Ferrer's song that says it best: "Todos por lo mismo."

Everybody for the same thing.

Between the pages of colonialism

Capitalists, homosexuals, atheists, spiritualists

Moralists

Everybody for the same thing.

[The tape plays several choruses until the end]*

---

*Pedro Luis Ferrer is represented in the United States by Caliente Music, Inc. We would like to thank Mitchell Morales, Vice President of Caliente Music, Inc., for allowing us to use the lyrics of "Todos por lo mismo" without paying the royalties. If any reader is interested in his music or that of many other Cuban artists, please contact him at (212) 960-5144 or by e-mail at calientemu@aol.com

My Grandmother Never Past Away:
A Stream of Consciousness
and Unconsciousness

Elia Arce

This work is an excerpt from *Stretching My Skin Until It Rips Whole*, a full-length solo performance work.

[The performer hangs a bedspring from the ceiling. The crooked bedspring floats in space. A black and white slide of her grandmother is projected from an antique suitcase on the floor, toward the upper corner stage right. The slide looks distorted by the angle. Shadows of the bedspring imprison the image in the wall. The performer sits in a rusted chair and breaks pieces of bread inside of an old tin bucket.]

When my grandmother Helida died, I was in the middle of puppet rehearsal. She had been in the hospital for a few days, and I hadn't gone to see her, because we were mad at each other. I can't remember what the argument was about, but she screamed at me from her bedside, "When I die, I'm not gonna leave you anything!," and I screamed right back, "I don't want anything you have anyway!" My grandmother was always in bed, she seemed to be very good with accidents, she had them all the time. The last one was on a coffee plantation. She loved to go and check on the coffee. If it was ripe, ready for picking, or if it was green, ready for waiting. She couldn't wait, she hated waiting. That's why she went that day with her cane, right after her doctor told her not to get out of bed. She slipped and broke the only part of her entire body she hadn't broken yet, her sacro bone. This time they couldn't even put on a plaster, and she was supposed to stay in bed until it healed naturally. Well, she was in her sixties and her body was already against natural healing, so I can't really remember her very clearly on her two feet. It seemed to me that she was only alive from her waist up. She looked like a pressure cooker ready to explode. And I would be terrified to walk into her bedroom every afternoon to comb her

(courtesy of Elia Arce)

hair. "When I die, I'm not gonna leave you anything!" My grand-mother was always screaming like that. That's why she had ani-mals all over her house. She had a zoo in her house. She had chickens from different parts of the world. And I would love to go and check underneath them for a warm, pinkish egg. She also had geese and a little pool for them that was always out of water. She had street dogs and pigs in the back. I didn't like to visit the pigs though, I didn't want to get emotionally attached. I always imagined a huge knife cutting its throat.

[A long screech]

She had about a hundred doves that became pigeons with time. And she would feed them every day at six o'clock in the morn-ing without delay.

[She throws pieces of bread toward the audience]

"Palomitas, palomitas!" she would scream out of the upstairs window, and they would all come flying to the zinc roof, "Prrra, prrra," the sound of the little pieces of old bread would stay suspended in the air like a huge cloud. She wouldn't let me feed the doves, though. She thought I was too small to reach the win-dow and I didn't have enough strength in my hands. I didn't believe her. I thought she just didn't want to share that with me. So when my aunt asked me if I would throw one of the female cats in the river if she gave me cinco colones, I considered it. My grandmother also had a room full of cats. She had about eighty-five cats in this room.

That was the room nobody spoke of, only my aunt, in secret. The room was dark and you could hardly see anything from the outside. I would sneak out the back door and put my face very hard against the window. But I could only see movement. Like rats, a lot of rats meowing all the time. My aunt wanted to get rid of the females, because those were the ones reproducing. But my grandmother knew each cat by name, and whenever one would disappear, she would get furious until the cat came back. They always came back. I guess when someone knows you by your name it is hard to resist. So I gave the cat-drowning job to my cousin Patty. Patty loved the job. She figured she was getting richer and richer as my aunt was getting poorer and poorer. Besides, my cousin Patty was always fighting me for one thing or another. She couldn't stand me being better than her in any-thing. I think it all started when her brother put his tongue in my ear when I was twelve. I didn't really want it, although it actually felt kind of good. But then I heard that he had been putting his tongue inside of all the maids' ears, who kept getting fired. I didn't feel that special anymore after that, and started feeling sorry about the maids. The last time I saw my cousin Patty was when I was twenty. I came into my boyfriend's house one morning, and she and my boyfriend were having coffee. She had spent the night, and they had been fucking all night long. It had been years since I had seen her. How and where she found out about him, I don't know, but I was happy to see her nevertheless. That was the last time I saw her, though; I guess she felt even after that. "Palomitas, palomitas…"

[She gets up and walks toward a small suitcase on the floor. Takes a white dead chicken from inside of it and, as she plucks the chicken, continues chanting "palomitas, palomitas" intertwined with the following text.]

Garbage
Broken pipes
Dirty dishes
Clogged pipes
Dust
Broken pieces
…palomitas, palomitas…
Dying plants
Emotionally clogged
Can't speak
Don't know what I'm feeling
Can't breathe
Smoke
…palomitas, palomitas…
No toilet paper
No soup
No soap
Papers, papers, and more papers
Saying yes to everything
Disappointing everybody
Nowhere and everywhere
Needy friends

(courtesy of Elia Arce)

Need
Hungry
No money
No time
Kentucky fried
Rash
Itchy
...palomitas, palomitas...
Growing mushroom
Fungus on my foot
Run out of toothpaste
Tar on my gums
Angry
Backaches
God delusions
Fascism
A dead leaf got caught in the seconds hand
And time stopped
and time
sssttoo...
aagghh...

[After a repressed scream, she slowly places the chicken back into the small suitcase, which is left opened. A small mirror inside the suitcase reflects the plucked chicken to the audience. She slowly walks toward the rusted chair and sits. With a red lipstick, she draws a line from the middle top of one foot, up the thigh, her chest, across her throat, toward a side of her mouth, and on her lips. Lies back and breathes.]

I was sitting naked on my couch, water still dripping from my body. I felt my head getting bigger and bigger in between my legs. It started to push and push through my mother's vagina. And that made me feel very sexy. And that made me feel very guilty. "Leche que nutre, leche venenosa." Nutritious milk, poisonous milk. I sit and I breathe. I don't want to feel all the things that I am feeling right now. I feel like I can't be sitting still one more minute. I shouldn't be feeling what I'm feeling... Oh...is coming...and I'm holding it in... I don't want to go around scraping memories from my bones...but the accumulation of them hurts more... hurts more.... Agghh... Sshh. I open my chest and I sit and I breathe. When I check my body to relax, I always notice that my legs are tight, that the insides of my thighs are pushing toward each other. And then an image pops into my head. When my grandmother Helida and I went to Honduras, we were all crammed in this pickup truck with my cousins. I wanted to ride in the open back of the truck, because it was sunny and it looked like a lot of fun. I was wearing a short green skirt that had hot pants underneath, and my older cousin, you know, the one with the tongue in the ears, was looking at me through the back window of the truck. All of a sudden, I started to feel this stare. It was my grandmother, who was motioning at me to close my legs, to close my legs. She was furious because I was sitting in an Indian position. She thought it was an inviting position, a provoking position. I couldn't understand what the big deal was at the time, but now I understand. I understand that even the way I sit now was decided by her twenty-five years ago. And that makes me feel like puking. That makes me feel like I just want to chew my roots and spit them out, chew my roots and spit them out! So I laid in my bed. I was touching my breasts in the dark, and it felt good, so I moved my hand to my crotch, it was dark and warm … and then this image popped into my head. I was six years old the day that my mother and my father left me with Miguel de San Isidro de Acosta to take care of me while they went to the movies. Miguel, Miguel, you son of a bitch Miguel. I hate you. I detest you. You marked my life forever, you are going to be impregnated in my feet, in my thighs, in my skin, in my hands. I have to expel you out of my body, you son of a bitch, la puta que te parió, I have to expel you out of my fingers, out of my guts, out of my vagina. I have to open my legs, open my legs in that Indian position, and I just give birth to you, motherfucker! But no, instead I started to touch myself. And imagined that I was with him, that I was with Miguel. And I wasn't a little girl anymore, I was a grown-up woman. And I just wanted to fuck his head off, I just wanted to fuck his head off. And so I just pushed him against the wall. I looked at him in his eyes and saw his burning desire to have me. And I just fucked him, and I just fucked him. And I left him there aching on the floor. I didn't even look back. I was satisfied. I guess sometimes you push your legs against each other, but my grandmother never taught me that sometimes you open them

(courtesy of Elia Arce)

up instead. My Goddess would agree with that. Maybe this is a
war of gods. I said, "I don't want anything you have anyway!"

*[She sings the following litany as it is sung in church, and distributes
amongst the audience the leftover pieces of bread from the tin bucket as if
they were communion wafers.]*

Cordera de Diosas
que quitas el pecado del mundo
ten piedad de nosotras
Santa Virgen de las prostitutas
…ruega por
nosotras
Madre de la Diosa
Madre sucísima
Madre promiscua
Madre puta
Madre con mancha
Madre corrupta
Madre insolente
Madre admirable
…ruega por
nosotras
Madre del mal consejo
Madre creadora
Madre destructora
Virgen imprudentísima
Virgen digna de compasión
Virgen digna de alabanza
Virgen poderosa
Virgen infiel
Ideal de ambiguedad
…ruega por
nosotras
Morada de sabiduría
Honor de los pueblos
Modelo de contradicción
Rosa despreciada
Fuerte como una torre
Hermosa como torre de marfil

Escarba los infiernos
Puerta del cielo
...ruega por
nosotras
Estrella de la mañana
Salud de las enfermas
Refugio de las pecadoras
Consoladora de las afligidas
Auxilio de las paganas
Reina de las matriarcas
Reina de las profetas
Reina de las apóstolas
Reina de las que no viven su fe
Reina de las no castas
Reina de todas las santas
Reina concebida con pecado original
...ruega por
nosotras
Reina elevada al cielo
Reina de la Santísima Rosaria
Reina de la paz
Cordera de Diosas que quitas el pecado del mundo
ten piedad de nosotras
NO NOS DES PAZ!

Scar

Caridad Svich

*A traveler comes to the edge of the millennium and spins a tale of hope
and apocalypse for a land called America. A pilgrim's solo flight in jazz
time. The following solo may be performed by a man or a woman. The
character is an androgynous soul, a battered survivor, a traveler in the
middle of the road. The time is the near future, a blasted landscape.*

[Light. The traveler appears, barefoot.]

We're in the middle ages, see
we're in the spit-fire of a chaotic age
ain't got to do nothin but look around
and you'll see
nothing but ash and crumble these days

some say it's the mighty cataclysm
I say it's the whole goddamn world
it's got itself hooked
two in the morning dry mouth hole in the gut HOOKED
on pain
and retribution

what it's got
is a taste for blood.

It used to be better if it was somebody else's blood
the farther away, the less recognizable,
the just plain SMALLER someone was
the better

now it don't matter
long as it's blood
we'll take it.
I guess you'd call it a loss of conscience

I think of it more as a natural state:
[Beat]

you want somethin, you get it
ain't goin your way, you get it OUT of your way
simple as that
it's fuckin' remorse that's kept us back all these years.

HALF OUR TIME

we've spent half our time
thinkin'
bout the other guy
nothin but feelin' sorry for ourselves
apologizin' for things we ain't even done
it's no wonder we got such a taste for blood
we goddamn lost our PIONEER SPIRIT

This land used to be
oh—this land was:

unbroken
the ribbon of it
stretchin curlin' unwinding it-self
for miles and miles
without end

solemn, it was
kind of land's forged in the fierce heat of war
merciless, unforgiving.

there was a call come over this land
in time past
shot out over prairie sky
and the dirt of Abel
come into the earth's skin
swift as Cain
sure in the claim
that its deep cry of battle
could never leave place

for surrender

we were warriors
[Beat]
When I think of it
oh–I think of it
keeps me AWAKE

"You find yourself, colonel? You find yourself?"
"How bout you, sergeant? You seen where you've been?"

I don't got to tell you
I don't got to tell nobody
we're just pickin up dirt now
all of us–warriors–pickin up
dirt

You know when you start lookin' at the ground?
how you get to fix on it with your eyes
fix on it
closely
like you're gonna let the particles in that strange earth
grab you by the hand, and take you
into their labyrinth?

it's DANGER lookin', it is
cause you can't stop your eyes once they're fixed
and you got no choice but to follow
'n the further you go
the further you see the ash 'n crumble
take you on past
until you are cock-sure you are in the ice age.

Now, I don't need to tell you: it's cold
just eyes and mouth peerin' out from under
"How'd I get here?" you think
"Where in God's name is the infinite peace
I have sought so long now that I find myself here
in this human-less
habitat?"

the sleepin' silence of the ice don't take long
it drowns memory and light in its quiet
but there is sound
and that sound is a RACKET
a clangin', 'teropsicatin' splendiferous roar
of bones bustin' for air
disarmin' for mercy

strange wonder.

So, you look up
you look around
you take your eyes
off
the ground
don't wanna give in to the ice
hell, that kind of peace is too much for human-kind

So you walk
you stumble
you trespass
Forward
don't look back
Forward
don't lose–step
Forward

You come upon:
what is it?
WHAT is it?
…Science.

the strangest of religions
and yet there it is:

atoms, protons, the nucleus of a hundred million stars
rescued from eternal mystery
by righteous human folly
oh–it does move us

it has made this un-broken piece of continent
uncircumscribed by definition
yet tiny
beyond reason

CHAOS.

[Silence]
The stars hold secrets, make no mistake
you wander up there long enough
you start to sense it
they don't tell you much, but what they do tell:

There was this green star
off to one side
it came up to me one day
it said, "how come you got to KNOW so much?
what purpose is there in your knowin'?
is not the brutality of time enough?"

"No," I said,
"No."
And I KILLED THAT STAR
I TORE OPEN ITS BELLY
AND SUCKED OUT ALL ITS LIGHT

"NO.
It is never
enough."

You see, I am a true citizen
I am a soldier, a brave
I can't stop myself from killin'
it's all I got

[Beat]
"Tell me, sir, what is the true price
of knowledge?"
"To kill."

yes.
to kill.

And when I am dead and buried
who will comfort me?
who will come
and silence
my dreams?

I think on this
I think
and I am shamed
There is no comfort in waking thought
There is no pleasure in the killing
a great hunger remains.

You ever feel a pain in your gut you don't know what to do?

There is a scar in my heart
deep is its wound
and it's cryin'
Sorrow
Repentance
as if someone could hear it

if only someone would

[Pause]

It's a kind of delirium, we're in
a half-crazed half-dazed perpendicular delirium
a steady stream of fire
is our companion through day and night
and all we do is stand still
in its haze
(letting the flames swirl through
the geometry of matter
while we set our thoughts
on some distant nebula of shame)
it's enough to make the whole planet

jump off
a roof

but we stay on
some of us
stay
we see no choice in absence

Perpendicular
we stand
drawing our swords
clinging to the earth's face
aimin' our metal
at barely guarded foes
it ain't victory no more
it's blood piss-red, common.

[Takes an old vending machine bag of peanuts out of pocket]

TAKE ME BACK

to ice
and stone

TAKE ME
I WANT TO FEEL

tender...

[Opens bag, eats peanuts]

and in the
sweet, hot
Can you hear me?

how bout now, pilgrim
what make you of this?
is your skin jumpin' out of itself?
(sweet exhilaration)
[Finishes eating all peanuts in bag]

oh—how weary you must be
how weary to be here

I am cold
...sorry

[Pause]

We're in a god-less age, see
smack in the hollow of an unjust sky
strange wonder
we're still

then again
not strange
we're hooked

the blood in the rock
creeps out
and we drink
without reflection

we're still warriors somewhere

(even if we're after
more conspicuous prey)

so, leave your mark
best to leave it
it will be cut down
quick
Tie the ribbon of road to your back
there is only one road
between the earth and stars
'n if you don't tie yourself to it
you'll fall
hard

Tremble

and see
if you can
feel it
a little

I will pour salt on my scar
let it burn
perhaps
something will
heal...

I can remember a time

I can't remember
a time
when everything
(every thing)
has been
so

small
forgotten
time

'n I got
a taste
in my mouth
righteous.

*[The traveler is standing. Lights begin to fade. The traveler turns slightly
toward the light.]*

[Fade to black.]

Mexican Medea:
La Llorona Retold

Cherríe Moraga

(Work in progress)

Performed at the Berkeley Repertory Theatre, Berkeley, California, on March 31, 1994.

Characters

MEDEA: *Chicana in her early forties, a midwife and curandera.*

LUNA: *Medea's lover of seven years, Chicana in her mid-thirties.*

SOCORRO: *Medea's aging grandmother, a Mexican Indian from whom Medea learned curanderismo. Also plays Nurse.*

JASON (pronounced Hasón): *Mechicano, Medea's ex-husband, Minister of Culture of Aztlán.*

CHAVO: *Medea's twelve-year-old son.*

SAVANNAH: *Luna's girlfriend, African-American, also plays Nurse.*

CORO OF CIHUATETEO: *a chorus of women who have died in childbirth. These Aztec figures wear the faces of the dead in the form of skulls. Their hands are shaped into claws. Their breasts appear bare and their skirts are tied with cords of snake. They are barefoot, their ankles wrapped in rattles made of shells.*

The CORO *should be played by four women independent of the cast. They appear in choreographed scenes, accompanied by American indigenous music and performing in the traditional style of the Aztec danzantes.*

Setting: *The play occurs at the beginning of the twenty first century. The revolution is over. The United States is now, like the U.S.S.R. of the early 1990s, split into various geographical regions along ethnic/racial lines. The Southwest is now the Chicano territory of Aztlán, the center of the country is made up of the Native American Confederacy, the South is African-American, the Northwest is reserved for the most extreme white supremacists, and the Northeast and other states scattered throughout the North American continent, referred to as*

Gringolandia, remain somewhat ethnically mixed, with lingering tensions between various "interests/identity groups." One such group, gays and lesbians of color, have been banished from their land of ethnic origin to a place named Tamoanchan, meaning "we seek our home" in Mayan. It borders Aztlán on the west and Africa-America on the east. It is essentially what was once the "Valle" of South Tejas. There MEDEA *and* LUNA *reside with* MEDEA's *twelve- year-old son. The setting and time of* Mexican Medea *move freely between the past at* MEDEA's *home in Tamoanchon, and the present, the psychiatric ward in Gringolandia.*

LUNA *enters. She turns on the message machine.* MEDEA's *voice can be heard.*

MEDEA *[Voice-over]:* I am swimming along with the black fish now. I know their names. I want to be left alone in the darkness of the water. My skin, scales. Oh my juventud, touch my scaling flesh, touch my old age, my barrenness.

*[*LUNA *crosses to the bedroom.* MEDEA *is laid out on the bed, thoroughly drunk.]*

LUNA: Medea.

[Sitting on the bed next to her]

Medea?

MEDEA *[Soft]:* Oh, it's you. *[Grabbing her sleeve]*

LUNA: What happened?

MEDEA: Take my body, baby.

LUNA: You saw Jasón.

MEDEA: I don't want to watch it descend into the earth.

LUNA: What'd he say to you?

MEDEA: Gravity, fucking gravity. The earth has become my enemy.

LUNA: C'mon, let me get your clothes off.

*[*LUNA *starts to undress her tenderly]*

MEDEA: I don't even remember being twenty.

*[*LUNA *smiles]*

MEDEA. Where have you been, amor?

LUNA: I was seeing about a job.

[Pulling off MEDEA's *stockings]*

MEDEA: I used to have spectacular thighs. Remember, Lunita?

LUNA: You still do.

MEDEA: I'd wrap 'em around your boy's face.

[Holding her face]
How come I called it a boy's face when it's so female?
[LUNA puts her face away, folds MEDEA'S *clothes onto the back of a chair]*
LUNA: Just butch.
MEDEA: No, not butch...boy. A boy's hunger, that's what I saw there in those dark eyes resting between my legs... Luna?
LUNA: Hmmm?
MEDEA: Why would you look at me that way?
LUNA: What way's that?
MEDEA: Like you didn't have what I had, like you didn't have nalgas, senos más firmes que yo, a pussy...that perfect triangle of dark hair...
LUNA: I'm just a jota, baby.
MEDEA: That's a stupid response.
LUNA:. Don't be cruel.
MEDEA: I'm not cruel, I'm dying. Dying to make sense of it. How does it start? How does it vanish? How is it you used to drink from me as if you yourself didn't taste the same coppered richness when you brought your own bloody fingers to your mouth? As if when you drew a woman's shape with your sculptor's hands, you didn't find the same diosa curves and valleys when you bathed yourself each day.
[Pause]
Eres mujer. But for you, falling in love is to think nothing of yourself, your own body. In the beginning, all was me.
LUNA: Yes, in the beginning.
MEDEA: And now...?
LUNA: It's different now. You get used to each other. It's normal.
MEDEA: I loathe normal. At night, I would lay awake and wonder...how is it she could worship me so and not be banished. But then you were banished. And now that's the road I walk, too.
LUNA: Medea, that was seven years ago.
MEDEA: I had always imagined I'd get to return to Aztlán, one day with my son, grown. I don't believe that anymore.
[Pause]
I am the last one to make this journey. My tragedy will be an example to all the women like me, vain women who only know

how to take the touch, to be the beloved, not the lover. Such an example I shall be that no woman will dare to transgress those boundaries again. You, you and your kind, have no choice. I see the difference now. You were born to be a lover of women, to grow hands that could transform a woman, like those blocks of faceless stone you turn into earth goddesses. I, my kind, is a dying breed of female. I am the last one to make this crossing, the border has closed behind me. There will be no more room for transgressions.

[Lighting transition. MEDEA, *now in a slip and barefoot, rises, crosses to psychiatric ward.* LUNA *watches her exit.]*

Interviews

Way Out Performance:
An Interview with Marga Gomez

Michelle Habell-Pallan

Marga Gomez is one of the most visible Latina feminist come-dian/performance artists to date; she is steadily inserting her brand of social commentary into the national consciousness. She has appeared on HBO's national cable-cast *Comic Relief.* She appears occasionally with the comedy group Culture Clash, both on their Fox-TV television program, *Culture Clash* (broadcast in the Southwest), and their live show, *Carpa Clash.* American Play-house has optioned her best-known and highly praised perfor-mance piece, *Memory Tricks,* for film production, and her subse-quent piece, *Pretty, Witty, and Gay,* has toured nationally. Before she achieved her recent success, Gomez studied drama and cre-ative writing at Oswego College in New York, then moved to San Francisco and became a member of the feminist grassroots theater group Lilith. When Gomez left that group in the early 1980s, she hooked up with Bay Area Chicana comedian Monica Palacios. Along with Palacios, she performed as an original member of Culture Clash for about two years. Later, she and comedian Palacios left the group and performed together throughout the West Coast. As a solo performer she has per-formed many stand-up shows in the past five years and has opened for Los Lobos, k. d. lang, and others.

Her most recent solo performances, *Memory Tricks, Pretty, Witty, and Gay* and *Half Cuban/Half Lesbian,* are compelling because they touch upon issues of immigration and assimilation anxiety as well as racism, misogyny and homophobia as they occur in the late-twentieth-century United States. Her next project is a performance piece about her father and the Latino entertain-ment world of the 1940s and 1950s in which he thrived.

As the Harlem-born daughter of Latino "show-biz parents," Gomez seems to be walking in their entertainment footsteps, though she has traveled a different path. Sometime in the late 1940s, both her Puerto Rican mother and her Cuban father im-migrated to New York City to escape poverty, hoping to play

MARGA GOMEZ

MANAGEMENT:
IRENE PINN

TRIAD ARTISTS, INC.
LITERARY & TALENT AGENCY

(photo by Irene Young)

the leading roles in their own American success story. Since both of her parents never fulfilled their dream–partly because of mainstream show business's bias against Latino performers– Gomez characterizes her parents' experience in this country as the failure of the American Dream. However, both parents had their moment of relative prosperity as successful entertainers in the New York Latino theater circuit before televised Spanish-language variety shows became popular. Gomez explains that the popularity of Spanish-language television was one of the major reasons for her father's fall from popularity. Willy Chevalier, Gomez's father, was a popular comedian, master of ceremonies, and producer of live variety shows who, in the early 1950s, enjoyed a large Spanish-speaking audience. But by the mid-1950s, people who at one time regularly attended live performances began to stay at home since telecast shows tended to follow the same format and feature the same performers (Celia Cruz and Tito Puente, for example) as the live shows Gomez's father had so successfully hosted. Unlike Gomez's mother, Chevalier chose to perform in Spanish. Thus he never enjoyed the appeal to English-speaking audiences that Gomez's mother did as she performed exotic dances in both Latino and Anglo nightclubs. Although he temporarily enjoyed the promise of the dream, he was never able to break into the television industry in a significant way, and died as poor as the day he entered the United States.

Her mother's story–the subject of *Memory Tricks*–is somewhat different. Performing as an "exotic dancer" (which, in the 1950s meant a variety of Middle Eastern and Afro-Cuban dance), Gomez's bilingual mother enjoyed popularity with New York's mainstream audiences as Margo the Exotic, as well as with Latino audiences as Margo Estremera. However, after she divorced Gomez's father and married an Italian-American man, she was forced to quit dancing and became financially dependent on her second husband. She now lives in a nursing home in New Jersey and is surviving Alzheimer's disease.

Despite the fact that (or maybe because of the fact that) she was raised by Latino parents and was greatly impressed by the Latino entertainment world to which her parents exposed her, Gomez makes a provocative claim: she does not see herself as a "real Latina," because she cannot speak Spanish fluently. Gomez says she has become totally assimilated into the "white supremacist social structure" that her parents encountered. Gomez seems to equate the loss of cultural authenticity with the loss of language, and at the U.S.'s fin de siglo, Gomez shares this opinion with others. In a *Los Angeles Times* interview, she jokes, "C'mon, I can't salsa. It's sad. Second-generation Latinos really feel a lot of angst over losing their language because it has to do with internalized racism."[2] Because issues of internalized racism and sexism are rarely discussed, and because Gomez knows so well the anxiety that Latinos can experience around such practices, some of Gomez's funniest material taps into the ambivalence and angst many second- and third-generation Latinos feel about issues of ethnic identity and identification, and demonstrates how these issues are complicated by and complicate issues of sexuality and class. In *Pretty, Witty, and Gay,* for example, Gomez explains that when she first arrived in San Francisco—knowing almost nothing about the city—she went to the Castro district, looking for her people (Cubans) and a Cuban-style restaurant that served beans and rice. Instead, to her delight, she found Coco the Transvestite at the restaurant, as well as a lively gay/lesbian subculture.

But others do not so readily agree with this notion that because Gomez, or any other Latina, cannot speak Spanish, she is not a "true-blue Latina." In her book on the production of oppositional cultural identity and identification, *The Bronze Screen,* Rosa Linda Fregoso questions the notion of cultural authenticity and argues against the production of ethnic identity (specifically Chicano) built on "a political model of subjectivity grounded in a notion of a fixed self. In this formulation, cultural identity appears as an authentic essence, located in a core subject, whose identity is one of 'being.'"[3] In contrast, Fregoso (expanding on Stuart Hall's theorization of cultural identity) understands identity as a formation—one becomes a "subject-in-process" and is never a "fixed self." This understanding allows one to recognize that the production of cultural identity is one that is dynamic and subject to historical, geographical, and political change. Thus what was once considered to constitute Latino identity is not completely lost in the past, but does in some way inform the construction of a future identity, though it does not necessarily determine it. Fregoso's argument assumes that categories of race/

ethnicity, gender, sexuality, and nationality are never biologically given, but are located in history, and are instead constructed through representation (or discourse). This assumption allows people (subjects) in their capacity as artists (and as everyday people) to reshape cultural/political identity. Fregoso's theoretical framework can be usefully applied to the construction of ethnic identity in general, but, of course, one would have to make adjustments for each particular ethnic group under analysis. It seems that Gomez's anxiety about cultural authenticity is informed by this notion of the "fixed self," despite the fact that she constructs new Latina subjects in her performances. In this particular instance, the authentic essence of Latino identity is the ability to speak Spanish—that which Gomez and others like her lack. Yet it seems that Gomez, in constructing herself as a certain subject—a Queer Latina who desires to reclaim her Spanish language and Latino culture—works against the notion of a fixed cultural identity. She is a subject in the process of "becoming." As she inhabits multiple subject positions as a Queer Latina, Latina lesbian, and feminist, she is enacting what Fregoso discusses at length—"an alternative formulation of cultural identity," one that does not force Gomez to choose between a strictly Queer or strictly Latino identity.[4] The tension Gomez jokes about as she is pulled by the two communities fuels her ambivalence, yet her identification with multiple communities (the gay/lesbian and Latino/Chicano) allows her to turn, what Fregoso so aptly describes, "the ambivalence of cultural identity into a politics of political identification."

One might say that Gomez's representation of Latina identity as constructed in the 1950s (in *Memory Tricks*) and 1990s (in *Pretty, Witty, and Gay*) demonstrates how that identity has transformed over time. In her performance pieces and standup comedy, Gomez constructs—for a relatively diverse audience—representations of the categories Latina and Queer that challenge those of the status quo. She is honest about her desire to succeed within mainstream popular culture, and she does see herself as part of a social struggle against Hollywood's refusal to allow Latino/a performers to represent Latinos and Queers more complexly. She has found that the more she attempts to whittle down her identity to a Hollywood cliché, the more complicated her representations become, as indicated in the title of one of her shows—

Half Cuban/Half-Lesbian.
Yet despite, indeed because of its tensions and contradictions, Marga Gomez's work is important in struggles against "the culture of the powerful,"[5] for at least four major reasons. Gomez's representation of "racial/ethnic" and sexual identity problematize notions of a "homogeneous" North American national identity. Gomez's performances of Latina experiences demonstrate the heterogeneity of this category, and her identification with both Gay/Lesbian and progressive Latino communities gives us insight into the way the construction of gendered, racial, and cultural identity and identification is negotiated by those theorizing outside of the university. Discussing the way that these categories overlap is important in order to understand how we might organize new types of coalitions against racist, sexist, economically marginalizing, and homophobic practices. Last, because Gomez's performance begins to map out common points of interest for those Latinos/as who do not feel "authentic," and for those antihomophobic and antiracist people who want to respond to those confused xenophobes who, as she jokes, "want all the Puerto Ricans to go back to Mexico." Precisely because her work is rich with interesting tensions and contradictions in regard to these issues, I structured my questions around issues of cultural identity and identification.

MH-P: Your dad was a Spanish-language comedian, right?
MG: Well, he also was an impresario, he put huge shows together, and he also wrote songs. But what he was best known for was being a master of ceremonies, and a comedian.
MH-P: Since he spoke Spanish, how did you understand him?
MG: Probably at the time I understood. Now I don't have a lot of recollection of it. I don't know if I really did understand him that much when he did his show, because by the time I started going to shows, when I was six or seven, I think I didn't know Spanish so well anymore. So I think I understood some things, but probably not that much.
MH-P: Wasn't it hard at home, then? How did you talk with your father?
MG: Well, no, he spoke English. On stage, he spoke Spanish, but at home, my parents spoke English to me. They weren't that concerned about me keeping the language. My father had more

pride in being Cuban than my mother had pride in being Puerto Rican. He didn't want to learn English that well. He tried to make it in Hollywood. He had his breaks and he had a screen test, but he didn't make it. He was pretty stubborn about learning English, he didn't want to. I'll never know really why they, or he, let it be that I didn't speak Spanish. But I think there was so much pressure in the 1960s to totally assimilate that he probably thought he was helping me. My guess is my mother set the direction for that.

MH-P: So he learned English in the U.S.?

MG: The story my mother told me was that he was in Cuba dancing on that strip of nightclubs in Havana as a comedy act. A talent scout from Johnny Walker Red saw him. At that time, he did a little comedy, a little dance. This scout said he was going to take him to New York, since he was doing really well in Havana. So he took my father, but I guess didn't realize that my father needed to speak English, since most of the venues catered to Anglo people who would come to see "the Latins." That was the new thing, the new trend.

MH-P: Where?

MG: I don't know the places, but there were a lot of clubs like that, because it was a new type of show, and the performers really had to be bilingual. Or really just speak English with a Latin "flavor." And since my father didn't speak any English, he got fired from this gig. He then tried to get into the Teatro Hispano and Puerto Rican theater, but they wouldn't give him a break. And so one night, he just jumped upon the stage and grabbed a microphone and started his comedy act and people really liked it, and after that, they had to hire him.

He was a comic and then became a master of ceremonies. Then he got involved in television. He got his diploma from a television broadcasting school in New York. And then he began creating his own television shows. In *Carpa Clash*, I did a piece about my father. I changed the situation, but basically I copied a character he created for television called Caballero Thirteen. Mr. Thirteen. He was the narrator, an Alfred Hitchcock type. He'd come out of his coffin, and then he would set up a scary story. He wrote the scripts himself. This was televised on channel 9 or 13 in New York. This was in the 1940s and 1950s, and there were a few hours of programming for Spanish-speaking audiences. In fact, Spanish television is what changed every-thing for my father—besides his own drinking and bad choices. I think Spanish television killed the live variety show in New York, because people just didn't bother going out anymore. They'd just stay home and they watched people on television. Families were starting to fall apart; the pressure from trying to make it in this country; people got cynical and jaded, and along with the fact that they could watch television at home, they never went out anymore. So his show really started to fall apart. But that's what he did, he was a real force in the late 1950s and 1960s.

And so this piece that I'm going to write about him…yeah, it's very hard, 'cause a lot of people are dead, I can't find people, and a lot of them were just out of it, nuts. So I'm going to try to do the research, but I might end up not making it so factual and just do the essence of who he was and what my experience was—mythologize him a little more. In *Memory Tricks,* the stories about my mother are things that actually happened. But with my fa-ther, I might not do it the same. I'm just thinking of having it be a little bit more abstract and using characters around his life. The thing is that I really love him, he treated me really wonder-fully, but he really wasn't around. He wasn't there for me. Even though my mother was involved in her career, she still tried to fulfill the role of mother—deal with my school. My dad just showed up, was around for a couple hours, and then he went and did his show. He was just more of a mystery to me. And then, of course, my parents split up, I went with her, I didn't really know as much about him.

You know, the research I'm doing about my father's life is difficult because I don't know Spanish. I have a few names in Puerto Rico. But the other thing is that a lot of people who knew my dad are still around. For some reason, with my mom, I wasn't thinking about those things, but after doing her piece, I'm a little shy about doing my father's story. Some of the things he did to women were intense, and some of those women are still around. And there's probably kids around. So I can't—if I told his story, I would have to make up another person. So I'm still trying to balance the two, which do I want to do—the factual or the fic-tional? Because it's very interesting, all the things he did, it makes a good story. But also, it's hard to give up the fact that he actu-ally lived, this is his name, these are the people. And if I do the factual, it's not going to be as honest. If I fictionalize it, I have the freedom to tell what happened. It will meet somewhere in between.

MH-P: *Memory Tricks* has recently been optioned to American Playhouse. Part of its wide appeal is that almost everyone can relate to issues concerning family relationships, especially dysfunctional relationships.

MG: Yes, it's particularly popular with Latinos and Jewish people.

MH-P: But the story you tell is so compelling because it is so specifically located in the history of U.S. Latino performance. As the daughter of Latino parents who immigrated to New York in the early 1950s, who left poverty to find success in the East Coast Latino entertainment scene, would you consider theirs an immigrants' success story? What were some of the challenges and obstacles faced by your parents?

MG: Well, I would call it an immigrants' quest-for-success story, but I would call it more a story of the failings of the American dream. That story focuses more on my mother. In her mind and in the minds of our very small world, she was a success. She came to New York as a teenager with her mother, very poor. She had certain values: to be very beautiful, the most beautiful, to be the most sought after. She wanted to be an actress. To be an actress, she had to take lessons, and to pay for the lessons, she started dancing. She wound up being known as a dancer instead of an actress. She wanted to be a Hollywood star, but that wasn't going to happen because of her accent. Instead, she ended up dancing for Latino audiences, and that's how she met my father. People said they were the Lucy and Ricky of their day; everybody loved them as a couple, but, of course, that little honeymoon was over right away. I remember them sleeping in separate beds.

When I was around eight or nine years old, my mother decided to leave the Latino scene and started to dance in the Anglo nightclubs. She was probably making more money in those places. She had an Anglo agent who sent her out to play Connecticut and that area. She was making more money than my father, and the marriage was lousy. By then, they were pretty much living their own lives. But yet she was still very beautiful, and everyone thought, Wow, she's got it all. And all she was doing, basically, was capitalizing on her looks and her dream to

MEMORY TRICKS
Written and Performed
by Marga Gomez

(courtesy of Michelle Habell-Pallan)

be an American; she really wanted to fit in, leave New York, leave Washington Heights. Well, eventually, she met this guy, an Italian guy but white enough, and he made lots of promises that he was going to make a lot of money. She really wanted to move to Long Island, into the suburbs. When you made it, you got a big house in the suburbs. So that's what she did: she divorced my father; married this guy; got a big house in the suburbs; couldn't dance anymore, because this guy wouldn't let her; was never accepted by the other neighbors; and, basically, became a prisoner in this house. There was nothing else for her. She really cut off her culture, she cut off everything, just to have this stupid house in the suburbs, and to be the only Puerto Rican for miles. She really tried to deny who she was and deny who I was. In *Memory Tricks,* I talk about her dyeing my hair red. So as my father continued in show business up to his last days, my mother gave it up. She gave up her career—in the traditional feminine role—for a man and for a white American man. So that was the failure of the American dream, because she wasn't coming to this country with all her identity, with a real sense of herself. She was coming with a sense of somebody else she wanted to be, and because of that, she lost it all. And then, as you see in *Memory Tricks,* her second husband just became more and more distant from her, and then her life was really hell. The time before she got sick was really a nightmare for her, and really terrifying for her.

MH-P: To go back to her early days as a dancer, what did it mean to be an exotic dancer in the 1950s?

MG: You're the second person who's asked me that in a week. It's different from what it meant back then. Now it means being a stripper. As far as I know, she was never a stripper. I think once you become a stripper, that's it. First she started out doing Afro-Cuban and merengues. She had beautiful little costumes—she had a cat costume—and she did burlesque numbers. I don't mean by burlesque that she would strip, but they were just dances. She would probably take off the cat suit and have a bathing suit type of costume underneath.

MH-P: In terms of cultural mixing, it's interesting that she as a Puerto Rican woman was doing all these various dances.

MG: Well, those were the dances that the solo performers were doing then: merengues, Afro-Cuban, mambo. She did them all.

At that time, those dances were really hot. So she was doing that—she was doing all kinds of numbers—with lighting and different types of effects. A real presentation there. So when she became an exotic dancer, she started to play in the white clubs; that's when her stage name became Margo the Exotic. Dancers always had to change their styles according to the trends, and since Afro-Cuban dancers were no longer the rage, she became an exotic dancer. It was the new thing, and everybody was looking for exotic dancers. Exotic dancers could go to Japan. She had the opportunity to go to Japan, but I was too little, and she didn't want to leave me. So I think she was dabbling in a few different dance routines and styles. But then she mostly started doing the exotic dancing. That would be the belly dancing with a little Middle Eastern music.

MH-P: Interesting, a Puerto Rican woman performing Middle-Eastern dances.

MG: In those clubs, exotic meant the same thing: you could either be from Iran or from Puerto Rico, it was all considered exotic. Plus, she had bleached blonde hair, so it was pretty crazy.

MH-P: I guess the question is, exotic for whom? But since we have a short amount of time, do you mind if I switch gears a little? You mentioned earlier that you observed that there is not a lot of documentation of Latino performance in this country. So do you see yourself as a historian of sorts, a chronicler of a different kind of history?

MG: I kind of wish that was true, but I don't know if I have the discipline to do all that work.

MH-P: But I mean in a different way—a different kind of historian, what they call an organic intellectual. We have this term *organic intellectual*, which is an intellectual not produced by the university. So what I was trying to ask—since there is an impulse in mainstream culture to deny the full range of the contributions people of color have made to the economic, political, and cultural fabric of the U.S.—is if you see yourself telling about an experience that isn't considered history and telling it differently in a different form than we are taught history should be told in. Do you think about your project in that way?

MG: Well, that's what I hope to do, but I don't feel that's what *Memory Tricks* is... *Memory Tricks* has just a hint, a suggestion, of what was. For some people, I guess that's big news. For me, that's how life was. When I read *Mambo Kings* [by Oscar Hijuelos], I was very moved, because he captured a lot. For example, what it was like doing a gig and taking the subway home; although my father always drove Cadillacs and my mother always took taxis home. The movie was a disgrace to the book, it was totally whitewashed, but I was inspired by that book, and I thought I would like to add to that. I would like to bring out the details of my parents' lives. But I'm finding it hard to get information. I just try to interview people, like my mother's old friends, and they are so reticent to talk. The thing is—I don't know if this is just a Latino thing—but we're really very private. So a lot of people I talk to don't really want to say too much, because they really believe in privacy. And then, I have to honestly tell them that I'm going to do this film and do a piece, and that makes things even harder. There's someone who could tell me so much, but it's like pulling teeth. But even just a little is fun, and plus I have tons of pictures that I haven't even looked at yet and little clippings. Some of the material, though, that I'm going to put in these pieces about my father is going to be part imagination and intuition. If you can't remember the past then you just make it up! So it's going to be somewhere between history and myth.

MH-P: Can you remember if your parents were involved in any actors union or organizations?

MG: Yes, they were in a group for artistas. I think my father was the president, and they made it up. But all they did was have parties, and then they got very criticized because there were dues being paid, and people thought all they did was do parties and didn't do very serious things. My parents really liked just having the meetings and my dad really liked being president and my mother was vice president. It was like this club where they said, "Yes, we have to do something," but they weren't real serious about it. In his story, I do want to recreate this little organization. Of course, they were in AGVA. I think the letters stand for the Actors Guild for the Variety Arts. They were both in that.

MH-P: What do you think is happening now in the development of Latino talent in the entertainment industry? What do you think has changed?

MG: Well, it's another chic—lesbian chic, Asian chic, and Latino chic. Everybody in Hollywood wants to have a hand in the Latino culture. I mean, Latinos have always been exploited and used by the industry and by advertisers. My father was really involved with that, in selling products, getting promotions going for whatever–Borden's or cigarettes or coffee. Usually, things that are totally bad for your health. Miller beer. In Hollywood, it's the same thing. They just want to make money, and so they think if they can make money off of us, they'll use us. They had their *AKA Pablo* show, which was a disaster.

MH-P: What was that?

MG: That was the Paul Rodriguez show about ten years ago. It was not written by Latinos, and he wasn't really ready for the show. He's a better actor now. That was a flop, and so what happened was since that was a flop, executives thought that Latino doesn't work on TV. So I've gone to meetings now where they want two different things. They want me to be a character for television who says something about being Latino, and then I go to other meetings where it is, "You're Latino, but it doesn't need to be the focus of the story." Which, really, for me, would be more appropriate, because I feel so assimilated, so cut off; that it's a source of shame and guilt for me. But at the same time, there are so many people like us [I told her I couldn't speak Spanish fluently either]. But it's hard, because for television, you have to be such a cliché almost. I don't know if it's serving us to do it.

For example (sigh), do you know that piece *Death and the Maiden*? It's set in Argentina. It's ready to play in Los Angeles at the Mark Taper Forum, with a Latina playing a Latina. But in New York, they did it with Glenn Close playing a Latina. It's about a woman who's been tortured, then comes in contact with her torturers many years later. So at the Mark Taper, they had a big controversy, because the big muca-mucas wanted to have a name, but then the people said, "No, this is bullshit, you can't try that in L.A." And now they are going to make a film of it, and Sigourney Weaver is going to take Glenn Close's place. And I'm just sick. They are very concerned with names. It's a catch-22. Now the names are Rosie Pérez. Of course, she can't do *Death and the Maiden* (imitating Pérez in a high Nuyorican-accented voice): "No, get out of here, my people will defeat you." Then there's Maria Conchita Alonzo. You can't really get too worried about her. They have to just open the doors. But there's no altruism in the industry. It's all about money. Someone breaks in once in a while despite all the obstacles, because they never just give, and there is no way to control them. I mean, we boycott the movies and they don't care. The only thing Latinos can do is somehow get behind Latino performers and really turn out for them. I don't know exactly how you do, but I guess when there is a Latino film, go see it. For instance, a lot of Latinos went to see *Like Water for Chocolate*.

MH-P: But *Like Water for Chocolate* is a film made in Mexico.

MG: Yes, it's not a Hollywood film. But *El Mariachi* that's done pretty good, that guy has gotten a lot of attention now. But, of course, in that film, a lot of people did get their brains blown out; so as long as you show that in a film, I guess it will do okay. I think that it's still really hard out there, and there's a lot of mixed messages. They say they're really interested, yet they can't seem to have the balls to bankroll anybody and give everybody else a break.

MH-P: Who are some of your connections in the world of Latino performers?

MG: Well, my major connections are Monica Palacios, Culture Clash; Luis Alfaro, I'm getting to know through Monica; and Beto Araiza. I've just gotten to know, she's not a performer exactly, Sandra Cisneros. That's really neat, because just as a writer, she's really inspiring.

MH-P: How did you get to know her?

MG. She came to my show—just a comedy show I was doing at Josie's Cabaret—not this New Year's Eve [1994], but the New Year's Eve before, and she introduced herself. She was being interviewed at the Herbst Theater, so I went to the interview, then afterward I said hi. Then I played in San Antonio, Texas, so I went and visited her there; we drank tequila and smoked cigars. I think that's probably it for my connections; everybody else is pretty peripheral. I've met Luis Valdez and José Luis Valenzuela. I met him at the Taper when he directed Culture Clash, and we had a real nice connection there.

MH-P: I understand that your work is influenced by your involvement with grassroots theater collectives, and I heard that you and Monica Palacios started Culture Clash together. How did that happen?

MG: Well, we didn't really form it. The person who formed

Culture Clash was René Yañez; Richard Montoya [a member of Culture Clash] calls him the Godfather. René was the director of the Galeria of La Raza on 24th Street in the Mission district [San Francisco]. Now he's at the Mexican Museum, and he's always got something going. Well, it was his job to organize something for Cinco de Mayo, and he wanted to do something different. Cinco de Mayo was always the same old thing. So he wanted to do a comedy show, and he had a connection with Monica Palacios— they had both performed at the Galeria—and he knew Richard [Montoya]. He asked Monica, "Why don't you have Marga come?" So it was Monica, me, Richard, and Tony Burciaga.

MH-P: That's Burciaga of *Drink Cultura* fame?

MG: That's right, he's a visual artist and a poet. So the four of us had a meeting. Then Hebert Siguenza came and Rick Salinas came, and we had our first show. It was just each one of us doing our own spot. The guys had never done stand-up before, and that's basically what it was. Each of us was doing stand-up comedy. Hebert was doing characters, Michael Jackson and Prince, and he was sort of in between the spots. Hebert would come out with different little outfits and do something like Tony Montana or Scar Face. That was the show.

MH-P: When was this?

MG: This was maybe in 1985 or 1986. Monica and I stayed with the group for about two years, and it was more or less like that. It didn't really take off until after we left, but I'm not saying it's 'cause we left! It was like we were all doing our own thing, and then we would get together and do a Culture Clash show. Culture Clash was like a secondary occupation. it was really neat for me, because before that, I had never played to Latino audiences. And one thing I had to learn was that Latino audiences are sometimes really religious (laughter). I thought Latino audiences would think it was really funny to make fun of the Church. But it was just the opposite, and I was having real trouble with a lot of my material, because I was still new at it. A lot of my material was just a reaction against all the oppressive things of my childhood. So I was really going after the Church and that was bad. We were doing a lot of shows to Republican Latinos, MAPA [Mexican American Political Association], and all those people. And Monica and I were just too feminist for these audiences. I don't even think we were doing any gay material, but we were not getting the same response as the guys. It just got depressing after a while. We had some good shows, and the women would always say, "All right!" But it was just hard not to have everybody with you. Since we were all new, it was important for the group to get smaller, and that's what happened.

MH-P: Do you think you influenced the group in a kind of feminist way?

MG: Monica was more outspoken. I was pretty unassertive. I was more passive-aggressive and I'd blow up. I couldn't really articulate what was bothering me, but Monica would. They knew what was up, they came from the community, too, they had to deal with strong women. But it was still a learning process and it was going to take them a while, and it was going to take us a while for us to feel comfortable. They continue, some people will say things about them. My experience has been pretty good this last time. In fact, they gave me all these male-bashing lines in the *Carpa Clash* show that everybody thought I wrote. But no, I wrote my monologue, but all the things I said to insult them, they wrote for me.

MH-P: So in this *Carpa Clash* show, you play a character named Mimi. I haven't seen the show, but one reviewer writes that Mimi is the daughter of Mexican entertainers. Could you tell me about how that character evolved? Why did you decide to present yourself as Mexican?

MG: Mimi is me. You know, I don't know how these reviewers get work (sigh). I spent the first five minutes of a fifteen-minute monologue talking about being Cuban and Puerto Rican. This guy could not have been Latino. No matter how much you try to explain that these are different countries with different personalities, different histories, to them, everybody's Mexican or everybody's Puerto Rican. It's the same to them: they think it's all Spanish. So, yeah, Mimi is me. They told me that all the guys in *Carpa Clash* had a clown nickname. So I figured I'd use Mimi. It's my nickname from when I was a kid, and I like the name; it sounded kind of clowny, too.

MH-P: Moving off the subject of reviewers and back to your work—your work is full of interesting tensions and contradictions.

MG: Thank you!

MH-P: As you travel to different venues, different performance spaces, you construct your identity differently in response to different audiences. In other words, you represent your "self," or your identity, differently to different crowds. Why do you do this?

MG: I'm not sure what you mean when you say that–when I'm addressing Latino crowds that I'm not addressing my sexuality? Can you give me an example?

MH-P: For instance, on the *Culture Clash* show, whose audience is primarily Latino, you tended to foreground your ethnicity and leave out discussions of lesbian sexuality. In contrast, when addressing queer audiences, on the HBO comedy special, it seemed easier for you to integrate comments about your ethnicity into your routine. This tendency to "shape" your identity is fascinating to me, because it demonstrates that identity is fluid, not fixed, and mutable. But could you explain why issues of lesbian sexuality; but not sexuality in general, tend to fade out when you address Latino audiences?

MG: Oh, okay. Well, I hadn't really thought about it that way. The reason I didn't talk about lesbian issues on the *Culture Clash* show is because the producer told me that the audience was full of a bunch of college-aged kids on dates, and since I was getting a break on television, I really didn't want to bomb. So I talked about growing up Catholic and having a chaperone named Hymenia Permanente. So I did talk about sexuality, but in a way that straight people could relate to. Since the HBO comedy special was focused on gay/lesbian comedy, I could joke openly about my sexuality. But what I've found is that jokes about relationships are popular with almost anyone, so I'm going to work on those for a while.

MH-P: Recently, a photo of you was featured in a special issue of *Time* magazine.[6] On the cover was the image of a mestiza who, the article explains, "was created by a computer from a mix of several races. What you see is a remarkable preview of the New Face of America." Under her image, the caption reads, "How Immigrants Are Shaping the World's First Multicultural Society." The funny thing is, we're not sure what this woman's ethnicity is or if she has one, nor is the late twentieth-century U.S. the world's first multicultural society.

A few pages into the magazine, we find an image of you. The

difference is that this mestiza's image is not computer generated, but can be traced to an actual Latina, you. And your image is interestingly marked as hybrid. Poised on a variety show stage, your long-haired figure is illuminated by candles with images of Catholic saints on them and holds a 1950s-style microphone as well as a rosary. Your pin-striped pant leg is almost wrapped around the microphone, and the men's high-top sneaker [a reference to U.S. mass culture] looks as if it might come crashing down on the candles. Or maybe it's being energized by them. The caption labels you a "Latin actress." Given that your image appears in this special issue, what would you say if I said that this representation constructs a new image of a U.S. citizen or subject?

MG: Well, I don't think so much about this country as I do the planet, and sometimes I do feel very out of it—being an American, that is. Living in San Francisco or living in Santa Cruz is not like living in America. I don't know, because I really always felt out of the mainstream, on the fringe. I don't know if I'm the new kind of citizen, because a U.S. citizen, to me, is really into being in a group, really into shared experiences like Super Bowls and all that stuff. That's not for me. I feel more like an expatriate who lives here (laughter).

MH-P: Right, except that there are many of us who have a shared experience of feeling like we don't belong, and whose communities have been disenfranchised from political and economic power. So I think that there is a different version of U.S. citizen emerging because of the historical conjunctures, and though you have concern for the planet, you've lived or experienced certain historical moments. From the 1960s to the 1990s, you've witnessed the world change in certain ways. You've seen how the influx of Latino immigrants has changed the cultural fabric...and we've all witnessed this too, and experienced...this constructed image of what it means to be a true American (blond, blue eyes), which excludes the full range of what constitutes "American," more specifically, North American. I think that we are more representative (not that any one image can represent everyone), but that your story is just as American as that of the constructed ideal—blond, blue-eyed, straight subjects.

MG: I feel more, to use an old term, like a citizen of the underground.

MH-P: Well, there's a quote by a poet, Bob Kaufman, he was from the Bay Area, and he used to say that "...'way out' people know the way out."[7] What he meant is that sometimes way out people, people on the fringe, can sometimes show us the way out—out of this homophobic, misogynist, racist climate in which we live. So what I mean by that is people living on the fringe.

MG: Yes, I see where you're going. You know, I had a little rap I used to do called "The Way Out." This was about the time of the NEA censorship and all that. I used to do it all the time, and I used to have go-go dancers behind me. I would sing a little Spanish, and it would go to Santana's tune "Evil Ways." I had sampled Mellow Man Ace, and he samples Santana. Olivia Records might have a video of it. It goes like this (Gomez starts to sing).

Check it, homies, we got problemas grandes, porque our libertad is being [Gomez forgot the word] by a honky. Senator Helms, he hates the arts endowment. He's got a flag up his ass. Hey, don't have a cow, man. Who told Jesse he's got taste? He's just a big pendejo, our culture is just too good to waste. Don't cut off my dinero. A mi no me importa, if I do not get a grant. The show must go on, 'cause we have a brand new dance. I warn you, if you're prudish or fanatically devout, no mires este baile que se llama "Way Out." It's homo and erotic and you move your crotch about, it's a real ice-breaker and it's called the "Way Out" (and I'd have the dancers come on). Carmen and Diane are here to show you, when you do the "Way Out" people get to know you. First you lick your lips like a nasty thing, mirando y templando and flapping your left wing. Then you give your partner a gentle thrust; if you like, rub your chichis, that means "touch your bust." You can "Way Out" on the job, and you can "Way Out" in the car. Got the same sex cravings? The "Way Out" will get you far. If you are in the closet, but you feel like shouting, express yourself. Honey, do the way outed. I remember the day I "Way Outed" to my parents, they were angry, enojados—a little bit embarrassed. But then my parents changed. Now they're real proud of me, y siempre me gritan. Marga baila—"Way Outing"—this is my handle, this is my spout, this is how you do—the "Way Out." I hope you didn't mind the "Way Out" exhibition, we want to do it now, before they have a prohibition. I know that it's not a Disney creation; to me, it's art, to others, deviation.

I can't remember the rest of it, but I have it somewhere. I did that rap for a couple years and people would always ask for it. But I lost the tape. I could start using it again, but, you know, it's not a topic anymore...but it was great 'cause everything came together. I was able to put some Spanish in there, even though I didn't know very much.

MH-P: The titles of your shows are funny and highly suggestive (Marga laughs), especially titles like *Pretty, Witty, and Gay* or *Memory Tricks. Pretty, Witty, and Gay* suggests different things to different audiences. Maybe Latinos think of *West Side Story*, but in the Castro district, it means something else. What were you trying to say with that title?

MG: Oh, both things. I have a little bone to pick with *West Side Story.* When you watch it, it's hard not to laugh. There's the terrible accents and makeup jobs. But then, at the same time, I'm very attached to it, so I always wanted to do something about it in stand-up. The first time I did anything about *West Side Story,* I did a three-minute-twenty-second version of it. Did you ever see that? This is when I did my Spanish talk show host has-been named Filumena Fabulosa. She had a show called *Noche Line.* So that was my first experience satirizing *West Side Story.*

And still a lot of times at events they will play "I Feel Pretty" or "I Want to Live in America," some stupid song from *West Side Story.* That music will haunt Puerto Ricans 'till the end of time. So I decided it was time to get them back, get it back, get our shot. And a lot of times in stand-up, you need to have little slogans to describe yourself, and I thought it was just a good-sounding sound bite. So I decided to do the show that way. And to bring up shades of *West Side Story* was appropriate, too. That song was written at a time when the term *gay* meant something else, and, of course, its meaning has changed and can't really be used again. It just worked out nicely.

MH-P: Some fans wanted me to ask you if you were trying to make a political move by using *Pretty, Witty, and Gay* instead of *Pretty, Witty, and Lesbian.*

MG: (laughs) Well, I don't think they got the *West Side Story* connection. Did they think it should be *Pretty, Witty, and Lesbian?* To tell you the truth, I prefer the terms *gay* or *queer. Lesbian,* to me, just, it's just too charged. Monica Palacios does a whole bit about claiming the word *lesbian.* To me, I just don't like it. I was involved in lesbian separatism. I just have had too much lesbian—it's not just a word that describes sexuality to me, it describes almost a very strict way of living. I identify more with gay men (laughter). But that's a whole other performance piece.

MH-P: Going back to your days in New York—you joke about how you could speak Spanish until the "pack of wild Irish women who raised me, beat it out of me. Back in those days, we called those Irish women nuns." Did the nuns really beat it out of you? I wouldn't be surprised, because in the U.S., there's a history of violence that surrounds language and issues of resistance.

MG: I don't know, they beat us, they just beat us. I was a very, very good girl in Catholic school, because I didn't want to get hit at all. I don't know if they would hit us exactly for speaking Spanish. But what they did was they really favored the Irish kids in class, because the neighborhood was Puerto Rican, a little of Cuban, and Irish. They always favored the Irish kids. They just made you feel bad for speaking Spanish, for being darker. It was a psychological beating, but combined with the physical punishments we'd get for breaking a rule, it all became part of the same thing. I just wanted to survive and be on the nuns' good side. I'd do whatever it took. So the threat of punishment was really an encouragement to finally complete the process of total assimilation and that's what I did. Total detachment from my roots—in which I feel my mother was a collaborator, she's the one who started the whole thing. I know it had to happen somewhere, because when I learned to speak, it was in Spanish and in just a few years, it was gone.

MH-P: I think that happens to a lot of people. Although there is nothing inherently wrong with speaking Spanish, we get rewarded not to, and the English-only laws reinforce prejudice against speaking Spanish. But you answered my next question: Was your school culturally and racially mixed?

MG: Yes, it was at least 50 percent Latino, if not more. There was this feeling from the nuns...this school probably was there in the '40s or '50s then suddenly in the '60s there was just this wave of all these little brown kids. I think they couldn't stand it that their neighborhood was just changing. The school was pretty much in a white neighborhood.

MH-P: So there were no African-American students?

MG: Well, everything changes in the space of one block. So yes, there were African-American students, in fact, that area was considered Harlem. But there were a few black kids in the class. In a class of twenty kids, there would be four or five black kids. They really got trashed unless they became total super nerds. They could never do nothing wrong, or else they would get beat.

MH-P: Because you grew up in Harlem, the press constructs you as child of the city, which is true, but they do it in such a way that it seems as if you were underprivileged. But you went to private school and had nannies. Can you tell me about how issues of class figured in your inner-city experience?

MG: It was really bizarre, because the neighborhood was working class. Everyone was struggling and getting poorer and poorer as the years went by. We were rich, in the eyes of the neighborhood and in our own eyes. I thought we were rich because my father drove Cadillacs, my mother had minks, she had housekeepers, and we took these trips to South America. We had tacky French furniture and statues. And I grew up with a false sense of being upper class, when we really were not. They spent a lot of money on junk, and suddenly there was no more money. My mother just married someone who strangled her financially. My father had one bad business thing after another. He died in poverty, on Medicare in a little place. Since my mother didn't really have any of her own money, she ended up where she started. My mother is now in a nursing home. I wasn't able to put her in the one that I wanted, because I didn't have the money. They started really poor, grew up in poor circumstances-shacks, no running water. They came to this country, struggled, and had a few years of prosperity. My mother's lasted a little bit longer, but as the property of a man. So you see, it's really hard to define my class position. I really did live as a rich kid for a few years, at least the years that are most formative. Everybody envied me and I enjoyed that I was a little brat.

MH-P: How do issues of class come up in your work now?

MG: Issue of class? Well, I don't know, it's complex, it's not that simple. You have money, you have illusions. I think that the symbols are there, but they may not be obvious. In *Memory Tricks,* when I tell the story about my mom and her father...she was an illegitimate child, and her mother would go and take her to see her father; that's when issues of class come in. He had money, she didn't have money. So you see, she came from poverty. When somebody comes from poverty in Puerto Rico, it's sort of like being in a caste, and, of course, in the piece, you can see she came to a bad end.

And even if I do manage to prosper, I'm still always going to have this sense that this is going to be taken away from me. I have so much anxiety about making money or being homeless. I mean, you do have to take care of yourself, especially when there is no one else. I think the problem is that some people don't put a limit to it. People start to acquire and then they can't have enough. But there are certain basic things that you do need to provide for yourself as far as your health and old age.

MH-P: Yes, it's especially difficult for women, especially working-class immigrant women, to get the kind of health care they deserve as they age.

MG: And that's why I worry.

MH-P: You seem to be de-essentializing Latina and queer identity. In other words, your work complicates any notion that Latina or lesbian identity is lived in any one way. Your new stand-up show is called *Half-Cuban/Half-Lesbian*. What are you suggesting with the title?

MG: *Half-Cuban/Half-Lesbian?* Well, it's always come up in my stand-up. I try to keep my stand-up simple, so I want to do jokes about being Puerto Rican. But I'm also half-Cuban. So I've tried to deal with that in stand-up. I don't even know that much about Cuban culture, although I know more now that I'm researching this for my father's piece.

MH-P: But you know what it is to be Cuban-American.

MG: Kind of…or more American-Cuban, I guess. I don't remember how I put that title together, and of course, I don't say "half-Cuban, half-Puerto Rican, half-lesbian." (pause) I know why. It's because I played in Miami, so I wanted to get the message across to gain the audience of Cubans, but I did not need anybody there who was going to flip out when they realized I was gay. So that's the reason for the title—I wanted to hit my target audience. Not that my audience was just Cuban lesbians, but that anyone who thought this was pretty cool would come to the show. But I continue to use that title because it's catchy. Even though I don't like to define myself as a lesbian comic, it helps me take the worry out of a situation where I'm traveling hundreds of miles to face people. This way, they know where I'm coming from.

And it's funny, because it's like lesbian is almost a sort of ethnic root. In a way, it is a culture unto itself, and the two meet in interesting ways. I think the title works whether people see it or not, because a lot of people don't think of Latinos as being queer at all. It's a message...and it also refers to the conflict that I've gone through with both cultures. The same goes with Puerto Rican. This is just easier, it just rolls off the tongue easier.

MH-P: Have you seen the work of Luis Alfaro? I think he negotiates ethnicity and sexuality in different ways than you do. Alfaro refuses to separate his sexuality from his ethnicity. He explains that he cannot be Chicano without being gay, and vice versa.

MG: Well, Luis is very uncompromising. I, on the other hand, come from show business parents. So I'm trying to remain true to myself, but, at the same time, I'm going to have my hand in a few different things. I do try do make things accessible, but still have some kind of integrity. I try to expand my audiences. And it's not out of any kind of idealism, it's dollars and cents. I'm trying to provide for myself, since no one else does. I'm honestly afraid of being old and homeless.

MH-P: You once said that you've been received by the mainstream press because of your lesbian profile. Why do you think issues of sexuality are more accepted than those of class, race, and ethnicity? Or is that the case?

MG: It's easier to follow, because I'm a really assimilated Latina. So I don't have that essential Latino quality.

MH-P: But none of us do.

MG: Right. But it's not good, it's very hard to get sound bites out of me about being Latino. My stories are kind of short about it. I'm really trying to get back to it now, but the lesbian chic thing? Well, I've been living in the Castro, so I'm pretty much closer to this culture and to this community.

MH-P: So you feel like this lesbian chic has made it okay to be lesbian now?

MG: Oh, yeah, but we don't know how long that's going to last. There has been a taboo on homosexuality and bisexuality. But it's finally being lifted. For so long, people of color have tried to get attention and get a dialogue going. With just being queer, we can't. We can't even write about this, we can't even talk about this or see what you do. So now it's almost like the first time it's in the open. That's why it's new and the information has got to get out up to the plateau. It's really how much we're going to plateau out, how much are they going to be able to take, and it's really a mainstream kind of thing, homosexuals that they're talking about. There is lesbian chic. k.d. lang came out and Martina [Navratilova], and that's made a big difference. They really can't argue with the way k.d. sings or the way Martina plays. Actually, I've gotten the most attention from the press for *Memory Tricks*. It's my struggles with my Latino heritage and my mother that have gotten the most interest and attention.

MH-P: Marisela Norte is a spoken word artist whose writing, at times, shares similar themes with yours. In one piece, she has written that she is the one who "cuts the label out." My reading of that line is that she cuts the label out of the category *Latina/ Chicana* in order to represent a different image of what it means to be Latina. You, too, do some "cutting out." I think that's important, given that some people don't realize that the category *Latino* is quite heterogeneous, that Chicano culture is different from Puerto Rican, from Cuban, and other Latino cultures.

MG: Oh, yeah, but I still get mistaken for being Chicano, especially working with Culture Clash. At the end of Culture Clash shows, they have a question-and-answer session. One time, Richard [a member of Culture Clash] said that Chicano is a state of mind; that's the way I feel about being queer. It's not so much about who you sleep with, instead it's this openness. So I thought, Okay, I can be a Chicana, or I can even be a Chicano.

I think I'll be a Chicano (laughs). It happens constantly. And it works the other way. If I were a Chicano living in New York, then everybody would think I was Puerto Rican.

MH-P: To me, the fascinating thing about your performances are that they mutate the dominant story of what it means to be Latina or queer in the U.S. They also alter the story of what it means to be a U.S. citizen in 1994. Even though you may not intend to make a huge political statement about such issues, well, maybe you do…or at least it can be interpreted that way.

MG: The only thing I do is be honest, and that has not been that easy. And that's what I try to stick to. I guess with my cultural identity, I do two things: I hold it up and I try to strip it away at the same time. It's confusing. But I guess it's the honest approach.

MH-P: Do you have any advice for aspiring comedians?

MG: Write down what you think is funny and don't steal jokes.

Or just don't steal my jokes (laughter).

Thanks to Professors Dana Tagaki and Donna Haraway for giving the interviewer the time to develop this interview in the Winter 1994 graduate seminar entitled "Cultural and Historical Studies of Race and Ethnicity." Gomez's interview took place on February 28, 1994, in San Francisco.

Notes

1. Culture Clash performed *Carpa Clash* in the spirit of the original carpas. *Carpas* (literally, "tents") were used by Mexican troupes who toured Chicano communities in the Southwest in the 1920s and 1930s. The troupes were named for the portable theaters in which they performed vaudeville productions, which included sketches about current topics as well as songs and dances.
2. "Pretty, Witty and Mainstream: Lesbian Comedian Marga Gomez Says There Are Signs of Acceptance," *Los Angeles Times,* Calendar Section, Oct.13, 1994.
3. Rosa Linda Fregoso, *The Bronze Screen* (Minneapolis: University of Minnesota Press, 1993), 31.
4. Ibid.
5. Stuart Hall, "Notes on Deconstructing the 'Popular'," in *People's History and Socialist History,* ed. Paul Kegan (London: Routledge, 1981), 239.
6. "The New Face of America." *Time* Special Issue (Fall) 1993.
7. Maria Damon, "Unmeaning Jargon," *South Atlantic Quarterly* (Fall) 1988, 708–709.

The Gaze of the Other:
An Interview with Cherríe Moraga

Ellie Hernández

Poet, playwright, essayist, and teacher Cherríe Moraga's directorial influence as artist-in-residence with Brava Theater Company has produced numerous productions by lesbians and
women of color. Part of her residency with Brava includes a
number of theatrical ventures that have placed Moraga on the
cutting edge of Bay Area theater production. Moraga's first major production with Brava, *Watsonville,* brings together a story of
the women in a small agricultural coast town in Northern California. This highly dramatic piece weaves the dimensions of three
sensational events that have placed Watsonville, the town, at the
center of collective action in Chicana/o politics. The events that
eventually developed into a major production in San Francisco,
include the cannery strike, the Loma Prieta earthquake of 1989,
and the "image" of the Virgin de Guadalupe emblazoned on a
tree near the town of Watsonville. Moraga's continued success
in the area of stage production culminates with yet another production—Brava staged a rehearsal of *Mexican Medea,* set to debut
in the Fall 1997 season. *Mexican Medea* proves to be a quintessen-
tial Moraga stage production, which employs the lyrical Chicana
lesbian in conflict with social mores. But unlike previous stage
productions, *Mexican Medea* is a complex narrative that turns this
dramatic piece into a mature expression of Chicanas dealing
with the traditional trappings of female subjectivity. Cherríe
Moraga's style this time around is meticulously crafted as well
as moving. Moraga rewrites the female script to reshape the ideologies within Chicano theater.

And yet, much of what we are familiar with in Chicano theater centers around the very private delineation of Chicano and
Chicana communities: the home, identity, and sexuality all
bound within an intimate space. How those intimate spaces intersect with each other is what Moraga is interested in rewriting.
Moraga's work has certainly come to represent the privation of

familia and the problematic of living in the shadows of historical marginality in Chicana subject formation. As we approach the next millennium, I, as well as other emergent Chicana intellectuals, have recommitted once again to working within our community's best interests, that is, to write from the space that creates these realities we call criticism. It is for this reason that I took the opportunity to write about someone who has indelibly marked my very own consciousness. I believe that because Cherríe Moraga understands the function of memory so well, her work will naturally symbolize the struggle of the Chicana lesbian imagination for generations to come. In my role as the interviewer, I could not help but feel the performance of our bodies in the presence of the tape recorder: In other words, do we stage ourselves as we craft our ideas? Here we were, two presumably self-avowed butch women talking about the formation of the self–her mode, the dramatic political stage, and mine the academic political scene. But I think that what most moved me was seeing Cherríe Moraga between the outlines of her strong butch exterior tenderly holding her newly born son. I really believe that she is rewriting the script for all Chicanas.

As our world grows increasingly smaller, the sense that we have arrived at another location from which to view our condition as Third World women living within the exhausted paradoxes of our modern condition seems all the more real. Cherríe Moraga remains one of the most telling writers of our time. In many respects, Cherríe Moraga has redeemed the role of Chicana intellectual. As a critical thinker, Moraga has offered a vocabulary for new visions. As a playwright, Moraga has redefined performance and spectacle at the very core of identity by asking us to look at the ordinary situations in people's lives and to make them come to life. Throughout all her work, we have the sense that she points to the future while remembering the past with the sagacity of aged wisdom. Moraga never ceases to transgress the boundaries of intellectual, critical, and practical means of reclaiming a sense of being. In this interview, the very intentionality of her work articulates the gaze of the other.

EH: So much of your literature has changed in the last fifteen years. Let me briefly outline some of your published and staged work to date. You started on the East Coast with two collaborative efforts, namely, *This Bridge Called My Back* and *Cuentos: Stories By Latinas,* followed by your own collection of essays and poetry in the highly acclaimed *Loving in the War Years.* Then, in 1986, you published *Giving Up the Ghost,* a play in two acts, with the debut of the play here in the Bay Area, followed by numerous other stage productions, such as *Shadow of a Man* and, later, *Heroes and Saints,* not to mention your most recent collection of essays, *The Last Generation,* published in 1993, and your most recent collection of plays, published this year, titled *Heroes and Saints and Other Plays,* and, now, your work with Brava. We will get back to your work with Brava later. However, this is perhaps the best place to recapitulate the literary turn you have taken as a dramatist. What motivated you to take to the stage?

CM: In 1983, after I published *Loving in the War Years,* which were primarily autobiographical poems and essays...

EH: So you do regard *Loving in the War Years* as an autobiographical form?

CM: Yeah, of course, there are some things in there that are fiction. But essentially...more and more, even when I am writing things that are essentially autobiographical, I feel that right to create characters. All the genres are starting to fuse for me, so you'll never know what is really real and what is not, in the sense that the essays and the poems come out of a personal kind of urgency and biography that forces me to take pen in hand, which is a very different process for me than why I write a play. I started writing theater, as I said, after I finished *Loving in the War Years,* and the reason for that...that is—it [writing plays] actually happened to me very organically; it was because after I had finished *Loving in the War Years,* I felt I had finished with my own story. There is a certain way in which the completion of that book left me with a sense that I had some room inside, that I had emptied myself inside of some stuff and I had some room; because of that room, I started writing in journals again, and this character Corky came to me. And that wasn't me! Just suddenly there's a young girl, Corky. She started writing and talking—she was talking and I was recording what she was saying. I immediately liked her and thought that she was a much more interesting child than I ever was, and she was the sort of child I wished I had had the guts to be. I found her very fascinating.

I also was in a relationship at the time, a very brief relation-

ship, and that was really the first time I had been with an osten-
sibly heterosexual woman. There was a sort of a need that I had
to understand the relationship. What I would have typically done
is express that in poetry or an essay. What I found instead is that
this woman started speaking to me, this heterosexual woman
started speaking to me who wasn't my lover but was someone
who inspired me by that experience. She was explaining to me
heterosexual desire. It's something that I realize as a lesbian writer
that I really wanted to write for the larger Chicano community
without sacrificing my own lesbianism. I knew that I would not
be able to speak to other Chicanas unless I could understand
heterosexuality, not just compulsory heterosexuality, but heterosexual desire—that it was a real thing, and I had to understand it, and if I could understand it, then maybe I would be
able to speak to a larger community. What I started to find is
that through characters, *my* characters could teach me things
that my own autobiographical writing couldn't do. It was much
more limited. The way it came to me was not through internal
monologue. It was voice. It was out loud. It wanted to be told; it
wanted to be spoken; it wanted to be heard. That's how *Giving
Up The Ghost* came about, where I suddenly realized I had a
journal full of monologues. The people were not necessarily talking to each other, but worked within earshot of each other. The
book is really within the realm of *teatro poesía*. It really reflects
my transition from being a poet to being a playwright. The majority of the play is monologue. It's not me, it's not my story.
What I discovered through the act of doing theater, unlike essay
and poetry, was that you can present, as with fiction, characters
full of contradictions. They can reflect the complexity that is
very difficult to work out on the page in an essay, or analyti-
cally, or even in a poem. The characters are just themselves: full
of contradictions. There is a certain joy I get out of writing characters and a certain sense of completion and a sense of satisfac-
tion that I don't feel with other kinds of writing. I think that
comes from the fact that I don't have to explain anything. In
essays, I have to explain myself. In theater, I don't have to explain. I can take what are my pressing concerns and what I perceive as being *real* issues within our community by simply putting them on stage and let the characters try to play it to each
other.

EH: In all of your work, there appears a very strong connection to *la familia* and, with that connection, a strong critique of the participants in the family drama. Does stage production allow you to capture the complexity of the family on stage as opposed to the narrative or the poem?

CM: The beauty about theater is that you can present those contradictions and complexities, such as in *Shadow of a Man.* I always feel, on a certain level, that the things that I am writing are in dialogue with not only the Chicano community at large but also Chicano theater. As a lesbian writer, they had always presumed that I was essentially antifamily, simply because I had written *Giving Up the Ghost.* What is Chicano theater going to do about that, because it is so lesbian? But, on the other hand, lesbianism is also born out of families…out of Chicano families. We come out of Chicano families. They create us just as much as they create heterosexuals. I wanted to show family situations that did blur the lesbian, but also to show the hierarchies, sequences, and silences in the family. The thing about being a lesbian is that in all my work, I am really interested in the subject of desire. In every single member of that family, they are dealing with desire, and the only one who has made peace with that in *Shadow of a Man* is Rosario; everyone else is tormented by that desire. In the family, you can show all these dynamics. Because everybody has to have a full life on stage, you have to give each character a sexuality. And all of those sexualities are in the same room. It is enormously complex and, in that sense, it is fulfilling and satisfying to me, because it comes closer to any reality, certainly better than any of my essays.

EH: Also, in relation to the previous question, is the male figure in *Shadow of a Man* a critique of Chicano culture, such as the arguments you raised directly in *Loving in the War Years* with the subjugation of female sexuality in the oedipalized family structure?

CM: The play went through a lot of versions, and some feminists liked earlier versions better, when the men weren't even present. Some of them have been ghosts…sometimes they were not even there…

EH: Even the title suggests that the presence, or shadow, of men might not be necessary to uphold the patriarchal forms of masculinity in our culture.

CM: Of course, but women are *still* living under the shadow of this man. That was one version of it. However, I was not satisfied with this version. Because by virtue of making the men shadows, they were ultimately given even more power.

EH: So what you are saying is that men did not need to be present and accountable on stage in order to exemplify their power in society, that by being absent and oftentimes silent, men can still uphold existing modes of power that are, by all accounts, institutionalized in our everyday lives?

CM: Exactly. They were even more powerful by not being present. Once Manuel got on stage, he turned out to be the weakest person. He ended up being a man who exerted power in the family by virtue of his hierarchical relationship in the family. All the women and children had to twist and turn themselves in order to coexist with him. He definitely had power in that family. But once the man began to take flesh, his own weakness became clear, and it is that very weakness, then,…of a person who is weak and in a position of power in the family, that I wanted to expose, the effect that he has on those individuals below him in the hierarchy.

EH: So it's very important to your feminist position to make men present and accountable on stage?

CM: Yeah, some people didn't like that change. They said that somehow now the play became about Manuel. I thought it was really strange that some of the mainstream critics, like the *San Francisco Chronicle,* for example, focused on Manuel. They didn't focus on any of the women. And yet, when you look at the amount of time that Manuel spends on the stage, it is minimal compared to all the complexities the women bring up. I think that's a measure of our own set of institutionalized and internalized sexism. Well, the story was never about Manuel. There was one story in the play: It was my belief that men love each other so much and disregard women so much that a man will give up his own wife to keep a man he loves. That is the secret in the play–Manuel loves his compadre so much that he would give up his wife to keep that man. On a certain level, the point of the story is about Manuel, but that was actually true whether Manuel was on the stage or not, through his inability to really claim his own desire, to name his desire, name his love, by virtue of the fact that men are in power situations over women.

But the fact that a man is in a position that he is in that family and is not willing to deal with his own desire, then he perverts the lives of everybody in his whole family. The goal of that story is to equally describe how each female member of that family responds, copes, and survives or creates options for herself. So that Leticia, for example, dealing with a mother who is completely male identified, who worshipped the little dick, can say, "I got me one, too, Mama." But that is not going to name her, she is not named by that dick when she says, "I fucked him." She did that because she wanted to give up her virginity, because she did not want any man to put his name on her sexual identity.

I remember I was discussing this with a friend who felt that little dick scene with the mother was a little too much. In this case, Leticia is the antidote to that, as much as she can be within her constrained environment. When you're talking about fiction, you can't create ideal characters. You have to make characters who are real, and when you're talking about Mexicans, you're talking about people who are constrained by their environment.

EH: I find the relationship between sexuality and the speaking voice the most illuminating aspect of your work. You present this combination especially well in *Giving Up the Ghost* not just with Corky's rape, but also with the tribulatious of lesbian sexuality, coming out, the family, and, especially, how silence severs desire from the body. How do you explain women's desire to actually write or speak with our sexuality in our culture…as lesbians?

CM: I think they come out of the same origins. In the same sense that Yvonne Yarbro-Bejarano mentions in the relationship between mouth and voice and pussy, and I'm not the first one to say this, yet it's all the same business with all of us, and this is that sexuality gives voice, as does the mouth give voice, as the vagina is the place from which to speak. She [Yvonne] had an interesting line about "La Ofrenda." In her critique, the narrator is making love to this Tiny character, and Tiny is this big bad butch, right, and Tiny is going, "Fuck, fuck," like that, and the narrator shuts her up and says "Tell me something…" and she continues by saying, "So I didn't kiss her…I kissed her in that other place," which is her vagina, "that place where she had never spoken." It goes through this whole list of all the things she had been called: manflora, bulldagger, dyke, etc. The mouth knows all that language, what the vagina knows is a different kind of language, the language of self-love. For me, those things have been intricately tied. Particularly, *Loving in the War Years* has all this mouth stuff. It's the voice and since, as Chicana lesbians, having the right to speak is such a measure of our autonomy and therefore our self-love, both have been denied: voice and desire have been denied. When you look at *Heroes and Saints,* this becomes especially clear, because you are working with a character that has no body, but she has a goddamn mouth that knows how to speak.

EH: Would you elaborate a little more about your most recent work, *Heroes and Saints,* and could you describe that piece and compare it to the writing and staging of *Shadow of a Man* and *Giving Up the Ghost?*

CM: I always feel that I am in dialogue with Chicano theater. I feel like I've always tried to write work that is going to reach the Chicano community and that looks recognizable to them or that does not compromise all the issues for me as a lesbian and feminist. *Heroes and Saints* was my attempt to write a community-based play, where there is a real materially conditioned problem—which is pesticide poisoning. So you have a character, a girl, who is born only a head, because her mother was picking in a pesticide-sprayed field. I was inspired to write the play after I watched a United Farm Workers film that showed a little boy without arms and legs. I was very shaken by this. When I think about the head, the main character, Cerecita, is also a Chicana who was denied the right to a body. So it becomes a feminist play. In terms of the Chicano community, it is the first play that has been embraced by the Chicano theater community. The fact of the matter is that the play is as feminist as anything else. The girl, unlike everybody else in the play, speaks very loftily. She is highly educated and reads and reads and reads...and she is like a mind.

EH: It sounds like an allegory for the Chicana intellectual, through the denial of her body.

CM: Yeah, exactly, but the trick about her is that she does not want to deny her body. She says to the priest, when the priest has failed her and eventually betrayed her, "If I had your arms and legs, I would give healthy children to every woman who

wanted one, and I'd even stick around to watch them grow up."
What she is saying is that if she had that power to be a man, she
would do many things that she can't otherwise do, because as
women, we are denied the power to take action, which becomes
a critique of men. To me, it's so obviously feminist, and yet no
one sees the feminism in the play.

EH: Could you describe your current work with Brava? What is
Brava about and what kind of theater is Brava producing?

CM: I am an artist-in-residence at Brava, and through that, I
teach two courses. When I got the residency, which is funded
through the California Arts Council, I had two communities that
I really wanted to work with: one was gay youths of color and
the other one was Chicanas and Native American women. I had
two different motivations: with the Chicana/Native American
women, I wanted that base of writers whose core connection
was indigenous to the Americas; and I wanted to connect with
the gay/lesbian youth movement here in the Bay Area. They
write and perform their own work. And their work is braver and
more cutting-edge than anything else that I have read from my
own gay/lesbian counterparts. It's amazing stuff and quite an
inspiration. I also produce and direct my own work out of Brava,
which makes the practice of theater even more worthwhile, because you're not just sitting around and writing them, but you
also work with the movements, actions, and the people who
make the ideas real.

EH: If you could select a piece of writing from your extensive
repertoire, what project stands out in your mind, that is, is there
any work that continues to amaze or confound you?

CM: Cerecita this head character, in *Heroes and Saints*, she was a
gift from somewhere. She still amazes me... I am still very moved
by that possibility–that someone so disempowered could have
a voice, and the fact that she is just a head and a Mexican female. She is really a hero in that sense: somebody with everything against them insists on having a voice, and that sort of
continues to inspire me. I really like "La Ofrenda" and parts of
Giving Up the Ghost. Fundamentally, I guess that as a Chicana
lesbian, there is a place about trying to talk about Chicana lesbian desire that really is important to me. In fact, the new play
that I am writing, *Mexican Medea,* is about lesbian desire again.
Just when Chicanos think that I got my politics right, about pesticide poisoning, I go and write another play about dykes.

Black Opium:
An Interview with Migdalia Cruz

Tiffany Ana López

They took him into the playground and threw him down into the sand-box. Everybody stood around him and screamed at him. You couldn't even understand what they were saying…
    He tore her clothes off with his teeth. He ripped her open with his teeth. His teeth were yellow and sharp, like gold. Golden teeth. Now he had vomit and blood caked onto his teeth. They weren't so pretty like they used to be. They looked good now. Like they were supposed to look.
    We keep away from the sandbox now. It's strange when people from an island are scared of sand.
    —Migdalia Cruz, "Sand," in *Telling Tales*

Migdalia Cruz is a Nuyorican playwright from the South Bronx who has been an NEA and a McKnight Playwriting Fellow and is currently a TCG/PEW National Artist-in-Residence at the Classic Stage Company. Her work has been commissioned by the Cornerstone Theatre Company *(Rushing Waters)*, INTAR *(Welcome Back to Salamanca)*, The Working Theatre *(Broccoli)*, The American Music Theatre Festival *(Frida)*, the Theatre for a New Audience *(Dreams of Home)*, Playwright's Horizons *(Cigarettes and Moby Dick)*, and the Arena Stage *(Latins in La La Land)*. She has also been a participant in INTAR's Latino Playwright's lab with Maria Irene Fornés.
    Cruz's work has been produced by Latino Chicago Theater, Playwright's Horizons, INTAR, Cornerstone, the WOW Cafe, DUO, BAM's Next Wave Festival, and the Houston Grand Opera, among other theaters in the United States and abroad. Her work has been published in Theatre Communications Group's Plays in Process *(Miriam's Flowers)*, and in numerous anthologies, including *Shattering the Myth (Miriam's Flowers); The Best Women's Stage Monologues of 1990, The Best Scenes for Women from the 1980s* (selections from *Lucy Loves Me, Miriam's Flowers,*

and *The Have-Little); The Best Short Plays of 1991–92 (Dreams of Home);* and *Telling Tales.*

Theater has become an important artistic arena for Latinas working through issues of women's identity and cultural development, particularly in regard to their representation of two marginalized groups in American society: women and people of color. Cruz is one of the most prominent Latina dramatists on the East Coast. Her work brings to the surface some of the most difficult and taboo issues of female sexuality. As she states in this interview, she writes about the poverty of women. Consequently, the body becomes the only physical thing her characters fully own. In the terms presented by their world, it follows that sexuality becomes an important means by which these characters explore conflict.

Many have labeled Cruz's characters—homeless women, junkies, and prostitutes—as stereotypes. In the media of film and television, such characters have been made into stereotypes. As part of her artistic commitment to write about women and Latinas, Cruz sees it as important to fully explore who these characters are as people, beyond what we've learned about them as stereotypes. The goal of her theatrical work is to give spirit and voice to those characters who might otherwise remain invisible in our communities and to build a theatrical space where people who might otherwise not be able to do so will come together.

The following interview took place during the Pacoima, California, run of Cruz's *Rushing Waters* (1992), commissioned for the Cornerstone Theater Company. The play addresses Pacoima, a predominantly African-American and Latino community in Los Angeles, and its shared history, which includes colonization, drug wars, the Los Angeles rebellions, and issues concerning the emerging multicultural family amid a changing California population. This community theater project is designed to bring together the various ethnic groups of Pacoima by foregrounding their history, and providing members with an active voice through the theatrical performance. Cornerstone's goal is to set up and leave theater for the community. As of the final revisions of this writing, in Summer of 1994, many of the members of the cast of *Rushing Waters* have continued the project with the first Los Angeles Community Bridge Show, which brings together the three communities that hosted Cornerstone residency projects over the past three years.

TL: How do you see yourself as a Latina?

MC: I think of myself as a Puerto Rican-American, and before that, I think of myself as a Nuyorican, Puerto Rican from New York, which is a whole other thing. Being Nuyorican means starting from the bottom up, rather than coming from a place where you've ever felt entitled to the culture. I've been a person forced to assimilate with America as my home, not Puerto Rico, which is where my roots are and where my parents are from.

A lot of Puerto Ricans write from an unempowered place, searching for power. I don't know if that's true for all Latinas. I don't think so, because I think that Mexicans have their country. Puerto Ricans don't, really; we have a commonwealth, whatever that means. And it's always been a part of this country. They've fought for it, settled for things, yet not been able to vote for president. This made my parents unambitious. They thought, if we can make enough money to keep our children safe and fed, then we've achieved the American dream.

My dream is different, because I'm from here, and I see what other people have. I aspire to other things, like having my parents be people who are respected. But that's probably true of all writers: you want to pay respect to where you came from. But for me, it has significance because it's a place that not a lot of people write from, especially from a woman's point of view. I write about poverty from a woman's point of view.

TL: What was your childhood like, and how does your childhood play into your writing? How did it prepare you?

MC: When have you learned what you need to know to be a writer? George Bernard Shaw says by the time you're ten, you know everything you need to know. You've formed your personality, decided your views on life, and met the most significant people. I think almost all of my writing comes from there. In a lot of my writing, I do write about my neighborhood and the people I knew. But they're all composites.

People always think I've had this tragic childhood, and that all of these horrible things I write about have happened. In real life, I had a great childhood; I just had a bad neighborhood. (Laughs) I had friends who weren't as lucky as I was, as far as their parents, their upbringing, and their self-respect goes. I think self-respect is the one thing I learned from my parents. That kept me sane. All of my sisters went to college, which is really

(courtesy of Tiffany Ana López)

unusual in the neighborhood. My parents didn't go. My father went up to eleventh grade, and my mother to the sixth. They both had to work. But we always knew the importance of education, family, dressing nice, having self-respect.

TL: How did that contrast to the other images in the neighborhood? How was your house particularly different? For example, the point of view in *Telling Tales* seems to come from someone who has that real sense of self-respect, who is also viewing these photographs from the neighborhood that go completely against that.

MC: We all were poor. It was a Puerto Rican and black neighborhood. When I was growing up, it was a tense place to live, a time in which blacks and Puerto Ricans weren't getting along. Our house was a Puerto Rican building, so it got burned down by a black gang, that kind of thing. But my best friends were always black, so there was this strange "the outside world and the actual world," which were two different things. It affected me because that was just a part of life. I never thought, Oh, I live in a ghetto; it was just where I lived. I think it's strange that a lot of people want to categorize that I just do one thing, write about this one little neighborhood in the South Bronx.

That bothers me most, because all writers write from very specific points of view. In writing beyond the mainstream, if you're not a white man, your work immediately becomes categorized as not being as important or as being important only for a certain group of people. I would hope my writing would be good enough so that everyone could relate to it in some way or another. And you know, dysfunctional families are in all cultures. Not all of my plays are about dysfunctional families. There's a certain kind of prurient value, in which people think, Ooooo, this is how Puerto Ricans are. But that's *not* how Puerto Ricans are: that's how these characters I wrote are. There are many different types of Puerto Ricans. When you look at the work of people of color, people who are not of that race, culture, or religion will think that everyone is like that. When I did my play *Miriam's Flowers* in London, it was very strange. They couldn't understand that they were in the Bronx, not in Brooklyn. They think the only ghetto in New York City is Brooklyn. What they couldn't understand was this was about a certain family's voyage through mourning, and it wasn't about how every Puerto

Rican in the world is.

My character in *Miriam's Flowers* happened to be a self-mutilator; not every Puerto Rican is a self-mutilator, or nymphomaniac, or whatever it is I choose to write about. My characters are always experiencing a certain kind of pain. And some people think I couldn't have possibly made it up, because it doesn't fit the image of how they think it is. So they say, "Well, this must be how it really is." And that's not the case at all. I write fiction.

TL: How did you come to be initiated into the theater?

MC: I used to write puppet shows when I was six and do them for my parents. My dad built me a puppet theater, and we'd make puppets out of Spalding balls. I used to do these very socially conscious plays about the Ku Klux Klan and crosses burning. (Laughs) It was the '60s and I was obsessed with civil rights. I thought about things I saw on TV, and things that I saw in my neighborhood that were different from the TV images in that it was black against Puerto Rican, black against brown, as opposed to white against everyone.

I did these shows to the age of twelve. I didn't really think of myself as a writer. I always kept a journal. I read and wrote about things I saw around me that were upsetting, along with other incidents in my life. Like in *Telling Tales,* the story "Sand" is about a girlfriend of mine when I was eight who was raped, murdered, and thrown off the roof of our building. Things like that weren't common, but there was something about it we all sort of accepted in some way. The violence in the neighborhood was just part of the world.

I went to Stuyvesant High School in Manhattan, a science and math school. I really thought I was going to be a mathematician or something. I used to write musicals intended to make my friend Ana Martinez, who's Cuban, and myself famous. We used to play hooky and go to Central Park to write such things as *I Was Framed, I Was Fried,* the story of a convict, a chorus line thing inside a prison. It was really ridiculous. It didn't make us famous!

When I went to City College in Queens, I was signing up for courses, and I saw one on Beckett. I was interested in history, so I thought it was about Thomas à Becket; the course turned out to be about Samuel Beckett. I just started to read and thought if I could do this, it was what I wanted to do. I didn't know why.

The way he used language jumped out at me. This was a very important thing to be able to do. From then on, I wanted to write plays, not really knowing what they were, just sort of thinking about them.

Then I got a B.F.A. in playwriting, then an M.F.A. And I still didn't know how to write a play. I didn't know how to tell the truth. Not yet. That's what I learned from María Irene Fornés. I was in her workshop for about five years. That's really where I learned to write. Or where I learned to find the place in myself where I could be a writer. She was very tough on me. And I'm very grateful that she was, for if she hadn't, I probably would have been writing the same old junk that I wrote when I was six! (Laughs) No real meaning, but sort of thinking, these are the things I should be writing, or, this is how writing sounds, or, this is how you sound intelligent. Instead, she made me look inward and think about how people talk, and what people say, and who are the people I know I could really write about. Because, actually, that's all I'm entitled to in a way. I think you really have to know who you are writing about and at least try to pay respect to them in some way. That's where I am right now.

TL: What was the INTAR experience like? I'm also interested in hearing about how INTAR helped you to better define yourself as a playwright, and if this led you to see yourself in even broader terms, such as a performance artist.

MC: No. I don't consider myself a performance artist at all. What bothers me about performance art is that it denies the existence of the writer. Plays give writers power and, obviously, as a writer, that is what I lean toward.

At INTAR, because it was all Hispanic writers, I really learned about how much we all had in common and how our voices were different from others, as well as the need to learn to pay respect to that and appreciate where you come from. This confrontation was deep. I was this Nuyorican who didn't speak Spanish, surrounded by people who, when I tried to speak Spanish, would make fun of me. Which is what always kept me back, because I feel very nervous about it and very intimidated. At the same time, I also feel very sad I don't have that. My parents talk to me in Spanish, and I answer in English. It's not that I don't understand it, it's just that I never allowed myself to be a part of both cultures in that way.

A big part of INTAR was it made me feel it was okay to be Puerto Rican. Not that I ever felt it was not okay, but I always felt that you weren't supposed to be. The whole idea of assimilation is to be like the other and be like yourself. INTAR gave me courage, so I could simply be myself.

TL: What did you see were the things that brought the various Latinas in that workshop together culturally, and what did you learn were some real and distinct differences?

MC: You just sort of have the same sense of humor, a feeling that you were getting together with people who always felt they were on the outside. But the exception to that, of course, was Cherríe Moraga, who was very bold and militant. I learned a lot from her, too. She gave me a lot of courage, because she is so…so who she is! (Laughs) Not taking any shit. And I was used to taking shit. Maybe that's a Caribbean thing; maybe it's a Puerto Rican thing; maybe it's just a Migdalia thing. But it's the ability to follow through, to make waves—like talking loud in public. Using Spanish. Dealing with how people stare at you. All that stuff was something I learned from just being around more Latinos.

But the other thing I learned after working in Latino theater for a while was it's not the only place I wanted to be. And it's not to reject that. There's one theater I would work with all the time in Chicago called Latino Chicago Theater. It's run by Mexican-Americans. I feel it's a home for me. And it's good to have a home, but it's also good to challenge yourself and the world.

TL: Do you see there being a particular space for Latina works and, if so, does your own work fit into that space?

MC: That's a difficult question to answer. I think I definitely want to keep working in Latina/o theater. But right now, I don't see that particular space happening. I think theater, like everything else, is still run by men, whether they be Latino or white! (Laughs) Unless women get behind the scenes more, that space won't necessarily open up, as something that specific. But there are places, there are programs. Even bigger theaters have workshops, what they call "Hispanic labs," whatever that is. But these often turn into a way of keeping us all together and not producing us in a bigger venue. It's ghettoizing. Because it's not Latinas/os doing it for Latinas/os. It's someone else doing it, and it's saying, you're in this part, you're in the second season, or you're in the workshop, you're not on the main stage. Once again, it's a way in which they can say, well, we've given them this much, so we are helping this group of people, and that's the end of our commitment. But the commitment should be about the work, and the work Latinos are doing now is as strong—if not stronger—than anything anybody else is doing. So it makes no sense to me that it's still so separate. But it's about the state of the world, which is still so separate.

I was doing a play at INTAR, and a Puerto Rican woman working in the office said what a wonderful writer she thought I was, "But…" she asked, "Why are you always writing about junkies and pregnant teens? Our community has moved beyond that." I said, "Well, there are lawyers and doctors, but I don't know any lawyers or doctors. But if that's where I came from, I would write about that. But, frankly, I don't find lawyers and doctors interesting. These are the people I find interesting and poetic, and these are the people I love. I don't love you, so leave me alone!" (Laughs) I didn't say it quite like that, but something like it. I was taken aback by her understanding of what I should be writing about as a Puerto Rican would be so exclusive.

Many stereotypes have been written, and that's one of the reasons I write, because I feel like they've now been explored as people. From what you see on TV, the drug dealer's mother just says "¡Ay, mi madre!" and that's the character. I think the Puerto Rican or Colombian drug dealer's mother is probably a really interesting woman and must be going through an awful time, and that's what I like to write about. In writing about those things, I find hope. Unless you look at something, you can't define it. And until you define it, you can't fix it. For me, my plays are very helpful. The other thing I'm criticized for is that in my plays, there's no redemption, the new word in theater these days. I don't even think I know what that means. Do you mean that somebody comes in at the end and saves the day? Is the world suddenly changed? Suddenly there's fireworks and everything's okay? That's not how people are. I believe in the power of people to heal themselves. That's really important to me. I do feel I have a sense of spirituality in my plays. I think all of it is about people finding their own spirituality and finding their own way, their own journey.

TL: Who do you see as your role models and your influences?
MC: María Irene Fornés, definitely. Lorca, Cervantes,

Shakespeare. I like the "big picture" writers, like O'Neill and Williams. Adrienne Kennedy, I think, is a wonderful writer. And then there are a lot of other wonderful writers who are my contemporaries that I admire. I'm also inspired by novelists and poets, such as Toni Morrison, Maya Angelou, James Baldwin, and Piri Thomas. Thomas was an influence that I had forgotten about for a while, actually. One of the first novels I ever read about a Puerto Rican experience was *Down These Mean Streets* in junior high school. It was cool to read. Everybody got it because of the dirty words, it it was an amazing thing, because he wrote the truth, which I had never thought about before. His was the first work I'd read that was actually about my culture. He was one of my first influences. There's also Piñero, but his point of view is so narrow and hard. It's very different from mine, but he's definitely someone I would think of as having an influence.

But our influences are also very subtle. I think you don't know what influences you until much later. I was talking to my father, and I was saying how weird it was that I'm the only artist in the family, and he said, "Yeah, we think it's weird, too." And I said, "It's so strange, because we never read poetry at home, and I never remember doing those things." My dad suddenly recited this really beautiful poem in Spanish. It was sad and made me cry. It was about this boy who felt like he was an orphan, walking through a storm. I said, "That's amazing. How'd you learn that, Dad?," and he said, "Well, you know, I wrote it in high school." That's the first time I ever knew my dad wrote poetry. (Laughs) This was six years ago, maybe five. That made me think, Wow, maybe there is something in how you learn to see the world from your parents. His poetic soul was something I would have never thought about. I knew he was a sensitive guy, but I never thought of him as that. He was just Dad. Dad the poet was a new thing for me.

TL: Many critics have noted that Latina writers tend to pay tribute to their female ancestors. I definitely see this as a part of your work, especially in *Frida, Dreams of Home,* and *Telling Tales.* Yet, again, there seems to be a real—and I guess I'll bring up the word that others have used to describe your work—"darkness," used to expose the destructive side of female ancestors, particularly in scenes which reveal the hurt, the hate, and the violence that can lie within relationships between women. A lot of times, it seems, women writers, in particular, will not show such a dark side in relationships between women, but you don't seem to hesitate about doing that.

MC: Yes, I'm very determined to do that. I don't think I consciously set out to show both sides, but I think I tend to see the darker side. To me, that seems the natural way to explore a character. I don't think it has to do necessarily with a cultural thing, but more so with my personal journey to write down these dark things and to find hope, love, and truth.

I made a choice a while back to write my female characters as composites of men I've known, to experiment with that and its effects on portraying the character of women. So often in women's plays, you get a lot of back slapping and "Right on, sister" stuff, which I think is kind of bogus. We all know from our relationships with our own families, there are good and bad sides, especially to women. I've been criticized a lot, actually, for showing both sides of women, that I should be more "positive," whatever that is. I think about who these people are and what are their issues. I'm very analytical and I tend to be very hard on myself, so I'm hard on my characters. If I sat down and said, "I'm going to write a really positive play," I don't know what that would be. I think all of my plays are very positive plays! People think unless people are enjoying their lives every minute of the day and everything ends happily that it's a negative thing. I think the reality of our lives is you have to find the positive in everything. Happy times don't come that often; that's why they're so wonderful when they do come. I think if you had a completely happy life, there's something wrong with you! (We laugh) Or you're not admitting something. Good for you, but that's not reality.

TL: In all of your plays, the characters work through their pain and other issues through their sexuality, for example, the self-mutilator in *Miriam's Flowers*. Sexuality seems to be a very important means of working through conflict for you.

MC: I've thought about that a lot. I think part of where it comes from is that the one thing women always own is our bodies. For me that's always been the center of who I am. I think women use their bodies differently than men do. Men always feel entitled to their bodies; women think that they're supposed to act certain ways with their bodies, do certain things, or have them acted upon. So as a woman, you have a different sense of that. The body is the only concrete thing you have. For my characters, sexuality is the only thing they feel particularly empowered with. It's their one tool through the world. They don't have money, they don't have good jobs. They don't necessarily have a good education, and, even if they do, it always breaks down into their giving up their bodies and exploring what it means to do so. How do you give it up? And if you give it up, do you do it gladly or is it painful?

I think the more self-esteem you have, the more you can control and have pride in your body. The lower your self-esteem, the more the body becomes a tool to get what you want. I saw that in many a cousin and many a friend, including myself. It was a way to feel…important. To be a sexual person, to be desired; the physical part of you is how you first relate to everyone in your life. And it seems to me that it's really important how you feel about yourself at those moments. If your self-esteem is high, you almost always look better than you normally do. It's really such a matter of your mind, more than your body.

For example, in my play *Lucy Loves Me,* the character Lucy is really beautiful, but has absolutely no self-esteem. She brings home a serial killer in order to have someone flatter her. That's not a sane way to deal with people. And yet I think it's a very true way for people with low self-esteem. I think a lot of that does come from inside me in regards to my self-esteem, which goes up and down constantly. It's kind of been on an upswing lately. But, you know, that's a hard thing to talk about.

TL: Do you find that there is something culturally specific about it, especially in terms of media images? When I teach issues of race and gender in my classes, we specifically talk about how images of beauty are those of white women and how women of color, even light-skinned women of color, will always know that these images are not theirs, that we can never be that. Do you see that kind of culturally specific view of beauty informing the way you are trying to work out tensions around sexuality and self-esteem in your work?

MC: I don't think I've ever sat down to really think that through when I've been writing. I write about the one thing that I know: that's me. And that's not mainstream. Obviously, that's part of my work, but also that's not necessarily conscious. I can't control who I am. I would have no idea how it would be to be blonde and blue-eyed.

TL: Could you elaborate about some of the recurring images that pervade your work, for example, the destructive relationships that can occur between mother and daughter, self-mutilation, images of the grotesque, sexual abuse, baptism by blood, sexual violence, and men whose sexuality is dangerous and threatening, as well as men who seem to be the betrayers of the family?

MC: All that comes from my Catholic upbringing. I was obsessed with the church when I was a kid. The blood rituals and the eating of Christ's body and drinking his blood is part of every Sunday mass, which is a bizarre, strange, cannibalistic thing that was kind of sexy, too. It was mysterious, so sacred and vulgar. The whole idea of priests being celibate, the choir boys running around in those dresses…It's very bizarre! (We laugh) The church is a weird place, but, for me, that was the first theater. All of it was just such a spectacle. That's also the place where I was first really aware of smell, because of church incense. I was always in love with that smell. To me, that's a very powerful, evocative thing from my childhood.

I wanted to, in some productions of *Miriam's Flowers,* burn incense. I did research on exactly what that smell was, and the only thing I could find close enough to it was called "black opium." I thought, That's perfect, because the church is like this drug. It's hypnotizing, mesmerizing, dramatic, and scary. But in the end, everything comes out all right. Maybe. As long as you go to confession on Saturday and everything works out. I don't consciously set out to write about blood. I think I only have one play with self-mutilation–I hope I only have one play with self-mutilation–and that's in *Miriam's Flowers.* People think that's the only play I ever wrote. They say, "Everyone's always mutilating themselves in your plays. Are all Puerto Ricans like that?" It was interesting, because the people who would talk to me the most about self-mutilation were not the Latinos. It's a lot more prevalent among white women than Latinas.

TL: How are such issues as those we've just discussed perceived by a community in which they are traditionally taboo? It's interesting when you talk about Catholicism as being the ultimate theater, in which all these bizarre things do happen, but at the same time those issues are extremely taboo in our culture to explicitly talk about, let alone put into a dramatic space in which you become involved in the performance of the taboo.

MC: Some people relate to it, and some people don't. Some might think that I write these really weird things. I don't know. I think people outside the culture accept it more easily, but what they accept is that everyone is like that, but that's not what it's about either. People who have been in relationships with an alcoholic, or have experienced the death of a young child, have gone through the kind of mourning that could make you hurt yourself, and that's what they relate to. They don't think about it as self-mutilation. And I actually didn't think of it as self-mutilation initially. I thought about it as trying to be a saint and the need to make your own stigmata. Instead of waiting for it to come upon you, you cut into yourself and try to create some kind of spiritual healing this way. In African cultures, it's quite common to cut yourself for spiritual reasons. I'm sure it's been done for a very, very long time.

TL: This takes us back to the body as a site which is often the only locus one has to speak from.

MC: Yes, but it's also about what happens if you strip a person of all their things. The body is all you'll have. That's when you search for symbols. If you're looking at a naked body and you want to show mourning, you could cover the eyes or pull them out. It depends upon how much pain you're in. How do you make that theatrical? I think the greatest vehicle of an actor is their body: how they use it and what they do to symbolize what the words are saying.

TL: Where do you envision your work going in the future?

MC: I'm feeling that I'm getting tired, like it's all so hard. Not that I'm going to stop writing, but what exactly am I pursuing? What's the goal? Will I ever get paid as much as a man? No. Not in my lifetime, anyway. Will I go to these big theaters and my name be known among the names of Lorca and O'Neill? Not in my lifetime, if ever. Am I doing enough for change by just being an artist? That's something I've been thinking about a lot, particularly with the work I've done with Cornerstone in Pacoima. What, exactly, is the responsibility of theater? There's a case to be made that it's enough you bring up the issues so people can discuss them. But I do wonder if that's enough. Especially if your work doesn't go to the places or to the people who have the money to make changes, because in this country, change comes from money and the people willing to support it.

On the other hand, working in a community is so great, to see people grow and see how well they do, and how interesting they are, having them explore their talents and seeing them get self-esteem, see their English get better, in some cases, or see people who have never spoken in Spanish sing Spanish lyrics. All these things, to me, are very exciting. And that is about very positive change. But who'll come see this play? And what will it be?

TL: Where do you see Latina drama in the future in terms of playwrights and the production of works?

MC: Certainly, there are Latino theaters that are doing more women's work, like Latino Chicago Theater Company. The building of a Latina audience is the key. A space needs to be fostered where Latinas feel like they have theatrical homes to come home to, where they can feel comfortable growing and being themselves. Part of that is also doing things such as productions in Spanish, or bilingually, or whatever it is, so that Latinas/os feel they can enter their own culture and not some foreign place. There are more of us writing than ever before, so there's more of an opportunity now to see stuff. It's crucial to have Latina/o-based theaters, because of the potential of their impact on those first, formative experiences with theater. Consequently, it's important for Latinas and Latinos to say "Let's go to the theater on Friday," or "Let's go to a performance instead of a movie." In general, theater is not that popular in our cultures, or even in American culture. But it would be nice if it were.

Storytelling as a Source of Healing: Talking with Elvira and Hortensia Colorado

Michelle Macau

Telling stories is an ancient human ritual. Springing from a need to describe personal experiences to other tribe or clan members, oral traditions have been part of cultures throughout the world. It is a mode by which the customs, morals, history, religion, social and political practices, proverbs, myths, legends, crimes, horrors, jokes, anecdotes, and so on, of a culture are handed down from one generation to the next.

"There's a magic that's carried from the breath of a storyteller [to the listener]; your breath and the storyteller's breath join together and share in that magic," says Joseph Bruchac, a Native American storyteller.[1] He asserts that to the Native American, stories are literally alive and palpable, carrying the spirit of the people, their history and culture.

Elvira and Hortensia Colorado inherited the gift of storytelling from their mother, who gathered her large family in the TV-less living room of their house and entertained them, bringing to life the stories of her ancient tradition. Their mother also loved fiestas and performances and sent her daughters to La Escuela Lázaro Cárdenas, where they learned and performed traditional songs and dances. While in high school they became members of the Chicago Fiesta Guild, performing throughout the city of Chicago.

They came to New York in search of careers in theater and encountered rejection, both in the Anglo and Latino communities, fitting into neither. They have been accused of looking "too Indian" for commercial work. They performed on and off Broadway and played prostitutes and maids in films. They were becoming disillusioned with the commercial world of show business when they encountered Spiderwoman Theater. Thrilled to see three Indian sisters creating and performing their own style of theater, the Colorados were inspired.

In 1984, after collaborating on several projects with Spiderwoman, Vira and Hortensia began their own theater company, Coatlicue/Las Colorado. Storytelling is the framework of all their performance pieces. They tell personal stories that unlock the secrets of their familial past. These secrets have kept them silent, imprisoned, and feeling worthless for many years of their lives, creating nothing but pain, anger and rage. Once exposed and expressed in a theatrical form, the secrets no longer hold the power they held in silence. Storytelling, for them, has become a journey of self-discovery, leading to healing and acceptance.

The stories deal with the pain of denial, racism, poverty, incest, and alcoholism they experienced as children in Blue Island, Illinois, where they grew up. The family are members of the Chichimec nation of Mexico, but the Spanish blood that mixed in their mother's veins was held in higher esteem. Photographs of their mother's family were proudly displayed, but those of their father, who was nicknamed Red by members of his own community, were buried in a trunk in the basement of their home. In school, they were harshly criticized for speaking Spanish. At home, they were not allowed to invite friends to visit, lest their poverty be judged by outsiders. This experience of isolation created a great shyness that confined and imprisoned them, and storytelling has been their release from this border of silence. It is through the confrontation of these secrets, including familial incest, alcoholism, and gambling addiction, that the sisters have begun to heal.

In the midst of these painful memories, they laugh. Their laughter rings out with a positivism and ecstasy of living that they say offers a balance, a release, necessary for survival. Humor is hope.

The sisters interweave tales of their personal experiences with those of women of past generations. They include stories of their ancestors, their cosmology, and of Mexican and indigenous women, who have played a role in carving out the history of both Mexico and the United States. By giving voice to women, who have been silenced through the ages, and to contemporary women, who continue to be silenced today, the Colorado sisters link the past with the present, making time all one.

Storytelling is "a sharing of heart and spirit," according to Ruth Sawyer in The *Way of the Storyteller*.[2] By sharing their hearts and spirits, Vira and Hortensia connect very strongly with their audience. By revealing to them their secrets and the secrets of crimes committed in the past, audience members are empowered to confront their own lives and begin individual journeys of self discovery. And people do come up to them, talk to them, expressing how deeply they relate on a very basic human level. In San Antonio, where they performed for their first audience of Mejicanos, they encountered a reception of such warmth and empathy that they were emotionally overwhelmed. It was while in San Antonio that they began to seek out and meet members of their father's family. For them, it was an incredible experience, touching something very deep. Their indigenous roots, which had been denied for so long, were finally affirmed.

The need to tell their own stories and those of others has provided a rebirth for these two actresses. Storytelling inspired them to start their own theater company; it encouraged them to become writers and take control of their artistic expression; and it has linked them to the Mexican and Native American communities throughout the United States and Mexico. Most important, storytelling empowers them to confront the social and political injustice, genocide, and racism they and others continue to confront today.

MM: How do you develop your work?
VC: First it comes out of an urgency. That's how we develop a theme. We get an idea for something and we say, "We have to talk about this, or we have to address this." Our material comes from so many different sources.
HC: We've been reading and cutting out stuff about Chiapas...
VC: We have files, files...
HC: We have a whole thing on radiation.
VC: On immigration. Because that's another whole thing about the people that are here as illegals. Illegals in their own country!
MM: Once you establish a theme, what's your artistic process?
VC: We talk a lot.
HC: We tell stories.
VC: When we talk about the particular theme that we're developing, it brings in stories from our families, from our history, and that brings another idea and that brings another story.
MM: What's your rehearsal process? Do you write first?

HC: We keep talking and writing through the rehearsal process… What happens is, Vira has a story, I have a story. We take them apart and begin to weave them together, making connections; sometimes just using one sentence, one word, an action.

VC: Or, we break up the story. Maybe not the whole story will be told in one section. Maybe we'll tell the beginning part of the story, and then we'll go on to another story, and then we'll tell the second part of the story in another section.

HC: And maybe we won't tell our own story. Maybe I'll tell Vira's story, and Vira will do an action or a movement that enhances the story. We start layering, coloring, putting the piece together.

MM: How long does it take you to develop a piece?

HC: From the time we actually start…maybe a couple of months, but not in a structured way. Well, yes, our own structure, nonlinear. It's probably a month. But before that, it could be a couple of months before we do it. Sometimes in a day or a few hours, we develop a skit.

MM: Let's talk about your relationship with each other.

HC: I'm the oldest.

MM: Do you feel that you provoke each other in a positive, creative way?

VC: Oh, definitely, because there's a lot of times when we're developing a piece, there are things that maybe Hortensia doesn't want to talk about. And I'll say, "Well, you've got to talk about it," or "That's a story we have to include." And she'll say, "Well, I don't know." So we kind of prod each other. Or she'll say something that will spark an idea or bring back a memory. And a memory, you know, is a story.

HC: I remember, this was kind of, for you and me, it was kind of a hard thing, about the red coats. That was hard.

MM: Is this a story that you're putting in one of the pieces?

HC: Yeah, it's in one of our pieces. It's the story of when we were growing up and Mama, all the stuff we would grow in the garden, she would can. And we had these two big tins, round…for bathing, canning.

VC: But I do remember something with hot water, and I do remember something about running…but now it seems like a vague memory. Now I'm not sure if I remember it or it's something that you, because you brought up the story, that I remember it…

HC: Or even though I brought it up, you don't want to remember it. Mama used to can and she had these big, round tin tubs, that you would do the wash in, those tin ones. Well, she'd put all the Mason jars in them. And she had them right in the middle of the kitchen, boiling water. And me and Vira were running back and forth…

VC: But it's not like you did it deliberately.

HC: Well, I don't know. In playing–deliberate, not deliberate– I don't know. We were running back and forth. It was in playing.

VC: So it wasn't deliberate.

HC: Where do you draw the line? We were running back and forth, and we both had these same little red coats…

VC: Unless you were angry.

HC: No, we weren't angry. Little red raincoats. Well, we were running back and forth, and she kept telling us…but she was so busy, both my older sister and my mom were busy canning, so they were kind of, "Get out of the way, mosetonas, get out of the way. Cuídense. Cuídense. No corran. Stop running like crazy." So we were running from the kitchen to the living room, back and forth. And what we were doing was throwing the coat over each other's head. One would get the coat and then throw it over the other one's head. We couldn't see, running with the coat over our head. On one of those times, Vira had the thing over her head. And I remember pushing her. That's what I remember. Pushing her. And she fell in.

MM: Into the hot, boiling tub of water?

HC: Yes. Anyhow, I have lived with that, that has haunted–it has been in my head since that happened. It's one of those things that never leaves your head. It was during *Coyolxuahqui* that we put it in. I never told her that. And every time she would say, "Oh, I have all these scars here." Every time she would say that, I would go, "Ohhhhh, ohhhhh." (She cries in pain) And so, so there are real scars and there are… I had to talk to her about this, and she said, "I don't remember that. You didn't do that." And I said, "Vira, I did it. I know I did it."

VC: I don't remember. I just remember Mama saying that they tried to take my clothes off, but all the skin came right off; so then they just wrapped me up in a blanket and took me to the hospital. And they thought I was going to die, because they had me in this incubator, and Mama prayed, she made lots of novenas.

HC: So.

VC: So that's one of the stories.

MM: Where did this take place?

HC: We were both born in Blue Island, Illinois, a big hub for Mexican people, lots of industry, the stockyards, steel mills, working in the fields, the railroad.

MM: What did your parents do?

HC: My dad worked for the Rock Island Railroad. He left Mexico as a teenager, working his way to Chicago…Blue Island.

VC: My mother is originally from a small rancho in Guanajuato, my father was originally from San Luis Potosí.

MM: How did your mother get to Blue Island?

VC: Mama was married at the age of thirteen to a wealthy landowner. She lived at the time of the Mexican Revolution. She had four children with her first husband, one died, and he died of a heart attack, leaving her with three small children to support. She had a lot of wealth, but was young, naive, and uneducated. His relatives came and took all his money. She had relatives in Los Estados Unidos, and they told her to come, that there was lots of work.

MM: Were you the only two siblings from that marriage?

VC: Yes. Our brothers and sister from the first marriage were much older. And we were poor, we were very poor. We were raised with all our nieces and nephews, so we had a full house.

MM: How many people are we talking about?

HC: My brother had about six or seven kids in his family. My mom would take care of them, plus the two of us, plus my sister with her two daughters and her husband. We all lived in the same house. We had a garden, raised chickens and goats, grew vegetables.

VC: My mother grew everything in the garden.

HC: Except for big sacks of rice and big sacks of beans and big tins of lard. We'd go to the city, to the Mexican commodity store, and get those on weekends, once a month, and then from the sacks she'd make underclothes for all of us.

VC: My mother would make big pots of soup and chickens that we raised, and we had all those natural things like herbs that she grew in the garden. Whenever we got sick she cured us with herbs, istafiate, yerba buena, so we grew up with all of that traditional stuff. We talk about that in one of our theater pieces as well, because we use a lot of…everything…all the stories and things that we grew up with…in our theater pieces, because we draw from all of that.

HC: It's stories. It's stories of our lives as we grew up, of our lives—

VC: —and growing up also, too, with the racism.

HC: We grew up with the thing of color in our family.

VC: Color played a large part of our growing up. Like my nieces were very light-skinned. My mother, brothers, and my mother's son were light-skinned. So when my sister and I were born, we came out very much looking like my father, very indígenas. I don't know, I think my mother was embarrassed of the way we came out, so she rarely took any pictures with us, it was always with my nieces, who were light-skinned and had curly hair, ringlets, like Shirley Temple, and our hair was straight, so straight. What they would do was, they'd cut it and give us a permanent, and these permanents would never take on our hair, they would just come right out. Our hair would never curl!

HC: The thing about color, there was the denial of being Indian all the time. The denial was so strong that we didn't know our father's side of the family.

VC: We had to say that we were Spanish and not Mexican, because to be Mexican was…

MM: Was this among the Mexican population as well?

VC: Right in our own families. In the community. In the school. In the society in general.

HC: In spite of Mama's denial, we grew up with all the traditions.

VC: My mother would cook all the traditional dishes, we would celebrate all the different fiestas, and…

HC: She used the metate and the molcajete.

VC: She would be on her knees, and she would moler the chile on the metate, and that's the way she did it all the time.

RC: And that's a very Indian thing, so you know, she denied it and yet, you know…

VC: I think my mother secretly would have liked to have been a performer herself. She had a beautiful voice and was always singing around the house, and also she was a wonderful story-teller. We didn't have a TV, so she would entertain us with her stories about La Llorona and Brujas. It goes way, way back to our oral traditions. Also, we began performing from the time we were six or seven years old.

HC: We would go into the city of Chicago to a woman who came from Mexico. Her name was Señora Celia Pedroza; and she would teach us all the songs, she would teach us how to make special things, certain crafts. She would put on plays. The woman was everything: she was director of the show, she painted the scenery, she taught us the dances, she taught us the songs. She's kind of an inspiration that we have, too, for theater. You think of her and you think, this woman did everything. She schooled all these snotty-nosed little Mejicanitos, she's something like a light we have to go by.

MM: Where was your father in all of this?

HC: Our dad was very quiet, he was very, very quiet. He would drink, he would drink quite a bit. He was a gambler.

VC: There was…everything you could possibly think of, we had it in our families. Alcohol, drugs, incest, denial…we grew up with all that, we thought it was normal…because all of this was covered up with religion. My mother was a very religious woman, and religion was shoved down our throats till we couldn't take it. My father was not a religious person in the sense of going to church and praying, in that way.

HC: I have a short story about my dad. Daddy would come home with a six-pack, and he'd sit at the table and I would sit there with him, and he'd drink, very quietly, he'd sit there and drink, and I would sit there, and it was as though we were having a conversation and we never said anything. And it's not till now that I realize, Why didn't we talk? Why didn't we…why didn't he share his thoughts? Why didn't I ask him? There was nothing spoken. It's very funny, it seems as though we were talking, though, but nothing was said.

MM. Did your father deny his heritage?

HC: He didn't talk. He drank beer and he gambled.

VC: My father was raised by his godmother, because his mother gave him away when he was a baby. We don't know why she did, what was the reason for that, and why he left Mexico at such a young age. That was one of the secrets.

HC: On my mother's side, my grande chiquita had "cara de India." She was Chichimecaotomi, and my grandfather, his people came from Spain, and he had been married before. My grandmother used to work for him and his wife, for the family.

When his wife died, my grandmother became his wife. We have been thinking, Did he marry her? Did he just take this Indian woman? Was it again the taking of an Indian woman, which goes back to the conquest?

I think my mom told me this story: When my grandfather's family would come to visit, they would come to visit him, and my grandmother would get locked in a back room, because the family did not want to see her Indian face. That's how deep the denial is. That is the little that we know, which tells a lot and it's so minute and it's so deep. So we have to go back to my mother's place, we have to go back to my dad's place. We have to talk to whoever is there now.

We feel very strongly that we, the ones who are here right now, Vira and I and even my son, we are the ones that have to give voice to my mother, for her shame; voice to my father, for his silence; voice to my grandmother, for silence and shame. We are their voices now. The voices of all those who have gone before us. We have their blood. That's very important, because that blood was passed on to my son, and it's going to be passed on to generations. And even if it doesn't get passed on to generations, us doing our theater and talking, it gets passed on that way.

VC: And also, the type of theater that we do is not only entertainment, it's educational, because we educate people with the stories that we tell, and sometimes people see themselves in the stories. Once we voice these stories, the process of healing begins, of healing ourselves, our community, and, hopefully, the people that come to see and hear our theater. They're really survival stories.

MM: Tell me about your first theater piece—*Tlatilco* [mid-1980s].

VC: It was a piece we collaborated on with Gloria Miguel [of Spiderwoman Theater]—*Our Goddesses, Ourselves.* We took the different deities in relation to ourselves and how we identified with them and the transformation of all the goddesses. All the goddesses have different aspects of each other. They are really all one and the same, because they all have this power to transform themselves, so we took that as a premise for collaborating on this theater piece, *Tlatilco: The Place Where Things Are Hidden.* Muriel Miguel [of Spiderwoman] directed that piece.

MM: What was it you wanted to say?

HC: I guess that we have the powers, that we have those powers and that we can take the power that's within ourselves.

MM: To do what?

HC: To transform ourselves.

MM: Into what?

HC: Into women of power. Like, sometimes there's that lack of security, you don't have the trust in yourself that you are capable of being a whole woman, a complete woman, that you are capable of being a woman that has beauty. That you're not just a dumb Mexican.

MM: So it's about empowerment?

VC: Yeah, empowering ourselves.

MM: What did you want to say in your next play, *Walks with Indian Women* [1989]?

HC: It's like in our history. You go back and forth in time, and it's like when someone says to you, "But why are you talking about being Indian, that was a long time ago?" It's a long time ago and it's now.

VC: Because in our cosmology, it's really the past, the present, and the future. It's all one and the same, nothing is separated—it's all connected.

HC: These women that come from way back up to the present that go back to the past and come—constantly going back and forth across these borders. These are some of the women who have not been written about in history books, women like the revolutionary women, Las Adelitas.

I mean, these women have names, these women were very powerful women, they were colonels that fought in the Mexican Revolution; the women in our families who were also very strong, very powerful women and warriors. So it's giving voice to those women, the unsung heroines. What's her name…Julia Pastrama: the woman with hair all over her face, who's still traveling in London.

VC: She was a Yaqui Indian woman from Mexico, and she was born with hair all over her body and she was exploited. She worked in the circus, she sang, she danced. She had a beautiful voice, she spoke three languages, one of them her own native language, and I think she was with Barnum and Bailey Circus, and other competitors were interested in her, and so her promoter, in order to keep her, married her. She always felt that he loved her. She had a child, but the baby looked the same as her, with hair all over his body, and the baby died right after it was born. And then shortly thereafter, Julia died, too, and her husband just couldn't bear the thought of losing the money that he was making on her, so he had them both stuffed and exhibited all over the world, and they are still being exhibited, which means that her spirit is not at rest. Another example of exploitation.

HC: It, again, is really the genocide of indigenous people.

MM: Talk about *La Llorona* [1990].

VC: There are all kinds of stories about La Llorona that go all the way back to before the conquest, pre-Colombian, and the deities and the Cihuateteo, the women who died in childbirth. There are so many different transformations of La Llorona.

MM: What's the basic legend of La Llorona?

VC: Some say she was Malinche, Cortes's mistress and interpreter. Some say she represents the cry of women who died in childbirth. They were considered warriors, because they took the path of the sun, just like the men who died in battle. They would have that status of being warriors. It goes back into our history and into the present of women warriors living today. The women now, the activists, the farm workers, the women in the Chicano movement...all these women are considered warriors. La Llorona represents...it's a cry of pain, it's a cry of joy.

HC: Or La Llorona lives in the South Bronx. She's a Mejicana who came here from Puebla, and her kids are joining street gangs there and she's, "Oh, hijo, hijo, cut it out, hijo. Don't do that. Follow the right way, hijo." That's her cry. La Llorona lives here in the South Bronx...it goes back to cosmology...

VC: Yeah, to cosmology...

HC: Because that's what they became—the stars—these women who died in childbirth. They followed the path of the sun. It's the cry of joy, the cry of pain, the cry of loss, the cry of love, the cry of ecstasy.

VC: Hope.

MM: Let's move on to *Coyolxuahqui: Women Without Borders* [1990].

HC. We got the idea from the slab of stone that was found under the subway [in Mexico City] of Coyolxuahqui, the goddess who was killed by her brother.

VC: He killed her and severed her body, cut it up in pieces, and threw it down Snake Mountain. She is reborn every month as the moon, the various parts of her body become the different phases of the moon.

HC: So from that, we said...women are cut up sometimes. Women are silenced. Women are...it's cut up, that was it, the word, that we are cut up sometimes.

VC: So many of the women in our family were silenced and didn't have a voice, and for a long time, we didn't have a voice, we were silenced. And so we felt this was a piece... All of our pieces have an urgency to them.

MM: What was the urgency about this piece?

VC: The urgency was the borders that we...

HC: –sometimes that are imposed upon us, sometimes we impose upon ourselves, society imposes upon us...

VC: The borders of class, race, genders. The borders of individuals.

HC: There's a piece that I put in there, and it was very hard for me to do. It was a piece that was on my back all the time, it was in my eyeballs, it was in my tongue, it was in my head, it was in my being. It was always with me. I left Chicago, I came here, I grew up with it. I went to confession with it, it never left me. This story had to do with incest. I don't know how to deal with it: can I tell it? It was something that had to be told. It was my brother and it was... I had this feeling, this hatred, hatred for my brother for the longest time. And I think around the time that I decided to use this piece to tell this story, I–somehow or other, the hatred diminished, the hatred diminished. I could not live with that hatred anymore.

VC: Because just by–I think your telling the story was a part of the healing process.

HC: And my mother knew about this, but it was also her son. I couldn't tell it to her, because I didn't think that she would believe me. I couldn't tell anyone. So right there in that story there are all the borders.

VC: And silences.

HC: We looked at them as borders.

VC: They were borders we imposed on ourselves sometimes. We kept silent a lot of times. So we imposed those borders on ourselves.

HC: Because you weren't, I guess, there was no worth to you...

VC: It's making you feel worthless... Oh, that's another thing. When I went to the passport office–that brought up another story. I went to get my passport, and I was standing in line and the clerk said, "You don't have sufficient documentation. You'll have to come back tomorrow with your birth certificate." So I went back with my birth cettificate the following day, and they told me, "No, this still is not enough. You have to come back with somebody who's known you for ten years, so they can prove that you are who you say you are." By this time, I was really, really upset. And I said I had to speak to the supervisor. The guard told me, "No." He says, "Lady, look, you better go stand in line like everybody else." I said, "But I just need to ask the supervisor a question. I already stood in line." Then he started to come toward me, this big guard, and he said, "Lady, if you're not going to stand in line, you're going to have to get out. Get out." And I said, "You can't talk to me that way." He said, "I can talk to you any way I want, because you're nothing, nothing, nothing, nothing, now get out, you're nothing."

VC: There's a lot of pain, a lot of anger, a lot of rage...

HC: And it puts those borders there around you.

VC: And again the silence. In each of these stories that we told, there was a silence, a silence at the end of each story.

HC: Again, going back to the goddess, she was silenced...cut off.

VC: Cut up. Being cut up, and putting the pieces back together, and being reborn again. Each time we're cut up, we try to bring those pieces back together, try to make ourselves whole by telling our stories as a way of healing ourselves and trying to heal those around us.

MM: Tell me about *Huipil* [1992].

HC: Well, you know, when you look at the huipil dress that the Indian women in Mexico weave and wear, each one of those symbols, animals, elements that are woven in the huipil come from their dreams. As they weave their huipil with things that they dream, we weave our huipil without dreams and our nightmares as urban Indian women living today in New York City.

VC: It can be our scarring...

HC: Yeah. That's what we weave in our huipil. That was the basis of it. We have these dreams and these scars as women here. When a woman puts on the huipil, and her head comes

through the opening, putting on her dreams...
VC: She stands in balance.
MM: Is the huipil the loom or the garment?
VC: The garment...her dress.
MM: The garment is a blouse?
RC: It can come down to your ankles. Different lengths.
VC: And the shape of it is in the four directions.
MM: Describe that.
VC: When the Spaniards first arrived in the center of the village, there was this enormous copal tree; and our ancestors would gather to exchange the goods...corn, squash, beans...they would share these with each other, because they knew by sharing, it would ensure the growth of the crops. But when the Spaniards came, they couldn't understand why our people gathered together and what this sacred copal tree meant to them. They thought it was evil and pagan, and so they decided that they were going to chop down the sacred tree.

They began to chop it down, but it was very, very difficult for them to cut it down. It took a lot of strength for them to do it. Finally, they succeeded in uprooting the tree. Out of the tree came all these colored serpents, red, blue, green, yellow, and so the Spaniards got scared and so they ran away. Then a woman appeared and she was wearing a white huipil. All these colored serpents attached themselves to her huipil in four directions, to the north, to the south, to the east, and to the west. A black serpent wrapped itself around her head. She was covered with serpents and protected. The Spaniards built a Catholic church over where the sacred copal tree once stood. They replaced the serpents with flowers, and they thought they stripped us of our power. At the end of that story, we say, "Where are the serpents of my huipil? Who has taken them? Dónde están las serpientes de mi huipil? Quién se las ha llevado?" [Then they ask the same question in their own language, Nahautl.] Because by taking, stripping the huipil of the serpents, which represented power and fertility, they thought they had stripped us of our power, but they couldn't, because the power is within us.
MM: Your next piece was *Blood Speaks* [1992].
VC: Uh-huh. That was a piece that we collaborated on with two other Native American women.
MM: Tell me what the piece was about.

VC: It was the role that religion played in the conquest.

HC: In the genocide of Native people. Because they conquered with the cross.

VC: We kept reading about Columbus, about all the conquerors, and then we said, "Yeah, but all these friars came over, too. The church had a very strong role in the genocide of Indian people."

HC: We have to tell our funny little story about how the piece was first conceived as a 10 to 15-minute piece, that's touring now as a video.

VC: We were invited to do a performance at A&S [Abraham and Strauss] Plaza for a Christmas show, and we decided to try it out there.

HC: This was in the middle—

VC: —of lunch hour shopping. Everybody was in A&S Plaza, doing their shopping. We got up to do our 15-minute performance piece, *The History Lesson.* We said what Columbus took and what he brought. (She laughs.)

HC: But we did it like two little kids.

VC: We did it like two little kids...

HC: Yeah, we had little party hats, because we were coming to Columbus's birthday party.

VC: In 1492, Columbus sailed the ocean blue in the *Niña,* the *Pinta,* and the *Santa Maria.* He brought gold, trinkets—

HC: —gonorrhea, and the cross—

VC: —the sword...syphilis...and he took gold, slaves, and he raped Indian women. And we went [intake of breath] "Noooooo, nooooo." We said it like two little kids, we were holding hands. And all over A&S Plaza, the word "gonorrhea" exploded. That's all everybody heard. Well, we finished our little piece. We went off and did our shopping. And all of a sudden, we heard all this commotion. The guards, the security guards and everybody... they called the police.

HC: We had to call the Community House lawyer...

MM: You were arrested?

VC: No, but that's what they wanted to do...

MM: What was the impetus for *Blood Speaks?*

HC: We both kept having dreams of the color red. That was the impetus.

VC: Blood...the blood that was shed... our blood that runs in our veins...

HC: We kept saying, "What is this? What is it? Why is this color red so important? It keeps coming up all the time." That's what prompted us. The blood.

VC: The blood speaks. When we went to Mexico, we saw all these human bones in the museums...all over, they have Indian bones.

HC: The stuff that's exhibited says, "Pagan. Pagan."

VC: And this is a country that sells its Indian image to tourists.

HC: What do you see but the pyramids in Mexico?

VC: All the ruins, the sacred sites. Religion played a role in our growing up, in our oppression. Because religion was a way of controlling us, too, and that's what religion did to indigenous people, it controlled them. It got rid of the culture...the language...it tried to erase all of that. We incorporated a lot of these stories. But we also had humor in the piece to break up the heaviness. We did a Columbus roast. We had blood sausage–

HC: –and finger food–

VC: –lots and lots of finger food. (She laughs).

MM: *Open Wounds* is your most recent piece?

HC: That's a work in progress.

VC: It has a lot to do with the abuse of the Earth, the land, the abuse of women.

HC: Because when you think of it, all the stuff they've taken, all the minerals, all the different–

VC: –the natural resources, how they've been ripped out–

HC: –it's like you're ripping stuff out of the Earth, out of a woman, you know–

VC: –and it's our mother, the Earth.

HC: We saw it when we went to Yellowstone and saw these geysers. This is part of the belly of this woman, this Earth. And what are people doing? They're ripping it out and then dumping it back.

VC: And then dumping toxic waste.

HC: Taking it out of the Earth and then making it a poison and then storing it back as poison into the Earth, into the womb of this woman, this Earth. How long can she take it? But you go to these geysers, and she's still bubbling, she's still strong, she's still there, she's a survivor, this Earth.

MM: How is what's happening in Mexico today affecting your work?

HC: It's a loaded question. What's happening in Mexico, I think we have to start talking about. It's happening in Mexico, it's happening in Argentina, it's happening wherever there are Indian people, it's happening all over Indian country.

VC: In a way, it's never stopped. It's ongoing since the colonization.

HC: I mean, there's Texaco going down into the rain forest in Ecuador and ruining the environment there for the Indian people.

VC: The Yanomani in Brazil—

HC: —the Yanomani in Brazil that are being killed off because the people that want gold want to come in there, and feel it's their duty to knock off these Indian people, because they're nothing, they are less than human.

VC: And the natural resources that are in Chiapas. They have all these natural resources but the people there, the indigenous people, what do they have? They don't even have a roof over their heads. They don't even have drinking water. They are dying of hunger. They don't have the basic necessities and over 1500 people, indigenous people, die a year from curable diseases. If they were able to get the proper treatment and care— but they are turned away from these hospitals and clinics that they go to.

HC: It's genocide, you know.

VC: So, in a way, what have they got to lose by fighting? They'd rather die fighting for a cause than die of hunger and starvation.

HC: What's happening is that Native people from Canada, Mexico, and the U.S., across the hemisphere, are dialoguing and supporting each other more. What has to happen more is that when you take the count here, when you say "Hispanic" and "Latino," you put all those Indians that come here from all those countries south of the Rio Grande, and you say that they are Latinos or Hispanic, but those are Indian people. We have to reeducate our communities.

VC: Again, that's another way of erasing, of killing us off…invisibility. We don't exist. Assimilation.

MM: How do you sustain yourselves?

VC: Whatever we can get.

HC: Anywhere we can get a job during the day. I don't make a living out of this theater. I have to do whatever I can lay my hands on, however I can make a nickel or a dime. That's very frustrating.

MM: What do you see in your future?

HC: We're going to keep on doing this. And we're passing it on to the next generation. That's what's important, that we are part of a continuation, that it's not going to die with us. My son is going to do it in his way, through his music, and he will pass it on.

VC: We would like to continue working with the Mexican community that is growing here in New York in leaps and bounds. It's overwhelming. That's something that has to continue, because when they leave Mexico, their culture doesn't have to die. Their culture can live here in New York City as well.

Notes

1. Evy Herr Anderson, "The Spell of the Storyteller," *Publishers Weekly,* 240, no.7 (Feb.15, 1993): 28–32.

2. Ruth Sawyer, *The Way of the Storyteller* (New York: Viking Press, 1962), 28–29.

Dos Lenguas Listas:
An Interview with Monica Palacios

Antonia Villaseñor

At a time when representations of Latinas in the mainstream media continue to lack authenticity, storyteller/performer Monica Palacios presents bits of everyday life in humorous narratives that have universal appeal. Dealing primarily with her life as a Latina/Chicana lesbian in her mid-thirties, Palacios weaves witty stories that disrupt stereotypes, make a public space for Latina lesbians, and, most important, make us all laugh.

Coming to Los Angeles in the late 1980s, via New York and San Francisco, Palacios began as a stand-up comic doing "straight" material. That was June 1982. By August, she was one of the nation's first openly Latina lesbian performers, coming out on stage as the "Latin Lezbo Comic," which was featured on PBS. Palacios soon gave up the mainstream circuit to do her own shtick as one of the founding members of the Chicano comedy troupe Culture Clash, and doing stand-up across the country in gay and lesbian clubs, community events, and colleges.

Recently, Palacios's work has been moving away from traditional comedy and toward storytelling and play writing. Her latest work, performed in the fall of 1994, "Confessions: A Sexplosion of Tantalizing Tales," has Palacios telling complete stories, with characters and plots, that do more to explore the lives of Latina lesbians and make personal connections with the audience, through identity, through universality, and through laughter.

These days when we all seem to take ourselves more seriously than ever, Palacios's gift is to break down those barriers that keep us apart, and then unite us through her humor. At the same time, however, her work is distinctly political. Part of denying lesbians, especially lesbians of color, is misrepresenting their sexuality (at either end of a sexual continuum—as asexual or hyper-sexual). In her work, Palacios describes, frankly, and explicitly—but all the while with a respect lacking in most contem-

MONICA PALACIOS

(photo by Becky Villaseñor)

porary comedy–the intimate details of her lesbian libido.

Palacios's work also uplifts. In carving out a space for herself, she does the same for her audience–and not exclusively Latina lesbians. Within her narrative, Palacios is able to alleviate the strain of the everyday, not increase it; no groups are ever made fun of, no one person is the butt of her jokes (with the possible exception of herself and her partner, who does not seem to mind). Palacios finds the humor in what people do, not in people themselves, and shows the absurdity in our lives–from dinner with the family and shopping for sex toys to stereotyping and discrimination.

In person, Monica Palacios breaks what seems to be the number one rule of show business: she isn't always performing. Friendly, down to earth, and confident in herself, she easily laughs when someone else tells a joke–she doesn't demand the spotlight off stage. Through her involvement as a member of the board of directors of VIVA, Palacios is quick to share her support, talent and time. Since 1988, VIVA has been discovering, empowering, and promoting gay and lesbian Latino/a artists in Los Angeles. VIVA members organize events, curate exhibits, hold poetry readings, and produce performances. Palacios especially enjoys creating venues for those artists still developing their talent. As project coordinator for Teatro VIVA, she is responsible for booking performances that educate the gay and lesbian Latino/a communities about AIDS prevention. Moreover, since 1994, she has been coproducing and performing in "Fierce Tongues/Women of Fire," a festival of powerful Latina artists partly funded by the city of Santa Monica's Arts Division. Always generous and always quick tongued, Palacios not only breaks ground, but also cracks you up.

AV: I want to talk about your courage to go up on stage and perform. For me, there's a primal fear of being on stage and embarrassing myself. Do you have that fear? How do you deal with it?

MP: Are you kidding?! I live in constant fear. But seriously, folks... My first time on stage was doing stand-up and, yes, I was scared. But I had wanted to do stand-up for such a long time–I wasn't about to let fear ruin my stage debut. I turned my fear into fuel. I channeled (do I sound like Shirley MacLaine or what?) my fear into telling myself, You're going to be great. You know and believe in your material. You're a powerful writer. You look really cute. I actually went out and bought an outfit to do my first five minutes on stage. Yes, girl, I had to look good. I did the makeup, the hair–I used Latino Sheen for that wild Latin look. It was extremely important to me that I felt and looked great, because I knew I was going to be scared. So I needed to pump up my confidence.

When I started doing stand-up, I was given five minutes, so I had to gear myself for that. l knew that in the first minute, I needed to hook the audience. I did so by coming out and doing punch lines every twenty seconds. Then, after that initial intro, the audience warmed up to me, so I was able to do something a little bit longer. I would talk for about a minute and not really have a joke, just talk. And that's it, I had to be great in five minutes I would condition myself, I worked at it with my punch lines timed accordingly. My mission was to get to the end of the five minutes, and that was my goal. Plus, I had to be good. Even twelve years later, I still get nervous and scared before I go on stage. And still that fear pushes me out there and makes me a confident artist: A few times, it didn't work. I put my hook out, and I got no bite. But since I was committed to do five minutes, I had to complete my talk and, "Thank you very much. Good night." And that was it.

AV: And it doesn't devastate you?

MP: It can. I had a couple of times where I was devastated. I couldn't connect with the audience because, for one thing, I was at a straight club, feeling intimidated by the crowd, attempting to do mainstream material. And I just never got them hooked. I finished my five minutes, I left, and I was completely devastated. I kind of cried out the rest of the night. But at the same time as I was devastated, I was thinking, Man, next time I'm going to be better. I'm going to be greater. I'm going to be much more confident. I'm going to knock them dead. That's how I always felt. I never thought, Oh, my God, I should get out of the business. I was always thinking, Next time–oof! Hold me back.

AV: And how is it different now?

MP: It's different. Because I'm not in a club where people are conditioned to hear a joke every twenty seconds. I'm in a theater space, where people never really know what to expect. They're there to listen attentively, not listen full of alcohol.

They're there to give you their all. Since I use comedy in my theater performances, by the first five minutes, I've done some laughs. I don't think I've lessened my material. I just know that, for me, I need to hook them with a comedic situation within that five minutes. Then I can just kind of talk for a while and gracefully go into my next humorous anecdote—as opposed to struggling, looking at my watch. A watch is a comedian's best friend or worst enemy. The clubs give you a light—if you're not off by five minutes, they'll just yank you off. As a stand-up comic, you're really conditioned with timing, you really have to pay attention to that.

With my theater pieces, I'm working with a script that I have to stick to, because I have a certain story to tell. Also, I'm working with sound and light cues that my tech people need to follow, or else we'll be confused. Also, the audience knows they are going to listen to me tell a story. They are much more patient than a comedy club crowd.

AV: Once, I asked you to define being great on stage, and you said that it was when you connect with the audience. Could you talk about that connection?

MP: One time, I was at a women's festival, and there were seven days of performances. It was the last day, and I was the last act of the night. I had gotten there around 4 P.M., and I had to wait till around 10 P.M. to go on. It was at a college that shall remain nameless; there was a basketball hoop outside. So I did my tech, and I had about two hours to kill. I waited back there and I was shooting baskets. I went over my stuff; feeling good about myself, and really pumping myself up, giving myself a pep rally. You have to be big, you're the last act, last show, you have no choice.

The people before me, they were average—there was nothing really special about them that I could hear. They didn't sound like anything new or fresh. I just knew I had to really grab it. I had to go on stage and make it my own, and, sure enough, I went out there and I was huge, I was big, and I think I did my best performance. It was videotaped and that's the tape that I use for my demo tape, because it was so great. It was about getting myself together, pepping myself up—self-confidence, self-esteem. And being physical with the basketball was really great. It combined physical with emotional, and pumped up my performance. Because I ended the evening, and the festival I had chosen to be responsible for, with a big finish. People still call this festival [the promoters] and talk about me.

When I'm feeling good about myself, people really respond in a positive way to what I'm saying. Their response fuels me, because they are letting me know they can relate to what I'm saying or they are being supportive of my art. I have done my job when I get a laugh or an applause.

AV: Did you always know you were a lesbian?

MP: No, I did not. I just always thought I was some outsider, somebody who didn't fit into the crowd.

AV: Were you a comedian before you were a dyke, or were you a dyke before you were a comedian?

MP: I was a dyke before I was a comedian, and, actually, doing comedy got me into the whole queer scene. Because when I started doing comedy, I pretty much started out as a lesbian comedian. So that put me definitely into performing for lesbian crowds. I kind of learned about my queer culture through performing, really.

AV: So now you're moving into a new genre?

MP: I've already moved. I'm doing more performance work, more storytelling. I rarely do stand-up.

AV: Tell me about your new piece, "Seagullita."

MP: Celebration Theatre [the gay and lesbian theater of Los Angeles] asked me to write a playlet dealing with the theme of lesbian seagulls, which would be part of an evening of six short plays. So, of course, being a Chicana lesbian, I thought, Why not make a story about a Chicana lesbian seagull? It made sense to me. It's called "Seagullita," and I've loosely based it on the story of Cyrano de Bergerac. Seagullita comes upon this woman who has just been dumped by a lover she met recently. Seagullita tells her to get her back by wooing her with poetry. That's pretty much the story line. It has gotten great reviews. Two Los Angeles papers have featured it, saying, "Very funny...most successful offering" and "Strongest of the plays, surreal and sweetly silly."

AV: When was the first time others performed your work?

MP: Words Across Cultures, [a performance group] got my "La Llorona" story from the *Chicana Lesbians* anthology, and they asked if they could do a reading of it, using three characters. I said, "Okay." Then they asked if they could turn it into a little play, and I gave them permission. That was the first time. I felt the directing was quite impressive. "Seagullita" is the second time that other people are performing my stuff, and I think I want to start doing that now. I feel okay about letting my stuff go. At first it was so much a part of me—it was written especially for me. Now, I feel that I can write for other people. I'm extending what I'm capable of doing. And it's a good choice for me right now.

AV: Will you be producing or directing "Seagullita"? Are you interested in going in those directions?

MP: I would love to. Actually, when this gig was given to me, I thought, it would be great to write it and direct it. But it's happening now before my new one-woman show, and I can't be in two places at once. But I met with the director, and I really like where she's coming from—her background, her politics. She made it clear from the start that she enjoys working with the writer. So I felt really good about that. I think I'd be a little hesitant for somebody to direct my material who didn't know about me. A director with no comedic timing or sense would really freak me out. Because a lot of my stuff is humor. And to get humor across on stage, you really have to have it down. You have to know about timing; it's very important.

AV: In hindsight, do you regret your decision not to go mainstream?

MP: Absolutely not! There were so many problems that I was encountering when I was trying to be mainstream. For example, the homophobia, the racism, the sexism, the bullshit, the competition. I hated it. When I was trying to be mainstream, I wasn't myself; therefore, my performance, my art, really suffered, because I couldn't be a hundred percent. And in choosing to be my true Chicana lesbian self, I do more than a hundred percent. I really can feel what I'm about, what I want to project in print and on stage. Of course, I would be a lot richer if I had stayed mainstream and closeted, but I'd definitely be unhappy. This question has been asked of me a lot. Another interviewer asked me if I would take a job on television to play Al Bundy's wife (the *Married With Children* guy). No. No way. I would never do that I couldn't do that. Absolutely not. No, no, no.

AV: You've been doing this for twelve years. What has been most satisfying for you?

MP: The fact that I have chosen to be what I am about I don't have to fill up those little molds that Hollywood and the mainstream have you jump into so that you can be successful in their eyes. For me, it's such a relief that I am doing exactly what I want, when I want it, to whom I want to do it to. It's very freeing. It gives me peace of mind, and it gives me more energy to create.

AV: How do you define success?

MP: Success is creating my art. And if I think it's great, that, to me, is success. Being happy with what I'm about.

AV: Has your family seen any of your routines? And if they have, what do they say?

MP: The family member who's seen a lot of my stuff—too much—is my lesbian sister, Eleanor. She loves it. She completely gets behind what I'm saying. My older sister has seen some of my stuff; actually my more erotic stuff; and her comment was, "Wow, that's good, that's great." She didn't really go into detail, which is fine with me, because I know what she saw was rather intense. If I hadn't seen my work and I would see that particular piece for the first time, I think I'd be lost for words. At least she came to my show and stayed. She didn't leave in the middle of it. So that was a good sign. My mom has seen me perform standup many, many years ago. I'm not going to push my parents about coming to see my work. If they want to, fine. And if not, that's fine with me—it's their choice. They're very supportive of me being a lesbian and what I am doing. They're not disappointed, they've always said to me, as long as I'm happy with what I'm about, then they're happy for me. So I'm okay with that. I think if a relative saw my work and they were freaked out about it, and told me, "That's really terrible what you are doing," I think I would be angry and I would have to talk to them about it. Actually, my cousins have seen my work and they loved it, 'cuz they're lesbians, too!

AV: Your sister Eleanor seems to be a major influence.

MP: She's always been a role model to me in general. When I was growing up, when I still thought I was straight, she was always just very independent, bold, out there doing her thing. We came out at nearly the same time, 1979, 1980. It was great having this lesbian sister.

AV: Do you think your "relationship" has impacted your work?

MP: Absolutely. I talk about my marriage a lot on stage, because it's great. There are certain little things that we do that crack me up, that I think are funny, and I think other people can relate to them. That's why I talk about them. I mean, if I wasn't married, I'd have no show.

AV: What do you mean? You'd have a show; you had a show before you were married.

MP: Yeah, that's true. No, I mean, my marriage is definitely a big part of my life, and that's why I do talk about it. It's always these positive, funny little quirks that I think are worth mentioning. But, more importantly, I love who I'm married to. What's great about being married to this particular woman—an artist and a poet—she's given me many great ideas. Then I take them and I put them into my quirky form. So that's what I really love about her. She is an artist as well, so she knows where I'm coming from.

AV: I wanted you to talk about your political commitment to be queer on stage. How have you benefitted, how do you think your audience benefits from that?

MP: What it's done for me, it's reinforced who I am. If I was a queer comedian, closeted, doing mainstream stuff, I would not be a hundred percent. Here I am, a queer person performing queer stuff on stage in front of a lot of people. I think my biggest audience was when I did the San Francisco Gay Pride Parade, in front of hundreds of thousands of people. And there I was on stage queer, being accepted in front of throngs of people who were like me. So, yeah, it's really strengthened who I am. As far as my audience, what they get out of it is—I don't mean to say this in a cocky way—I'm a role model. I'm saying, Hey it's okay. It's okay to be queer. And not necessarily always queer, but it's just okay to be what you're about.

AV: In the lesbian communities, there are some heated discussions about who's lesbian or bisexual, and the politics of naming ourselves. What do you think about bisexuality and homosexuality and that whole dialogue?

MP: I think when I was younger—I'm aging now—I thought people definitely had to be straight or queer. I didn't really know about bisexuality. But now there are so many names people give themselves, like transgender and bisexual. I'm learning more about that now. As I go along and I'm seeing more performers who call themselves transgender or bisexual, I'm becoming more open-minded about that. And probably by next year, I'll be totally open-minded about that and have a sex change or get a perm.

AV: Open-minded about it in your life or just...?

MP: Just in my thinking, I believe.

AV: When you came out, did you come out as queer or bisexual?

MP: When I came out, probably for the first week, I didn't know. I didn't call myself a lesbian—definitely not. But then, by that second kiss, I was completely a lesbian. And I knew I wanted to be kissing women. It seems, in my experiences, and friends I've talked to about coming out say this, you're kind of confused, and you don't want to label yourself at first. But then you kind of figure out who you really are.

AV: Did your material start out political?

MP: No, absolutely not. When I first did stand-up comedy, it was purely what I found funny. I did these bits about Lassie, about sound effects, Johnny Quest, just really silly things I had in my body for all my life. I had had this comedic build-up in my head, and when I finally had the chance to do it, it was just strictly what I thought was funny at the time. And I was queer then, but I wasn't thinking it was going to be a queer thing—huh-uh—it was, What is funny? No politics, nothing. It was just these little silly, funny things.

AV: When did the shift to politically toned work come?

MP: When I decided that I was going to become a lesbian comedian in 1982. I started doing stand-up in June of 1982, and by August of 1982, I had chosen to go the lesbian comedian route. And, little by little, as I became more involved with the queer community, the politics were in my face.

Just the fact that I wanted to talk about the lack of Latinos performing on stage and in film, that really was a big turning point for me, and that truly happened when I jumped into the whole topic of racism—"Racism: The Comedy!"—when I came to L.A. Because I found L.A. very racist. Visually, to me, there were many boundaries here. Just the fact that I saw so many Latinos as workers, and treated like workers. It blew my mind and so I had to do something about that. I thought, Well, since I have the microphone, people will listen to me. And all the while, I thought I couldn't be very aggressive about it I didn't want to be like a jackhammer, in-your-face, "You're-white-I'm-oppressed-

and-you-did-it." I had to use humor; my tool for my art is humor. So I figured out how to talk about racism through comedy. For example, I do a game show called "Mexican Denial" and how I think los Angeles, particularly, is in Mexican denial. I come out as a host and I say, "I'm Hope Crane. I used to be Esperanza Garza, but the United States has me in Mexican denial." And I take you to this game show. At one point, I have packets of tortillas thrown at me, and I pick up the tortillas and I say, "Hey, it's the *Daily Tortilla*." This is where we have a Mexican family. We fly them to California, and the prize is that we fly them to Fresno, "where you'll stay in the lovely grape fields, working long hours in the hot sun, getting paid below minimum wage, receiving unnecessary harassment from Americans. So, hey, you get to enjoy the land that was once yours." I do that very game show-like, and people are laughing, I can see them laughing. But they're also soaking it in, thinking, Wow, that's really heavy stuff.

I've been asked, why do I deal with such a heavy issue in a silly manner. I think humor isn't as silly as people think; humor is strong, there's a lot you can do with it. I think people think that it's sometimes too slapstick or too Three Stooges, but I think that they're wrong. I think you can work a lot of heavy topics through humor.

AV: What is your favorite part about performing?

MP: The fact that I am saying something I think is either funny or poignant and having the audience agree with me, either through a laugh or applause. That, to me, is extremely satisfying. The connection with the audience is a great thing.

AV: Lately, your work has become more–

MP: –erotic, trashy, raunchy–

AV: –more explicitly graphically erotic–

MP: –erotic, erotic–

AV: –and not everybody is comfortable with it.

MP: 'Cuz I'm married to a sex kitten, okay? That's off the record. No, for one thing, I'm becoming more relaxed with my sexuality, and I like sex. People have a hard time with it; people have a hard time hearing lesbian sexual experiences, and I just want to let people know that we are sexual creatures. I'm sorry. Get over it. We don't go on a date and brush each other's hair. People believe lesbians have orgasms through giggling; that's not how it is. We don't just sit around and drink tea. We are sexual creatures. So 'fess up to it, ladies. It's interesting how sometimes when I'm in a group an audience full of women, sometimes they get really uptight about it, and I'm talking about *them*. I think my better-written stories and bits are talking about lesbian sexual experiences. I add a lot of humor to it, I have fun with it, I think it's great.

AV: Like your vagina song?

MP: Vagina medley. And you know, when I first performed that, it was like 1984, '85 and I thought it was a funny cabaret kind of thing. I believe I'm a lounge singer and I can sing like Bobby Darin—that's my belief. So I thought, What can I do to please my Bobby Darin self and do this vagina thing? let's take standard tunes and replace the key word with vagina. And, to me, it was just a silly thing, but people always find it empowering and political, and I guess it is. It's already been talked about by academics. Alicia Arrizón talked about it; it's like her favorite part of the show. She does this whole theory about the vagina medley, so I think that's very interesting. And sometimes when I do it, yeah, the last time I did it in front of a mostly straight audience, they were uptight about it.

AV: That's funny, because they have vaginas, too.

MP: I think so, last that I saw, heard. When I get that uptight response when I'm doing something really sexual, I feel sorry for them. At first I used to feel like, Oh, God, I should be more well rounded and not be so sexual. But lately, it's, Loosen up! For a country that's so sexual, I think, it's just so uptight. I think I've found as a writer that my best work has been about lesbian sexual experiences. I have a lot of fun, and it seems to flow really well when I add comedy to it. I think sex and comedy are two things that people can truly relate to, and I think those elements work really well on paper for me, so therefore when I perform it, it's even better.

There is one piece I do, "The Taqueria Tease," where I use food, sex, and comedy—a combo plate. I talk about how "I love watching her eat carne asada tacos from afar." I also have this short story called "Club." It's a fictional piece about this character's Latina lesbian group, Mari Macha. They go to a lesbian sex club. The character, Ana Mendoza, goes to a sex club, and she sees other women. The first line is "I met her at a sex club." Second line is, "I just walked right in there and started humping her leg." So right off the bat, I get right to the point. Ana sees this woman in the souvenir shop of this club; she's surrounded by her friends, and she's holding a "Big Souvenir." It's a dildo and they're laughing about it. In this particular piece, I really wanted to include the Latina kind of quasi-chola characteristic, and one of the friends says to her, "God! Dolores, put that thing down, you're going to put somebody's eye out." They're playing around, giggling. Ana goes throughout the sex club, keeping her eye on Dolores from a distance. And finally she catches up to her, where they are both looking at these two white chicks having sex on the floor, and Ana leans over to Dolores and says, "You would never see two Latinas going at it in public." And Dolores says, "No way, man, too much Catholic Latino shit."

Ana Mendoza is trying to pick up on Dolores-Dolor ("pain"). She plays with that word: "*Dolor*, is that pleasurable pain or ugly pain?" They do meet and they do talk and they take a walk outside. That's how it ends–they walk down Santa Monica Pier Boulevard, not really knowing where it's going to lead to. It's a hopeful ending. My stories usually end on an up beat. The main point of that story is I really wanted it to be as Chicana as possible including the sexual element, even the smallest details, like "I liked her wine-colored lipstick. It was Cholita by Max Factor." It was really important to me to maintain Chicana lesbian elements, because I have not read a lot of Chicana lesbian erotica that is playful and funny.

AV: What are your future plans?

MP: I want to continue to write a lot more, submit more short stories to anthologies. I would like to tackle a bigger play, as opposed to a ten-minute play. I really enjoy promoting new talent. I would like to produce shows, theater performance, spoken word, mostly focusing on getting queer Latinos out there, highlighting their work, giving them a place to perform. I coproduce an event called Chicks and Salsa through VWA, and it's really great to promote all these Latina lesbians who usually don't get that much attention, just because they're not "professional." We create this really safe, hip, happening environment for them, which allows them to really shine. And I want to win the lottery, so that I can travel around with my wife in comfortable cotton clothing that always looks neatly pressed.

Sometimes I think I have to stop performing so that I can write really great pieces, but I guess I'm going to continue to do both. I'm happy with both and I think people still want it: they like my work. Lately, I've been performing a short piece called "Picosa," and it's been quite a crowd pleaser. My plan is to try to book myself throughout the country. My work has been used in the colleges quite a bit, so I'm looking into teaching at the college level, as an artist-in-residence. In the last few years, I've been asked often if I was teaching anyplace, and I feel ready now.

Pocha or Pork Chop?:
An Interview with Theater Director
and Performance Artist
Laura Esparza

Marguerite Waller

Laura Esparza is one of the few Chicana theater directors active in the United States today. She had worked extensively in community theaters in Seattle and San Francisco when she was accepted in Jorge Huerta's graduate program in Latino theater at the University of California, San Diego. While she distinguished herself in the mainstream UCSD Theater Department, she also did less traditional performance art work with the women's art-making collective Las Comadres.[1] Upon receiving her M.F.A. in 1992, she became artistic director of San Francisco's community-based Teatro Misión, and she soon became deeply involved with another community theater, San Jose's Teatro Visión, as well. The following year, as a recipient of the prestigious Theater Communications Group NEA Directing Fellowship, she spent several months on the road assisting theater directors across the country. She assumed her current position with the Seattle Group Theater in July, 1994.

Throughout the very active years as a professional director, Esparza has also been experimenting with using her own and her family's history as source material for performances related to the work she did in collaboration with Las Comadres. Her discipline involves going deeply within herself to discover her own personal sources of pain and pleasure, of conflict and creativity, and using them to problematize any and all of the restrictive identities that have been offered her by the contingencies of history and geography.

I DisMember the Alamo, the autobiographical piece whose script is published in this volume, has been presented at the Centro Cultural de La Raza in San Diego and at the University of California, lrvine, among other venues, and continues to evolve, as Esparza explores the ramifications of belonging to a family that changed nationality four times (Spanish, Mexican, Texan, and U.S.) while remaining in the same San Antonio neighborhood for three hundred years. Recalling her decision to accept with pride the designation *pocha*,[2] for example, she remembers the cross-cultural malapropism of the Anglo friend to whom she proudly announced this self-empowering act. "Pork chop? You want to think of yourself as a pork chop? Why would you want to do that?" Literalizing the pun, she flagellates herself with thick California supermarket cuts of meat, while contemplating the possible meaning of being a pork chop as well as a pocha. The pun accurately designates her position in language—any language—as relative, fluid, and multidimensional.[3] She is free to play, and to play on, the pivotal role of manipulator of multiple codes. Why not a pork chop, an Anglo mishearing of a Mexican misperception of Chicana identity? The multiple border crossings inscribed in "pork chop" incorporate the continuous parallax shifts, and the fluidity of categories, that can unravel the binary, either/or logic that enables minoritizing and exclusion in the first place.

Pervading *I DisMember the Alamo* is a powerful awareness of the effects of binary logic on constructions of gender and sexuality and, concomitantly, of constructions of gender and sexuality on the writing and rewriting of history—including the history of Esparza's own family. Wearing heels and fishnet hose, with a man's shirt and bow tie, she announces that she is giving away the family jewels—at once a euphemistic and raunchy, off-color characterization of her rocky passage from patriarchal, dualistic history to a more carnivalesque, multidimensional mode of representation. She retells the bizarre tale of her great, great, great grandfather's death on the inside of the Alamo, with the American "heroes" fighting against the forces of the Mexican leader Santa Ana. "Inside" is, for once, the wrong place to be, since the defenders of the Alamo were all killed. Her great, great, great grandfather, though, had chosen to remain there out of loyalty to an Anglo Texan friend who had once saved the Mexican Texan's son from drowning. Later, of course, when the descendants of the American defenders of the Alamo came to benefit politically and financially from their status as sons and daughters of the Alamo, the Esparza family, as Mexican, were disenfranchised and impoverished.

In Esparza's retelling of this story, the tragedy lies not with the characters but with the narratives (liestory) that cannot accommodate a Mexicano in the Alamo or a non-Spanish speaking Chicana (herself) in modern San Antonio. These narratives, furthermore, leave out her great, great, great grandmother, Ana, left with "four babies and a bloody corpse," living on past glory, through the hype of history. Looking through Ana's eyes suggests a double irony, a double disenfranchisement, that involves a binary gender system no less specious than the dualistic border that so poorly maps the complex history of the neighborhood which her family has never left.

Esparza's performance, through these and other strategies, systematically dissolves the linguistic and cultural binaries that have separated her from "real Americans," all of whom, she concludes after questioning audience members, have also suffered losses of ancestral lands and languages. As pocha (or pork chop, or both), she gains access to a global community of immigrants and refugees. Her dismemory/dismembering of patriarchal, nationalistic history leads not to an alienated (national/ethnic/sexual) identity, but to accountable citizenship in a serious but carnivalesque world whose energies flow with, rather than against, her multidimensional Chicana subjectivity.

MW: How do you see yourself as a Latina?

LE: When people ask me this question, I have to dwell on what it means to be from somewhere. I am really fortunate, because I have a long history in one place. My family has lived in the same neighborhood in Texas for over three hundred years. I grew up with a sense of my family's history and the history of the city, San Antonio. So whenever I'm asked where I'm from, the first thing that comes to my mind is that I am a Chicana from San Antonio. *Chicana* is not a term that's used freely in San Antonio, Texas, but it's something that I really feel myself to be, because it identifies me as a bicultural person and a person who is aware of her relationship with the particular politics of race and culture in this country.

This country has a history and a culture of race and racism that are unlike those of other countries. We have a particular sensitivity and pain. I feel that *Chicana* identifies me in relation to that struggle. One of the things I've had to work on in my life is creating a positive myth of myself as a Chicana from San Antonio. An important part of my myth is the heritage I have from the city. I feel the land and location of Texas in my blood and bones. I know that place as my body. Also important was growing up on the west side of San Antonio with that particular culture but not speaking Spanish, because my parents felt that somehow we would progress in life further than they had if we didn't. They discounted the racism that had kept them in their place for so many decades, so many centuries, really. I grew up feeling censured by the society around me because I didn't speak Spanish—an experience of Chicanos or Latinos who are growing up bicultural everywhere. And it's not just Chicanos. People, both immigrant and indigenous, are dealing with this issue of language.

MW: Yes, that's the issue in one of the most striking moments of *I DisMember the Alamo*.

LE: It's an aspect of all of my work.

MW: You identify your relationship to language with that of everybody else, rather than seeing it as different.

LE: This came about as a result of my having to do so much work about being monolingual. The Latino culture really judges you on whether you are monolingual or bilingual. People from other ethnic backgrounds identify with this, people who were of Russian or Italian heritage were able to respond to my work. They had the same kind of struggle in their families. It's not just a Latino struggle, but a "United Statesian" struggle.

MW: Can you remember a time when you thought about your linguistic situation differently?

LE: Yes, definitely. The flip side of all these stories is the subjective experience of feeling negated and rejected by my own culture as well as by the mainstream culture. And most of us live much of that reality very painfully through the first two or three decades of our lives. I've been able to get some perspective through my work and through the way people respond to my work. What I feel it means to be a Latina has expanded to a more global vision, perhaps because I have felt a simpatía, a kind of onda, with people of different cultures, particularly South Korean, Italian, and other Mediterranean and Middle Eastern cultures. Perhaps Latino culture is more global than Spanish-speaking culture. Beyond the language, which I think is a superficial characteristic, is a kind of simpatía that we share with people

(courtesy of Laura Esparza)

of other races and other cultures, and I think this feeling is as real and as legitimate as the language marker.

MW: Could you say more about the sense in which you feel a South Korean is like a Latino?

LE: Sometimes it has to do with the way you consider family. It's a kind of inner warmth. And sometimes it's a sensitivity to the inarticulate languages of culture–the way you bargain in a market, for example, or the way you make someone feel welcome in your home. It may be a relationship to food or to color or to other things that go beyond language. It's a feeling of being related that goes beyond surface relations of language or family–an onda, or wave, of familiarity. I was speaking recently with an Italian woman, a theater director in Minneapolis, who remarked that she feels this way about Israelis. It's surprising, but I've made this discovery with Irish people, Italians, Middle Easterners, and South Koreans. It could be anybody, perhaps.

MW: This makes Latinismo a majority rather than a minority characteristic.

LE: Yes. I'm beginning to think that way. It is part of the struggle to stop minoritizing myself. Sometimes I feel different. Sometimes I don't feel different. But part of the struggle of the early part of my life was getting over being a victim or feeling like a victim because I was a member of a minority group in relation to the United States culture. My strategy, I've found, is to travel more, to connect more with people from other countries, so that I feel more related to people than not, without losing any of the distinctness of my culture. Perhaps this is what it means to be a global citizen.

MW: This strikes me as a very original model of claiming one's identity. How did you hit upon it?

LE: Two things experienced when I was growing up: When I was a young Mexican-American girl growing up in a cloistered Latino family, certain inhibitions were built in. They had to do with travel and with education. Talking to Latinas around the country, I've found that many of us have experienced the same inhibitions. I grew up feeling that I didn't have a right to be in the world, a right to travel in the world, or the right to be where I was when I did travel in the world. People have different ways of describing it. I feel as if I'm a spy when I'm in other parts of the world–when I am in places where Latinas have not gone before, where I'm the only one.

I also feel as if I've been let out. This is partly because I'm one of the few Latinas who has been in the places where I've been. But it's also because being cloistered has made me feel minoritized. Unless you can imagine what it feels like to be free, then you can't be free. Unless you start acting as if you are free, particularly intellectually, then you can't be free.

MW: Do you recognize any particular role models or guides in your struggle for freedom?

LE: It was Gandhi's idea that, unless you can believe and act as if you are free, then your struggle will persist. So I have tried to break the myth of my Latina childhood and create a new myth of myself. Otherwise, I walk around the world trying to make work while imagining a little holy card of myself as a Chicana schoolgirl in a blue, pleated Catholic school uniform.

MW: There's an idea for a performance.

LE: Yes, the people, the neighbors, the families, and the images of the people I have seen in my childhood and beyond are all part of my source material, but I can't really make the work unless I transcend the definitions that are imposed on me by that myth. So I'm always balancing.

I have this idea about my next-door neighbor, who, like my mother, raised six children and is a housewife. The image I have is of the Chicana housewife behind a screen door—looking distanced, disillusioned, and tired—at her six children playing in the yard. If Ninfa got to be a theater director, what would she say? That's sometimes how I see myself, as a voice for my people. At the same time, I can't allow that voice to inhibit me as an artist, as a woman, as a traveler, or as a world citizen.

MW: Do any women like her come to work with you in the neighborhood theater in San Francisco?

LE: Oh, all the time. I work with this wonderful group in San Jose called Teatro Visión. They're a group of women who have worked together in Teatro for twenty years while raising their kids, getting their separations and divorces, and working their jobs. They are very connected to the life and politics of their community. They're all activists, but they care to make theater.

MW: What kinds of theater do you make together?

LE: Popular theater. We have a mostly Mexican and Mexican-American audience in San Jose. I like San Jose a lot, because it has a Chicano community like San Antonio's.

MW: Do you develop original productions with them?

LE: I have done plays with them, but the next thing I am doing with them is an original production. We're working from a play called *Las Nuevas Tamaleras* by Alicia Mena, but we wanted to work on an idea that never really gets developed by the play. It's the idea of cultural amnesia. Three modern Chicanas get together to make tamales, but none of them can remember how to make them. We wanted to explore the idea, not only dramatically, but in other modes of performance. So we're creating a Chicana carpa, to go around the play. The carpa features a comedian emcee, Rosa Maria Apodaca, who introduces the show. There are also a magician and an accordion player. We meet the characters of the play as clowns, and we learn a little about them through their clowning around. Then we do the play followed by a reprise of some interior moments of the characters who are going through a kind of cultural amnesia, the self-censorship of their culture, and the guilt of not being fully "Chicana."

MW: How does it come out?

LE: It comes out as a comedy of contradictions, which is the life we live. There is no resolution to this contradiction. The contradiction of biculturalism is a continuing comedy. Going around the country, you meet all kinds of Latinas, and you know that they are Latina. Some of them speak Spanish and some of them don't; some of them remember how to make tamales and some of them don't. But you still know that they are Latinas by that simpatía, by that onda, between you. And they'll become gay or feminist or liberal or conservative and right wing. All the variations of people on this earth may be represented by them, and you'll still know they are.

That's the sense that you have to believe in, not these superficial markers of nationalism, one of which is language. I don't believe that language really is a true marker. And we serve ourselves better by making coalitions across the borders that we set up among our own people—borders of homophobia, or sexism, or monolingualism.

MW: Is it something like collective performance art that you are creating in San Jose?

LE: It's a carpa. Carpa is a traditional Mexican vaudeville form of the nineteenth century that was very popular across the Southwest, up until the talkies in the early part of this century. It was a variety show in which there was an emcee comedian, some theater, music, and magic. They sold tamales. It's part of our theatrical heritage.

MW: Were they traditionally political?

LE: Yes, they could be, and many of them were. They were political in that they were venues in which a community could discuss an event in their community that was very politically charged and could not be safely discussed otherwise. So it was a way to discuss something without being arrested or beaten up for discussing it in public.

MW: Do you encounter any conflicts or problems developing this material with this group of people?

LE: Not really. One of the things we have as a foundation is that this group has been working together, so they're already an ensemble. We have a pretty common set of beliefs. Our politics are really in sync, and there is a real joy among these people. There are the usual problems: lateness, babysitting the kids. But the wonderful thing about doing Latino theater is that the whole family gets involved. Your kids are there, your husband is there; your sister is there, and your mother is there, and they all work on the show, or not. But they're there. They usher or whatever. And the kids of the performers sometimes stand around the stage or stroll backstage or into the house. The rules have to be relaxed when there are kids around, and I like that feeling in the theater. I like feeling that they are breaking the rules of the typical theater experience– you know, sitting in your seat and being quiet. I find that very joyful.

MW: I was wondering, after seeing the San Francisco Mime Troupe production *Offshore*, whether your group in San Jose has taken up any contemporary border issues–the border closings in Texas or San Diego, for example, or NAFTA?

LE: No, this theater still focuses on a kind of cultural Chicanismo. There are two basic subjects in a lot of Chicano plays–identity, and assimilation. I think these need to be rolled around a bit longer to allow a greater part of our people to think about these issues. But I also think that my new Latino theater should be creating coalitions among people who are Chicano, but who have different orientations.

I also want to say that I am very lucky in my life. I'm very lucky that I got to graduate school, and made it through. Going through an academic system that is still very ethnocentric and doesn't value your literature or your language really abuses your psyche. I'm very lucky that I participated in Jorge Huerta's graduate program at the University of Catifornia, San Diego, where a lot of Latinos from different cultural backgrounds were making theater together. I was also very lucky to get the Theater Communications Group (TCG) NEA directing fellowship, which allows me to travel and work with the U.S. directors of my choice. I think there were 140 applications this year for only four fellowships.

But... I don't know how to put this... that education and those experiences that I've had away, where I've tried to enrich myself or my work in order to bring something back to the culture, have also separated me from my community. I feel a suspicion toward me for having education, opportunity, travel, and experience away from the cloister of the family and the culture. That's a contradiction of my biculturalism, of my belonging to my Chicano culture and to the larger U.S. theater culture. I have to live with it. The suspicions are strange. People wonder whom you are loyal to if you are going out into the world working with French directors. What are my loyalties if I go to graduate school?

MW: So this coalition-building is not an easily negotiated trajectory at all. What plays did you perform in San Jose?

LE: We did Josefina Lopez's *Food for the Dead*, and we did Denise Chavez's *Novenas Narrativas*. We did *Roosters*. And now we're doing this one called *Las Nuevas Tamaleras*. I'm also directing a show in San Antonio called *When El Cucuy Walks*, by Roy Convoy. That's coming up in February at the Guadalupe Cultural Center. Then I'm directing the first Latino Equity show ever to be done in Seattle—*Harvest Moon,* by José Cruz González. I'm really excited about all three of them. They're different, and they're the same.

MW: Do you feel a conflict or a preference between your personal performance pieces and the more traditional plays you direct?

LE: No, I don't see any conflict whatsoever between these types of work, berause my play work must be as personal and as urgent, must have the same kind of playfulness, as the solo work. There's no difference, really, in the intention or the spirit with which the work is made. I'm also working on an idea that Luis

Valdez was working on at the Teatro Campesino. I'm thinking about the collective memory of my audience, of my Mexicano, Chicano audience, and looking at the pre-Columbian roots of our thought. I'm finding that a lot of the dynamics of that thought closely mirrors the dynamics that I try to bring into the building of a play, which is what Luis Valdez was trying to do. I'm after a fully integrated approach to gesture, symbol, architecture, kinesthetic relationship, and tempo (these are Ann Bogart's terms for the basic elements of the theater). On the stage, everything is part of one system. Everything is alive. Every object, every part of the set, every word, every body is alive and part of the same energy system.

MW: Who are the directors whom you will be visiting this year?

LE: Ann Bogart is the principal one, because she has an approach to theater that encompasses the basic belief system of Taoism, which I think is synchronous with pre-Columbian philosophy. Then I worked with Peter Sellars in Los Angeles, watching him set up flic *Persians* in the Taper (The Mark Taper Forum Theater). After that, I worked with a theater in Minneapolis called Teatre de la Jeune Lune. Jeune Lune does a lot of very big, spectacular fairy-tale work, myth work, with a lot of puppetry and a lot of big staging. They reminded me a lot of Latino theater in being very family oriented. They have been working as a collective for fifteen years—and they are bilingual. That bilingualism really enriches the process of building a play.

MW: Is that English/French?

LE: Yes. I think it really adds a dimension. I'm doing another project with Ann. We're doing *The Women* again, at the Hartford stage. And then, I don't know, I'm thinking about visiting Urban Bush Women, and Antunes Filho, a Brazilian, who has also created a movement system around Taoism.

MW: Where do you see yourself going over the long term?

LE: I think that I have to write. I cannot not do it anymore. I've already reworked *I DisMember the Alamo*. When I got a little distance from it, I could see that I was trying to use the metaphor of the Alamo to describe the Alamo of my childhood—its bicultural conflict. I've also done a new piece in which I try to work out the voice of my great great great grandfather's brother Francisco, who was on the other side, in Santa Ana's army. I was trying, with no information, because there really isn't any, to work out where he was coming from. I've been trying to devise a myth of Francisco and his journey—how he got to this battle, how he discovered my great great great grandmother Ana when she left the Alamo, and how they discovered the body of her husband, his brother. I've written this and I'm really excited about it.

MW: How do you coordinate so many different, ambitious projects?

LE: I bought a laptop. And in July, I'm going to take an ongoing position at the Seattle Group Theater—a theater I used to work at when I lived in Seattle before—as their associate artistic director. The theater is making a commitment to producing Latino theater in Seattle. This is good, because there should be more Latino plays done on main stages with Equity shows and decent production values, as well as community-based Latino theater that is bilingual for Mexican and Mexican-American audiences. I will continue my connection with Teatro Visión and with the theater I founded in San Francisco, the Teatro Misión.

Notes

1. For an extensive account of Las Comadres and of the performance piece, "Border Boda" that Esparza developed in collaboration with several other of its members, see my essay, "Border Boda or Divorce Fronterizo?" in *Negotiating Performance: Gender, Sexuality, and Theatricality in Latin(o) America*, ed. Diana Taylor and Juan Villegas, Durham: Duke University Press, 1994.
2. The masculine word pocho is a pejorative term used by Mexicans for U.S.-born children of Mexican descent.
3. For an excellent theoretical elaboration of the notion of multidimensional discourse I allude to here, see Emily Hick's *Border Writing:The Multidemensional Text,* Minneapolis; University of Minnesota Press, 1991.

Criticism

Latina Playwrights, Directors, and Entrepreneurs: An Historical Perspective

María Teresa Marrero

Hypothesizing about the Past and the Present

It is the goal of this study to trace the role of Hispanic women in theatrical activity in the United States from the late 1800s to the present. I focus upon the women who were company owners or directors during the first half of the twentieth century, and those who are playwrights contemporarily. Although many of the women company owners and directors were also highly successful performers in their time, I highlight the aspects of their career which placed them in positions of decision-making power. During their particular historical moment, these creative women of vision inserted themselves into an arena historically commandeered by men: the theater.

Very little has been published that offers testimony to Hispanic women's participation on stage prior to the 1960s. Although much more information is available regarding Chicana and Latina women's participation in contemporary theater and performance, relatively little has made its way into print.[1] This study draws on available, published studies on the history of Hispanic theater productions in the United States prior to the 1960s. The second part of the century (from the 1960s to the 1990s) offers a different paradigm: since the advent of the Chicano, women's, and other civil liberties movements in the United States, there has been a marked increase in the visibility of Chicana/Latina women in public spheres. Of particular noteworthiness is the increased numbers of Latina playwrights as of the 1980s, and the gender-sensitive subject matters being addressed by them.

Unlike the historical past, where the structure of Hispanic theater in the U.S. revolved around traveling vaudeville (*carpas*, *teatro bufo*) and operetta (*zarzuelas*, *sainetes*) theater companies, the structure of Latino theater today varies. There are basically three models for Latinos: the continuation of community-based theater organizations (such as the Guadalupe Cultural Arts Center Theater in San Antonio, Texas, and Su Teatro in Denver, Colorado); the professionalization projects, which aim to introduce Latino plays into mainstream, Anglo theaters (South Coast Repertory's Hispanic Playwrights Project and New York's INTAR Playwrights-in-Residence); and independent performance artists, whose performance structure rejects traditional notions of dramatic structure and production (Carmelita Tropicana, Las Comadres, Emily Hicks, Laura Esparza, Yareli Arizmendi, Teresa Chavez, Belinda Acosta, and Elia Arce).

Between the 1960s and the 1990s, the number of Latina college graduates increased significantly. The present generation of Latina playwrights, such as Cherríe Moraga, Dolores Prida, Josefina López, Edit Villarreal and Sylviana Wood, and directors such as Laura Esparza, Amy González, and Susan Tubert, have all benefited from some form of institutional or academic education. Access to university theater training programs and Latino/a playwrights' development projects have highly refined the writing and production talent of contemporary Latinas. But how did women insert themselves into the spheres of production and direction during the first half of this century? What avenues were available to them, and how do we know this information?

Insertion, according to common dictionary definitions, is both the act of inserting or introducing something into the body of something without force or artifice, and also with force or artifice (American College Dictionary). This equivocal definition suits the case of Hispanic/Latina women in theater rather well, because the act of insertion into center stage as decision-makers has historically taken both roads. I suggest that during the first half of the twentieth century, women employed tactics of insertion that were available to them through the organizational structures of theater at the time (traveling, semipermanent performing companies versus the Equity theaters of today). I hypothesize that university and other institutionalized arts programs existing since the 1960s have altered the model of insertion, particularly for Latina playwrights.

I use the term *Hispanic* to describe theatrical activity in the historical past, as researched by the published sources previously mentioned. I also use the term *Hispanic* when a contemporary writer applies the word to describe herself; the same is true for the term *Latina*. *Latina* offers the benefit of being gender-specific, as opposed to the neuter *Hispanic*. *Latina* also connotes a politicized point of view regarding questions of gender and identity.

The presence of persons of Mexican, Cuban, Spanish, and Puerto Rican descent in the United States before the 1960s is a historical fact. Traditional comic forms, such as the Mexican *carpas* and the Cuban *teatro bufo*, as well as Spanish musical theater (*zarzuelas*) all influenced the contemporary aesthetic of the theater of the 1960s. Contemporary *teatro* Chicano is embedded in the rich *carpas* and *corridos* (ballads) tradition; Cuban audiences in Miami continue to enjoy theater in the *bufo*/comic tradition, and New York Puerto Rican and other Latin American writers create dramatic works often described as "magical realist."

The value embedded into this analysis is feminist, which means that I offer a rereading of canonized notions of contemporary Chicano/Latino theater histories.

About the Centers

How central can Latina women be in the development of U.S. Latino theater, one may ask, if their participation, historically, has been invisible? In *The Power of the Center: A Study of Composition in the Visual Arts* (1982), Rudolf Arnheim describes a curious phenomenon in the visual perception of pictorial compositions that challenges common notions of centrality. Arnheim states that "only in geometry is a center always in the middle because in geometry a center is defined by location alone."[2] If, then, as Arnheim suggests, the center and the middle are the same only if defined by the geometric computation of a physical space, what else counts as a center? "When we speak of a center," Arnheim writes, "we shall mean mostly the center of a field of forces, a focus from which forces issue and toward which forces converge." Furthermore, a center can be visually present without being marked explicitly (which would constitute a "retinal" presence). The marked, physical presence of a center can easily be ascertained by deduction; the center of a field of forces can be ascertained by induction. Through induction, the viewer can perceive balance or imbalance in a picture, and can perceive any absences.

"Centrality" in theater has been valued as a physical and a metaphorical descriptor of placement, prominence, visibility, and importance. The very nature of the traditional proscenium stage as a framed visual experience and the importance of the center stage justifies the analogy. The pioneering efforts of Hispanic/Latina women company owners, directors, and playwrights have not been treated as central subjects of academic inquiry until very recently,[4] consequently the scant published material makes a comparative history impossible. There is only one text on the history of Hispanic theater in the U.S. which includes data preceding the 1960s. *A History of Hispanic Theater in the United States: Origins to 1940.*[5] Methodologically, this historical reconstruction was conducted by unearthing Spanish-language newspapers published in what is now United States territory. The small, regional Spanish-language newspapers during the late nineteenth and early twentieth centuries often published extensive literary and cultural articles, which closely documented the social activities of a given community, such as New York, Los Angeles, San Antonio or Tampa. Due to the ephemeral, self-consuming nature of the acid paper used in newsprint, many of these publications have either disintegrated or are undergoing what library experts call "acid burn." Library special collections, such as the ones at the New York Public Library, the Center for Puerto Rican Studies at Hunter College in New York, the Chicano Special Collections at the University of California, Berkeley, and Stanford University, offer newspapers as a source of primary materials. Many also have unpublished play scripts and billboard and performance information. Very few of the plays documented in *A History of Hispanic Theater* exist in published form today. The history, then, that can be reconstructed today represents the record of past events, but not the presence of printed texts as evidence of that historical record. The very important participation of women impresarios, directors, and playwrights are documented in Kanellos's text, Armando Miguelez's study of Teatro del Carmen in Tucson, Arizona, and Tomás Ybarra-Frausto's study of San Antonio vaudeville actress La Chata (Beatríz Escalona) Noloesca. These scant publications count for most of the printed history of women's participation in Hispanic/Latino theater in the United States prior to the explosive 1960s. A close reading of these sources, however, echoes Arnheim's description of invisible centrality: women have constituted and continue today to constitute a notable, yet overlooked, presence in U.S. Latino theater. The problem of relative invisibility, due to the lack of published material (plays, publicity, academic studies, and so on) still poses problems today for Latinas, a situation of which contemporary Latina playwrights are highly aware. Documentation of the contemporary performance scene for the historical record methodologically requires not archival research but rather fieldwork.[6] Therefore, researchers today must develop numerous interdisciplinary skills, from archival recovery to journalistic and anthropological techniques of fieldwork.

Popular and Powerful Hispanic Women in Theater: 1866–1950

It is evident from Nicolás Kanellos's research of nineteenth- and twentieth-century Spanish-language newspapers that much theatrical activity by Hispanics existed in what is now the United States. Due to the discardability and fugacity (high acid content) of the newspaper medium itself, it is reasonable to assume that newspaper records cannot be counted upon as a complete and thorough source of historical information. Nevertheless, from available sources, Kanellos reconstructs a picture of busy theater companies that travelled extensively from Mexico, Cuba, and Spain throughout the northern territories of Texas, Arizona, California, New York, and Tampa. These companies satisfied the entertainment needs of resident Hispanic populations in various concentrated areas, who either were already here when the territory became part of the United States (such as the former Mexican Southwest with the Treaty of Guadalupe Hidalgo in 1848), Cuban tobacco workers who came to Florida during the last few decades of the 1800s, and Spanish expatriates who fled Spain for the eastern coasts of the United States during the Spanish Civil War.

The first mention of a woman in *A History of Hispanic Theater in the United States: Origins to 1940* (1990) is the description of the allegedly lovely actress Estrella del Castillo, wife of the prominent Mexican-born leading man and later director of the touring Compañía Española, López del Castillo. Kanellos quotes an enthusiastic reporter for the California-based newspaper, the *Los Angeles News* on January, 26, 1866:

> Mr. and Mrs. Castillo will rank with the best performers in the state. Mrs. Castillo's imposing and attractive form, handsome features and graceful and charming ease with which she moves through all her representations is alone well worth the price of admission. When fond of looking at a beautiful woman in the theatrical costume, we would advise you to purchase a ticket.[7]

Two important factors emerge from the example that this quote represents. With variations, what is alluded to here is repeated a number of times in *A History of Hispanic Theater:* the popularity that gave Mrs. Castillo a certain "star" quality had the potential of providing her with an equal footing on stage with her partner; and the professional association with her husband lent her a measure of respectability, despite the risqué nature of the profession. Both of these, I hypothesize, are key elements in the emergence of Hispanic women as powerful figures, not only on stage, but subsequently behind the scenes as company directors and impresarios. Not unlike in the film industry today, actresses and actors who became very popular with the public gained in box office prestige. The past resembles the present in this sense, particularly if one looks at contemporary film stars such as Julia Roberts, who have become powerful in Hollywood terms due to box office appeal.[8]

Getting to be a popular "star," yesteryear, however, involved a different route from that of "stardom" today. At a time in which women generally did not receive higher education and when university curriculum in theater arts was not the generalized norm, an actor or actress learned the trade from other, more experienced actors and actresses in a type of apprenticeship of dramatic, declamatory, comedic, and singing techniques. One's insertion into an apprenticeship required that the actor or actress join a traveling company. One can hypothesize that for young women to leave the protection of their homes without the sanctity of marriage would not have been generally acceptable. The case of the reporters' respectful, yet glowing comments about Estrella del Castillo's physical beauty may be in part due to the fact that she held a "respectable" position as the wife of the theater company owner. In other words, she was not a "tramp." It seems reasonable to assume that in the nineteenth century, marriage was the only legitimate and "decent" way for presumably Catholic, Hispanic women to legitimize their presence on the stage (following the patriarchal logic that if the husband condones his wife's actions for God and the world to see, then it must be all right, because no man would willingly disgrace his family name or honor).[9] Therefore, it is not demeaning to women in this sociohistorical context to underscore the legitimacy that marriage afforded them within the rather risqué business of the theater.[10] While not all of the women company owners or directors became prominent through their husbands, a number of them did. Examples from Kanellos's *History* suggest that prominent women, such as dramatic actress Estrella del Castillo, or the Texas vaudevillian La Chata Noloesca (Beatríz Escalona), or the exotic Italian-born singer/dancer Dorita Ceprano, came into their own through a large dose of personal talent and charm, but not without the advantage of being married to a prominent theater director. La Chata Noloesca began her training with the famed Cuban Areu Brothers Theater and was later married to José Areu. Dorita Ceprano was married to Enrique Areu.[11]

The clout that translated itself in economic terms, often turned into opportunities for a "star" to become director of the company, or even branch out to form their own company. While there are many more instances of men coming to this position of power, there are numerous instances mentioned in Kanellos's account in which evidently the "star" quality of actresses afforded them the economic solvency to become company and theater owners and directors.

The case of La Chata Noloesca provides an excellent example of the combination of the two factors already mentioned: entering into the theater world through marriage in the 1920s, she became a huge success who overshadowed her husband and later, in the 1930s, branched out on her own. A theater attendant in San Antonio, Texas, her ardor for the stage led her to meet her husband. They married in the 1920s, and her talent was nurtured and matured as a fast-talking, quick-witted *peladita* of the Mexican *carpa*-style, low-brow, popular comedy. By 1924, La Chata "began to ascend as a musical comedy star and overshadow the Areu brothers."[12] By the late 1920s, La Chata's character had fully gestated as a *pícara*, a *tandas de variedades* (vaude-

(courtesy of Benson Latin American Collection, Univ. of Texas at Austin) ville), comic character actress.[13] And, by the end of the 1930s, La Chata launched her own company, Atracciones Noloesca, Variedades Mexicanas, which made its debut in the Teatro Alcázar in La Habana, Cuba.[14] Neither of the historical narratives mentions the fate of José Areu and La Chata as a couple after she became a company owner. The subtext suggests that this occured after the marriage broke up.

Another key female figure to emerge in the early twentieth century mentioned by Kanellos is the very beautiful Mexican leading lady and traveling theater company owner Virginia Fábregas. The Fábregas Company played an important role in encouraging the development of local playwrights in the Los Angeles area.[15] Rather than only performing popular zarzuelas and melodramas by renowned Spanish authors, Fábregas would often buy the work of local Los Angeles writers, and produce it while on tour. She thereby served as a type of traveling literary agent, giving new talent much-needed exposure. Her tours traveled from coast to coast and on to Madrid and even the Philippines.

Mrs. Carmen Soto de Vázquez poses a different historical example. In 1915, in Tucson, Arizona, she built a 1,400-seat theater on a lot of land her husband gave her as a gift. The theater bore her name: Teatro Carmen. According to Armando Miguélez, Carmen Soto de Vázquez was an important cultural figure who strongly promoted the Spanish language and culture of that city.[16]

In the 1920s, Pilar Arcos emerged as a very successful actress and singer of Spanish *zarzuelas*. In a variety of entrepreneurial partnerships, she became an active figure in New York City, performing, promoting, and directing in a variety of theaters. In an attempt to establish Spanish-language theater companies in New York City, Arcos, among other entrepreneurs, would frequently rent already existing theater buildings.[17] Arcos seemed to have had numerous dynamic empresarial relationships. She is first mentioned as the director of the Compañía de Zarzuela Española Arcos-Sardina, and later she is mentioned as having developed a longer-lasting partnership with Fortunato Bonanova; together they formed the Compañías Unidas during a run at New York's Lyric Theater.[18]

During three decades–the 1920s, 1930s, and 1940s–Spanish-born actress, director, and playwright Marita Reid (her father was English; her mother, Spanish) also carved out a name for herself in New York City. She did everything from acting and directing standard melodramas, *zarzuelas*, and comedies to directing a group called the Spanish Players at the Centro Libertario, where she produced some of her own work, including her entremés, *Sor Piedad.* An avid antifascist, she championed Spain's right to become a republic in the 1930s.[19] Marita Reid's successful career extended into the 1960s, in English-language mainstream theater, including live television drama, such as *Armstrong Circle Theater, The U.S. Steel Hour,* and *Studio One.*[20]

There are two significant leads, then, that emerge from analyzing the scant historical narratives available on Hispanic theater in the United States. First, there were women who were highly active on the stage, not only as actresses, but also as directors and entrepreneurs. Secondly, with the lack of institutionalized support for theater training such as we have today in college and university curricula, most male and female actors began as apprentices in actual, and often traveling, theater companies. The trend to ascend from actor or actress to director or company owner, was, no doubt, conditioned by the level of success of the particular "star." Through a combination of personal talent, wealth, marriage, and box office success, Hispanic women in the late nineteenth and early twentieth centuries displayed a remarkable breadth of professional theater activity in the United States.

This brief historical sketch provides some evidence of the means available to women to enter into the directorial and creative echelons of Spanish-language theatrical life. With the exception of Marita Reid, no mention is made of Hispanic women playwrights prior to the 1940s in the United States in the Hispanic theater histories available to date. The 1950s is a lacuna, and the explosion of documented sociocultural activity in the 1960s is the beginning of what is called contemporary Chicano/ Latino theater.

Rereading Chicanas in the *Teatro* Movement of the 1960s and 1970s

The Teatro Campesino's history and evolutionary dynamic is inextricable from the development of the Chicano/Latino the-

(all courtesy of San Antonio Conservation Society Foundation)

ater as a whole. A rereading of the paternalistic nature of the collective Chicano theater structure has been the subject of heated debate recently. Chicana creative writer and critic Roberta Fernández's essay "Abriendo Caminos in the Brotherland: Chicana Writers Respond to the Ideology of Literary Nationalism—Women Writers in *El Grito* and *Caracol*"[21] lays the groundwork toward articulating the complicated relationship between Chicano cultural nationalism and the interests of Chicana feminists. Fernández, Gloria Anzaldúa, Cherríe Moraga, Yvonne Yarbro-Bejarano and Yolanda Broyles-González are examples of Chicanas involved in rewriting and inserting her-story[22] into literary historical narratives.

In "Women in El Teatro Campesino: '¿Apoco estaba molacha la Virgen de Guadalupe?,' " Yolanda Broyles-González discusses her observations from her oral history project about the women of El Teatro Campesino. Broyles-González's discomfort regarding the lack of female presence in *teatro* histories sprang from a 1980 performance by Socorro Valdez in El Teatro Campesino's 1980 European tour of *Fin del Mundo:*

> The spirit of the group commitment was still alive in that production, and that energy obviously contributed to the rare power of that performance—a power which visibly transmitted to German and French audiences in spite of language or other cultural barriers. My own dissatisfaction with the piece sprang from the portrayal of Chicanas. The women characters in the show felt like an eerie rerun of earlier Teatro plays: the saint-like wilting wife, the sleazy whore, and the grandmother figure. Compared to the male characters, the females seemed one-dimensional and relatively insignificant. Among the male characters, the most notable in terms of expressivity was the Pachuco youth nicknamed "Huesos." It was Huesos who most controlled the audiences and the motion on stage. I was astonished backstage after the performance when I discovered that Huesos was played by a woman: Socorro Valdez. Her performance was unforgettable. And yet her presence in the Teatro had never been described by scholars or historians of Chicano drama. Why?[23]

Any reconceptualization of a canonic image requires its destabilization and recollection. It requires a jarring reframing. Socorro Valdez makes some interesting observations about the women's growth process within the Campesino fold in the past nearly thirty years. She was a girl of fifteen when she began acting in the *teatro*. She is now an adult woman: "There is more of a consciousness of women–in oneself–than there was then." With this maturity came the awareness that the roles in which women were cast generally had a limited range: "You were either the novia, la mamá, la abuela o la hermana. And most of the time these characters were passive. The way those females are laid out are for the most part very passive and laid back, y lo aguantaban todo."[25]

This coming of age of women in *teatro* is paralleled by similar observations made by Latino actors in commercial theater. In a number of personal interviews Diane Rodriguez,[26] founding member and performer in the popular Los Angeles comedy foursome Latins Anonymous (Rodríguez, Louisa Leschin, Armando Molina, and formerly Rick Najera, now Chris Franco), opted to coalesce because, she said, "We were tired of what Hollywood had to offer: stereotypical parts as the drug dealer, the maid, or the hot Latin señorita.[27] The stereotypes may be different between one hegemony and the other, however, the same type of frustration is expressed by the limitations imposed upon performers due to race or gender by the "powers that be," who claim power over their representation. *Teatros*, governed by the same inherent patriarchy as society at large, perpetrate(d) and impose(d) a similar repressive standard of values.

In this case, Chicanas came up with creative alternatives in light of what they perceived as a lack of adequate roles for women. Within the example of El Teatro Campesino, Socorro Valdez and Olivia Chumacero opted to play male roles in disguise, or to play nongendered roles (La Muerte). Another option was to branch off and do independent performance work. This last option significantly influenced the development of the *teatropoesia* (a linguistic combination of theater and poetry) aesthetic of the San Francisco Bay Area. *Teatropoesia* is a gender-based, alternative created by Chicanas to deal with the overall lack of concern for Chicanas in general in the artistic arena of the Chicano social movement.

In 1974, Dorinda Moreno and Las Cucarachas performed *Chicana,* which included a blend of dance, music, poetry, and prose. In 1979, Olivia Chumacero and Rogelio "Smiley" Rojas presented a *teatropoesia* piece, *Cabuleando in Motion* at a number of Northern California community centers. By 1981, a number of groups emerged doing *teatropoesia,* including Valentina Pro-ductions[28] of San Jose, California, who presented a piece called *Voz de la mujer.* The group disbanded shortly after the perfor-mance; however, the impact of the freer form of the combina-tion of poetry and performance had left an indelible mark.

Subsequently, another major event of *teatropoesia* held in San Francisco was *Tongues of Fire.*[29] Two important factors manifested in *Tongues of Fire* can still be seen in the 1980s and 1990s work of Chicana playwrights and, particularly, performance artists. They are the centrality of writing as an activity of self-creation and a way out of a psychological underclass; and the willingness and freedom of women performers to experiment with their own bodies as artistic and sociocultural metaphors outside the limi-tations set by a proscenium stage.

Performance art does not require a proscenium stage, which subsequently does away with the established hierarchies inherent in the sociology of traditional theater (an artistic director who chooses the play, a director whose vision the actors must act out, and so on). The freedom afforded in performance art al-lows for either one-woman shows or collective creation. An in-creasing number of Chicanas and Latinas are using this art form: from the Cuban-American Carmelita Tropicana, to Chicana Belinda Acosta (who performed her one-woman show, *Machisma,* at the 1992 TENAZ XVI), to the San Diego/Tijuana collective Las Comadres, to director and performance artist Laura Esparza. *Border Boda,* a collectively created piece by Las Comadres (a multiethnic group), performed at the Plaza de la Raza in Balboa Park in 1990, reflects a junction between the *teatropoesia* of the late 1970s and early 1980s and the techniques of current U.S. avant-garde performance art (including the works of Ana Mendieta, the Border Arts Workshop, Emily Hicks, Laura Esparza, Yareli Arizmendi, Eugenia Vargas Daniels, Teresa Chavez, the Guerrilla Girls, Marguerite Waller, and the Urban Bush Women). Las Comadres took as a theoretical and literary base Gloria Anzaldúa's *Borderlands/La frontera. Border Boda* starts off with a poetic narrative, and expands into focusing on Chicana and nonChicana women's bodies as a metaphor for political and philosophical analysis. It is set within an art installation space in which the real/metaphoric geographic spaces are divided into three: the kitchen/Mexico side, the barbed-wire border region, and the technocratic/U.S. side.[30]

Within the contemporary Chicana feminist stage, the influence of Cherríe Moraga and Gloria Anzaldúa presents itself in Chicano theater history as a forceful insertion that threatens the status quo. The first all-woman playwrights' panel held in Chicano theater history was held on November 12, 1992, at the TENAZ XVI international festival of Chicano/Latino Theater at the Guadalupe Cultural Arts Center in San Antonio, Texas. The forum was moderated by Paulina Sahagún, and the participants were Cuban-American Dolores Prida and Chicanas Belinda Acosta, Beverly Sánchez-Padilla, and Cherríe Moraga.

Moraga challenged the participants to image the unimagined: to break the traditional structures of thought that keep us from reinventing ourselves as a creative construct. Echoing her original statement in the first feature article on Chicano/Latino theater in *American Theater* magazine (November 1992), Moraga calls into question women's participation in contemporary Chicano theater. "Largely we are allowed to write comedies... If you're committed to writing complex theater about what is the specificity of the female condition, that is still completely taboo." About the collective-writing system, which is often remarked in theater histories as a major breakthrough in the radical Chicano and Latin American theater movements, she commented that:

I think the structure of the collective in Chicano theater was a sort of an extended family... But in that extended family, the father was the patriarch, and the rest are his little children, and the women on one level had to function as modern-day Adelitas. The Adelitas were the women who fought in the Mexican revolution...essentially they had to fight them, fuck them and feed them. *(American Theater* 17)

Moraga represents the junction of several socially difficult positions: in no particular hierarchical order, she considers herself a lesbian, a Chicana, a feminist, a playwright, and a thinker. On the subject of the representation of alternative sexuality and lifestyles, Moraga and gay playwright Eddie Sánchez[31] can corroborate my assertion that gay and lesbian sensibilities are still a strong taboo in Chicano and Latino theater organizations. Moraga, like other Latinas, has had to go outside of the Chicano Latino establishments and turn to women's producers and publishers to get her word out.

Latinas In Contemporary Theater

The Chicana contribution to the development of a performance aesthetic is, by no means, the only one. The dramatic production by Chicanos and Latinos since the 1960s has been canonized with a beginning, a "father" figure which precludes all others: that of Luis Valdez and El Teatro Campesino. I would like to destabilize this narrative of contemporary Latino theater history by suggesting that there are two women who mark the vigorous reinsertion of Latinas into U.S. theatrical culture: Puerto Rican Miriam Colón Valle, initiator, director, and producer of the Puerto Rican Traveling Theatre/Teatro Rodante Puertorriqueño,[32] and Cuban-born, New York resident Maria Irene Fornés, playwright and director of the INTAR Playwrights-in-Residence Laboratory. I suggest with this alternative historical point of reference that *her-story* in *teatro* has a unique and different genesis and subsequent trajectory than *his-story*. And while the two "stories" are intertwined, they are quite different, affected by numerous factors, not the least of which is gender.

The Teatro Campesino's genesis is usually dated to 1965. In 1967, Puerto Rican actress Miriam Colón founded the Puerto Rican Traveling Theatre/Teatro Rodante Puertorriqueño in New York City with a grant from then Mayor John Lindsay. The company's first production, *The Oxcart (La carreta),* by Puerto Rican playwright René Marqués, featured the now legendary Raul Julia, whose professional training is owed to the Puerto Rican Traveling Theatre. It is considered to be the first professional, bilingual Hispanic theater company in the United States. While the careers of Miriam Colón, and Carmen Zapata (founder and codirector of the Los Angeles Bilingual Foundation for the Arts) somewhat follow the early twentieth-century pattern of actresses switching into directorial positions by means of their acting acumen and popularity, Miriam Colón's company is significant because of her vision. Her company is a pioneer in creating playwriting workshops which have proven to be crucial in the creation of a Latina dramatic aesthetic. The company's goals are to create a professional, bilingual theater

which would emphasize the contribution that Puerto Ricans and other Hispanic writers have made to the canons of dramatic literature while highlighting new plays by Hispanic playwrights living in the United

States and to make these plays accessible to the widest possible range of people.[33]

The playwrights' unit of the Puerto Rican Traveling Theatre began in 1977. The list of recent accomplishments by the playwrights' unit is impressive, and it includes the work of playwrights (for example, Lynette Serrano-Bonaparte, *The Broken Bough*, and Lynn Alvarez, *El Guitarrón)* and directors (for example, Susana Tubert, *Real Women Have Curves),* whose development can be traced through a number of such playwrights' projects.

Also in the 1970s, another very important playwrights' development project emerged. Designed to promote Hispanic talent, the INTAR Playwrights-in-Residence Laboratory was conceived and is still directed by Cuban-born playwright and director Maria Irene Fornés.[34] Chicano and Latino theater experts, such as Jorge Huerta, say that Fornés's influence in the past twenty years warrants that her playwrights' laboratory is reckoned as the generator of a kind of *Who's Who* in contemporary Chicano and Latino dramaturgy.[35] Fornés is the only Hispanic woman to have been honored with several Obies, including one for sustained achievement.[36]

Ms. Fornés's INTAR Hispanic Playwrights-in-Residence Laboratory has nurtured the talents of Hispanic men and women for many years. By the 1980s, a strong body of Latina talent could claim the INTAR Lab as a place where their talent was strengthened and reinforced. Among this contemporary generation of talented playwrights are Milcha Sánchez-Scott; Cuban-Americans Ana María Simo, *Going to New England;* Dolores Prida, *Beautiful Señoritas* and *Botánica,* Ela Troyano, experimental filmmaker, and Caridad Svich, *Gleaning/Rebusca, Alchemy of Desire/Dead Man's Blues;* New York Puerto Rican Lynette Serrano-Bonaparte, *The Broken Bough;* Migdalia Cruz, *Fur;* Chicanas Cherríe Moraga, *Shadow of a Man, Heroes and Saints, Mexican Medea;* Josefina López, *Simply María* and *Real Women Have Curves,* and Edit Villarreal *My Visits with MGM (My Grandmother Marta)*; Evelina Fernandez, *Luminarias.*

Where to from here?

Chicana and Latina women are not a homogeneous block, either ethnically or ideologically. Many of them still pursue traditional theater forms. In this area, too, Latina playwrights have been gaining ground. A look at the available historical records shows that a significant difference between the late nineteenth century and the late twentieth century is the increase of Latina playwrights and the decrease of Latina theater company owners and directors. Latinas as production directors today are still highly underrepresented. The best-known theater directors are Argentinean-born, East-coast-based Susana Tubert; Cuban-American, San Francisco-based Amy González; and Chicana, San Francisco-based Laura Esparza. Carmen Zapata and Cuban-American Margarita Galván still direct the Los Angeles Bilingual Foundation for the Arts. Miriam Colón is also still the director of the Puerto Rican Traveling Theatre. In Phoenix, Teatro del Valle was founded in 1988 by Trini Yañez Hale (Teatro del Valle took a children's piece written by Terry Tafoya Earp called *Laura's House* to TENAZ XVI in San Antonio). New York Puerto Rican Rosalba Rolón codirects the very active Pregones in the South Bronx. Former El Teatro Campesino member Diane Rodriguez is now at the Los Angeles Music Center's Mark Taper Forum. She cofounded the very popular, professional Los Angeles-based comedy group Latins Anonymous (Louisa Leschin, Armando Molina, and formerly Rick Najera, now Chris Franco).

One-person shows and individual performance artists have begun to carve a space for their often transgressive art form. Carmelita Tropicana with her *Milk Of Amnesia*, Monica Palacios with *Greetings From A Queer Señorita*, and Coco Fusco and Nao Bustamante's *Stuff* are prime examples.[37]

This new generation of Latina/Hispanic/Chicana playwrights, directors, and independent performance artists are deeply aware of their talent and their potential. Their voices, however, are not homogeneous. Some are deeply committed to community-based theater, others court the professional stage, and yet others prefer an experimental, mixed-media approach. Ideologically, they differ. Josefina López and Dolores Prida both rebutted Moraga's comments at TENAZ XVI that as Latinas, what we are "allowed" to write are comedies, implying that this form is "light" and inconsequential. "Through the comedy," said Josefina López, "you can slip in many more things than you can if you were serious… You get them laughing, then soon they stop and think: Oh, my God what am I laughing at?" (TENAZ XVI Women Playwrights'

Forum, November 12, 1992). Prida, on the other hand, takes the position—following that of Maria Irene Fornés—that being "Hispanic" or "Latina" is not the most important thing about her work. Performance artist Belinda Acosta discussed the difficulty of being published as an experimental Chicana writer/performer. Actresses in the audience asked the playwrights to create more challenging roles for them, and to get them published and available.

Once the lack of Latino and Latina talent on the professional stage was explained as a lack of refined or professionally trained talent. Now Latinas are challenging this, and claim their ability to write, produce, and direct plays. It is the strong wave of college-educated, professionally trained Latinas, not men, who are in the vanguard of this challenge. They often make alliances with ethnic and non-ethnic women's groups in order to find a space for their work. (Cherríe Moraga and Caridad Svich are examples.) However, there are two fields yet to be "cracked": mainstream producing organizations and the publishing industry. All of the women playwrights at the 1992 TENAZ are profoundly aware that they will not exist in the histories of theater unless their work is published. They have learned the lessons of history well by analyzing the scant historical material published not only about Hispanic women in theater but about all women in theater. Although women in *teatro* today no longer need to marry into it or own a company in order to be able to direct it, we are still subject to a number of hegemonies, from insidious, institutional patriarchies (academic and professional) to the commercial marketplace economy.

The preservation of the past historical record of Latino cultures in the United States is an urgent task that has been undertaken by a number of historically oriented literary projects.[38] However, another urgent need exists: that of documenting the historical present as it unfolds. I pose to you the following question: What kind of a history could our great-grandchildren be able to reconstruct from the present coverage by either Spanish- or English-language newspapers, magazines and journals of Chicana/Latina theater in the United States since 1960? Even the well-intentioned feminist theater critic Sue-Ellen Case, after devoting a chapter to "Women of Color and Theater" in her 1988 ground-breaking book *Feminism and Theater* comes to the following conclusion: "Though Chicanas in theater have created an organization for their needs as well as their own form, they do not enjoy a stable of playwrights."[39] I am pleased to be able to emphasize (and I believe Professor Case would also be pleased) that the content of this paper emphatically does not corroborate her statement. However, it is understandable how she came to this conclusion: there is a severe lack of publications that focus on contemporary developments in *teatro*, particularly the centrality of Latinas.

Women have always been resourceful in the development of ways to insert themselves onto the center stage. The urgent task now is to recognize and publish this historical fact.

Author's Note

A version of this paper was originally delivered at the University of Houston, November 21, 1992, at "A Joint Conference: Recovering the U.S. Hispanic Literary Heritage and Two Decades of *The Americas Review*," coordinated by Teresa Marrero, Recovering the U.S. Hispanic Literary Heritage Project coordinator, and Marina Tristán, assistant director, Arte Público Press. The three-day conference was sponsored by the Rockefeller Foundation, the Texas Committee for the Humanities, Arte Público Press, AT&T, Tenneco Oil, and Exxon.

Notes

1. Although Estela Portillo Trambley, Maria Irene Fornés, and Dolores Prida have had anthologies of their work published, it was not until 1992 that the first anthology of several Chicana and Latina playwrights (*Shattering the Myth: Plays by Hispanic Women*, Arte Público Press) was published.
2. Rudolf Arnheim, *The Power of the Center: A Study of Composition in the Visual Arts* (Berkeley: University of California Press, 1982), 2.
3. Arnheim, 2.
4. Chicanas Yvonne Yarbro-Bejarano and Yolanda Broyles-González have led the way in the area of scholarly research. Cherríe Moraga's work crosses the boundaries between the creative, the feminist, and the scholarly. Anglo feminist Sue-Ellen Case devotes a chapter to women of color in theater in her book *Feminism and Theater* (London:

Macmillan, 1988). I have been devoting attention to the work of emerging playwrights, such as Chicana Josefina López, New York Puerto Rican Lynette Serrano-Bonaparte, and Cuban-American Caridad Svich; the performance work of the Chicana/multiethnic collective Las Comadres; and the work of director Laura Esparza.

5. Nicolás Kanellos, *A History of Hispanic Theater in the United States: Origins to 1940* (Austin: University of Texas Press, 1990).

6. I have conducted field research in Latino theater since 1984, concentrating primarily on a number of playwrights' laboratories designed to polish and professionalize the talent of emerging Hispanic/Latino and Latina playwrights in California, New York, and, recently, Texas. However, I am also familiar with the work of community-based *teatros* nationwide.

7. Kanellos, 8.

8. See the *Los Angeles Times* Calendar, June 9, 1991, p. 8, headline story "Pretty Powerful Woman," by Elaine Dutka.

9. The concept of "honor" is a thoroughly documented social phenomenon predominant in traditional Spanish-speaking societies on both sides of the Atlantic.

10. More than one hundred years later the legitimation of a woman's social position through marriage has not disappeared. Feminist writers, such as Susan Faludi allege that women actually have lost ground since the 1980s in almost all areas of public life: from reproduction rights to equal opportunity to wages. See Susan Faludi, *Backlash: The Undeclared War Against American Women* (New York: Crown Books, 1991; second editon, New York: Doubleday Anchor Books, 1992).

11. Kanellos, 93.

12. Kanellos, 38.

13. Tomás Ybarra-Frausto, "La Chata Noloesca: La figura del donaire," in *Mexican American Theater, Then and Now,* ed. N. Kanellos (Houston: Arte Público Press, 1983), 45–46.

14. Ybarra-Frausto, 49.

15. Kanellos, 19.

16. Armando Miguelea, "El Teatro Carmen (1915–1923): El Centro de Arte Escenico en Tucson," in *Mexican American Theater, Then and Now,* ed. N. Kanellos (Houston: Arte Público Press, 1983), 52–67.

17. Kanellos, 111.

18. Kanellos, 114. The organizational structure of Kanellos's account, by geographic location—in other words, by local city activity, gathered from local archival collections—makes the tracking of key personal figures extremely difficult. For instance, in the case of Pilar Arcos, she is mentioned on fifteen separate pages, often with little filling the gaps between the occurrences of each mention. Therefore, what happened between her directorship of the Compañía Española Arcos-Sardina

and the emergence of the Compañías Unidas is not clear. This may also be due to the lack of primary information.

19. Kanellos, 144.

20. John C. Miller, "Hispanic Theatre in New York, 1965–1977," *Revista Chicano-Riqueña* 9 (1978): 40–59.

21. Roberta Fernández's paper was delivered at the University of Houston, November 20, 1992, at "A Joint Conference: Recovering the U.S. Hispanic Literary Heritage and Two Decades of *The Americas Review.*"

22. I would argue against Linda Gordon's point in "What's New in Women's History" that "naming the new women's history 'herstory' does us no favor," *Feminist Studies/Critical Studies* (1986): 20. I would agree with her, however, that women's stories are part of the overall historical narratives, and not a separate (but unequal?) story line.

23. Yolanda Broyles-González, "Women in El Teatro Campesino: '¿Apoco estaba molacha la Virgen de Guadalupe?,' " in *Chicana Voices: Intersections of Class, Race and Gender* (Colorado Springs: National Association for Chicano Studies, 1990), 163.

24. Broyles-González, 165.

25. Broyles-González, 166.

26. Diane Rodriguez's acting career can be traced through the whole *teatro* movement: she began with El Teatro Campesino, later joined Teatro de la Esperanza, and subsequently has worked in films, television, commercials, and *teatro.*

27. Personal interview with Diane Rodriguez, August 1990, University of California, Irvine.

28. The Valentina Productions members were Irene Burgos, Rosie Campos-Pantoja, Clara Hill de Castañón, Liz Robinson, and Juanita Vargas.

29. Yvonne Yarbro-Bejarano, *"Teatropoesia* by Chicanas in the Bay Area: 'Tongues of Fire,'" in *Mexican American Theater, Then and Now,* ed. N. Kanellos (Houston: Arte Público Press, 1983), 80.

30. *Border Boda* by Las Comadres (1990). I conducted an interview with Laura Esparza in August 1990. See also Marguerite Waller, *"Border Boda* or *Divorce* Fronterizo?," in *Negotiating Performance: Gender, Sexuality, and Theatricality in Latin/o America,* ed. Diana Taylor and Juan Villegas (Durham: Duke University Press, 1994), 67–87.

31. Eddie Sánchez has a beautiful play called *Trafficking in Broken Hearts,* in which the characters—three men—are gay. The play represents these characters' sexuality in a direct but not explicit manner. The subject is not homosexuality itself, but the lives of three men who are homosexual. The play received a second public stage reading at the South Coast Repertory Hispanics Playwrights' Lab in 1989. In my most recent communication with Eddie Sánchez, he told me that this play has not been blessed with production offers. His subsequent play, *Doña Flor and Her Trained Dog,* a psychological drama of *implied* incest and

homosexuality, has fared much better. This says something about the way in which producing organizations believe that the public will "buy" a homosexual theme.

32. The Puerto Rican Traveling Theatre's address is 141 West 94th Street, New York, N.Y 10025.

33. From a press release, "About the Puerto Rican Traveling Theatre: History and Purpose." I received the packet of information from Vera Ryan, Development Department of the PRTT, dated January 18, 1988, after a visit to the theater in New York.

34. Her first play, *Tango Palace,* appeared in 1963. Other titles include *Promenade, Fefu and Her Friends, Mud, Sarita, The Danube, Abigdon Square,* and *The Conduct of Life.* She directs her own work, and has presented her plays at the Theater for the New City (New York), at INTAR, and at the Padua Hills Playwrights' Festival in Claremont, California.

35. Jorge Huerta's comment corroborates my personal observation at the TENAZ XVI International Festival of Chicano/Latino Theater, held at the Guadalupe Cultural Arts Center in San Antonio, Texas, November 10–15, 1992.

36. Elizabeth Osborn, *On New Ground: Contemporary Hispanic American Plays* (New York: Theater Communications Group, 1987), vi–viii.

37. For an anthology of Latina/o performance art, see Teresa Marrero and Caridad Svich, *Out of the Fringe.* New York: Theater Communications Group, Fall 1999.

38. For example, Henry Louis Gates's Afro-American Periodicals Project and Nicolás Kanellos's Recovering the U.S. Hispanic Literary Heritage Project.

39. Sue-Ellen Case, *Feminism and Theatre* (London: Macmillan, 1988), 109. Professor Case teaches theater at the University of California, Davis. We met during a quarter-long focused research seminar, Contemporary Latin American and Chicano/Latino Theater at the University of California, Irvine, in the fall of 1990. Although not an expert in this field, her very valuable contributions came from a feminist perspective. In her chapter on women of color, Professor Case discusses the difficulty she experienced in finding printed materials by and about Chicana/Latina women in theater.

Contextualizing Chicanas: The Emerging Female as Subject on the American Stage during the Mexican Revolution

Elizabeth Ramírez

U.S. Latinas/os are the fastest-growing population group in the United States today, and Chicanas/os constitute the largest particular ethnic group in the Southwest.[1] Some important sociological and political histories about this presence have emerged in recent years and have brought about a better understanding of Chicana/Chicano contributions to U.S. and world history.[2] In theatrical history, scholars have only begun to investigate Chicana/Chicano participation and to make information available in English about this activity. Clearly, further research is needed in order to comprehend the vast richness of this particular tradition.

During the nineteenth century, and even earlier, the Spanish-language professional acting companies that arrived in the United States from Mexico formed a lasting tradition. This theatrical heritage stemmed from a long history of both amateur and professional Spanish-language activity, originating in Spain. Few scholars have noted that the Golden Age of Spain coincided with the entry of Spain into the New World. The conquistadores' arrival in New Spain awoke an interest in dramatic literature. More significantly, the conquistadores also gave the first dramatic performances on American soil.

Although chronicled in the first volume of G. C. D. Odell's *Annals of the New York Stage,* theater historians rarely mention Spain's unique contribution to American theater and its impact on the New World. Overall, scholars are just beginning to investigate the rich performance heritage of indigenous Americans, since before the conquest, from the Mayan and Aztec, to the Chicana/Chicano oral traditions. Clearly, this unique theatrical heritage has made significant contributions to the annals of theater history, but we must continue to broaden the scope of this historical inquiry.[3]

Although my research on the history of Mexican-American professional theater in Texas has uncovered a distinct tradition of dramatic acting companies that lasted from 1875 to 1935, further research on this particular activity now reveals significant contributions by women to this tradition; furthermore, these have yet to be chronicled in English.[4] One such example occurs around the time of the Mexican Revolution, a period in which radical structural, demographic, and behavioral changes within U.S. history stand out.

The history of Chicanas and other Latinas in theater in the United States during the period of the Mexican Revolution has not undergone a detailed analysis. What were the cultural, social, historical, and political effects on a people who had been under a dictatorship, left it behind, and emerged within a democratic society in the United States? The time during the years of Mexican turmoil, 1910 to 1924, may serve to judge the effects of a changing political, social, and cultural milieu that has yet to be investigated in relation to U.S. history. In regard to theater history, Chicanas participated in a major theatrical movement in the United States during this time, and their distinct role in this period of upheaval can be analyzed in order to comprehend the significance of women in this history.

Although the Mexican and Spanish professional theatrical companies established a long tradition in the United States, the effects on these groups of moving from a dictatorship to a democratic society have yet to be analyzed in terms of theatrical activity. Because women played an important part within this legacy, this article will attempt to reveal their impact through an examination of language, gender, race and ethnicity, politics, and performance. Although no known plays by women are available, women's unique place within the cultural, social, and political context in which they appeared in performance may be evaluated in order to understand the broader sociocultural implications of their work. This study thus begins to contribute to the goals of American Studies and Cultural Studies to focus on a broad understanding of all aspects of American cultures.

We have extant play texts from this period of a great influx of immigration into the United States from Mexico, which can serve to document the broader Latina contributions to American theater. By contextualizing the emerging Chicana during this time of political crisis, we can begin to unveil and understand the role these women played in theater history. Through this analysis of two extant play collections available at the Mexican American Project Special Collection of the University of Texas at Austin, Benson Latin American Collection, we can begin to understand how women were placed as subjects in the reconstruction of the immigrant newcomers' fusion of "old and new behavioral strategies to meet the continuing demands of survival." Although these plays are known to have been performed in Texas, there is evidence of a broader presence outside the state as well.[5]

In the drama that appeared on the Mexican-American stage during the Mexican Revolution, women's roles were largely constructed and controlled by male dramatists. Their drama was rooted in romantic tragedy that idealized the past through connections with Mexico as the mother country. The representation of women on this stage reveals how the female body and subject were used as tools of cultural and social formation and as a political weapon in support of sustaining ties with the past, reconnecting with the old order, and constructing a new community. Given the importance of the visual gaze in relation to desire and object, and amid this culturally specific political climate, Jill Dolan's questions are especially pertinent to this study: "How does a given performance—the dialogue, choice of setting, narrative voice, form, content, casting, acting, blocking—deliver its ideological message? How does it convey its assumptions about its relation to social structures?"[6]

The promptbook of *La Llorona,* a four-act drama in verse by Francisco C. Neve, was copied by Luis Hernández in San Antonio, Texas, on 31 August 1911. Hernández was one of the members of the Compañía Hernández-Villalongín, a company that performed in and around the northern provinces of Mexico and in Texas, until the Mexican Revolution made the company decide, in 1911, to reside permanently in Texas. One of the surviving informants and several supporting documents and reviews indicate the popularity of this play. The Compañía Hernández-Villalongín was only one among several that produced this work. In the case of the Compañía Hernández-Villalongín, we know that the play was produced often and with great success.[7]

The story of "La Llorona," "The Weeping Woman," is an old and well-known tale among Mexican people. Clarissa Pinkola

Estés, in *Women Who Run with The Wolves,* notes that although some say the tale originated in the early 1500s, when the conquistadores invaded the Aztec/Náhuatl peoples of Mexico, the story is far older. In some cases, the story is related to that of La Malinche, the native woman thought to have been the translator and lover of the Spanish conqueror Hernán Cortés. Whenever it originated, the story itself may have to do with a woman haunting a river in search of her children.

In a tale bearing similarities to the Medea story, a poor woman bears a rich Spanish nobleman two sons before he announces that he will return to Spain to marry a rich woman chosen by his family. Knowing he will take his sons with him, the young, virtuous woman attacks him savagely, and, in her crazed state, takes her two sons to the river and throws them in. The children drown and she expires in her grief. Instead of being allowed directly into heaven, however, she must first find the souls of her children in the river. Thus the woman is said to be constantly searching for these lost souls.

When this story is told, it is generally related as a warning for children to stay away from the river after dark, in case the weeping woman mistakes them for her own children and takes them away instead. Estés includes various modern versions of this tale, and adds that this kind of "river story" overtly entertains, but is meant to cause listeners "to experience a shiver of awareness that leads to thoughtfulness, contemplation, and action."[8]

The plot of the popular romantic tragedy differs from the folktale in several ways. The playtext of *La Llorona* seems to indicate that prevailing themes and ideas were transformed by the repertory of resident companies in order to make the story distinctly specific; after all, the story was speaking to a displaced people living outside of their homeland. Because the play was performed immediately after the first wave of exiles reached San Antonio, this method of address to Chicanos stands out in its politically manipulative discourse aimed at a newly forming marginalized group.

Francisco C. Neve's tragedy revolves around Ramiro, the son of "Hernando" Cortés, obviously implying a reference to the historical figure Hernán Cortés. Here, Ramiro has a son by Luisa, someone he met in "el Oriente," that is, the Orient/East, during "an orgy born one morning...amidst the vapors of wine."

In his delirium, he saw a bright light shine upon his encounter with this "kneeling angel of God." Although he loves Luisa, the demands from his mother and his status as a Spanish nobleman require that he marry a noblewoman, serving as "a soldier for his country and for the Cross." When Luisa discovers that Ramiro plans to take his son with him, she kills the child in a crazed frenzy resulting from this rejection, and is hung for her crime.[9]

Zavala, newly arrived in "New Spain" (Mexico), has also been struck by this "perfection" from the Orient. In Zavala, Luisa has someone to avenge her death. As her servants affirm "the tale told in the barrio," the ghost of their mistress, with a dead child in her right hand, walks at the stroke of midnight. Zavala leads Ramiro to see the haunting figure of Luisa lamenting for her lost child. Zavala, who once saved Ramiro's life, now serves as Ramiro's conscience and seeks retribution for Luisa's sake, making him confront his deed. In his remorse, Ramiro expires upon hearing La Llorona's "sorrowful lament."

Luisa appears on the Texas stage during a time of political unrest. As Jameson suggests, instead of examining "the denunciation of the centered subject and its ideologies," we should study "the subject's historical emergence, its constitution or virtual construction as a mirage," which may also stand as "an objective reality."[10] It thus seems that what needs to be analyzed here is how the figure of Luisa is being presented to the Mexican populace in their exiled state. In regard to "the weeping woman," we must ask, Why is Luisa from the Orient? What representation emerges with a figure that Zavala ridicules as "the inheritor of that valor of the great progenitor that put a world at his feet," referring to Ramiro who is, on the other hand, described by a courtier as "the son of the great Cortés and richest inheritor?" Why is the avenger coming from the colonizer's homeland?

This play was chosen by a male actor–manager to be presented for a Spanish-speaking audience that was composed of at least three distinct groups: they belonged to an immigrant group newly arrived in a land formerly part of their past, or to a native population that had always lived in their own land, or to a group newly exiled from Mexico because of political strife. Just as Said views "the Orient that appears in Orientalism" as a "system of representations framed by a whole set of forces that brought the

Orient into Western learning, Western consciousness, and later, Western empire," here Orientalism emerges as a distinct product of political forces and activities that cannot be overlooked.[11] Luisa's Orientalism stands out as difference, as sensuality, as something separate, and, ultimately, as something that can be abused and destroyed but never legitimized. She is positioned as the weak outsider who seems to give power and superiority to Ramiro, who represents the imperial Western European oppressor. Luisa has been displaced, and only someone who can understand displacement, such as Zavala, who is struggling with his own disassociation from his homeland, can defend her.

Zavala recognizes that, just as he was awakened by the brilliant sunshine from "el Oriente," reputed to be the place of "pleasure of Mexican mornings," so too his "will" has been subjugated" by something "grand and fierce" in Luisa; he has been drawn "like a magnet to steel."[12] Ramiro, on the other hand, is always drawn by the power of her love for him and his own desire to own her, but he remains the disreputable "mal hombre" or "evil male" throughout, not only the destructive imperialist but also the conqueror of her very soul. In effect, by this portrayal of Ramiro on the Spanish-language stage, the colonizer emblematically retains the space of the dominant force over the weaker, or underdeveloped, regions, such as the Orient or the dark passages in which Luisa appears only elusively.

What, then, does this tale tell us about the sociopolitical and cultural status of Chicanos in the Southwest during the Revolution? As already noted, Mexicans were coming in droves into the promised land, searching for economic opportunities, exiled from their motherland, or already permanent residents of the United States. In the case of the large number of men leaving Mexico and remaining in the United States, we may view the drama as a means to remind them about the need to keep the family together. But this view can be sustained only if we allow Luisa to represent the Mexican woman as the outsider, the non-American, the one left behind who may, in the end, no longer be attainable.

Unquestionably, Ramiro emerges as the villain with regard to both women. He not only disrupts his contractual agreement with Luisa, which was made under the eyes of God, but he also disrupts his man-made contract with Ana, which was made through legal marriage in the Church. In contrast to this despicable male figure, the image of woman is constructed as honorable and morally flawless. Both Luisa, from the lower class, and Ana, from the nobility, are portrayed as absolutely virtuous in character. Although Luisa has obviously sinned by slaying her child, it is clear that circumstances led her to an understandable and unavoidable moment of insanity, and she visibly suffers greatly for her wrongdoing. The image of honor is reinforced when Luisa appears as the ghost figure at the end in the emblematic garb of "Justice." A woman symbolizing a divine justice that is ultimately avenged, she walks in front of Ramiro, the bloody clothes of her dead child in her right hand.

Perhaps the voice of the male dramatist supports the lament that women must suffer at the hands of men, but another message seems to be at play here as well. It seems that the audience is also being reminded that leaving one's distanced and elusive place of origin will undoubtedly bring suffering, as both Luisa and Zavala illustrate. Luisa has left the Orient, and Zavala, his native Spain. Zavala says, "Why did I leave my enchanted land?"[13]

Noticeably missing is the river imagery, which plays such a significant part in the folktale as we hear it even today in the Southwest. That omission may signify a permanent rupture with Mexico, given the Rio Grande's role as a geographic and symbolic border. Or, more likely, it may indicate the fact that the border was not the inclusive or exclusive barrier that Mexicans would encounter later.[14] The river is simply not an issue in this play, and perhaps it was not an issue in those times; the important message seems to be one directly targeting that large population mentioned earlier, men who had left families behind in Mexico and would not always return.

The warning may be that the search for a life of wealth and a new homeland may cause severe loss: loss of family, roots, and culture. The strongest message may be that these men should sustain their family ties; regardless of the seemingly insurmountable obstacles set before them. These obstacles might include other women with more money or offering better living conditions, or, in the case of women, being used by white men and then forgotten, or intermarrying and severing their ties with their blood families.

Another message is connected to religious belief for a strong adherence to Catholicism and is evident throughout. The young child is described as being "like an angel of the Spanish Virgin," and Ramiro says he serves his country and "the Cross."[15] There are continual laments to God and to heaven for justice and peace. Zavala's final appeal for eternal justice coincides with a lament for pity from heaven on those below. Although Mexicans were Catholics traditionally, the Catholic faith had helped to unite rural and urban Mexicans, and even helped to bring them together in support of traditional ways of doing things.[16] Thus Catholicism became suspect in the eyes of the rebel leadership. It is not surprising, then, that these performances, situated on the U.S. side, promoted Catholicism, for they were presented primarily to the growing number of exiles that were from the upper class, which was aligned with the fallen Díaz regime.

Other themes are family duty, defending one's honor, parental pressure, and the dangers of resistance. In all of these matters, Zavala continually offers Luisa a better life far away in his homeland. By distancing Spain, political references emerge, such as a notable rising unrest among some Indians that is sharply censured by the aristocracy in the drama, in contrast with the Creoles, who are described as "men of valor and prestige" in their defense of King Philip II.[17] Such a defense of patriots obviously spoke directly to those exiled former defenders of the dictatorship.

In regard to race and class, not only does the verse form call considerable attention to class distinctions, but the overall story makes specific distinctions of status. Luisa comes from the lower class and speaks in prose with the servants, but her speech becomes noticeably loftier verse when in the company of Ramiro. Her material and class gains are marked not only through language; her devaluation emerges as well in her subjugated status as mistress. Although she is worthless to Ramiro in terms of class and race, when he recognizes that his line will end with him, he decides that he must take his child from Luisa. The entire weight of race and nobility lies in his role as descendant of Cortés, and he cannot allow that lineage to end.

This connection to Cortés continually recalls the mythology of La Malinche as the primary informant to the telling of the weeping woman story. Jean Franco, in *Plotting Women: Gender and Representation in Mexico,* describes the figure of La Malinche as "the medium for conquest." Franco also says, "The scarcity of documentation enabled her to become a literary function (the 'helper' of the hero story), the medium-translator (traitor) of conquest and the flawed origin (mother) of a nation who would make her the symbol of the schizophrenic split between the European and the indigenous."[18] Luisa's role as subject on stage, like La Malinche, is to represent someone who has sold out her own race, perhaps reminding the audience that intermarriage is as fatal and tragic as the drama itself. As Franco notes, Octavio Paz, in *The Labyrinth of Solitude,* located the "Mexican disease" precisely "in this ambiguous subjectivity of the sons of the Malinche who were shamed by her rape (conquest) and thus forced to reject the feminine in themselves as the devalued, the passive, the mauled and battered, as *La chingada,* the violated, the one who has been screwed over, fucked, and yet is herself the betrayer" (xix). La Malinche became Cortés's mistress and interpreter, bore him a son, and continued to serve as interpreter after being exchanged and given in marriage to one of his captains. Just as La Malinche is inextricably tied to Cortés, La Llorona is bound to Cortés through his descendants.

The role of La Malinche as the "site of representation of sexuality for a culture" is an area that Yvonne Yarbro-Bejarano has studied in relation to female constructs in contemporary Chicano theater. Yarbro-Bejarano views this figure as a means of shedding light on the construction of gender. Thus, through her sexual union with the white conqueror, "the defeat of a people and the destruction of their culture" ensued, producing the "half-breed," or mestizo, race. La Malinche thus becomes emblematic of the construction of " 'woman' as object, as other, reserving the active subject role for the masculine gender."[19]

Verena Stolcke goes even further in her analysis of this role of La Malinche in regard to Latina/Latino representation. In her article "Invaded Women: Gender, Race, and Class in the Formation of Colonial Society," Stolcke begins a much-needed examination of more far-reaching, ideological dimensions of the conquest than sexual violence. Her exploration focuses on how social and racial conceptualizations brought over by the colonizer were disseminated and transformed by colonial elites, and how these changing values affected women in particular. In this process, certain conceptualizations were reformulated, adapted to local circumstances in order to legitimize and perpetuate a new hierarchical social order.[20]

The role of "woman" in La *Llorona* is rather ambiguous, because Luisa is always referred to as good, honorable, and an angel with "Roman virtue," but in using her to construct a national identity, she further represents a displaced, distanced, and strange woman from the Orient that seems to mold different races into one. If she is responsible not only for killing the legitimate heir of Cortés but also his child, then her treachery is comparable to the conquest and defeat of Mexico itself. The power her figure wields here contains the ability to eradicate an entire nation. Luisa, then, like La Malinche, is made to bear the burden of responsiblity for a people's fall. However, the play also presents her as an angel figure, allowing her to appear as the almost mythical counterfigure of La Malinche, who is also responsible for the end of this lineage.

The larger discourse, however, seems to revolve around an even more prominent issue, the fact that the downfall occurs because the family unit has been so severely ruptured that it cannot ever be reconstructed. The fact that the family unit was changing was evident even as early as 1911. As Elaine Showalter points out, although most of the women in the work force at the turn of the century were certainly no threat economically, a few privileged and exceptional women were alarming for men to contemplate. In the case of Chicanas, they were just entering the work force in San Antonio, largely in such jobs as pecan shellers, garment workers, and maids. Why, then, would they, as Chicanas and women, be perceived as the "potential disrupters of masculine boundary systems of all sorts?"[21] Elaine Showalter suggests that women have "traditionally been perceived as figures of disorder" due to the fact that "women's social or cultural marginality seems to place them on the borderlines of the symbolic order, both the 'frontier between men and chaos,' and dangerously part of chaos itself, inhabitants of a mysterious and frightening wild zone outside of patriarchal culture."[22] But the overall message of La *Llorona* seems to be that of reaffirming the importance of the family. Showalter quotes the Reverend W. Arthur in 1885: "In all countries the purity of the family must be the surest strength of a nation." And family strength is constructed as being dependent upon steadfast gender roles which, as the play suggests, were publically encoded and enforced.

The investigation of the emerging Chicana as subject on the American stage can go even further by examining another playtext, *La mujer adúltera (The Adulterous Woman)*. This four-act drama, with a seven-scene prologue, written by Juan P. Velásquez, contextualizes the Chicana in an even broader landscape than the earlier text allowed. The promptbook, dated 1907, lists the itinerary of a tour taken by the Compáñía Villalongín y Guzman in 1916. The tour included unspecified cities in Arizona (21 February), as well as Cananea, Sonora (25 February), and Nogales (29 February), although it is not indicated whether it was Nogales, Mexico, or Nogales, Arizona. Hence, this playtext is representative of work that appeared at the peak of the period under discussion.

La mujer adúltera is set in Santillana del Mar (a town found in the region of Santander, Spain). This setting is relevant, because the Spanish colonists in New Spain took its name for a new military settlement that extended from the northern Mexican region of what is now Tamaulipas to the lower Rio Grande valley on the Texas side, from Laredo to the Gulf of Mexico, or "Mexican Sea." Magdalena, described as the "pearl" of her surroundings, has an unclear origin, but she seems to have come from the sea. In this play, water and sea imagery have an important function. Described as unusually ambitious, and apparently with a mind of her own, Magdalena is no sooner married to Angel than Fernando, a wealthy nobleman who has seen her portrait, proclaims that he must have her. Fernando comes to claim her, and she leaves her new husband for a presumably better life.

Always unsettled and haunted by her deception and abandonment of her husband, she is soon confronted with her past. Although it had been reported that Angel was lost at sea, he soon reappears. An artist had captured her with her husband on her wedding day. This portrait has been exhibited at a highly publicized Exposition and she fears being discovered upon hearing that the painting has been bought. She soon learns that Angel is alive when he confronts her as Sandoval. When Magdalena begs forgiveness, as God forgave Maria Magdalena, Angel tells her that even Maria Magdalena sought peace before she was forgiven.

Upon discovering that Angel is still alive, Fernando abruptly abandons Magdalena. She, in turn, begins to seek peace and forgiveness. She goes to her father, who reveals that her own mother was also an adulteress. Her father has gone insane from the shock of his daughter's infamy. She then goes to Angel to ask that he forgive Fernando, who robbed her of happiness. She begs Angel not to seek revenge. Angel reveals that Fernando has died, and that he has forgiven him. Achieving the peace she desires, Magdalena expires, thanking Angel and asking for his pardon even at the end. Angel's final words are that she dies just as his hope has died, and he asks God to pardon her as he has.

In both of these plays, men have plotted women. It is significant that in one, the female figure appears as a virtuous victim, and in the other, she appears as an opportunistic adulteress. In both cases, the women suffer and die without attaining happiness on Earth and without final absolution for their sins. How male dramatists have written these women and the fact that male actor-managers have chosen to illustrate them on the stage may shed light on how gender is to used to represent the problems of the Mexican nation as a whole. The fact that neither of these gender representations achieves emancipation may, in fact, be inextricably bound up with the fate of the larger community and the censuring of behavioral patterns in both men and women as Mexicans became more firmly entrenched in their new country.

Jean Franco reminds us that "the constitution of Mexican nationalism was a long process that had its roots in the criollo nationalism before Independence and that received a new impetus with the Mexican Revolution during its earlier segment, that is, 1910–1917, a revolution in which the peasantry played a major role." With the postrevolutionary society came a populist nationalism that tended to obscure the Mexican state as an instrument of capitalist modernization. Starting in 1917, women were on their way to attaining the national vote, with the issue of women's emancipation a "part of a major campaign against the obscurantism of the Church, and some revolutionary leaders supported emancipation because they saw women's religious fanaticism as an obstacle to revolutionary ideology." Supporters of women's emancipation included men such as Venustiano Carranza, the first president of postrevolutionary Mexico. Yet official ideology would return to the idealized patriarchal family that the literature under examination here supports. Recording women's stories was obviously obscured by the political aspects that dominated both the new social order in the United States and Mexico's emerging modernization and populist nationalism.[23]

In the case of *La mujer adúltera,* specific textual references indicate that the intent is to provide parallels between the homeland and America. Not only is there the direct connection between Santander, Spain, and the "New Santander" of the borderlands, but other links between Spain and "New Spain" also abound.

A missionary arrives from California, giving good counsel to Magdalena; Angel has been away at sea near Ecuador, and when Angel visits Fernando, the Compañía Villalongín y Guzman's copy indicates a textual change from Fernando's reference that Angel comes from "another world" to "America." This historical attention to place seems to want to imply the United States as center. Its dominant representation is in contrast to the marginalized Other in the unspecified outer boundaries that mark Magdalena and Angel, both having emerged from that unknown place of the sea.

It seems most apparent that the heavy emphasis on water imagery calls specific attention to the fact that the border was now firmly entrenched; the water imagery is a signifier of loss of country, rupture with one's homeland, and a place of racial inferiority. Moreover, with Magdalena stemming from those unknown depths, her function as a disrupter of domesticity is apparent. Unquestionably, she has violated the marriage contract and permanently severed relations not only with her family but with the extended family that surrounds her. Her actions affect Angel's parents and their relations in the community, and she causes an even further disjuncture with her father, who is also a friend of the larger family. By the very fact that Angel, too, serves as a subsequent disrupter of the presumed safe haven of feigned marriage and family that Fernando and Magdalena represent, we find that this drama serves as a representative of an ideology that places the family unit at the core of community; it is only through its cohesive force that chaos and tragedy can be avoided.

In trying to understand gender representation on this stage, it is important to consider the role of women as performing subjects. One known star in the roles of Luisa and Magdalena was Concepción Hernández. She was the leading actress in the Cornpañía Villalongín, and she also represents the performers who remained in Texas to continue a theatrical tradition through the resident company. Thus she is one of the first Chicanas on the American stage.

The features most often noted by newspaper critics were an actress's intelligence, ability to comprehend her part, and skill in presenting a well-studied role with clarity in diction, all of which Hernández accomplished on the stage. However, her primary strength was a unique vocal range. In one review, she was said to have had a "potent voice" that "ranged from a ferocious roar of injured dignity; to the soft cooing and billing of a dove, sweet and harmonious, as a murmur of breezes from the fjords," when the character she portrayed, "for the first time…felt the beating in her heart of the sweet sensations of true love."[24] The style of the period required that the declamatory actress perform in moral and instructive dramas, suitable for the entire family. The fact that Concepción Hernández was performing in a family enterprise, always accompanied by her mother, sisters, and other relatives, probably enhanced the image of wholesome entertainment that the Compañía Villalongín was said to have provided. In Concepción Hernández, the reinforcement of family as a visual ideological site was further sustained both in front of and behind the footlights.

Hernández's training began in childhood, and she grew into the parts she played. Her parents were actors and managers of the Compañía Hernández prior to its merger with the Compañía Villalongín. Concepción's sister, Herlinda, was also an actress, but upon her marriage to Carlos Villalongín, Herlinda turned her attention to other matters, such as rearing nine children. Thus Concepción was almost exclusively the leading lady of the company, and she served as a role model for her niece, María Luisa Villalongín, who grew into Concepción's roles. Among Concepción's principal roles were María Antonietta, La Llorona, and Doña Inés in *Don Juan Tenorio*.[25]

The Mexican Revolution had caused Carlos Villalongín, his family, and some other actors to remain in San Antonio, where the company performed at the Teatro Aurora, instead of returning to Coahuila, where the company had held temporary residence. Coahuila was among the northern Mexican provinces that were at the heart of the political struggle of the time. Thus the Mexican Revolution enabled the tradition of Spanish-language drama to continue on the American stage through resident companies. Carlos Villalongín's children, among them my informants, were among the first known Spanish-language performers born in the United States. María Luisa Villalongín de Santos, who still resides in San Antonio, was among them.

Several individual performers and performances made important contributions to the theater. The professional Spanish-language companies were instrumental in introducing and popularizing new ideas and practices, and women made distinct contributions as actresses, managers, and part of the family nucleus that composed these companies. How these women were read within the roles they performed has yet to be examined fully. In the case of the period being discussed, women as subjects were placed within a context that had a serious and deep-rooted cultural, social, and political impact on the audiences they served.

Some of the problems theater historians often encounter in trying to assess the contributions of women lie in the evaluation of extant data. For example, in Nicholas Kanellos's book *A History of Hispanic Theater in the United States: Origins to 1940*, (Austin: University of Texas Press, 1990), his discussion of activity in San Antonio seems to dismiss completely the leading actress and her place in history. Nevertheless, enough evidence exists to substantiate the significant role of Chicanas/ Latinas in American history, even if some writers fail to assess them properly.

Mexican-American theater thrived for a long time in Texas. It died down during the Depression and arose again in the 1960s with the Chicano theater movement. Luis Valdez, the director of El Teatro Campesino, and other Chicano dramatists and performers have looked to pre-Columbian rituals and ceremonies, along with the amateur dramatic tradition, as the primary sources from which to draw. Yet the period of Mexican revolt may also serve as a rich resource for those groups. Contemporary Chicano theater companies, always in search of plays drawn from their own experience and background, can draw from this source of plays and performance tradition and reinterpret these works for contemporary audiences, as many resident companies throughout the country are doing with the classics of world drama. More broadly, it is time to challenge what Oscar G. Brockett describes as the "consensus" point of view in history, the preoccupation with tracing the development of the mainstream English-language stage.[26]

We must expand the scope of historical inquiry by including such traditions as those provided by Chicanas/Latinas on the American stage if we are to reveal the multicultural richness of our past. We cannot afford to omit, disregard, or misinterpret the significance of women in theater history. Just as Gayatri Chakravorty Spivak calls for a "recoding of diversified fields of value" in attempting to "imagine 'identity'," we must also examine techniques of knowledge and strategies of power through the question of value.[27] Chicanas on the American stage, as characters and as performers, have served as a means of empowerment and an exercise of power even through male constructs. Without the distinct voice of female playwrights, it seems that we can only rely on an analysis of women in performance and the roles that men engendered in order to arrive at their significance. Fortunately, contemporary Chicana playwrights are fast emerging. We can thus begin to examine more fully their women's voices as a powerful weapon of desire and identity within the cultural, social, and political context of American history and American literature.

Author's Note

This study was partially funded by a National Endowment for the Humanities Travel to Collections Award to facilitate travel to the Mexican American Project Special Collection at the Benson Latin American Collection of the University of Texas at Austin in 1993. This article is also part of a larger, book-length study, "A Latina/Chicana Theater History," which has received funding from the NEH Summer Research Program Special Initiative, 1994–95.

Notes

1. The term *Latina/Latino* is used here to designate the larger U.S. population of women and men descended from Spanish-speaking

groups. The term *Chicana/Chicano* is used for women and men of Mexican descent residing within the United States for any length of time. Although the term has certain ideological and political meanings connected to the Chicano movement, this researcher supports the view that this term is generally accepted as appropriate for this particular underrepresented group in the United States. Because of the issue of gender in Spanish words, the slash is used for inclusion of women and men as appropriate.

2. See, for example, Ricardo Romo, "The Urbanization of Southwestern Chicanos in the Early Twentieth Century," *New Scholar* 6 (1977): 183; David Montejano, *Anglos and Mexicans in the Making of Texas, 1836–1986* (Austin; University of Texas Press, 1987); Ronald Takaki. *A Different Mirror: A History of Multicultural America* (Boston: Little, Brown and Company, 1993), 311–339.

3. An excellent example is Lillian Schlissel, Vicki L. Ruiz, and Janice Monk, *Western Women: Their Land, Their Lives* (Albuquerque: University of New Mexico Press, 1988), 2, 342.

4. Elizabeth C. Ramírez, *Footlights Across the Border: A History of Spanish-Language Professional Theater on the Texas Stage* (New York: Peter Lang Publishing, 1990); and "Hispanic American Women on the Texas Stage," in *Women in Texas History: Selected Essays* (Austin, Texas: Texas Historical Association. May 1993).

5. Romo, 200; Mrs. María Luisa Villalongín de Santos, Private Collection, San Antonio, Texas; Carlos Villalongín, "Memoirs" and "Promptbooks" in the Compañía Collection in the Mexican American Project Special Collection, Benson Latin American Collection, The University of Texas at Austin.

6. See Laura Mulvey, "Visual Pleasure and Narrative Cinema," in *Modern Feminisms: Political, Literary, Cultural,* ed. Maggie Humm (New York: Columbia University Press, 1992), 347–353; Jill Dolan, *The Feminist Spectator as Critic* (Ann Arbor: The University of Michigan Press, 1988), 17; and Gayle Austin, *Feminist Theories for Dramatic Criticism* (Ann Arbor: The University of Michigan Press, 1990), 1–2, 83–85.

7. Elizabeth Ramírez, "Compañía Juan B. Padilla" and " Compañía Villalongín," in *American Theater Companies, 1888–1930,* ed. Weldon Durham (Westport, Conn.: Greenwood Press, 1986), 353–358, 449–453.

8. Clarissa Pinkola Estés, *Women Who Run with the Wolves* (New York: Ballantine Books, 1992), 303.

9. Francisco C. Neve, *La Llorona.* Promptbook #84 in the Carlos Villalongín Collection in the Mexican American Project Special Collection, Benson Latin American Collection, The University of Texas at Austin, 16, 17.

10. Fredric Jameson, *The Political Unconscious: Narrative as a Socially Symbolic Act* (Ithaca: Cornell University Press, 1981), 153.

11. Edward Said, *Orientalisn* (New York: Vintage Books, 1979), 202–203.

12. Neve, 23–24.

13. Neve, 31.

14. The Border Patrol of the Immigration Service was not established until 1924. As Carey McWilliams tells us, "Prior to 1924 the border could be crossed, in either direction, at almost any point from Brownsville to San Diego, with the greatest of ease." See Carey McWilliams, *North from Mexico* (New York: Greenwood Press, 1968), 59–62.

15. Neve, 86–87.

16. Ramón Eduardo Ruiz, *The Great Rebellion: Mexico 1905–1924* (New York: W. W. Norton & Company, 1980), 412–413.

17. Neve, 51.

18. Jean Franco, *Plotting Women: Gender and Representation in Mexico* (New York: Columbia University Press, 1989), xix.

19. Yvonne Yarbro-Bejarano, "Female Subject in Chicano Theater," in *Performing Feminisms: Feminist Critical Theory and Theater;* ed. Sue - Ellen Case (Baltimore: The Johns Hopkins University Press, 1990), 134–135.

20. Verena Stolcke, "Invaded Women: Gender, Race, and Class in the Foundation of Colonial Society," in *Women, "Race," and Writing in the Early Modern Period,* ed. Margo Hendricks and Patricia Parker (New York: Routledge, 1994), 274.

21. Carol Pateman, quoted in Elaine Showalter, *Sexual Anarchy: Gender and Culture at the Fin de Siècle* (New York: Penguin Books, 1990), 7.

22. Showalter, 7–8.

23. Franco, xix.

24. Villalongín, "Memoirs," 123.

25. Concepción Hernández received many gifts from people offering tokens of admiration and friendship, some of which are in the Villalongín Collection in the Benson Latin American Collection. In one poem, for example, we get a glimpse of her unique qualities: "The inspiration of your creations is born in your soul; and you lovingly make it [the melodrama] live in the hearts of everyone. You create a reality of both suffering and feeling. Your modesty is [a] gift of art!... you move everyone's soul."

26. Oscar G. Brockett, *History of the Theater,* 6th ed. (Boston: Allyn & Bacon, 1991), 637.

27. Gayatri Chakravorty Spivak, "Imperialism and Sexual Difference," in *Contemporary Literary Criticism,* 2d ed., ed. Robert Con Davis and Ronald Schleifer (New York: Longman, 1989), 517.

No More "Beautiful Señoritas": U.S. Latina Playwrights' Deconstruction of Beauty Myths and Gender Stereotypes

Alberto Sandoval Sánchez

To Karen Remmler, con todo mi corazón.

Men look at women. Women watch themselves being looked at. This determines not only most relations between men and women but also the relation of women to themselves. The surveyor of women in herself is male: the surveyed female. Thus she turns herself into an object—and most particularly an object of vision: a sight.[1]

What is a "Beautiful Señorita"? I guess I do not have to answer that question, although it is not simply posed as a rhetorical one. All of us have seen or, have had close encounters one time or another with, "Beautiful Señoritas," either on television, in movies, theater, advertisements, or in a midnight drag show. We can easily recognize them, because we have internalized, in one form or another, all of those Carmen Mirandas, Chiquita Bananas, and Charo "cuchi cuchis" as the stereotypical images in the United States of Latina femininity and gender relations, as portrayed by the hegemonic Anglo-cultural and ideological apparatus of patriarchy.[2] Nevertheless, what processes are at work when we spot a " Beautiful Señorita?" Is it just a matter of reactivating the idealization and mythification of Latinas as objects of beauty , exoticism, passion, and desire of/for Otherness? What is a "Beautiful Señorita" when staged as a dominant cultural configuration on Broadway and Hollywood with women as spectacle, and as models of/for gender-identity for Latinas?

Close your eyes and you will see the theatrics of the "Beautiful Señorita" from South of the Border as a cultural exotic construct and as an object of entertainment and (sexual) pleasure. Picture it. Lawrence Welk, that "American Institution," announcing Anacani, the lovely little Mexican girl from Escondido: "Ah One, Ah Two. Here she is, our own Beautiful Señorita singing "Cielito Lindo."[3] Neither can we forget about *West Side Story,*

(courtesy of Alberto Sandoval)

where Rita Moreno played the loose and loud Spanish Señorita and Natalie Wood played Maria, the most pure, virginal, and angelic "Beautiful Señorita" of them all, singing in front of the mirror: "I feel pretty,/ Oh, so pretty,/ I feel pretty, and witty and bright, / And I pity / Any girl who isn't me tonight!"[4] Neither can we disregard Linda Ronstadt, that born-again "Hispanic Beautiful Señorita" of the 1980s who took "America" by surprise, flaunting her Mexican roots. She toured with her musical show *Canciones de mi padre: A Romantic Evening in Old Mexico* around the country and even on Broadway. There she was, putting on the show of ethnicity: cross-dressing into a sweet and lovely indiecita or mestiza with trencitas and bright dark eyes, colorful flowers in her hair, and a brilliantly multicolored zarape. I even remember vaguely a commercial with the most eccentric "Beautiful Señorita" I have ever seen and imagined. She was wearing a Spanish flamenco dress crowned by her peineta and mantilla, had a flower in her mouth, was dancing a tango, and had a Mexican accent. Indeed, she was an incredible collage of images of womanhood from Latin America to Spain, which converged into a bizarre folkloric monstrosity and queer feminine idealization in excess. Not even a drag queen would have done such a hilarious *sui generis* campy act in his/her impersonation of a "Beautiful Señorita." But there she was, performing alone of all her sex, staging her gender attributes, and displaying her ethnic hybridity. Once a "Beautiful Señorita," always a "Beautiful Señorita," making a spectacle of herself and masquerading ethnicity in order to please the Anglo-American audience and to fulfill the horizon of expectations of Latina stereotypes according to the Anglo ways of seeing in their cultural imaginary. There she was, silent, without a discourse or a subjectivity, like Linda parroting las canciones de su padre and looking at herself through the eyes of the Father. She was simplemente Maria, an image to be looked at, an object to be possessed, an Other to be exoticized, a speaking I to echo male speech and desire.

Although the cultural trope of the "Beautiful Señorita," as already discussed, materializes in a series of representations, Carmen Miranda constitutes the most eccentric, exuberant, stereotypical, and popular manifestation among them.[5] The fiery Brazilian singer and dancer with her picaresque eye movement, hips in motion, tutti frutti hats, and exotic language hypnotized and electrified audiences on Broadway and Hollywood in the 1940s.[6] She not only impersonated Latin American women but Latin America itself by becoming the ambassador for the Good Neighbor policy in her function of reasserting the U.S. government commitment to hemispheric unity.[7] She made a spectacle of herself, of Latin American women, and Latin America. After becoming a sensational celebrity, Carmen Miranda became part of the Anglo cultural imaginary as a "Beautiful Señorita," who would always entertain with her comic excess, zesty image, heavy accent, elaborate and colorful costumes, exotic jewelry, exaggerated turban headdress, and five-inch platform-soled slippers.[8] Since then, her image has been constantly imitated, in campy cross-dressing acts by actors, or parodied by actresses, in the theater, movies, commercials and TV. Her imitators include Imogene Coca, Mickey Rooney, Joan Bennett, Jo Ann Marlow, Milton Berle, and Willard Scott.

Carmen Miranda is both a stereotype and a caricature. She not only embodies the construction of Latinness/South Americanness in the 1940s and thereafter, but she also registers a spectacle of difference, using her body and sexuality as a locus of exoticism as well as a locus of racial and ethnic Otherness.[9] Film scholar Ana López has interpreted Carmen Miranda's function as precisely a spectacle of sexuality and ethnicity:

Miranda functions narratively and discursively as a sexual fetish, freezing the narrative and the pleasure of the voyeuristic gaze and provoking a regime of spectacle and specularity… But she is also an ethnic fetish. The look she returns is also that of the ethnographer and its colonial spectator stand-in. Her Latin Americanness is displaced in all its visual splendor for colonial appropriation and denial.[10]

Indeed, "Beautiful Señoritas" such as Carmen Miranda, Latin bombshells, and "Mexican Spitfires" are the fabrication of voyeuristic conventions, constituted by ethnic and gender-role misrepresentations, misperceptions, and misconceptions of Latinas in dominant Anglo social imaginary. U.S. Latinas with a feminist consciousness could not any longer tolerate or identify with such negative stereotypes; they could not remain trapped as "Beautiful Señoritas" in mainstream culture. Most important, they had to challenge patriarchal imagery, male desire, and the perpetuation of a visual pleasure registered as a "to-be-looked-at-ness" condition in dominant representations. They had to deconstruct such discursive models of femininity that simply pleased the Anglo gaze and fulfilled their desire of/for the exotic, ethnic, racial, and sexual Other.[11] Since the 1970s, U.S. Latina playwrights, as feminist critical practice and as an act of resistance, have responded to the iconic formation and fixation of the "Beautiful Señorita" in the Anglo-American cultural imaginary. Latinas have started to refract, disrupt, resist, and destabilize the male gaze and dominant cultural patriarchal conventions of dramatic representation. They call into question the traditional and pleasurable ways of looking at the ethnic, racial, and sexual Other. These playwrights stage-manage and move center stage the sexualized, objectified, erotic body of the Latina from a revisionist and resisting position. Thus their works debunk and demythify patriarchal and imperialist fantasies and ideals of feminine stereotypes of Latinas in Anglo sociocultural reality. However, their feminist intervention and critical revision could not be limited to deconstructing stereotypes in the dominant Anglo cultural realm. They also have had to question and reevaluate stereotypical representations and gender roles of women in Latin American culture. Consequently, U.S. Latinas have had a double task: to deconstruct both Anglo and Latin American representations of gender and to create a space for self-representation and U.S. Latina experience.

I

This essay analyzes how U.S. Latina playwrights question dominant stereotypes of Latina femininity and sexuality through their own politics of representation, discursive practices, and the construction of gender identity. I focus on the works of Cuban-American Dolores Prida's *Beautiful Señoritas,* and Puerto Rican-American Janis Astor del Valle's *Where the Señoritas Are,* in order to show how these plays inaugurate a discursive space for ideological contestation where Latina identity formation is in process, multiple, and always shifting, according to power relations. I examine how these plays represent strategies of resistance to stereotypes, and question taboos of female sexuality. From this perspective, these plays aim at deconstructing essentialist notions of U.S. Latinas as "Beautiful Señoritas" and try to re-con-

(courtesy of Alberto Sandoval)

struct a female subjectivity in all its contradictions, multiplicities, and ambiguities, not only by remapping the body but by subverting official cultural constructs of Latina ethnic and sexual stereotypes.[12] Such acts of apprehension, appropriation, and self-recognition lead to a political re-vision and re-affirmation that re-define women's roles and identities in Latino culture. From this feminist critical practice and political agenda, their goals are the staging of the questioning of sexual taboos, reversal of stereotypes, dismantling of "machismo," destabilization of gender roles, and recognition of the female body and sexuality as a body politic.

In these plays, U.S. Latinas explore their own personal experience in introspective monologues and testimonial tableaux; they stage their phases of life as rites of passage; they do not hesitate to enunciate their erotic desires and experiences; they negotiate identity and permutations of self not only in a woman's life but across generations of women; and they denounce male dominance, exploitation, sexism, and chauvinism. In these plays' denunciation of male domination, Latinas redefine their cultural roles as part of a process of self-examination. They claim control of their bodies and advocate self-determination in social and gender relations, both in Anglo and Latino cultures.

II

When Duo Theatre produced Dolores Prida's *Beautiful Señoritas* in 1977, the Latino audience was confronted for perhaps the first time in Latino/a theater with issues of gender and feminism.[13] The play constituted a conscious response to the absence of positive female characters on the stage as well as to the virtual invisibility of Latina playwrights.[14] Prida's play was an act of intervention to debunk dominant images of femininity and to deconstruct stereotypes of Latinas. In her own words, *Beautiful Señoritas* is a feminist play, a very early feminist play.

It dealt with stereotypes about Latin women. "What I do is I use all these characters, the Carmen Miranda types with bananas on her head, the Latin bombshell, la madre sufrida, and all of them go through a process where they take away all this superficiality and dig inside themselves, to find who they are. It's a búsqueda, a search."[15] Indeed, *Beautiful Señoritas* center stages the process of being born a woman, of being trapped in gender roles in a patriarchal world, of being Latina in the United States.

The play, a musical, opens with the birth of a baby girl, whose future life as a woman is projected in a series of vignettes. The girl learns what it means to be a woman by going through the experience of a beauty contest. As the contestants parade in front of the girl, the participants provide her with the necessary props, adornments, and cosmetics to express her femininity in a patriarchal world. The beauty contest also functions as the medium that brings to the stage all the stereotypes that limit Latinas from being themselves: the Carmen Mirandas, the Latin bomb shells, las madres sufridas, prostitutes, beauty queens, Chiquita Bananas, la guerrillera, and so on. As the contest unfolds, these stereotypes are attacked, along with patriarchy, machismo, and the exploitation of women. Through comedy, satire, parody, irony, cynicism, and sarcasm, Prida denounces a patriarchal world, where women are victims of machismo, misogyny, and compulsory heterosexuality.[16] By doing so, Prida challenges patriarchal institutions that oppress, exploit, marginalize, and silence woman such as Catholicism, the family, the media, beauty myths, and so on. While the girl is processing and assimilating all the images of what she is supposed to be or could be, at the same time she and the audience are exposed to and engaged in a process of questioning, dismantling, and demythifying images of Latinas in Latin American and Anglo culture.

The process of deconstruction starts with the opening scene, when the audience is put face-to-face with male chauvinism. Without any delay, machismo is promptly attacked in the portrayal of a father who is expecting to have a son. As he waits for the birth of the child, he becomes a caricature of machismo: "Come on, woman. Hurry up. I have waited long enough for this child. Come on, a son. Give me a son... I will start training him right away. To ride horses. To shoot. To drink. As soon as he is old enough I'll take him to la Casa de Luisa. There they'll teach him what to do to women... My name will never die. My son will see to that."[17] His masculinity is undermined when the midwife informs him that it is a girl. His reaction is total disappointment: "A girl! ¡No puede ser! ¡Imposible! What do you mean a girl! ¿Como puede pasarme esto a mí? The first child that will bear my name and it is a...girl! ¡Una chancleta! ¡Carajo!" (20).

This sexist response positions the spectators vis-à-vis rampant machismo and misogyny in Latino culture. As he is ridiculed, patriarchy, patrilinearity, and primogeniture are called into question, in order to devalue male chauvinism and sexism. After mocking the father's behavior and value system, this opening scene stages a feminist agenda when the midwife becomes the bearer of a feminist consciousness:

He's off to drown his disappointment in rum, because another woman is born into this world. The same woman another man's son will covet and pursue and try to rape at the first opportunity. The same woman whose virginity he will protect with a gun. Another woman is born into this world. In Managua, in San Juan, in an Andes mountain town. She'll be put on a pedestal and trampled upon at the same time. She will be made a saint and a whore, crowned queen and exploited and adored. (20–21)

Consequently, the midwife's role is to disauthorize the male figure and to introduce the feminist agenda of the play. The message is clear and direct: Women are oppressed and exploited in dominant cultural representations and patriarchal discourses.

In the next scene, the midwife is interrupted by the voices of "Beautiful Señoritas," who sing a rumba and perform for the girl. These women, who are dressed as Carmen Miranda, Iris Chacón, Charo, and María la O, embody the stereotypes of women in Latin American and Anglo culture; moreover, these are precisely the role models that the girl has to emulate and idealize. These images offer the girl a series of gender-specific roles and a construct of femininity that perpetuate the representation of women as spectacle and their disposition to please the male gaze and sexual desires. In these images, women are objectified and denied a subjectivity up to the point that they internalize negative stereotypes of women: "We Beautiful Señoritas / mucha salsa and sabor / cuchi cuchi Latin bombas / always ready for amor." In order to deconstruct these images, the girl is taken to a beauty contest, where women parade their bodily assets and contribute to the perpetuation of sexism. However, what is at stake here is a parody of dominant representations of women and beauty contests in order to raise feminist consciousness in the girl as she grows up. The ultimate spectator is not the girl but the audience themselves, who are being entertained and educated on women's issues.

If the father is a chauvinist pig, so, too, is the emcee of the beauty contest, who perpetuates the stereotypes of Latinas as beauty objects:

You will have the opportunity to see the most exquisite, sexy, exotic, sandungueras, jacarandosas and most beautiful Señoritas of all. You will be the judge of the contest, where beauty will compete with belleza; where women of the tropical Caribbean will battle the Señoritas of South America. Ladies and gentlemen, the poets have said it. The composers of boleros have said it. Latin women are the most beautiful, the most passionate, the most virtuous, the best housewives and cooks. And they all know how to dance to salsa, and do the hustle, the mambo, the guaguancó... And they are always ready for amor, Señores! (24–25)

At work here is not only a battle of the sexes, but a battle of stereotypes, both in Anglo and Latin American culture. The Latinas start to parade in order to display their stereotypicality and to enact their "to-be-looked-at-ness," as predetermined by gender conventions. As they walk on the ramp, they become a parody of gender roles and femininity. In this way, stereotypes are dynamited in a humorous and ironic manner.

Ms. Little Havana's only assets are her body measurements (36-28-42); Miss Chile Tamale is an illegal alien who wants to marry an American; Ms. Commonwealth from Puerto Rico wishes only to be a mother and a housewife; and Conchita Banana brings to life the commercial cartoon, which stereotypes and degrades all Latinas in Anglo culture. These stereotypes are juxtaposed with a choir of women's voices who instigate feminist consciousness about women's silence, oppression, and objectification. This spectacle is performed solely for the girl, who finds herself within a process of assimilation and imitation. In her effort to imitate the contestants, she applies an exaggerated amount of makeup that results in "her face made up like a clown."(24). This grotesque image is a distancing technique to make the audience constantly aware of women's dependence on beauty myths and woman's complicity in making a spectacle of themselves to please males.[18] In this sense, women's pressure to look feminine and the desire to make themselves the object of the male gaze are unveiled as patriarchal constructions that women must decenter and resist.

Unquestionably, the purpose of having the girl participate in a beauty contest is to challenge and undermine dominant representations of femininity. In many scenes, the ultimate goal is to break away from sexual and cultural taboos. In one, for example, the Señoritas' open confession of their sexual desires and sexuality serves to present an attack on the Church for restricting women's sexuality. This satirical assault on Catholicism contributes to liberating women from guilt and to controlling their own bodies and sexuality. Throughout the play, the girl and the audience are engaged in questioning traditional ways of seeing and of making their sexuality and bodies desirable. The Señoritas' disciplined and tortured bodies must do away with patriarchal control and women's submission to the Church. Most important, women must interrogate positions of obedience and chastity in order to de-stabilize patriarchal dominance. As a result, the girl and the audience locate themselves in a critical perspective where gender attributes and behavior imposed by the Church are questioned. Under these circumstances, the audience also acquires the necessary tools to dismantle traditional roles assigned to women by the Church and society at large.

Act 2 centers mainly on demythifying male-female relationships where women are passive and submissive. The women as wives, mothers, and martyrs are portrayed as the stereotypes of women who internalize abuse and domesticity. The sacrificed, abused, pregnant, and abandoned women must wake up to domestic violence and victimization. Between the lines, the audience can read that women who do not live for themselves and who are there just to please the males must become independent, self-assured, and self-reliant. It is the guerrillera who mobilizes the community of women: "We can change the world and then our lot will improve… We, as Third World women…are triply oppressed, so we have to fight three times as hard!… Have your consciousness raised! Come with me and help make the revolution!"(36). As a matter of fact, the guerrillera does not escape stereotyping when the women think of her as being a lesbian. Also, the irony is rampant: although the guerrillera is successful in raising consciousness, once they hear the voice of a man—"Is dinner ready?"—they all run to comply with their domestic duties and to show obedience to their husbands:

Woman 1: ¡Ay, se me quema el arroz!
Woman 2: ¡Bendito, las habichuelas!
Woman 3: ¡Ay, Virgen de Guadalupe, las enchiladas! (39)

The women leave the guerrillera alone as they rush to their daily tasks at home. For now, women's liberation will have to wait.

The next scene centers on demythifying the popular belief that women's work at home does not compare with a man's job. Although women work all day, their work, to men, is meaningless. By accentuating men's unfairness and lack of consideration, the play challenges the stereotype that women belong at home. The message is that if they stay home, they still have to do all the work: cleaning, cooking, raising the children, and pleasing the husband. Also in this scene, the male is condemned when he harasses the social worker and asks for a date after his wife goes to bed. His behavior is not only indecent, it is clear that he does not respect his wife or women in general. The same applies to the father of the girl and the emcee of the beauty contest.

In a dramatic and serious scene that contrasts with all the humor and parody in the play, a group of women–who really are a choir of consciousness raising–condemn the suffering of women. They enunciate the crimes: women are abused, victimized, raped, and killed:

Woman 1: Sometimes, while I dance, I hear–behind the rhythmically shuffling feet–the roar of the water cascading down the mountain, thrown against the cliffs by an enraged ocean.
Woman 2: ...I hear the sound of water in a shower, splattering against the tiles where a woman lies dead. I hear noises beyond the water, and sometimes they frighten me.
Woman 3: Behind the beat of the drums I hear the thud of a young woman's body thrown from a roof. I hear the screeching of wheels from a speeding car and the stifled cries of a young girl lying on the street... The string section seems to murmur names...
Woman 4: To remind me that the woman, the girl who at this very moment is being beaten...
Woman 1: raped...

Woman 2: murdered…
Woman 3: is my sister…
Woman 4: my daughter…
Woman 1: my mother…
All: myself… (47–48)

This denunciation and act of solidarity that condemns crimes committed against women and their bodies is followed by the emcee's announcement that the choice has been made. The new beauty queen is Ms. Senorita Mañana. Obviously, patriarchy is indifferent to women's oppression and exploitation. The emcee must go on with the show.

To everyone's surprise, the new beauty queen is a mess. She is wearing all the items she picked up as she encountered all the stereotypes and images of woman: the tinsel crown, the flowers, a mantilla, and so on. The choir of women surround her, realizing that they have confused the girl. The only one to blame is the emcee and his beauty contest. Ironically, this confusion leads to the final scene, where the women clean the girl's face, removing the excessive makeup, and give the girl final advice:

Woman 2: Honey, this is not what it is about…
Woman 1: It is not the clothes.
Woman 2: Or the hair…
Woman 4: Or the cooking.
Woman 3: But… What is it about?
Woman 4: Well… I was 13 when the blood first arrived. My mother locked herself in the bathroom with me, and recited the facts of life, and right then and there, very solemnly, she declared me a woman.
Woman 1: I was 18 when, amid pain and pleasure, my virginity floated away in a sea of blood. He held me tight and said; "Now I have made you a woman."
Woman 2: Then from my insides a child burst forth…crying, bathed in blood and other personal substances. And then someone whispered in my ear: "Now you are a real, real woman." (43)

The choir of women start to articulate a subjectivity in process at the moment that they recognize their own bodies and experiences based on menstruation, loss of virginity, pregnancy, and childbirth. In this way, the women's act of intervention is a definite feminist praxis to foment consciousness raising. Given that the play is an effort to explore female identity, the final message is that women must articulate their own subjectivity and enunciate their own experiences. In these terms, there is a reminder that all stereotypes must be debunked in order to construct a new Latina identity. This objective is summarized in the following way: "In their songs they have given me the body of a mermaid, of a palm tree, of an ample-hipped guitar. In the movies I see myself as a whore, a nymphomaniac, a dumb servant or a third-rate dancer. I look for myself and I can't find me. I only find someone else's idea of me" (43).

Undoubtedly, *Beautiful Señoritas* is a musical that embarks on a search, a self-examination, and a critical inquiry of stereotypes that culminates in Latinas celebrating their bodies and subjectivity as they "look at each other as images in a mirror, discovering themselves in each other" (44). The final act of resistance is to look at themselves face-to-face, displacing the patriarchal gaze. Like other patriarchal stories and discourses of power that manipulate and dominate women, "Mirror, mirror on the wall…" (44) becomes obsolete once women start telling their own stories. In this way, the male gaze is bounced back. The women are not going to look at themselves through patriarchal imagery any longer. Enunciating their independence and freedom, the women look at themselves and refuse to make a spectacle of themselves. They are ready to celebrate their own lives, their bodies, and their stories. At this point, and only then, male sexist ways of looking are totally reversed: they are the ones who look at him looking at them in the process of subverting his self-flirtation. "Mira Mami, psst, cosa linda / Look at me looking at you."[19] Now, she has the final look and the final word. She is free at last to articulate her Latina identity.

The girl (as well as the audience) will be able to define *woman* in a new way. Indeed, before the play closes, the girl, pronounces her first words in the play: "… that there are possibilities. That women that go crazy in the night, that women that die alone and frustrated, that women that exist only in the mind, are only half of the story, because a woman is…" (44). With the other women, the girl starts a process of self-definition and self-realization which is concretized in the action of looking at one another face-to-face, in order to discover what a woman is. The girl's new (feminist) identity is articulated in a song: she has found her own speech, becoming the subject and decentering woman as spectacle and object of visual pleasure in patriarchal discourse. The women, who are no longer typical "Beautiful Señoritas," proclaim their independence and affirm their self-esteem and liberation in the song "Woman Is a Fountain of Fire." The girl represents a new generation of Latinas who are liberated and empowered after breaking the patriarchal mirrors and shattering the myths that imprisoned them.

Even though *Beautiful Señoritas* unveils sexual and cultural taboos while the protagonists in their cultural critique debunk myths and deconstruct stereotypes of Latinas, sexual orientation is still a taboo. In Latina/o theater, a very early attempt at breaking the silence on lesbian desire, rape, incest, and violence against women is Cherríe Moraga's *Giving Up the Ghost*.[20] Chicana critic Yvonne Yarbro-Bejarano lucidly states the following about the politics of representation in Moraga's play: "[The protagonists] Marisa and Corky do not conform to the codified gender representation of 'woman' on stage, neither in their appearance (hair cut short, clothes, etc.) nor in the way they move... The text explores the ways in which Chicanas, both lesbian and heterosexual, have internalized their culture's concepts of sexuality."[21] This process of exploration and construction of a lesbian desiring subjectivity is fully accomplished with Janis Astor del Valle's 1993 lesbian romantic comedy, *Where the Señoritas Are.* Because the action of the play centers on lesbian desire and identity, it represents the ultimate attempt to give up the ghost of "Beautiful Señoritas" and compulsory heterosexuality in Latino culture.

Where the Señoritas Are was produced at the Nuyorican Poet's Cafe in September 1994. In 1995, it received an award at the eleventh annual Mixed Blood Versus America contest, sponsored by the Mixed Blood Theatre Company of Minneapolis.[22] The action takes place on Cherry Grove Beach, Fire Island, where two Puerto Rican friends spend a women's weekend together. Luli, who is a lesbian feminist, has invited her best friend, Maxie, who is a homophobic, flaming heterosexual, without informing her that the Grove has a predominantly gay and lesbian population. Their friendship, which goes back to adolescence, takes a new turn that weekend, when they experience their first sexual encounter with each other. The play portrays, through Maxie's case, the vicissitudes of coming out through the exploration of lesbian sexuality and the experiences of lesbian relations. By focusing on lesbian desire, the play calls into question internalized heterosexism and homophobia, in its effort to break the taboo of lesbian sexuality in Latino/a communities. By exposing lesbian sexuality, the protagonists disrupt patriarchal discourses and horizons of expectations that employ femininity to secure and perpetuate male power relations.

Astor del Valle's title, *Where the Señoritas Are,* contains an ironic intention with the purpose of deconstructing dominant stereotypes of Latinas: the Señoritas here are not traditional representations of heterosexual Latinas who flaunt their femininity and dispositionality to attract males. These Señoritas happen to be proud Latina lesbians who are not in the closet anymore. Where are the Señoritas? Where they are is unimaginable in Latino/a culture: they are spending a weekend in a lesbian and gay environment. What are the Señoritas doing in that space? The lesbian "Beautiful Señoritas" are coming out and coming to terms with their lesbian desire and identity. In this context, the horizon of expectations of a heterosexual audience is subverted, but what is most important is that the play opens up an alternative space, where lesbians and gays interact, displaying their sexuality and erotic desires. Given that the action takes place in a location frequented and appropriated by lesbians and gays, the audience is forced to recognize the existence of such an alternative space as well as the existence of Latino/a lesbian and gay identities.

The opening scene introduces the audience to Maxie's problematic and abusive relationship with her boyfriend, who has told her that he needs his space. Her friend Luli responds with an attack on male mistreatment and manipulation: "You're a pendeja, Maxie, letting these guys live with you, rent-free, cleaning up after them while they don't lift a finger around the house or anywhere else" (1). Luli's response reveals her feminist consciousness as well as a critique of male sexist abusive behavior. Ironically, Luli is also a pendeja ("And you call me a pendeja— Look at you, you're a mess!") (4) for allowing her ex-girlfriend Maria to mix her up. In this direct mode and without any apologies or taboos, Luli's sexuality is exposed. Her lesbian relationship with Maria has come to its end because Maria is supposedly bisexual and is having an affair with a man. Furthermore, the relationships mirror each other's dysfunctionality without regard to sexual practices. That is to say, once the butch-femme roles reproduce the heterosexual model, they also replicate its dysfunctionalities, which are based on the uneven power relations of the patriarchal (Latino) model.

As they enter the ferry to go to Cherry Grove, Maxie notices that the sexes are divided into two lines. Maxie's homophobia is reactivated once she realizes that Luli has tricked her. In these terms, Maxie enters an alternative space of lesbian and gay sexual relationships, where her heterosexuality is not the norm. Luli promptly reminds Maxie that when they are together, they only frequent straight places. Without any doubt, Luli is willing to introduce Maxie to gay and lesbian lifestyles. In this alternative space, heterosexual relationships are put aside while lesbian and gay sexual relationships take the center stage. In this space, lesbian existence is not denied or made invisible. Indeed, lesbian representation is a feasible task once heterosexuality is displaced, especially once the male gaze is interrupted and dislocated.

Maxie's panic arises from the possibility of becoming an object of desire for women. Although she accepts Luli as her best friend, women desiring women, women seducing women, or women having sex with women is repulsive to Maxie: "I accept you, I just can't—the physical part…it grosses me out."(9). In spite of the fact that Luli reassures Maxie that no one is cruising her, Maxie's homophobia progresses as she fears that people may think that they are a couple. After they come to terms with their differences, Luli hugs Maxie who, not feeling comfortable, rejects her immediately: "Okay, don't hold me so long, people will think we're—"(13). Maxie is so homophobic that she cannot even pronounce the word *lesbian.* In this sense, she has not only internalized homophobia, but she is an accomplice to sexual taboos in Latina/o culture, which erase lesbians, making them invisible and silent.

At the beach, Luli runs into Maria, who still wants her. And Maria is not the only one after her: there are two bailadoras/dancers that appear constantly to Luli in her imagination. These bailadoras embody the stereotypical Anglo image of Latinas:

they are "Beautiful Señoritas" dressed in flamenco regalia, performing a seductive tango. Given that the "Beautiful Señoritas"
are two lesbians, these apparitions contribute to the
demythification of femininity and women as spectacle and objects of desire to please males. Their function is to seduce Luli
that weekend, a seduction that is doubled in Luli's and Maxie's
sexual attraction. These bailadoras–who provide a lesbian role
model–allegorize Luli's relationship with Maxie: they appear
specifically when they are bodily close. For example, when Luli
applies some gel to Maxie's back, the bailadoras seduce her,
inciting sexual desire. Such a seduction is emblematized by one
of the dancers: "Toma, mami, toma"(34). Whatever she is giving and offering is not clear, but what is indisputable is that lesbian desire, pleasure, and sexuality are incarnated in the
bailadoras and their seductive tango. In any case, if anything is
being offered at all, it is the dancer's lesbian body. These visions
occur with more regularity and with growing intensity until Luli
and Maxie themselves become the dancers.

At the end of act 1, Maxie and Luli miss the ferry to return
home, and this time it is Maxie who wants to stay and have fun.
Act 1 closes with Luli and Maxie dancing to disco music while
Juanita and Maria feel jealous. In a disco scene, Maxie and Luli
on the dance floor literally become the seductive dancers of Luli's
visions. Such duplication demonstrates how Astor del Valle has
refocused the male gaze in order to validate and authorize lesbian existence: women look at women. Once lesbian existence
enters representation as an act of resistance to male voyeurism,
the outcome is an act of subversion that gives visibility to lesbians and their ways of seeing and being.[23] This transgressive act
also allows for a lesbian subject position in Latino culture and
the expression of erotic attraction and desire between women.

At the beginning of act 2 Maxie and Luli are spending the
night at a gay friend's beachfront cottage. Jesus offers them his
place to stay after they miss the ferry. Their sexual encounter is
predestined by the fact that there is only one bed. Not only that,
but the bailadoras make their appearance and perform for Luli
once more. As before, Luli is the only one to see them and to be
seduced. While the bailadoras surround Luli, she responds with
the desire to possess them. However, her efforts are in vain:
"Luli may even reach out to a bailadora, but every time she

does this, the dancer should move away from her. Bailadora #1 is seductive, taking the lingerie from Luli, teasing her and trying to bring Luli out of herself, to let loose her true, innermost desires and identity" (70). Luli's lesbian imaginary is exposed through the fantasy of seductive dancers; her desire becomes a reality when Maxie comes out of the bathroom wearing lingerie. What is at stake here is a process of substitutions and transactions where fantasies may become reality while, at the same time, those fantasies embody Luli's ultimate desire to become a "femme" seducer and possess Maxie. Through her fantasies, Luli also deals with how she projects herself in a lesbian relationship. She wants to play femme, not butch.[24] When Maxie asks Luli to wear lingerie—which, ironically, belongs to Jesus—Luli realizes that Maxie perceives her as butch. If lingerie inscribes gender roles and images of femininity in a heterosexual world, these gender attributes are subverted with a butch-femme relationship, which distorts the heterosexual model.[25] In these terms, when traditional gender conventions are appropriated by lesbians, such an appropriation becomes a gender performance, a campy act of excessive femininity/masculinity that parodies, like camp and drag, heterosexual gender roles. Alternately, the butch-femme couple constitutes an act of subversion by the mere fact that it questions and denaturalizes traditional gender-specific conventions and categories. Judith Butler's theorization on gender identity, when parodied in the cultural practices of drag, crossdressing, and the sexual stylization of butch-femme identities, applies to Luli and Maxie's negotiations with butch-femme categories:

[G]ender practices within gay and lesbian cultures often thematize "the natural" in parodic contexts that bring into relief the performative construction of an original and the true sex... In imitating gender, drag implicitly reveals the imitative structure of gender itself—as well as its contingency. Indeed, part of the pleasure, the giddiness of the performance is in the recognition of a radical contingency in the relation between sex and gender in the face of cultural configurations of causal unities that are regularly assumed to be natural and necessary. In the place of the law of heterosexual coherence we see sex and gender denaturalized by means of a performance which avows their distinctness and dramatizes the cultural mechanism of their fabricated unity.[26]

Luli is very conscious of butch-femme roles when she challenges Maxie with her own politics of representation: "A piece of clothing ain't what makes somebody butch or femme... Being butch or femme is more of a state of mind–something so deep, it's rooted in the heart and soul; it's a spirit, an attitude–an aura!" (71). For Luli, butch-femme roles do not mean gender performance and/or gender-specific behavior that register visual markers of masculinity or femininity; rather, for her, butch-femme is the process of articulation and constitution of a given lesbian identity. This subjectivity in process appropriates heterosexual gender behavior in order to construct a lesbian identity, which continually destabilizes traditional gender roles and behavior. In doing so, butch-femme couples enact in their imitation an act of resistance and appropriation, which permits the formation of lesbian identity and validates lesbian sexual relationships. On this matter, Teresa de Lauretis theorizes the following:

The butch-femme role-playing is exciting not because it represents heterosexual desire, but because it doesn't; that is to say, in mimicking it, it shows the uncanny distance, like an effect of ghosting, between desire (heterosexuality represented as it is) and the representation; and because the representation doesn't fit the actors who perform it, it only points to their investment in a fantasy–a fantasy that can never represent them or their desire, for the latter remains in excess of its setting, the fantasy that grounds it even as it is deconstructed and destabilized by the mise-en-scène of lesbian camp.[27]

In these terms, if Luli's notion of being butch or femme is a "state of mind," clearly being butch or femme implies an ontological outlook that comprises the impossibility of linguistic representation. Consequently, for Luli, lesbian identity, sexuality, and desire demand a subject position and lesbian agency in which butch-femme representation is a matter of desire, fantasy, and subjectivity. Luli's definition does not limit gender to a performative act that is readable on the surface of the body; gender performance also depends on the not-said, the not-represented of a given interiority that strives for its representation without achieving it.[28]

Luli and Maxie's preparation for their inevitable sexual encounter is introduced in two ways: through the bailadoras and through Maxie's curiosity to know in detail about lesbian sexuality. On the one hand, the bailadoras surround them, embracing and dancing to the rhythm of Afro-Latino music. On the other hand, Maxie's curiosity about lesbian sex prepares her for their sexual encounter. Luli explains to her the sexual act: "The mouth is a whole organ unto itself" (74). And "Dental dams go between the chocha and the tongue. Or the culito and the—" (75). After such a sexual and erotic preamble, which even puts into practice safe sex, the unavoidable sexual scene takes place when they start a pillow fight. At that moment, a Virgin hanging above the bed crashes to the floor and breaks. This breaking is an act of transgression that signifies shattering myths of virginity imposed by the Church and the patriarchal order. The breaking of the Virgin is a sign of liberation from idealized chastity and motherhood in the patriarchal world. Although they wish to have sex and to enjoy it without guilt, Luli is terrified, because she sees the breaking of the statue as an omen of bad luck. As they kiss, Maxie coaxes Luli: "Forget about la Virgen tonight." The bailadoras reappear doing a tango that validates lesbian sexuality. Their dance not only projects Maxie and Luli's sexual act, it also concretizes the possibility of lesbian desire and sexuality. At this point, the "Beautiful Señoritas" are no longer objects of pleasure and desire for males. Moreover, the protagonists are equipped to see themselves as the subject of desire, refusing to be men's object of desire and sexuality.

At the end, Luli breaks up definitively with Maria and starts a relationship with Maxie. Maxie's coming-out experience and her sexual relationship with Luli empower her: "Luli, no one has ever touched me the way you have—and I'm not just talking sexually—you've always been there for me, the one person I could always count on, the most positive force in my crazy, mixed-up life" (90). Their relationship is not limited to sexual pleasure. It evidences what Adrienne Rich calls the "lesbian continuum". "I mean the term lesbian continuum to include a range—through each woman's life and throughout history—of woman-identified experience, not simply the fact that a woman has had or consciously desired genital sexual experience with another woman."[29] Their sexual act contributes to the solidification and strengthening of their love and true friendship.

Maxie and Luli are not alone. There is a gay community that supports them. Indeed, it is from their friend Jesus that they learn the most as he advises them to put aside their fear: "Sí, el miedo, el miedo es como un parasite, feeding on the dark side of your mind, staying with you like a deep sickness, eating away at your heart, blinding your soul, until you no longer see what is good, you can't remember what's pure" (94). Jesus has learned to be strong from the AIDS crisis, which, in turn, has given him the tools to be confident, be proud of being gay, and live with dignity:

Mija, I spent the last ten years watchin' all my friends die. That's scary. One by one, they just started getting sick, and never getting better… And I was the only one who wasn't gettin' sick. I started to feel un poquito guilty, tú sabes? Like, 'Why me?' I told myself, 'Jesus, si Dios quiere, you just got to be strong for them.' I didn't think about bein' strong for myself… And that part of my life seemed to pass como un blur…going from hospital to hospital, breakfast for Carlos—he used to love my harina de arroz—lunch for Victor, dinner for Lydia, changing sheets and cleaning bedpans for all of them… Nights were my saving grace; I'd do my shows and rush home to Joaquin…in his arms, I could feel like everything was gonna be all right. Until he got sick. Then I felt everything inside of me just fall apart…he was the only man I ever really loved, tú sabes…and within six months, he was gone…taken away from me, just like that…pue, we had seven precious years together; I only wish to Dios we could have had more… Mija, I'm tellin' you this, because I seen the way you look at Maxie and I seen the way she looks at you—it's the same way Joaquin and me looked at each other…and that kind of love only happens once in a lifetime. (94–95)

At work here primarily is a politics of affinity resulting from the tragedy of AIDS in the gay and lesbian community. AIDS has pushed men and women out of the closet, forcing them to recognize the power of true friendship and the meaning of love. Nothing can stop them, not even fear, as Jesus' advice bears witness to his courage and survival in the age of AIDS: "But you girls have got to get over it, pafuera el miedo, and get your shit together because love is the most precious thing on this Earth!" (95). Luli echoes Jesus' words after coming to terms with having a relationship with Maxie. Finally, Luli and Maxie are able to articulate a lesbian subject position that validates their lesbian existence. Furthermore, their lesbian agency provides them with a series of positionalities where class, ethnicity, and even AIDS intersect. In this sense, lesbian identity is de-essentialized as they inhabit multiple subject positions and take control of their sexuality and desires. Luli and Maxie are mapping a new Latina identity, which allows for diversity and difference among Latinas. It also proposes an alternative way of building community. Once Latina lesbians and Latino gays come out, their act of resistance empowers them to intervene politically in all kinds of cultural practices through cultural critique and transgressive strategies of lesbian and gay representation. In doing so, they bring to an end lesbian and gay invisibility in Latino culture: they are willing to stage their own self-representations in order to dismantle homophobia, disrupt compulsory heterosexuality, and, in solidarity, fight AIDS.[30]

There is no doubt that the new assumed U.S. Latina subjectivity-in-process and growing feminist and lesbian consciousness put to work a theatrical agenda—a system of expectations for developing new strategies, new visions, and new options—that shall engender Latinas' bodies and em-body diversity and plurality from female experiences and points of view. In this way, these plays give evidence to a U.S. Latina agency based on negotiations, difference, and oppositional subject-positions. By no longer staging "Beautiful Señoritas," the theatrical space is now open to that new Latina subjectivity that Gloria Anzaldúa dramatically defines as the new mestiza.[31]

Latina theater since the 1980s has become an accomplished and fruitful enterprise that embodies a heterogeneity of voices, a plurality of discourses, and a diversity of experiences. Latinas in the theater have come a long way. Playwrights such as Dolores Prida and Janis Astor del Valle have opened the doors to a new way of doing theater, both in subject matter and in dramatic structure. As a result, they are mapping their female bodies, voicing their silences, dismantling sexual and cultural taboos, exploring difference and diversity, and constructing multiple subject positions on the center stage of the theaters of the Americas. And the rest is her/story.

Author's Note

For their careful critical reading and suggestions, I would like to thank Diana Taylor, Nancy Saporta Sternbach, Silvia Spitta, Elizabeth Young, Julie Inness, and Alida Montañez.

Notes

1. John Berger, *Ways of Seeing* (New York: Penguin, 1972), 47.
2. I use Jill Dolan's definition of "gender" and "sex." See "Gender Impersonation Onstage: Destroying or Maintaining the Mirror of Gender Roles?" *Women and Performance* 2.2 (1985): 6. As for "patriarchy" I use the following definition which appears in *A Feminist Dictionary,* ed. Cheris Kramarae and Paula A. Treichler (London: Pandora Press, 1985), 323: "An important term used in a variety of ways to characterize abstractly the structures and social arrangements within which women's oppression is elaborated. Means an ideology which arose out of men's power to exchange women between kinship groups; as the power of the father; to express men's control over women's sexuality and fertility; to describe the institutional structure of male domination;" quoted in Sheila Rowbotham, "The Trouble with 'Patriarchy,' " *New Statesman*, 28 (December 1979).
3. See William K. Schwienher, *Lawrence Welk: An American Institution* (Chicago: Nelson-Hall, 1980); and Lawrence Welk, *Ah-One Ah-Two! Life with My Musical Family* (New York: Prentice-Hall International, 1974).
4. Arthur Laurents, *West Side Story* (New York: Dell, 1965), 195–196. See also Alberto Sandoval Sánchez. "Una lectura puertorriqueña de la América de *West Side Story,*" *Cupey: Revista de la Universidad Metropolitana* 7.1-2 (1990), 30–45; and Alberto Sandoval Sánchez, "La puesta en escena de la familia immigrante puertorriqueña," *Revista Iberoamericana* 162–63 (enero-junio 1993*), 345–359.
5. In this essay, I do not attempt to trace the genealogy of the "Beautiful Señorita" in mainstream discursive representations. Nevertheless, I would like to point to some specific historico-cultural constructions of the trope. For example, Harry L. Foster, in *A Gringo in Mañana-Land* (New York: Dodd, Mead and Company, 1924), dedicates a chapter to "Those Dark-Eyed Señoritas!" During the 1940s many songs from Broadway and Hollywood centered on Latin America promoting, in a propagandistic way, the "Good Neighbor Policy." Some of the songs portraying "Beautiful Señoritas" are "Conchita, Marcheta, Lolita, Pepita, Rosita, Juanita Lopez" (from Paramount Pictures, *Priorities of 1942)*; "Lily-Hot from Chile," "South of the Border," "Nenita," and "Sing to Your Señorita" (from 20th Century Fox, *Down Argentine Way* in 1941). In the 1940s, United Fruit's creation of the commercial cartoon Chiquita Banana was the most stereotypical impersonation of Carmen Miranda; see Cynthia Enloe's "Carmen Miranda on My Mind: International Politics of the Banana," in *Bananas, Beaches and Bases: Making Feminist Sense of International Politics* (Berkeley: University of California Press, 1989), 124–150. Consult John J. Johnson's *Latin America in Caricature* (Austin: University of Texas Press, 1993) for the representation of Latin America as a "Beautiful Señorita" in political cartoons from the nine-

teenth century to the present. In the 1990s, Carmen Miranda has even been appropriated by gay men in order to survive the AIDS epidemic; for example, see John Glines' one-act play "The Demonstration," in *Art and Understanding: The International Magazine of Literature and Art about AIDS,* issue 14, 4.1 (Jan–Feb. 1995), 8–11, where a lover dresses as Carmen to perform a hilarious and campy act that will entertain his partner and make him laugh on his deathbed.

6. For a biography of Carmen Miranda, see Martha Gil Montero, *Brazilian Bombshell: The Biography of Carmen Miranda* (New York: Donald I. Fine, 1989).

7. Allen Woll, *The Latin Image in American Film* (Los Angeles: University of California Press, 1977), 56.

8. Woll, 68; James Robert Parish, *The Fox Girls* (New Rochelle, N.Y.: Arlington House, 1971), 507.

9. Ella Shohat, "Gender and Culture of Empire: Toward a Feminist Ethnography of the Cinema," *Quarterly Review of Film and Video,* vol. 13, 1–3, (1991): 68.

10. Ana M. López, "Are All Latins from Manhattan? Hollywood Ethnography and Cultural Colonialism," in *Unspeakable Images: Ethnicity and the American Cinema,* ed. Lester D. Friedman (Urbana: University of Illinois Press, 1991), 418–419.

11. Laura Mulvey, in "Visual Pleasure and Narrative Cinema," in *Modern Feminisms: Political, Literary, Cultural,* ed. Maggie Humm, (New York: Columbia University Press, 1992), relates the male gaze to the pleasure of looking at women. I go a step further by including ethnicity as the pleasure of exoticizing, displaying the Other. Such is the case with Carmen Miranda.

12. See Lou Rosenberg, "The House of Difference: Gender, Culture and the Subject-in-Process on the American Stage," in *Critical Essays: Gay and Lesbian Writers of Color,* ed. E. S. Nelson (New York: Harrington Park Press, 1993), 97–110.

13. Dolores Prida, "Beautiful Señoritas," in *Beautiful Señoritas and Other Plays,* ed. Judith Weiss (Houston: Arte Público Press, 1991); all further references are included parenthetically within the text.

14. Dolores Prida wrote the play after attending a *festival de teatro* in Venezuela in 1976. The play was a response to the absence of plays centering on women's issues and representation (personal interview, March 1995). Also, see Dolores Prida, "The Show Does Go On (Testimonio)," in *Breaking Boundaries: Latina Writings and Critical Readings,* ed. Asunción Horno-Delgado, Eliana Ortega, Nina M. Scott, and Nancy Saporta Sternbach (Amherst: University of Massachusetts Press, 1989), 181–188; and Wilma Feliciano, "Language and Identity in Three Plays by Dolores Prida," *Latin American Theater Review,* 28.1 (Fall 1994), 125–138.

15. Luz Maria Umpierre, "Interview with Dolores Prida," *Latin American Theatre Review* (Fall 1988): 82.

16. For a definition of "compulsory heterosexuality," see Adrienne Rich's well-known article "Compulsory Heterosexuality and Lesbian Existence," *Blood, Bread, and Poetry* (New York: W.W. Norton, 1986), 23–75; Sue-Ellen Case, in *Feminism and Theatre* (New York: Methuen, 1988), summarizes Rich's argument in the following manner: "Rich identifies two ways in which heterosexuality is made compulsory: through 'the constraints and sanctions that, historically, have enforced or ensured the coupling of women with men' and, in a phrase she borrowed from Catherine MacKinnon, 'the eroticization of women's subordination.' Rich places lesbianism in the context of patriarchal oppression rather than in the bi-gender context of homosexuality. The lesbian, she suggests, performs an act of resistance to the patriarchal assumption that men have the right of access to women"(75).

17. Prida, 20.

18. For an analysis of woman's image as a fulfillment of male desire, see Jill Dolan, *The Feminist Spectator as Critic* (Ann Arbor: University of Michigan, 1988), 54. For studies of women and the beauty myth, see María Teresa Marrero, *"Real Women Have Curves:* The Articulation of Fat as a Cultural/Feminist Issue," *Ollantay Theater Magazine,* 1.1 (Jan. 1993), 61–70; and Naomi Wolf, *The Beauty Myth: How Images of Beauty Are Used Against Women* (New York: Anchor Books, 1992).

19. This line was eliminated in the publication of the play. It appears in the manuscript (1980) as one of the lines in the song "They Do It All For Me."

20. Cherríe Moraga, *Giving Up the Ghost* (Los Angeles: West End Press, 1986).

21. Yvonne Yarbro-Bejarano, "The Female Subject in Chicano Theatre: Sexuality, 'Race,' and Class," *Performing Feminisms: Feminist Critical Theory and Theatre,* ed. Sue-Ellen Case (Baltimore: Johns Hopkins University Press, 1990), 145. Also, see her article, "Cherríe Moraga's *Giving Up the Ghost:* The Representation of Female Desire," *Third Woman* 3.1 (1986) 113–120.

22. Janis Astor del Valle, *Where the Señoritas Are,* unpublished manuscript, 1993; all further references are included parenthetically within the text. An excerpt of the play is published in *Torch to the Heart: Anthology of Lesbian Art and Drama,* ed. Sue McConnell-Celi (Newark, N.J.: Lavender Press, 1994), 83–96. I would like to thank Astor del Valle for providing me with the manuscript of the play.

23. Jill Dolan, in *The Feminist Spectator as Critic,* says the following on lesbian representation: "A body displayed in representation that belongs to the female gender class is assumed to be heterosexual, since male desire organizes the representational system. Disrupting the assumption of heterosexuality, and replacing male desire with lesbian desire, for example, offers radical new readings of the meanings produced by representation." (63)

24. For a theorization of butch-femme role playing and lesbian spectorial desire and identification, see Sue-Ellen Case, "Toward a Butch-Femme Aesthetic," in *Making a Spectacle: Feminist Essays on Contemporary Women's Theatre,* ed. Lynda Hart (Ann Arbor: The University of Michigan Press, 1989), 282–299; Teresa de Lauretis, "Film and the Visible," in *How Do I Look?: Queer Film and Video,* ed. Bad Object Choices (Seattle: Bay Press, 1991), 223–276.

25. As Jill Dolan suggests in "Gender Impersonation Onstage," "In gay male drag, women fare no better. Female impersonation here is usually filtered through the camp sensibility, which removes it from the realm of serious gender play and deconstruction... [Women] are non-existent in drag performance, but woman-as-myth, as a cultural, ideological object, is constructed in an agreed-upon exchange between the male performer and the usually male spectator. Male drag mirrors women's socially constructed roles" (8).

26. Judith Butler, *Gender Trouble: Feminism and The Subversion of Identity* (New York: Routledge, 1990), 137–38.

27. Teresa de Lauretis, "Film and the Visible," 250–251.

28. Indeed, Luli's definition does not imply gender understood as a role. Judith Butler exposes in "Performative Acts and Gender Constitution: An Essay in Phenomenology and Feminist Theory" the fact that "gender cannot be understood as a role which either expresses or disguises an interior 'self,' whether that 'self' is conceived as sexed or not. As performance which is performative, gender is an 'act,' broadly construed, which constructs the social fiction of its own psychological interiority." This quote appears in *Performing Feminisms: Feminist Critical Theory and Theatre* ed. Sue-Ellen Case (Baltimore: Johns Hopkins University Press, 1990), 279.

29. Adrienne Rich, "Compulsory Heterosexuality," 51–52.

30. Latina lesbian performers are also opening a space for lesbian representation. For example, in their performances, Marga Gómez and Carmelita Tropicana deconstruct dominant stereotypes of "Beautiful Señoritas" from a lesbian perspective. On Carmelita Tropicana, see Lillian Manzor Coats, "Too Spik or Too Dyke: Carmelita Tropicana." *Ollantay Theater Magazine* 2.1 (Winter/Spring 1994), 39–55, and her essay in this collection.

31. Gloria Anzaldúa, *Borderlands/La Frontera: The New Mestiza* (San Francisco: Spinsters/Aunt Lute, 1987), 79.

Subverting Scripts:
Identity and Performance
in Plays by U.S. Latinas

Yolanda Flores

Women of color, a term originated in the 1970s to represent a challenge to the presumed homogeneity of voice and vision within the feminist movement, designates a political position that identifies North American women who face the triple burden of class, racial, and gender oppression. The contribution of women of color to the theater has been to bring to center stage their histories, traditions, and experiences, which affect the way they write for the theater, the way they choose to practice their art. Native American women, for example, reclaim their storytelling traditions. People of color are too often examined, defined, and labeled through the historical legitimation of the European-American perspective that renders all other perspectives secondary or inferior. Thus, a common thread that unifies the minority women playwrights who embrace the political category *women of color* is that, in one form or another, they attempt to validate cultural forms, histories, languages, and traditions of people not fully incorporated into or recognized by the dominant European-American culture. In using the term "political," I am not referring solely to actions originating in the government; rather, I wish to evoke the everyday negotiations of power, economics, ethics, education, culture, race, class, gender, emotions, intellect, and art that Amerasian playwright Valina Hasu Houston aptly designates "the politics of life."[1]

African-American women have been the pioneers and the first spokespersons for the movement of women of color. Similarly, they were the first women of color to achieve commercial and critical success in theater circles. Alice Childress's play *Trouble in Mind* won the Obie award in 1956 for the best Off-Broadway play of the season. In 1959, Lorraine Hansberry's play *A Raisin in the Sun* won the New York Drama Critics Circle award for best play of the year. Adrienne Kennedy, in 1964, earned an Obie Distinguished Play award for *Funnyhouse of a Negro.* And in

1970, Ntozake Shange's *for colored girls who have considered suicide when the rainbow is enuf* was a commercial success on Broadway.[2] Although most of these playwrights center their work on their experiences as black women, some explore the position of African-American women and mainstream theater. By mainstream theater, I mean large commercial houses that principally produce plays written by European-American male authors or by deceased Europeans. Alice Childress's *Florence* (1949) and *Trouble in Mind* dramatize the oppression African-American actors endure within their profession.[3] In *Florence,* the protagonist's only opportunities are to be cast in a Broadway play in which she performs the marginal role of a maid or to work in all-black productions, thus separated from the dominant culture.

Adrienne Kennedy has further explored the complex relationship between African-American women and the white theater establishment. In *A Movie Star Has to Star in Black and White* (1976), the protagonist, Clara, is an African-American dramatist who experiences difficulties in writing plays true to her life experience, that is, with black characters.[4] Hollywood's all-white glamorous actors and actresses constantly encroach on Clara's imagination, affecting her ability to write stories with black stars, because she has been deprived of the opportunity to visualize African-Americans as "Hollywood Stars." In this play, as in *The Owl Answers,* Kennedy insinuates the effects of internalized racism on colonized people.[5] She also shows the marginality and invisibility people of color experience in the prevailing system.

Making history's "invisibilities" visible is one way to describe Velina Hasu Houston's early work. In the trilogy of plays that culminates with *Tea,* Houston treats events of North American history not always acknowledged in contemporary American classrooms. In *Tea,* she examines critically the way traditional Japanese culture perceived the women who married North American soldiers after World War II.[6] Yet, the author maintains that same cautious glance at the racist relocation policies the U.S. government imposed on Japanese-Americans and the Amerasian communities during World War II. Houston, who is the daughter of a Japanese "international bride" mother and an African-American/ Native American father, in her personal life is engaged with activist community groups that promote the understanding of Amerasian culture. Although the playwrights

of color discussed thus far practice their art and political positions in various fashions, their work manifests how race, class,
and gender affect the art and personal experience of individuals
of that background.

Unlike women of color who are monolingual, bilingual Latina
playwrights run the risk of linguistically marginalizing themselves
even further from mainstream audiences and theater. Most Latina
playwrights today choose to write almost entirely in English,
with a few words in Spanish or Spanglish, the mixture of Spanish and English and the form of speech more in tune with their
personal experiences and their communities. But language, culture, and value systems are, at times, so interconnected that their
separation is impossible. Take, for example, *Coser y cantar* by
Cuban-American playwright Dolores Prida, where the dialects
of Cuban identity and Anglo-American assimilation are dramatized by a protagonist split into two: one speaking in English
and the other in Spanish, both selves competing to dominate
the creation of a whole.[7] Prida, in a gesture that simultaneously
embodies a sense of gleefulness and irony, describes her play as
one "which deals with how to be a bilingual, bicultural woman
in Manhattan and keep your sanity."[8] Nevertheless, even if a
play is written in English, with only a few words in Spanish, the
other language, the other culture, is still ever present.

Simply María or The American Dream by Chicana playwright
Josefina López, is a play that depicts the conflicting messages
that two cultures—Anglo-American and Mexican—offer to a
young woman caught between them.[9] What emerges is the creation of an identity neither wholly one nor the other: it partakes
of both. This experimental play adopts a nonlinear structure,
presenting a series of episodes heralded by titles that unsettle
the audience's expectation of suspense. Borrowing from Brecht's
notion of epic theater, it is a direct political critique of representational structures that mystify social relations.[10] Dismantling the
contrived nature of realist drama and its ideological implications, epic theater aims to empower its audiences by showing
them that in realist drama, as in life, hidden power structures
manipulate the construction of the real. Stressing narrativity
rather than plot, *Simply María* appropriates North American
and Latin American popular culture, subverting these forms
while incorporating them into the text. Its thematic ethnic con-

tent, as in some recent Chicano films, functions as a formal element that creates a style unto itself.[11] *Simply María* performs on stage the creation of a Latina American identity; in both form and content, this new bilingual/bicultural creation challenges dominant discourses, as it reflects the social and political oppression that people of color endure in the United States.

In contrast with both the earliest dramatic performances on North American soil and the more contemporary Chicano theater of Luis Valdez, where the presence of women is narrowed to their participation as actresses in secondary roles, *Simply María* centers on a young woman's search for independence from the cultural impositions placed on women by the traditional Mexican culture.[12] Ultimately, the heroine's quest is for the happiness promised by the American dream.

Dissenting against the narratives that inundate popular culture, *Simply María* is antiromantic. In this one-act play divided into twelve scenes, the literary encoding of the mise-en-scène is highlighted by constant references to popular culture's romantic scripts. The play's title itself, *Simply María,* alludes to *Simplemente María,* an extremely popular telenovela that aired across Latin America and in the United States through the Spanish International Network (SIN). As is characteristic of most popular soap operas, *Simplemente María* draws on the Cinderella theme of the beautiful young woman from the lower class who raises her socioeconomic status through marriage to a wealthy man.[13] Unlike the Latin American version, the unromantic narrative of *Simply María* is compared with the universal narrative of North American culture: the American dream. Thus it evokes the hybrid nature of this creation. In addition, by equating the felicity that the American dream brings to mind with the tide of a soap opera, a melodrama, it foreshadows the specific North American reception of Latin Americans, particularly the poorer and more ethnically marked, a differentiation that, as I will argue later, is based on race. Yet, the deployment of popular narratives, to which the play's title alludes, is not an isolated instance; rather, it highlights the beginning of a technique used consistently throughout the play.

The nonlinear structure of the text begins with the end: in a flashback, María enters the stage and sits down to watch the enactment of the creation of her adult character. With regard to the theatrical performance, this strategy foregrounds the fact that the audience can no longer maintain the illusion of being the unseen spectator at an event that is really taking place. Scene 1, set in a small village in Mexico, recreates the night María's parents eloped, an act conceived in the imagination of María's mother with expectations advanced by popular romantic tales. The escape of María's parents, Ricardo and Carmen, is introduced with an allusion to the primordial romantic narrative: "Romeo and Juliet elope" (117). But Carmen's running away from her mother's home is a distant reenactment of the fiction on which it is modeled. On the night that Carmen descends from her balcony to meet Ricardo, she asks him for the horse they will need for their flight. Instead of a horse, Ricardo has brought his old bike. Carmen reacts incredulously: "Qué! On that? No! How could you... Everyone knows that when you elope, you elope on a horse, not on a...Ricardo, you promised!" (117). Still, they escape on the ragged bicycle that, with difficulty, accommodates its two passengers. On one level, this scene elucidates the way in which popular culture informs people's imaginations and expectations of "the way things should be." López, in counterpoint, deconstructs these narratives by representing an outcome that is more realistic. In this initial framing scene, the playwright posits a theme that recurs throughout the rest of the theatrical performance: scripts are scripts and, as such, they can be rewritten.

Another manifestation of popular culture that *Simply María* blends into the construction of the play is film. Ricardo, in a charro's attire, engaged in the act of rescuing his young daughter and wife from the mob and confusion of downtown Los Angeles, borrows from the Mexican tradition of charro movies, in which the hero is always a man dressed in that sort of outfit. Even amid the array of characters that stroll down L.A.'s Broadway Avenue—preachers, street vendors, Chicano activists, Valley Girls, cholos, and bag ladies—Ricardo's entrance into this scene is monumental and a bit out of synchrony with the urban setting. His arrival is described thus: "Ricardo, dressed in a charro outfit, enters and gives some yells as if ready to sing a corrido. All the chaos of the city stops, and all the city people recoil in fear" (123). In contrast with the scene in which Ricardo and Carmen's realities override the romantic tale, the fictitious film narrative in this case nullifies the plausibilities of fact. López, in a sense, deploys this strategy to validate the Mexican cultural presence in this foreign land: only in the fantastic realm of the movies could a poor Mexican man be endowed with the heroic stature described in this scene; only in the movies could an otherwise vulnerable foreigner cause such an uproar in a setting designated by a slide on the top of the stage as "Los Angelitos del Norte." This scene, akin to the one analyzed previously, points to the double cultural reading encoded in this text.

The telenovela's intertext recurs in scene 9. Soon after a confrontation with her parents, who want María to relinquish her ambition to attend college and urge her, instead, to find a nice man to marry, María falls sleep. The three scenes that follow take place in her dreams. She sees herself married to a man who treats her like a domestic servant and objectifies her as his sexual commodity. In her nightmare, a pregnant María one day sits in her living room to watch a TV soap opera, *Happily Ever After*. The heroine of this story, Eliza Vásquez, is in the midst of walking out on a suffocating marriage and confronts her husband, Devero, with her dissatisfaction and desire to be free. "But I've given you everything!" says Devero, to which Eliza responds, "Everything but an identity! Well, Devero, Devero, Devero, I've discovered I no longer need you. There are unfulfilled dreams I must pursue. I want adventure" (133). The commercial that interrupts this segment of the soap opera ridicules the ideal traditional domestic wife: it shows a husband returning home from work with a precious gift for his wife: a can of Ajax. The wife receives it gratefully, claiming that it is an unmerited proof of her husband's devotion and generosity to her.

The self-reflexive element of these scenes necessitates further discussion: the soap opera and TV commercial sequences have been taped in María's living room and not in a TV studio. When, in her dreams, María sees a TV producer and actors in her apartment, she timidly protests their intrusion into her house, but readily acquiesces and lets the show be performed in her living room. Thus María watches a "fictive" resolution to the dilemmas affecting decisions that she should make when she awakens. Moreover, we, the audience of the play, are voyeurs of María's soap opera watching. In the theatrical event, this episode calls attention to the constructed nature of representation.

Interestingly, *Happily Ever After* does not honor the implied, anticipated ending alluded to by its title. Instead, it illustrates that this narrative is dispensed at great expense to women. The TV commercial that performs a cheerful version of the satisfied domestic wife underscores the disparity with the ending of *Happily Ever After*. López, in this manner, highlights the fact that women's roles and behavior are scripts constructed and imposed by a patriarchal ideology. From a different angle, given that community ethnic theaters are the most likely venues for producing this play and that the audience in attendance would most probably be Latino, López's self-referential technique of voyeurism performs for the Latino community the construction of a bilingual/bicultural identity, an alternative model nonexistent in the dominant culture.

Happily Ever After further explores the multicultural dimensions of North American society: the bicultural nature of this television production is not yet found in the North American version of soap operas nor in the Latin American telenovelas. From the Latin American telenovela, it borrows its clear-cut ending format; in its North American counterpart the ending remains open.[14] Yet, thematically, it departs from the romantic Cinderella formula common among Latin American telenovelas. Furthermore, by performing on stage the type of domestic problems that frequently arise after the amorous "happy ending," it demystifies romantic closures. From North America, it appropriates the cheerful notion of a "happily ever after." However, in staging Latinos as central characters in what appears as mainstream soap opera, it breaks boundaries placed on the representation of Latinos in Anglo-American television: no North American soap opera, to date, has permitted Latinos to be central characters in its stories.[15] *Happily Ever After* draws on both cultural traditions. From Latin America, it absorbs a tradition based on popular culture, which, in this case, is manifested in its deployment of soap operas to construct a meta-soap opera. A tinge of ironic playfulness accompanies the appropriations from North American popular culture: the barrio in which the poor, undocumented Mexican people live, among them María and her parents, is announced by a slide that reads "The Little House in the Ghetto." This title, of course, alludes to the "All-American" (white/European) family of the North American popular television series *The Little House on the Prairie*. The racial differences and their consequences are implicit in the shift.

These self-referential dramatic techniques beg for a closer examination of the construction of scripts, particularly those that have circumscribed women's lives and the roles they play. In scene 2, a slide reading "The Making of a Mexican Girl" advances the revelation of this creation. The wedding of María's parents as well as her infant baptism occur in the same ceremony, under the tutelage of the Catholic Church. As the priest places the baby in the center of the altar, three angelic girls sing beautifully the name *María*. This is followed by a recitation of the ingredients for "making a Mexican girl." From a long list, I extract the following examples: 1) as a nice girl, María ought to be forgiving and obedient; 2) she ought to like dolls, kitchens, cleaning, and caring for children; 3) María ought not to be independent nor to enjoy sex but must endure it in order to have children; 4) she ought never to shame her society; and, most important, 5) her goal in life is to reproduce; her only purpose in life is to serve three men: father, husband, and son (119).

The resonance of this trio of men with the Holy Trinity–Father, Son, and Holy Spirit–is not gratuitous: the Church, aside from offering its blessing, prescribes this behavior for women.[16] In the scene depicting Maria's dream, where she is marrying the "nice man" chosen by her parents, the sermon of the Catholic wedding ceremony dismantles the type of traditional matrimony Maria is expected to accept. The priest intones:

María, do you accept José Juan González López as your lawfully wedded husband to love, cherish, serve, cook for, clean for, sacrifice for, have his children, keep his house, love him even if he beats you, commits adultery, gets drunk, rapes you lawfully, denies you your identity, money, love his family, serve his family, and in return ask for nothing? (132)

Significantly, the baptism takes place in the Mexican village where María was born. The cultural baggage of these two scripts will accompany María's growth into womanhood, creating a source of conflict with North American society's freer values with regard to women. Together with her mother, María arrives in the United States as a small child; they come to join her father, who, since Carmen's pregnancy, has been saving money to send for his wife and child. Like that of many poor immigrants, Ricardo's reason for asking his wife and child to join him is to be able to offer them a better future, "In America," Ricardo tells his young child, "the education is great. You can take advantage of all the opportunities offered to you. You can work hard to be just as good as anybody" (124). Little María believes these words and begins to adapt gradually to U.S. values by showing a spirit of competitiveness in school sports and academics, behavior that her mother distrusts as unbefitting a Mexican girl. María's adolescence becomes a constant battle between, on the one hand, her parents' demand that she excel in domestic chores and, on the other, her yearnings for independence and the opportunity to go to college.

It is not accidental, then, that María wants to go to college to study to be an actress. For what is acting but the ability to transcend oneself, to become another person by performing a different script? This emphasis on acting in *Simply María* and, as I will discuss later, in *Latina*, goes beyond the use of game-playing as a mere theatrical convention, as some critics have observed to be the case of contemporary Latin American theater.[17] Rather than espousing the idea that life, like theater, is a game, López views the similarities between life and theater more as an enactment of scripts that are embedded in the culture in which one finds oneself. When those narratives prove inadequate, one has the potential to rewrite them. *Simply María,* it seems to me, is in tune with Elizabeth Burns' conception:

A theatrical quality of life...experienced more concretely by those who feel themselves at the margins of events either because they have adopted the role of spectator or...because they have not been offered a part or have not learnt it sufficiently well to enable them to join the actor—those who do not participate in a social system are less likely to see it as natural and are therefore more sensitive to its contrived or constructed quality.[18]

The notion of life as a game embodies a sense of playfulness that, although it has the potential to highlight relations of power, does not necessarily show how to change them. Moreover, Burns' comment contextualizes María's marginality in both Mexican and North American cultures. The role she ought to play is not yet written in either culture; she must write it herself. Once that script is written, she can empower herself by performing it, no longer confined to limbo by the confusion of not having an identity, a role to play.

The empowerment gained by performing a Latina identity can be appreciated when one considers that from the perspective of a woman of color, of a Latina within the North American context, acting out roles signifies one channel through which she can change the negative images Hollywood and Broadway produce of Latinos. Sarita, an actress and the central character of Milcha Sánchez-Scott's play *Latina*, echoing Alice Childress's *Florence*, voices the predicament of Latino actors by evoking the sort of Latino images on television programming. She laments:

I'll give you my credits. I was a barrio girl who got raped in "Police Story," a young barrio mother who got shot by a gang in "Starsky and Hutch," a barrio wife who got beat up by her husband who was in a gang in "Rookies." I was even a barrio lesbian who got knifed by an all girl gang called the Mal-flores... That means Bad Flowers. It's been a regular barrio blitz on television lately. If this fad continues, I can look forward to being a barrio grandmother done in by a gang of old Hispanics called Los Viejitos Diablitos, the old devils.[19]

Although, as Sarita observes, Latino actors still find their substance constrained by the desires of European-American producers, once a Latino actress or actor is well established within mainstream media, she or he has the potential to exercise influence to modify the negative roles and stereotypes of Latinos and to write better scripts for Latino actors. Josefina López's own aspiration to be a writer is born, precisely, of her desire to change the negative images Hollywood and Broadway circulate of Latinos and, especially, Latinas.[20]

Acting plays a pivotal role in *Simply María* and *Latina*. In *Latina,* the emphasis on performing assumes varied shapes that all lead to one end: empowerment. 1) Sarita fears that she will not get a part in the TV series for which she auditioned because, as she says, "I am too dark and freaky for 'Eight is Enough.' They don't have stupid Mexicans playing nurses on prime time, you know I might scare the kids." By the end of the play, this fear is dissipated, because she is finally cast in a non-stereotypical Latina role (93). 2) To support her acting career, Sarita works as a counselor for a domestic agency located in downtown Los Angeles, where the multiethnic composition of that city is, once more, highlighted. But unlike *Simply María,* which draws primarily on Mexican and Chicano presence and cultural forms, that is, cholos, Chicano activists, and Mexican corridos, through *Latina's* domestic agency circulate women from all over Latin America: Cubans, Peruvians, Salvadorans, Colombians, and Guatemalans, among others. Some of these women are undocumented and can barely speak English. To help them find employment, Sarita, in several instances, plays the employer and teaches them how to "act" more American in order to fit their European-American employers' demands. 3) In her role as a counselor, Sarita functions as a broker between the recently immigrated poor women and their white employers. Throughout the play, several European-Americans complain about their maids' inability to perform to their standards. On one occasion, an employer returns Almita, the maid who worked for her, as if she were damaged merchandise, to the domestic agency, claiming, "She has no respect for my blue and white Chinese porcelain, or any of our antiques and things that are irreplaceable" (109). A critique of the objectification of human beings and the human value attached to objects in consumer societies is implicit in this brief exchange. Still, Sarita never defends the maids, taking, instead, the side of the employer, and, by doing so, provoking resentment from the Latina women, who interpret Sarita's actions as a sign that she is ashamed of being a Latina and wants to be a "gringa desteñida" (112). Here, it is worth noting that the character of Sarita clearly embodies certain advantages–acculturated demeanor, and citizenship–that an illegal woman from Latin America lacks in the U.S. context.

Latina also dramatizes the exploitation of maids from their perspective. For example, Clara, one of the characters, describes her employer:

She like to talk. Eso de everybody equal. She go to meet with the other women, they talk everybody equal y de los husbands y como los hombres le tratan de mal. They talk how the women must be equal to men. Then she come to me and say, "Clara, you and me, equal." Hmmmmmph! I don't pay attention... She don't know nothing. I been taking three buses every day to clean houses for fifteen years and she...
(116)

Another character, Chata, articulates her own version of the complaint of women of color about the white feminist movement: "Comadre, you ain't equal to her. Any pendejo can see that" (116). The dehumanization of the domestic worker is expressed in *Latina* through Lola's confrontation with her employer:

Why, no one in your house call me by my name… All of you speak of me as your Mexican maid. Always you say, "Ask the maid, tell the maid." Each day you make me more nobody, more dead. You put me in nice white uniforms so I won't offend your good taste. You take my name, my country. You don't want a person, you want a machine. My name is Lola. I am from Guatemala. (139)

Sánchez-Scott clearly criticizes women who seek liberation at the expense of the exploitation of other women.

In the final scene, Sarita, for the first time, stands up for the Latina maids by rebutting the unjust accusations of an employer, engaging in physical contact with the aggressor. The women applaud Sarita's efforts to defend them; one of them says, "Sarita, I only wanted you to stand up for us, not to kill the woman. Andale un abrazo… Ahora, sí eres una Latina completamente Latina" (140). This example suggests that acting Latina is not so much linked to biological factors as it is to accepting an ideological position that recognizes the disenfranchisement of the Latino poor population. Through this recognition, a Latina identity acts in opposition to the forces that cause this oppression.

The interesting aspect of the preceding examples is that the value attached to acting derives from its practical purposes in seeking to empower the disempowered. Everyday "acts" constitute Houston's "politics of life." Similarly, López's and Sánchez-Scott's "acts" seek to change the artistic and social world they inhabit. For actors and playwrights, Hollywood and Broadway are sites in need of much change.

Simply María intimates reasonable root causes for Hollywood's acceptance of Latinos. Scene 3 stages the qualitatively different reception the Statue of Liberty dispenses to the European immigrant and to the non-European, in this case, the Mexicans. A giant sail enters the stage, brought in by four European immigrants: Italian, French, German, and Anglo; they all wave goodbye to their countries in their native languages. In the background, the sound of "America the Beautiful" is heard while three Mexican immigrants enter the stage. Ricardo is one of them. The Statue of Liberty recites the well-known verse,

Give me your tired, your poor, your huddled masses yearning to breathe free... I give you life, liberty, and the pursuit of happiness for the price of your heritage, your roots, your history, your relatives, your language... Conform, adapt, bury your past, give up what is yours and I'll give you the opportunity to have what is mine. (120–21)

Two of the Mexican immigrants accept this promise. One of them responds, "pues bueno, if we have to" (121). As lights flash, representing the celebration of the Americanization of the European immigrants, those same flickers become the glints of the helicopters that hunt the Mexican immigrants; the helicopters' lights are accompanied by the barking of hounds. The European immigrants join the Statue of Liberty in pointing to the Mexicans, so that they get caught. The scene ends with the European immigrants standing proudly next to the U.S. icon, while the Mexicans run offstage. As performed in this scene, there are no differences between the European and the Mexican immigrants except for race or color. Both groups are willing to abide by the demands of the North American foundational promise; yet the Mexicans are not welcomed.

But López is not the first playwright to point to the difference between North America's reception of the European and the non-European; other North American artists of color have made the same type of critique of the ideals of the Statue of Liberty. Amerasian writer Susy So Schaller, in her poem "Forget Me Not America," describes the sense of broken promises experienced by many Amerasians.[21] Extrapolating from these examples and from the constraints of North American history, one may extend this sentiment to immigrants of color, most particularly to those who are poor. Addressed to the Statue of Liberty, "Forget Me Not America" reads:

as you flock by the thousands to pay tribute
to a statue who represents your beloved ideals
falling short of our ideals,
have we settled for idle worship
making pilgrimage to stone?...

America, you fight for the first breath of the unborn
loose chains of your forgotten children
who remain wealthy heirs to two countries
yet without a home to call their own
whose only claim is an unmapped destiny
in a forgotten country called Amerasia.

Schaller's poem, in the second stanza, eloquently evokes the invisibility and the "unmapped destiny" of Amerasians left behind in Asia. The first stanza voices the sense of betrayal that Amerasians, like other people of color, often experience in this country. Likewise, López hints that the Statue of Liberty and the other immigrants do not welcome the Mexicans because they are not white Europeans. A similar attitude explains why the head nurse who delivers María's babies, the ones she gives birth to during the nightmare sequence, refers to them as "Mexican litter" (136). To borrow the title of a Cornel West book, in North American society, as in most societies, "race matters."

Josefina López's critique of North American racist practices is mild in comparison with other women writers of color, such as Audre Lorde, Patricia Williams, bell hooks, Gloria Anzaldúa, and Cherríe Moraga. López, in this play, never makes direct reference to race; rather, she quietly exposes representations of how that racism is enacted. Yet, neither María nor López can disassociate themselves from the implications brought about by their "raced" bodies in dominant white America. María's last words on stage as she prepares to abandon her parents' household in search of her independence are telling:

"Mexico is in my blood and America is in my heart" (141). Although both Mexico and the United States are equated with bodily organs, the heart is commonly associated with a state of mind, a set of ideas and values. Blood, in contrast, evokes, among many other things, a vivid color often associated with violence; it cannot be easily ignored: it is always a strong, notorious differential marker.

The cultural confusion between the Mexican and North American value systems that the play chronicles allows María to turn that confusion into a source of agency that gives her the courage to abandon her parents' household. North America has rewarded María's hard academic work by granting her a four-year scholarship to attend college. When María awakes from her sleep, she overhears her mother's cries as she argues with her husband– Carmen is confronting Ricardo about her suspicion of his infidelity; although initially he attempts to deny these accusations, Ricardo finally says to his wife, "Look, every man sooner or later does it." (140). Their argument reveals that Ricardo has been unfaithful to his wife many times before; Carmen knew this but chose to remain passive out of fear that her husband would send her and María back to Mexico (140). María recognizes that within the Mexican cultural framework, this is the type of future that awaits her if she is to follow her parents' values. Had she remained in the village in which she was born, María most likely would have had no option but to follow the traditional Mexican script. However, she is in North America, and she opts to fight for her share of the American dream, accepting the college scholarship that will separate her from her parents:

I want to create a world of my own. One that combines the best of me. I won't forget the values of my roots, but I want to get the best of this land of opportunities… Los quiero mucho. Nunca los olvidaré. Mexico is in my blood. And America is in my heart (141).

Mexican and North American societies, values, and popular narratives are the procreators of *Simply María*. Although on one level, *Simply María* is celebratory of North America, a counternarrative represents critically the racial prejudices dispensed to the non-European population.

The mainstream audience's reception of ethnic theater is indicative that North American society is still slow to accept cultural artifacts from traditions other than the white European. As mentioned before, López's plays have been produced in California by community theaters, that is, in ethnically based productions. Among Chicano theater scholars, the work of Josefina López has begun to be better known, thanks especially to the theater organization Teatros Nacionales de Aztlán (TENAZ), but Anglo-American companies have yet to take an interest in producing this play.[22] Perhaps their reluctance to undertake ethnic projects derives from the fear that they will not prove to be commercially successful ventures: the plays are too "ethnic" for white audiences. To a certain extent, it is true that ethnic plays tend to treat themes and cultural and linguistic forms that, in order to be fully appreciated, require explanation of their context.

These observations do not diminish Josefina López's artistic and personal achievements. And, despite all the limitations encountered in North America by a poor immigrant of color, where else could López, who lived undocumented in this country until a few years ago, at her youthful age, achieve so much? The character of López María is, after all, López's alter ego: *Simply María* draws heavily on autobiography. A native of Cerritos, San Luis Potosí, in Mexico, López came to this country with her parents when she was six years old. Now twenty-five, she has captured numerous awards; three of her plays, *Simply María or The American Dream, Real Women Have Curves*, and *Food for the Dead* have been produced in community theaters, principally in California;[23] and some newspapers have reviewed López's work warmly.[24] López identifies personally with the political label of a Chicana and views her role as a Chicana playwright as a commitment to changing the negative representations of Latinos, and especially Latinas, in the theater and in Hollywood.[25] Like María's decision to seek the fulfillment of the American dream, López's accomplishments as a writer are the fruits of the authors's search for that dream. Like the heroine of *Simply María*, artistically and personally, López has created her own world, one that combines the best of the scenarios she inhabits. For a change, the heroine of the play is an intelligent, independent Latina who demystifies Anglo-American images of Latinas. In *Simply María*, the Latino community has a playwright and a heroine to celebrate, and North America procreates a raced, gendered version of the Horatio Alger narrative.

Simply María and *Latina* draw from the author's personal experiences, dramatizing the creation of a Latina identity. In this regard, they echo Cuban-American dramatist Dolores Prida, who affirms, "Most of my plays have been about the experience of being Hispanic in the United States, about people trying to reconcile two cultures and two languages and two visions of the world into a particular whole: plays that aim to be a reflection of a particular time and space, of a here and now."[26] Like López, Milcha Sánchez-Scott immigrated to the United States, to Los Angeles specifically, as a small child. Sánchez-Scott's ancestry is Columbian, Indonesian, Dutch, and Chinese, but because her upbringing in California was heavily influenced by Chicano culture, she adopted that label for herself. *Latina*, like *Simply María*, draws on the author's personal experiences. In her more recent play, *Roosters*, Sánchez-Scott recovers her Latin American roots; she experiments with magic realism in a piece where the fictional space is an unspecified place in the Southwest.[27] However, the incorporation of other Latin American elements can be traced to her first play, *Latina*: the characters are immigrants from various Latin American nations and not simply from Mexico; Peruvian music accompanies the beginning and the end of the play; and references to the sculptures of Mexican–Costa Rican artist Francisco Zúñiga are a source of proud cultural identification to a young Sarita, who is struggling to find her identity. Latino ethnicities are complex and continuously evolving, but the term *Latino*, as opposed to *Hispanic*, allows commonalities to surface; working-class identification is an important one.

Rather than writing a story, López and Sánchez-Scott opt for the dramatic genre to display how gender roles and cultural values are scripts that can be subverted and rewritten. For, unlike the reading of a story in the privacy of one's home, theater has the advantage of showing, of "putting on stage," the gestation of a new creation. In privileging Brecht's notions of epic theater, López demonstrates how an individual is alterable and able to alter the course of events. *Simply María* and *Latina* illustrate how performative acts lead to the construction of gendered and cultural identities that are always embedded in social, cultural, and political contexts and in structures of power.

Latinas' presence on stage, as evidenced by the works discussed, promises to bring exciting challenges and important contributions to North American theater. These writers, like other women of color, incarnate in their dramatic productions a mixed blessing: although they sit in the margins of mainstream society, they are, nonetheless, at the forefront of ethnicity and gender awareness. This feature distinguishes them from their counterparts in Latin American countries, where a discourse on race, class, and ethnicity from the perspective of women who bear that burden, has yet to be articulated. As audiences and critics responding to Latinas' dramatic texts, we are moved to ask ourselves questions about the relationship between theater and life, art and society, and academic criticism and the social world, because all these realms constitute "the politics of life." In recognizing this challenge, the central remaining question is simply this: To act or not to act?

Notes

1. Velina Hasu Houston, "Introduction," *The Politics of Life: Four Plays by Asian American Women* (Philadelphia: Temple University Press, 1993), 8.

2. Ntozake Shange, *for colored girls who have considered suicide when the rainbow is enuf* (New York: Bantam, 1980).

3. Alice Childress, "Florence," in *Masses and Mainstream* 3.10 (1950): 34–57; "Trouble in Mind," in *Black Theater: A Twentieth Century Collection. The Work of its Best Playwrights.* comp. Lindsay Patterson (New York: Dodd and Mead, 1971), 135–74.

4. Adrienne Kennedy. "A Movie Star Has to Star in Black and White," in *One Act* (Minneapolis: University of Minnesota Press, 1988), 79–103.

5. Adrienne Kennedy, "The Owl Answers," in *One Act* (Minneapolis: University of Minnesota Press, 1988), 25–45.

6. Velina Hasu Houston, *Tea*, unpublished script.

7. Dolores Prida, "Coser y cantar: A Bilingual Fantasy for Two Women," in *Beautiful Señoritas and Other Plays* (Houston: Arte Público Press, 1991), 47–67.

8. Dolores Prida, "The Show Does Go On (Testimonio)," in *Breaking Boundaries: Latina Writings and Critical Readings,* ed. Asunción Horno-Delgado, Eliana Ortega, Nina M. Scott, and Nancy Saporta Sternbach (Amherst: University of Massachusetts Press. 1989), 185.

9. Josefina López, "Simply María or The American Dream," in *Shattering the Myth: Plays by Hispanic Women,* ed. Linda Feyder (Houston: Arte Público Press, 1992), 113–41. All further references are included parenthetically within the text.

10. See Bertolt Brecht, "The Modern Theatre is the Epic Theatre," in *Dramatic Theory and Criticism: Greeks to Grotowski,* ed. Bernard Dukore (Orlando, Fla.: Holt, Rinehart and Winston, 1974), 847–48.

11. Chon Noriega, "Between a Weapon and a Formula: Chicano Cinema and Its Contexts," *Chicanos and Film: Representation and Resistance* (Minneapolis: University of Minnesota Press, 1992), 154.

12. I am referring particularly to the culture of the small, poor rural villages of Mexico, which tend to be much more traditional than the lower-class and middle-class segments of Mexican urban centers.

13. See Livia Antola and Evere Rogers, "Television Flows in Latin America," *Communication Research* 11 (1984): 189–95.

14. Ana López, "The Melodrama in Latin America," *Wide Angle* 7 (1985): 8.

15. There are no references to suggest that it could be a telenovela aired through the Spanish International Network and, therefore, a Latin American telenovela. Furthermore, given Gutiérrez and Schement's observation, it seems unlikely that the thematic content would lure

SIN to program a U.S. Latino soap opera: "Both SIN and the U.S. television networks apparently discriminate against hiring Latinos. Mexican TV programs convey value systems that are not always relevant to the U.S. society in which U.S. Latinos live. For instance, surveys of the U.S. Latino show considerable dissatisfaction with SIN television programs especially by younger Latinos." See Felix Gutiérrez and Jorge Reina Schement, "Spanish International Network: The Flow of Television from Mexico to the United States." *Communication Research* 11 (1984): 241–259.

16. Other Chicana and Latina writers have denounced the oppressive nature of Catholic teachings as they pertain to women. For further discussion of this topic, see Bettina R. Flores, *Chiquita's Cocoon* (Granite Bay: Pepper Vine Press, 1990), particularly chapter 7: "Religion. Reality, or Repression."

17. See, for example, Jacqueline Eyring Bixier. "Games and Reality on the Latin American Stage," *Latin American Literary Review* 12 (1988): 22–35; and Catherine Larson. "Playwrights of Passage: Women and Game-Playing on the Stage." *Latin American Literary Review* 19 (1991): 77–89.

18. Elizabeth Burns, *Theatricality* (New York: Harper and Row, 1972), 11.

19. Milcha Sánchez- Scott and Jeremy Blahnik. *Latina,* in *Necessary Theater: Six Plays about the Chicano Experience,* ed. Jorge Huerta (Houston: Arte Público, 1989), 89. All further references are included parenthetically within the text.

20. Josefina López, "On Being a Playwright," *Ollantay Theater Magazine* 2 (1993), 44.

21. Susy So Schaller, "Forget Me Not America," in *Poster* (Seattle: The Amerasian Network, 1988).

22. This comment is made with full awareness that Josefina López's youth is a factor that affects this observation. López wrote her first play when she was seventeen; she has four plays to her credit. The fourth one, *Unconquered Spirits,* won an honorable mention at the 1992 TENAZ competition.

23. El Repertorio Español in New York City produced a Spanish version of *Real Women Have Curves* in January 1995.

24. See, for example, Nancy Churnin, "Simply Josefina López," *Los Angeles Times,* July 17, 1990, 8E.

25. Josefina López, *Real Women Have Curves* (Seattle: Rain City Projects, 1988), 44.

26. Prida. "The Show," 182.

27. Milcha Sánchez-Scott, *Roosters,* in *On New Ground* (New York: Theatre Communications Group. 1987). 243–80.

Conquest of Space:
The Construction of Chicana
Subjectivity in Performance Art

Alicia Arrizón

An analysis of contemporary Chicana/o theater must be mapped beyond the historical implications of El Teatro Campesino. The emergence of El Teatro Campesino as part of the Chicano theater movement in the Southwest (and parts of the Midwest) was oriented toward the cultural affirmation of working-class Mexicans. The social and political upheavals of the Civil Rights and the United Farm Workers movements were two of the main sources that influenced the beginning of El Teatro Campesino in the 1960s. Recent criticism on El Teatro Campesino's evolution reinterprets the company's history and analyzes the gender relations at work in its productions. As Yolanda Broyles-González points out, female roles in the trajectory of El Teatro Campesino have been subjected to reductive characterizations. She suggests: "Throughout the course of El Teatro Campesino's dramatic evolutionary process, the female roles have remained fairly constant in all the genres: variations of the same three or four types of categories. These characters are defined in a familial or age category: mother, grandmother, sister, or wife/girlfriend."[1] The designations of sisters, wives, girlfriends and mothers usually fall into one or two categories, *la puta* or *la buena,* the whore or the virgin. This dichotomy continues to characterize the female roles even after the period of the early *actos.*[2]

Broyles-González also examines both the working-class Mexican oral performance and the collective performance practices of El Teatro Campesino. Although El Teatro Campesino's collective system of production characterizes the power of group "action," the contributions of dramatists such as Estela Portillo Trambley in the 1970s, and, later, Cherríe Moraga in the 1980s, have created a broader space for Chicana/o theater and cultural development.[3] Estela Portillo's baroque and obscure play *The Day of the Swallows* (1976) and Cherríe Moraga's play *Giving Up the Ghost* (1986), precisely ten years apart, are symbolic of their decades as well as of the transition in representational strategies from the 1970s to the 1980s. The former plots a misogynist lesbian, Doña Josefa, who, trapped against her own will, prefers to die rather than accept her lesbian desire.[5] Later, in *Giving Up the Ghost*, the representations of both lesbian and heterosexual desire define the paradoxes of culture's concepts of sexuality. Yvonne Yarbro-Bejarano has studied the representation of female-desiring subjects in Moraga's *Giving Up the Ghost*. She suggests that the representational subjectivity as "sexual beings is shaped in dialectical relationship to a collective way of imagining sexuality."[6]

From Portillo's *The Day of the Swallows* to Moraga's *Giving Up the Ghost*, the transition breaks new ground in Chicana/o theater. Although Portillo's treatment of a lesbian character in her play was motivated by economic reasons, Moraga's political awareness deconstructs the cultural forces that have shaped the roles that men and women should assume. This significant transition in Chicana/o theater constitutes the opening of an alternative space. Since the 1980s, more emphasis has been given to the female subject in this alternative space, and more direct questions of sexuality have emerged.[7] In the 1990s, self-representation has become one of the most recurrent practices in Chicana performance art. Chicana performance artists such as Monica Palacios and Laura Esparza embark on a multifaceted process of recreating their own stories in an attempt to acquire a fuller sense of themselves as Chicanas, women, performers, and/or queers. Palacios's lesbian representation in the 1990s subversively enlarges this alternative space mainly to critique the reinscription of heterosexuality and homophobia in the public sphere.

Within the context of the cultural specificity of Chicana identity, I try to show some ways in which representation on stage involves a total rethinking of the gendered self as an autobiographical subject. In this sense, the gendered self is understood within a representational subjectivity in which the "real" person becomes a metaphor of representation. The technology of self-representation functions to perform the metaphorical resonance of reality, "a metaphor that functions as a trope of truth beyond argument, of identity beyond proof, of what simply is."[8] Analyzing the work of Monica Palacios, *Latin Lezbo Comic: A Perfor-*

mance about Happiness, Challenges, and Tacos, and Laura Esparza, *I DisMember the Alamo: A Long Poem for Performance,* I bring to focus the concept of the gendered self as an essential part of the representational "plotting" necessary for the performative space.[9] Both performance pieces are included in this anthology as documents that represent the possibilities of writing, recalling the memory of past productions. Although my analysis is based mainly on these "documents," I have definitely been influenced by their staging. Thus, in some instances, I include the reading of passages taken from performances I have seen on stage that are not in these published scripts.

Both Palacios and Esparza share the same concerns in unmasking the system of representation. While Esparza subverts the official history of the 1836 Alamo episode to invent "herstory"; Palacios is extremely humorous performing her struggle to come out in her Catholic Mexican/Chicano household and in show business. Moreover, in Palacios's *Latin Lezbo Comic* her politics of representation are based upon a notion of the self that moves toward integrating specifically sexual and ethnic components of identity.[10] As pointed out by Yvonne Yarbro-Bejarano, Palacios not only exposes her coming-out narrative and the homophobia of her "people," but "Mexicanizes the signifiers of European-American history and popular culture to negotiate complex relations of power and race."[11]

Judith Butler, in particular, has proposed ways in which naturalized conceptions of gender might be understood as constituted, but, have possibilities of being reconstituted differently. She has deconstructed theatrical or phenomenological models that situate the gendered self prior to its acts. In this context, Butler understands constituting acts not only as constructions of the actor's identity, but as "constituting that identity as a compelling illusion, an object of belief."[14] Theoretically, her argument deconstructs forced gendered identity and taboo. In practice, the gendered self conveys an open space to create and recreate the many possibilities of its construction. In the case of Chicana subjectivity and its self-representation, the construction of a plural gendered identity problematizes the relationship between self and other: marginal and dominant culture. Chicanas as creative subjects try to understand the self in relation to the paradoxes and contradictions caused by conquest, annexation, and assimilation. Subordinated to a superior system as a result of caste and class relationship stratified by racial and ethnic status, Chicana identity cannot be subsumed under the simple ideological category of nonwhite. In Gloria Anzaldúa's terms of the new *mestiza,* the Chicana has a "plural personality," thus "not only does she sustain contradictions, she turns the ambivalence into something else."[15] Ambivalence, then, becomes the process that enables, in practical ways, the necessary struggle for one's self-identification within the enactment of power relations.

As a cultural practice, performance art does not have an absolute definition. Diana Taylor problematizes the notion of performance as an autonomous system of production, separated from both the dramatic text and its representation. As Taylor puts it, "The term performance, and specially the verb performing, allow for agency, which opens the way for resistance and oppositional spectacles."[16] For performance artists such as Laura Esparza and Monica Palacios, the technology of self-representation involves the performative subject as an allegory of identity. Esparza and Palacios sardonically define the enactment of self-representation as a "narcissistic requirement of art," which, in essence, underscores the power relationships within theater, female representation, and performance art. This very notion of performance art pushes the boundaries of the institution of theater and its political economy, which historically has excluded the marginal subject.[17] As one of the main conditions of performance art, the representational strategy is produced within narratives of identity that are informed, in turn, by questions that link the gendered self with representation.

Although performance art engages diverse cultural, personal, social, and political systems of representation, it rebels against institutions or modernism. Many critics have explained this rebellion as the continuous struggle of twentieth-century art against commodification. For example, Jeanie Forte explains, "As a continuation of the twentieth-century rebellion against commodification, performance art promised a radical departure from commercialism, assimilation, and triviality, deconstructing the commercial art network of galleries and museums while often using/abusing their spaces."[18] Esparza and Palacios allude directly and indirectly to this "radical departure" suggested in Forte's text; they are particularly concerned with the political implications of performance as a transgressive display of self. The placement of the self is the "real" space of representation and can be seen as a model for contemplation. Within this context, the relationship between self and representation enables the (im)possibility of identity to be the subject of performance.

As is true of any performance, *I DisMember the Alamo* and *Latin Lezbo Comic* are representations without reproductions. According to Peggy Phelan, this process functions as a paradigm for another economy, "one in which reproduction of the Other as the Same is not assured."[19] Phelan suggests that performance art cannot truly be documented. If it is documented, then the work is represented by a photograph, a performance script, or a video tape. When a performance goes through this process, according to Phelan, it ceases to be performance art. Phelan indicates that: "the document of a performance then is only a spur to memory, an encouragement of memory to become present."[20] I concur with Phelan when she states that "performance's only life is in the present."[21] However, it is a very particular present, which can be transformed and modified once its spatiality has been recorded either as a visual or written text. It is a significant present with a memorable past in which future stagings or readings become the grand possibility of documentation.

In *Latin Lezbo Comic* Palacios's queerness is significant to the act of self-representation. She explains how she came to accept her sexuality:

MONICA: I'm so glad I've matured. And as I became more involved in the gay and lesbian community, I started using the word more. And one day I said the word a bunch of times. [*Repeats the word* LESBIAN *seven times*] AND I GOT OVER IT! Because, folks, it's just a word. I was making a big deal out of nothing. It seems to be the American thing to do! (See this volume.)

Just as Palacios exposes herself, connecting her sexual identity to the space within self-representation, her show goes beyond traditional stand-up comedy. It challenges this tradition by exploring the possibilities of one-woman performance. As a condition of performance art, the political economy implicated in a one-woman show has contributed enormously to broadening the space in Chicana theater.[23] This excerpt from Laura Esparza's *I Dismember the Alamo* graphically reveals this condition of performance art:

> Here I'm telling the family story as a performance art piece: that par
> ticular phenomenon in performance history driven by the economic
> requirements of American theater and the current government dispo
> sition on funding the arts; this particular chapter of performance his
> tory that clues us into the personal stories of every artist, actor, painter,
> poet or choreographer who has ever seriously considered the narcis
> sistic requirements of art. I am giving away the family secrets, per
> forming the family monologue, selling the family jewels, I'm coloniz
> ing myself! Y La Equity: ¡Chinga tu madre![24]

By telling the family story, Esparza gives away "the family
secrets." She sells the "family jewels," the privacy of her own
family, to recreate her personal story. Esparza's presence as the
act of self-representation involves her own performance as metaphor of her own identity. The role of the actress as the representer
of herself on stage positions the self to evaluate the power dynamics, which are expressed ironically, as "the current government disposition on funding the arts." This "disposition" is what
prompts her to give away the beloved secrets of her *familia*.

Palacios's aggressive approach attacks the power dynamics in
stand-up comedy show business. In *Latin Lezbo Comic,* Palacios
takes time off from her sunny pronouncements to reveal a crucial event in her career. She recalls the time when she was trying
to fit into "generic comic: straight, white, male" mainstream clubs:
"And every time I'd tell male comics I was from San Francisco,
they would respond with a stupid homophobic comment. I
wanted to smack them in their abdomens with an oar! Instead, I
walked away angry and confused. My tummy ached. So you
can imagine how I felt on stage." (See this volume.)

Latin Lezbo Comic goes beyond enjoyment and humor.
Palacios's performance is one of challenges (and tacos), where
comedy becomes the tool of reconstructing ways of understanding and of making visible the queer self. The practice of humor
that Palacios conducts interpolates audience members into a
dialogue that asks them either to identify with her or take responsibility for addressing the oppression, racism, and homophobia of their own lives. Palacios refuses to accept the "heterosexist"
world that denies her a space in show business:

> I just hated how comedy was and still is a boy's game.

Club owners don't like to book women because, quote, "They talk about women things and their periods." End of quote.
Yet guys would get on stage, grab their dicks, talk about shit, and talk about farts, and the audience would be on the floor! I wanted to make them stick their tongues on ice trays!
Bitter?! I'm not bitter. I'M A WAITRESS! (See this volume.)

Palacios's aggressive approach attacks the power dynamics in stand-up comedy show business, in which males are powerful and women are passive. It also subverts the rule of representation by placing the white heterosexual spectator in the position of passivity. Overall, the public is challenged with a humor that sardonically censures repression and, in particular, transgresses the order of tradition. As Yarbro-Bejarano points out, "Centering the Chicana lesbian subject also means decentering the traditionally privileged spectator, and Palacios's show raises the same issues of audience reception as Moraga's work for the theater."[25] Indeed, Palacio's lesbian representation "denaturalizes" the conventional and heterosexual spectator.

Her didactic spectacle intends to break heterosexist misconceptions about lesbians. As Palacios points out, "Most important for me, the show is out there hopefully educating people. I make it really funny, but I hope I'm out there making my point."[26] Palacios is also hilarious in presenting her struggle to come out in the private sphere; she recalls the time she first brought the woman she loves to a family reunion. Palacios performs the reactions of each member of her family. Although her precocious niece calls her "LEZBO," her older sister replies, "I'm not sure I understand it. Her girlfriend is nice–I GUESS THAT'S WHAT SHE CALLS HER! HER LOVER–PERSON?!" Through her enactment of the family's reactions, Palacios performs different voices as a way of presenting with sardonic pleasure the family story, what she calls, the "double dyke familia":

MONICA: But what a big burn on my family, because my other older sister is also a LESBIAN! You know, my family thinks–
FAMILY: Did you guys eat the same thing? How does this happen?
FILM ANNOUNCER: [*Commercial voice*] Just when this Mexican Catholic family thought they had one lesbian daughter, they actually have two! Experience their confusion in

DOUBLE DYKE FAMILIA!
Every year, the familia had that same holiday wish: "Por favor, let
them bring men home to dinner. We don't want to march in that gay
parade!"
DOUBLE DYKE FAMILIA! (See this volume.)

Palacios's personal narrative humorously affirms her individual
self as well as her collective sense of identity, making the audience "crack up." Within these comic narratives, the performance
of assumed ethnic and sexual identities transgresses the patriarchal and heterosexual privilege and indicates that it is not an
"accident" that lesbians and Chicanas are often marginalized in
and out of mainstream circles. In this context, the process of
self-representation as an act of resistance reconsiders (her) performance in relation to the centrality of the performer. Both the
lesbian and the Chicana are moved center stage.

In *I DisMember the Alamo,* Laura Esparza departs from the
Alamo's historical event to trace her family lineage. Esparza and
her collective self become the subject of performance. She exists because her great great great grandmother survived the Battle
of the Alamo in 1836. The construction of Esparza's identity is
based upon a collective subjectivity that transcends the excessive limitations of individualism. Esparza insists that the personal is the truthful history, that the story of the Alamo is
"herstory." She claims, "My body is the battlefield / of the colonized self. / The land where conquests of / Spanish, and Mexican, and American I have occupied my cells" (see this volume.).
This particular space of her colonized "body" must be interconnected to agencies that claim the history of the self from an identity that comes from somewhere else. Indeed, she sees herself as
an extension of a history. "An important part of my myth is the
heritage I have from the city. I feel the land and location of
Texas in my blood and bones. I know that place as my body."[27]
In relation to the way one conceives one's identity, Gayatri
Spivak suggests:

To an extent, the way in which one conceives of oneself as representative or as an example of something is this awareness that what is one's
own, one's identity, what is proper to one is also a biography, and has
a history. That history is unmotivated but not capricious and is larger
in outline than we are.[28]

Although Spivak is particularly speaking of Assia Djebar, the Algerian novelist, her remarks can be applied to other contexts. The basic understanding of the personal as the political "intermediary" of a collective consciousness involves the story of one's life with greater possibilities of representation–an identity that is constructed from other identities. Thus Esparza's self-narrative story cannot exist without Texan history and its transgression, or Palacios's self-identity enactment cannot be accomplished without the representation of her lesbian subjectivity. In this context, the process of self-representation is crucial to the philosophical "plotting" necessary for the politics of identity and its performativity.

The history of Texas is an inevitable subject in Laura Esparza's self-identity process of representation. Born and raised on the west side of San Antonio, Texas, Esparza rewrites history as a way of writing her own narrative. The cry of "Remember the Alamo," which became a call to arms for Anglo-Americans and Mexican-Americans in both Texas and the United States, is "dismembered" in Esparza's own version of history:

The history of Texas, to me, is a neighborhood I know by heart. The history of Texas is located here *in* my heart, in my blood. [*Lipstick X applied over heart*]
The history of Texas is never like a book or a movie. You can't put your hand on it. What happened can only be described one mirror at a time. (See this volume.)

Esparza's exploration of her Chicana identity and its multiple subjectivities leads her to "dismembering" the Alamo. Esparza's "dismemory/dismembering" is a critique of patriarchal and Anglo ethnocentric history.[29] Marguerite Waller has pointed out:

Her dismemory/dismembering of patriarchal, nationalistic history leads not to an alienated (national/ethnic/sexual) identity, but to accountable citizenship in a serious but carnivalesque world whose energies flow with, rather than against, her multidimensional Chicana subjectivity.[30]

In the opening scene of her performance, Esparza sings "Volver, Volver," a Mexican traditional song that translates as "return, to go back." It is a return to "herstory," the history of the Alamo, which defines her identity in relation to her ancestors who fought at the Alamo. She appears sitting behind a white rectangular screen, "or in a white tent, or better yet a white 1950s refrigerator with two white wings, somewhat resembling the Alamo facade" (see this volume). One sees her eyes through a hole cut in the screen and her wide open legs sticking out of holes.[31] There is also a television set. While the theme music from the movie *The Alamo,* starring John Wayne, is playing in the "preshow ritual," the movie begins to run on the television set. That is when she starts her show.

Esparza claims the history of Texas as the "story" of her family, showing family pictures and newspaper clips in slides projected through the white screen:

We have a family story,
A little familial history,
A ritual secret of sorts. We tell it to each other,
The family secret,
Our creation story of how we discovered
–ourselves. (See this volume.)

Esparza tells the family story, a history she thinks is important to "invent" as a way of empowering the self and its collective means. In order to do that, she subverts the official history of the 1836 confrontation at the Alamo between Texans and the Mexican army. For example, when she presents a slide of Jim Bowie, an "official" hero of the Alamo, she says:

There are some who say that Jim Bowie, hero of the Alamo, was protecting a hoard of gold he stole from the Apaches and hid in a well at the Alamo. Westward expansion, slaves, there was something for everyone, besides "freedom." And freedom for whom? Did Gregorio know what he was fighting for? (See this volume.)

The myths about the Alamo event portray heroes, such as James Bowie, as a defender of his home, a good Texan. Bowie was an infamous wrangler who made a fortune running slaves and had come to Texas searching for lost mines and money. Other "heroes" such as William Barret Travis, according to Rodolfo Acuña, "had fled to Texas after killing a man, abandoning his wife and two children."[32]

These men are portrayed as heroes who sacrificed their lives to defend their land and their comrades-in-arms. Esparza makes Gregorio Esparza, her great great great grandfather, the main protagonist of her own history version. In the first part of her performance, Esparza introduces her great great great grandfather as a hero of the Alamo. His name, Gregorio Esparza, is highlighted in the newspaper clippings projected on the screen. She uses the Alamo's historical event and *The Alamo,* the movie, to emphasize the role that Mexicans played in the battle. John Wayne directed, starred in, and produced the movie *The Alamo* in 1960. This movie and countless other Hollywood productions glorify the Anglo-American settlers who wrested Texas from Mexico. Esparza's performance humorously subverts this idealistic view:

In the family mantra
We have a grandfather
Actually, he's not my grandfather but
My great great great grandfather
or is it my great great great great grandfather,
I can never get it straight
Maybe only three greats for
old Gregorio Esparza.
Anyway, he's the star of the story. (See this volume.)

Although Esparza introduces Gregorio Esparza as the "star" of "herstory," it is precisely Ana, her great great great grandmother, who becomes "the real story." Esparza claims to be alive only because Ana survived. It is precisely the denial of women as active subjects in the Alamo's historical event that Esparza both foregrounds and subverts. Transgression within transgression functions as a system of subversion. Esparza begins her performance by making Gregorio Esparza the real hero of the Alamo event, but it is precisely the memory of Ana, Esparza's great great great grandmother, that is used to subvert both "official" Anglocentric history and Gregorio's patriarchal story:

1,920 acres of land she could not claim by her rights as a hero of the Alamo.
1,920 acres she could have tilled to feed her family. She fed her babies buggy meal to keep them alive.
1,920 acres she could not claim because her last name was Esparza, Mexicana like the land she stood on. An exile in her own land.

(both courtesy of Laura Esparza)

(courtesy of Laura Esparza)

Her cells are my cells.
Her grito is mine.
She lived past the glory the hype of history,
And I am here simply
because she survived. (See this volume.)

The power of Esparza's performance lies in the emphasis on personal experience and emotional material, such as family pictures. The slide projections of her loved ones on the white screen contain a truth-effect that stresses the process of self-representation. This effect becomes fundamental to enhancing the relationship between the representational and the real. "The real is read through representation, and representation is read through the real."[33] For Laura Esparza, the Alamo's intertextuality exists only as references that construct her family's historical background in San Antonio and deconstruct the legendary myths of the Alamo:

That's how I have this story to tell you now
because it was never found in history books.
It was part of being my name, part of my body,
my locus,
my tierra,
family rooted in story. (see this volume.)

Esparza invents a history as a way of constructing her identity. In her own version, only a herstory is the "real" story. Esparza's body is a result of and presented as a battlefield of "the profane war of lies" (see this volume.). Her body's presence becomes synonymous with her "locus" and "tierra." Her body "gives birth" to her story, as she presents family pictures and newspaper clips on the white screen. The pouring out of history functions as a discourse and metadiscourse of representation. Both discourse and metadiscourse narrate the dramatic story of los Esparzas: "That's how I have this story to tell you now, because it was never found in history books" (see this volume.). Discourse and metadiscourse are reinforced with visual images, photographs, and newspaper clippings, and convey meaning as an expression of self-representation.

The construction of the body reinforces Esparza's internal struggle and the Chicana's multiple selves: "The Indian in me will battle my Spaniard /My Spaniard will battle my Mexican and / my American will have its own internal Alamo with my Chicana" (see this volume.). Using lipstick on her naked chest and wearing a rebozo around her waist, Esparza ends her performance by drawing diagrams on her body. This ending responds to her multiple subjectivity as the reasoning of self-representation. She adds:

I am this:
an india
inside a mestiza
inside a gringa
inside a chicana.
I am all of these
and my psyche is like a road map of Texas
traversed by borders
with never any peace at these borders. (See this volume.)

The process of self-representation configures a particular space that inscribes a gendered ethnic identity within multiple border crossings. In this context, one must understand the very notion of identity as a dynamic process, one which is never static. Esparza's identity is defined within a narrative that seeks to construct a space conducive to a heterogeneous agent, which is the product of mestizaje and colonization.

Palacios's closing number is composed of a mixture of popular songs in which key words in the lyrics are substituted with the word *vagina:*

[*Sings to the tune of "Lullaby of Broadway"*]
C'mon along and listen to
My lullaby of Vagina.
The hit parade and bally-hoo,
My lullaby of Vagina.
[*Sings the next lines like a traditional medley, but replaces the key word with* vagina.]
I left my vagina in San Francisco…
Vagina Cathedral…
The days of wine and vagina… (See this volume.)

The playful substitution of *vagina* highlights the grammars of sexuality in a unique way that humorously honors womanhood.

Using the vagina parody challenges the social and cultural construction of female body and desire. The parody breaks the silence of sexual repression and inscribes an erotic space in which the gendered self centers the vagina not merely as object of female desire, but as the subject of transgression for gender-based structures of power. Moreover, the parody of the vagina serves as the focal point of her queer sexuality.

Laura Esparza's and Monica Palacios's performances and selves emerge as inherently political. Their performance art is the product of the relationship of women to the dominant system of representation, situating their gendered selves and ethnicity within a feminist critique. The technology of self-representation places the subject position exercising greater determination in the construction of subjectivity via performance art. Esparza and Palacios engage the process of self-representation as an act of resistance that reconsiders performance in relation to the centrality of the female ethnic "other." Both performances are autobiographical, grounded in the belief that representation is constituted through a performative space in which gender and identity (ethnic and/or sexual) involves constructing acts of the self. The performances of Palacios and Esparza demonstrate that the very identity-constructing acts create enough space to construe their representation. I read these performances as texts which attempt to theorize the performative space of Chicana identity and self-representation.[34]

Notes

1. Yolanda Broyles-González, *El Teatro Campesino: Theater in the Chicano Movement* (Austin: University of Texas Press, 1994), 135.

2. Broyles-González, 135.

3. The significant contributions of Josefina López, Denise Chávez, and Edit Villarreal have been representative in Chicana/o theater.

4. Cherríe Moraga, *Giving Up the Ghost: Teatro in Two Acts* (Los Angeles: West End Press, 1986).

5. Estela Portillo Trambley confesses in an interview that she wrote about a lesbian character, Doña Josefa, for economic reasons. She says, "The plot is about lesbians; I knew nothing about them, but I was going to sell it. Well, it got published, it appeared in four anthologies, I get invited to talk about it, it gets analyzed to death, and it's a play I wrote in a very short time and for a terrible reason! I was just being

mercenary." Consult Juan Bruce-Novoa, *Chicano Authors: Inquiry by Interview* (Austin: University of Texas Press, 1980), 170.

6. Yvonne Yarbro-Bejarano, "The Female Subject in Chicano Theater: Sexuality, Race, and Class," in *Performing Feminisms: Feminist Critical Theory and Theater,* ed. Sue-Ellen Case (Baltimore: Johns Hopkins University Press, 1990), 145.

7. Yarbro-Bejarano, "The Female Subject in Chicano Theatre," 133.

8. Leigh Gilmore, *Autobiographics: A Feminist Theory of Women's Self Representation* (Ithaca: Cornell University Press, 1994), 67.

9. Both pieces are included in the first section of this anthology, "Play and Performance Texts." All further references to these pieces are included parenthetically within the text. Palacios and Esparza have been performing their respective work throughout the country since 1991.

10. Monica Palacios performed at the University of California, Riverside, on March 2, 1993. Her performance was the major event that took place during the celebration of Semana de la Mujer. Co-sponsored by MECHA and the Chicano Student Program, Palacios's performance attracted more than 150 people to the theater. After this performance, she was invited in 1994 and 1995 by the Gay, Lesbian and Bisexual Student Program of this campus.

11. Yvonne Yarbro-Bejarano. "The Lesbian Body in Latina Cultural Production," forthcoming in *¿Entiendes?: Queer Readings, Hispanic Writings* (Durham: Duke University Press). I do not include a page number because I am quoting an early draft of this essay. I would like to thank Yvonne Yarbro-Bejarano for giving me the opportunity to read her unpublished work.

12. Judith Butler, "Performative Acts and Gender Constitution: An Essay in Phenomenology and Feminist Theory," *Theatre Journal 40:4* (1988), 519.

13. Butler, 520.

14. Butler, 520.

15. Gloria Anzaldúa. *Borderlands/La Frontera: The New Mestiza Consciousness* (San Francisco: Aunt Lute, 1987), 79.

16. Diana Taylor, "Opening Remarks," in *Negotiating Performance: Gender, Sexuality, and Theatricality in Latino/a American* (Durham: Duke University Press, 1994), 14.

17. By "marginal subject," I refer specifically to people of color, gays and lesbians.

18. Jeanie Forte, "Women's Performance Art: Feminism and Postmodernism," in *Performing Feminisms: Feminist Critical Theory and Theatre,* ed. Sue-Ellen Case (Baltimore: Johns Hopkins University Press, 1990), 251.

19. Peggy Phelan. *Unmarked: The Politics of Performance* (New York: Routledge, 1993), 3.

20. Phelan, 147.

21. Phelan, 3.

22. Phelan, 5.

23. Other Chicana performance artists who practice this tradition include Ruby Nelda Pérez, Carmen Tafolla, Denise Chávez, Raquel Salinas, Dolores Chávez, Belinda Acosta, Sylviana Wood, and Mary Sue Galindo.

24. This particular passage is very provocative and expressive. It serves as a good example to illustrate the act of self-representation as a condition of performance art. However, in the final written script of the performance, this section was not included.

25. Yvonne Yarbro-Bejarano, ¿*Entiendes?: Queer Reading, Hispanic Writings*. In this essay, Yvonne Yarbro-Bejarano relates the work of Palacios to other Latina artists. She uses as an example the work of Cherríe Moraga, Ester Hernández, and Marcia Ochoa to talk about cultural productions and the lesbianization of the heterosexual icons of popular culture.

26. Monica Palacios expressed this sentiment after she performed *Latin Lezbo Comic* at the University of California, Riverside, in 1993.

27. See Waller, *"Pocha* or Pork Chop?: An Interview with Theater Director and Performance Artist Laura Esparza." This interview is included in this anthology.

28. Gayatri Chakravorty Spivak, *Outside in the Teaching Machine* (New York: Routledge, 1993), 6.

29. The Alamo was a military defeat in San Antonio, Texas. However, it was a moral victory for Anglo-Texans and Mexican-Texans who supported the state as a republic with a provisional government and called for its independence. San Antonio became the leading city of the newly formed Republic of Texas until the Treaty of Guadalupe Hidalgo was signed, which, in essence, granted the whole Southwest to the United States,

30. Marguerite Waller, (see this volume).

31. In the performance, her spread legs, clad in heels and fishnet hose, mark the spot onto which pictures and newspaper clippings will be projected.

32. Rodolfo Acuña *Occupied America: A History of Chicanos* (New York: Harper Collins Publishers, 1988), 10–11.

33. Phelan, 2.

34. I would like to thank Juanita Heredia for reading an earlier draft of this essay. Her wise and useful comments helped me to consider the final title. This paper is dedicated to Monica Palacios and Laura Esparza, whose creative works have influenced my own.

From Minimalism to Performative Excess: The Two Tropicanas

Lillian Manzor

The body is the inscribed surface of events (traced by language and dissolved by ideas), the locus of a dissociated self (adopting the illusion of substantial unity), and a volume of disintegration. Genealogy, as an analysis of descent, is thus situated within the articulation of the body and history. Its task is to expose a body totally imprinted by history and the process of history's destruction of the body.

—Michel Foucault

All autobiographic memory is true. It is up to the interpreter to discover in which sense, where, for which purpose.

—Luisa Passerini

Exotic Games

The juxtaposition of Ana Mendieta (1948–1985) and Carmelita Tropicana might seem peculiar at first glance, given the dissimilarities in their aesthetic practices. In spite of their differences, I want to connect them in this essay in order to study the ways in which, precisely as performance artists, they utilize their bodies as both means and repository of a split historical and personal memory. Some biographical and artistic coincidences will serve as an introduction to their work. Both artists left Cuba very young during the early 1960s and were raised in the United States. Ana Mendieta died tragically, under suspicious circumstances, in 1985, the same year that Carmelita Tropicana began to perform. Taking elements from their personal lives and transforming them artistically in their art, performance was and is the "genre" of their work. Both artists began their "professional" work in Anglo feminist spaces: Mendieta with the AIR (Artist in Residence) collective; Tropicana with the women's group at the WOW (Women's One World) Cafe, in New York. Finally, both considered themselves cultural workers (as opposed to artists) and adopted the name Tropicana.

The common assumption of the name Tropicana highlights the need to study their work comparatively. Mendieta began to use the sobriquet in the last few years of her life, after she moved from Iowa to New York.[1] She reserved the name TropicAna for her most intimate friends. Carmelita Tropicana, on the other hand, is the name of a character or persona created by Alina Troyano. This character was born almost by accident.[2] Troyano was at the WOW Cafe one night when the emcee did not show up. She was encouraged to go on stage as the emcee's replacement. After some hesitation, Troyano went on stage as Carmelita Tropicana and, as she says, has never come off.[3]

Mendieta's and Troyano's differently inflected but nevertheless common use of the name Tropicana is intimately tied to Anglo cultural representations and constructions of Latin(o)ness, especially within popular culture. I write Latin *(o)ness* because in the United States, the specificity of Latin American "ethnicity" is usually fused with Latino under the name Hispanic.[4] While it is not my purpose here to trace a much-needed genealogy of this construction of Latin(o)ness, suffice it to say that—willingly in the case of Tropicana and perhaps unwillingly in the case of Mendieta—the two of them participate in a discourse that began at least in the 1930s with Hollywood's productions of Good Neighbor Policy films.[5] In performance, we could trace it back to Broadway's 1939 musical productions of *The Streets of Paris* with Carmen Miranda and *Too Many Girls* with Desi Arnaz.[6] Some characteristics of this construction are familiar: tropical rhythms, exotic clothing, colorful locales, and an exuberant body language.

The intersection of the ethnic and sexual axes further complicates this construction. For the Latina, specifically, the result of this conflation is a sexuality that is exaggerated, stereotypical, and mystified; at the epistemological level, she is usually represented as the "tropical bombshell" or the "Latin temptress," all part of the construction of what Alberto Sandoval Sánchez calls "Beautiful Señoritas."[7] Mendieta and Tropicana are aware that in the United States, being Latin(a) is synonymous with the exotic other, an import from a Latin America that has been fetishized by the Anglo cultural imaginary.[8] They know epistemologically and ontologically, that in the "best" of cases, the

Latin(a) exotic other is entertaining. But they are also aware that another stereotypical construction is at work. The Latin(o/a) becomes that foreign other that, because of its very exoticism, is considered savage, dangerous, a Bataillian corps étranger. Being typically portrayed as a political terrorist, illegal alien, gang member, drug pusher, or poor peasant, it is this construction that traditionally has kept Latin(o/a)s away from the residential and academic neighborhoods, and, especially, from the neighborhood of self-representation.

The name Tropicana is literally the name of a Cuban nightclub famous, before 1959, for its beautiful chorus girls. Even today, however, the Tropicana show, whether in Havana or in world tours, exhibits Cuban music and dances, men and women, as specimens of a "national" culture commodified for foreign consumption and taste. Mendieta's and Tropicana's appropriation of the name undoubtedly echoes the native's performance for a foreign, that is, "civilized" audience. Both of them, through their self-naming, assume this spectacular identity of exotic other. In so doing, they acquire both versions of the above construction: the harmless artist/entertainer as well as the dangerous other. This parodic appropriation, as a postcolonial tactic of intervention, constitutes a repetition but with a difference.[9] For Mendieta, specifically, it functioned as a self-parody of the stereotypical way in which she was seen by part of the Anglo art world of the 1970s and 1980s. Most important, however, is the hyphen, that division and pause that parodically deforms the name to underscore the bicultural and bilingual reality of a hybrid self. Half-English, half-Spanish: the name captures the very relational nature of postcolonial hybrid identity. This assumption, however, is never perfect or seamless. For both Mendieta and Tropicana, their parodic games and constant movement between self and other, English and Spanish, and identity and mask underscore that indeed, for bicultural hybrids or postcolonial subjects, this seam is proof of the performative nature of that self-naming and self-making.

The many interpretations of Mendieta's life and death, even of her art, have oscillated precisely between those two versions of otherness: the harmless, tantalizing entertainer and the dangerous other. For her husband, the well-known minimalist sculptor Carl Andre, Mendieta was his "darling, sexy, beautiful

Tropicanita."[10] On September 9, 1985, Ana Mendieta died from a fall from Andre's thirty-fourth-floor apartment window; the causes and motives of that fall have never been clarified.[11] Carl Andre was indicted three times and finally acquitted of charges of having killed Mendieta.

Mendieta's death split New York's art world in two. The power dynamics between those two groups are clearly delineated in the headlines of the *New York* magazine article "A Death in Art": "Did Carl Andre, the renowned minimalist sculptor, hurl his wife, a fellow artist, to her death ?"[12] As a sculptor whose "museum class" art was bought by modern art collections worldwide, indeed he had a name and an affiliation. Mendieta's name, on the other hand, disappears in and from the headline. Mendieta was a Latina artist who barely belonged to the feminist subculture of the art world. The article's headline aptly suggests, as it reproduces, Mendieta's relative anonymity and lack of affiliations. Indeed, although the article seems slanted against Andre, Mendieta is discursively constructed following the stereotypes of the cultural imaginary. For example, although Andre, the father of minimalism, is described as "sullen and taciturn," Mendieta is "boisterous and euphoric." And their marriage is characterized by Wadler as a "detached New Englander" marrying an "impulsive and outspoken young woman from Havana."[13]

Yet, these representative stereotypical quotes cannot be seen in isolation any more than Mendieta's death can be seen merely as a result of gendered hysteria, or, as Howardena Pindell might have it, the result of a "segregated" art world: "I know if Ana had been an Anglo and if Carl had been black, the art world would have lynched him."[14] Rather, these quotes underline that Mendieta, as a Latina, was indeed seen at the intersection of those two types previously discussed. As the Latina/exotic other, she was beautiful, sexy, and entertaining. However, when it was needed, her "untamed" and "wild" nature was quickly interpreted as a mimetic reflection of the cultural imaginary's construction: no longer entertaining, she was discursively constructed, even by those who were favorable to her, as a threatening creature. Oddly enough, even her death, in spite of or perhaps because of its mysteriousness, was attributed in part to her misunderstood interest in santería as a religious practice.[15]

The descriptions of Carmelita Tropicana reflect a similar discursive construction within Anglo culture, that of the Latin(a) as the entertaining, fun-loving exotic other. The press has referred to her as a cross between Ricky Ricardo and Lucille Ball, probably because of her overacted heavy accent and red hair. The *Village Voice,* for example, in an article on Candela y Azúcar, describes Tropicana as "a flame-haired heroine who dreams of dance."[16] And Robert Sandia, of *Dance Magazine,* describes Tropicana in the following fashion: "With her fiery temperament and impenetrable accent, Tropicana is a cartoon of the hot tamale; she's so outrageously Latin that she makes Charo look like Estelle Getty."[17]

"Flame-haired," "fiery," "tempestuous," "hot tamale": undoubtedly, these are the most predominant stereotypes of the outrageous Latin(a). But there is another agenda driving Tropicana's performances, which the Latino magazine *Más* seems to recognize: "Carmelita *pretends* to play with Latin stereotypes but what she is *really* doing is playing with your head. She is a cultural terrorist, a Carmen Miranda cloaked in dangerous fruits."[18] It is interesting that even *Más* uses these constructions to refer to what it does not quite understand or does not want to name. Yet the reader never finds out exactly what *Más* detects in Carmelita Tropicana that is both terrorizing and dangerous. The comparison to Carmen Miranda is clever and appropriate. As Ana López has demonstrated, Miranda, a Hollywood construction, functions "as a fantastic or uncanny fetish. Everything about her is surreal, off-center, displaced on to a different regime: from her extravagant hats, midriff-baring multi-colored costumes, and five-inch platform shoes to her linguistic malapropisms, farcical sexuality, and high-pitched voice, she is an 'other,' everyone's 'other.' "[19] Carmelita Tropicana wears and performs Carmen Miranda's excesses, but with a difference: Tropicana's excesses are "indigenized" and recast self-reflexively as stereotypes of Latin(o/a)ness. In Carmen Miranda's films, that rhetoric of excess "carried over onto the mode of address of the films themselves."[20] The mode of address in Tropicana's performances is altogether different, and reflects her different conception of excess. Carmelita Tropicana "pretends to play" not only with stereotypes of Latin(o/a)ness but also with both Anglo and Latino stereotypes of masculinity and femininity. She does so in the lesbian address of her performances, which decenters the Latina heterosexual spectator as well as the Anglo lesbian spectator. As a gay self-parody of Carmen Miranda, then, Tropicana's performances open up the space for a different kind of self-representation, one that constructs female bodies that resist fetishization while undermining traditional ethnic and gender representations.

Rituals of Recuperation

I am overwhelmed by the feeling of having been cast from the womb (nature). My art is the way I reestablish bonds that unite me to the universe.[21]

Ana Mendieta belongs to a generation of conceptual artists who are interested in working with the "raw" physical presence of the human body. So-called "body art" or "conceptual performance art" is a minimalist and austere work that investigates and takes physical risks while avoiding signs of theatricality and interaction with a consuming audience.[22] For Mendieta and other conceptual artists, the ephemeral nature of performance is an alternative to the commodification of art "in the age of mechanical reproduction."

Traditionally, Mendieta's work has been approached from two different angles. It has been seen as a programmatic exponent of a universalized feminism, on the one hand, and, on the other, as an expression of an exotic mysticism misunderstood by the Anglo criticism that describes it as mysterious or exotic. In other words, her art has been reduced to either "feminist" or "Hispanic"; the two never appear together. Such analyses, products of a monocultural critical approach, are insufficient if one wants to understand precisely the hybrid nature of Mendieta's art.

By contrast, Luis Camnitzer, a Latin American art critic, refers to Mendieta's art as "Spanglish": "In relation to art, Spanglish represents the merging of a deteriorating memory with the acquisition of a new reality distanced by foreignness…It accurately represents the fact that one came from one place and went to another, and it functionally bridges the abyss left by that travel."[23] My interest in Mendieta's work resides precisely in that network of bridges, in all of its nuanced complexity. How does the feminist in her work inform, indeed could one even say, how is it produced by the Spanglish and vice versa? What role does memory play in the bridge between gender and race? How is memory materialized in and through the sexed bridge-body? Like Mendieta's and Tropicana's art, my theoretical strategies respond to and have been produced by the intersection between a common Cuban culture, North American education, and models of analysis adopted and adapted from the feminism of Chicanas and other U.S. "women of color." This conjunctural approach accounts for the fact that Latinas and other U.S. women of color are situated within different hierarchies of social power and discourse; we exist precisely "within the overlapping margins of race and gender discourses and in the empty spaces between them."[24]

An intersectional approach to Mendieta's work, then, needs to read how her hybrid performances, executed in direct contact with nature and with the earth, respond to both her feminist and Spanglish artistic practices. Mendieta's performances were ephemeral pieces subject to the changes of nature.[25] The elements she used were expressly the basic ones: earth and sand, water, fire, blood, and her own body. These came mainly from two fields of reference, which are inseparable in her art: her childhood remembrances of Varadero Beach, Cuba, and the syncretic Afro-Cuban world vision of santería. As I have examined elsewhere, santería, or the way of the saints, is a syncretic religion brought by the slaves from Africa to the New World.[26] I say "syncretic" because santería, at least as it was and is practiced in Cuba and the Cuban communities of the diaspora, is a mixture of old African traditions, mainly Yoruba, and Catholicism. Indeed, in the New World, the Yoruba were forced to adapt to a different religious system. This co-optation signaled at once resistance to the Catholic tradition and accommodation to its values. It came to be known as *santería*, "the way of the saints," because its practitioners continued to follow the African gods or orichas "beneath" the images of the Catholic saints. What originally constituted a strategy of subterfuge eventually became an integral part of the religion: the Catholic saint and the oricha are now considered to be different manifestations of the same religious entity.

Like many other Cuban and Caribbean artists in the United States, Mendieta became interested in santería because its prac-

Silueta, Mexico, 1976
(All photos in the chapter courtesy of Lillian Manzor)

tice in the United States constitutes a tactic of resistance against cultural amnesia and assimilation. For many Latinos/as and Afro-Americans, the survival of santería practices has become emblematic of the survival of cultural memory, as it once was for the slaves. Santería, then, offered Mendieta a way of reconnecting with her ancestors and relocating her land:

"Through my earth/body sculptures I become one with the earth. This obsessive act of reasserting my ties with the earth is really the reactivation of primeval beliefs."[27] She also learned formally from santería that which she already had intuited: the Earth is an organism from which one can borrow energy and power. Nature, a manifestation of the gods/orichas, serves as a medium, or vehicle, to contact the orichas and, through them, our ancestors.

She believed that by creating her works in unison with the Earth, she could share the ashé of the gods; ashé is something akin to the power or energy resulting from the grace endowed by the orichas, a life force. This was manifested in her performance art. In the different versions of the series entitled *Siluetas (Silhouettes,* 1975, 1976, 1979), for example, the creation process was similar. She traced her silhouette on the earth or sand with fire, flowers, or blood. Through the use of her own body to create the form and shape on the earth, Mendieta reestablished a union between herself and the land. In the final piece, however, Mendieta's physical body was not literally present. Rather, its silhouette became a figurative depiction, and a figurative vehicle that offered broader significance. Whether in a river or on a mountain side, those silhouettes eventually became one with the forces of nature: they disappeared downstream, or the next rain made them invisible within the earth or its surroundings. It is difficult to separate Mendieta's use of her body as vehicle from her creative process and the pieces' eventual transformation into nature. Mendieta's performances were precisely this whole process: from the cleansing of the space, to the silhouette's disappearance into and transformation of nature. Read within the codes of Mendieta's feminist/Spanglish artistic practice, the *Silueta* series interweaves elements taken from both santería and the experiences of migration and exile. Within these two systems of signification, the silhouettes function as a ritualistic dramatization of birth, death, and rebirth, which metaphorically constitutes a staging of the constant processes of subjectification of a hybrid female self.

The other elements that Mendieta utilized in her work have to be read within the same double iconography of personal remembrances and santería. Her predilection for water, for example, suggests both the beaches of Varadero, where she grew up, and the sea that surrounds Cuba. Mendieta's *Ritual a Ochún (Ritual to Ochún,* Miami 1980), enacted at the beach in Miami, was one of many examples of performance pieces with water. With this piece, as with all her art, Mendieta tried to cross figuratively that sea which is the geographic dividing line between Cuba and the United States, that same sea that until August 1994 was being physically crossed daily by thousands of Cuban balseros (raft people) in search of the promised "American Dream." Most important, Mendieta's *Ritual a Ochún* is an excellent example of how she borrowed elements from santería and then reworked them in an artistic and pseudo-ritualistic context. The key elements of this performance piece are Mendieta's female body in the sand, the two snakes, the head, and water. Water, in the Afro-Cuban religions, is considered the primordial element of all life. In any of its forms—sea, rivers, lakes—it is sacred. In the pantheon of santería, Yemayá, the oricha of maternity, is the Universal Queen precisely for being the oricha of the water. Yemayá's sister, Ochún, named after an African river, is the oricha of the rivers and fresh water.

Any believer of santería will recognize that in Mendieta's *Ritual a Ochún,* as in most of her performances, the different elements borrowed from santería's belief system are transformed or juxtaposed. The most obvious one here is the fact that the ocean is not Ochún's territory: it is Yemayá's. Moreover, snakes are usually associated with Yemayá and not with Ochún. However, if one compares the way that Mendieta placed the snakes with Afro-Cuban sacred writings called anaforuanas,[28] the two snakes could literally be read as an inscription meaning "separation." Figuratively, this separation can be read as Mendieta's own cultural deracination. As a matter of fact, the position of Mendieta's own body in the sand, present in the piece only insofar as the snakes outline its shape, reproduced Mendieta's presence/absence relation to her home country.

Mendieta's use of her own body in this piece must, once again,

Ritual a Ochún

be read in a multilayered manner. Her body is a vehicle for the creation process, but is present in the piece only through its absence, delineated by the two snakes/separation. Thus in order to participate in this dramatized ritual of departure and return, her body, once again, is transformed into both a figurative depiction and a figurative vehicle. Ultimately, the performance enacts a beautiful metaphor of Mendieta's quest for that double return, or reunification of the physical and spiritual.

The use of blood as a medium was, finally, one of the most controversial but key elements of her performances precisely because of its doubled inscription in ritualistic and body systems of signification. At first glance, it suggests the internal splitting of her being, exiled from its native surroundings. But blood also functioned for her as a metaphor for violence at the macro- and micro-political level, a metaphor for the vulnerability of women's bodies. Mendieta's pieces based on a ritualistic use of blood are the most interesting and complex, because of the ways in which she hybridized the Anglo feminist aesthetic practice of women's rituals with santería images. Within the world vision of santería, blood, like the earth, gives ashé, or power. Utilized in purification rites, blood is believed to have a regenerating force in an indefinite cycle of life and death. *Rastros corporales (Body Tracks*; filmwork, 1974; restaged at Franklin Furnace, New York City, 1982) was exemplary in this regard. In a space with walls covered with white paper, Afro-Cuban batá drums began to sound. Mendieta walked in with a bucket filled with blood. She immersed both of her arms and hands in the bucket and began to leave their traces, very slowly, on the wall as she went from a standing to a kneeling position. After she reached the floor, she exited the space, and the drums continued to be heard. She used blood here as ink, leaving, in a symbolic gesture, her own anaforuana, or sacred writing. The body tracks created and left during that performance resembled the body she created with the two snakes in her *Ritual a Ochún*. In the photographs of this piece, those imprints appear as tracks of a body violently torn apart, of a body in pain.

Mendieta's restagings of blood spilled in violence were neither purely a feminist protest statement against the ways in which women's bodies are defiled nor a direct cleansing ritual. From *Bird Transformation* (Old Man's Creek, Iowa, 1972) to *Rastros cor-*

porales, these reenactments suggest that, indeed, for Mendieta, blood did not have a negative connotation: "I started immediately using blood, I guess because I think it's a very powerful magic thing. I don't see it as a negative force."[29] As a matter of fact, these performances transformed santería's view of blood as the essence of life into a hybridized feminist and Spanglish ritual of empowerment. Through these performances, which dramatized a personal and cultural exorcism, blood cleansed Mendieta's own body and all women's bodies.[30] Furthermore, by sharing ashé with other women and with the gods, Mendieta aspired to the personal and collective self-empowerment needed to regain control of women's bodies.

In 1980, Mendieta traveled to Cuba for the first time since her departure. During that trip, she explored the possibilities of returning in order to do some of her works in Cuba. In 1981, sponsored by the Cuban Ministry of Culture, she returned to do her work in Jaruco. Until this point, her work was an obsessive act intended to reconnect herself with the earth, to reunite herself with the ancestral origins from which she was torn apart. Her pieces in Cuba, *Esculturas rupestres (Rupestrian Sculptures,* Jaruco, 1981), were, without a doubt, the culmination of that long internal process. Her Cuban executions initiated formal changes in her art, which she maintained and developed up to her last pieces in Rome: experimentation with new media and with drawings, exploration with floor pieces suited for indoor exhibition, and a heightened sensuality in the female forms, which became less personal and more abstract and emblematic.[31] It was as if Mendieta, after finally sharing the ashé, the power and strength, coming from the direct contact with her native earth, found less of a need to reconnect to it symbolically.

As ritualistic dramatizations, all of Mendieta's performances had a double function. On the one hand, as in the various Afro-Cuban religious ceremonies, through her performance/ritual she tried to establish "contact with the disappeared predecessors, with the world 'beyond' and with the mythical origins of the sect."[32] On the other hand, Mendieta's performances as art pieces were—like the fruits and flowers of Afro-Cuban altars—in and of themselves her offerings to the orichas. In her double role as executioner and image, as oricha and devotee, Mendieta sought to evoke the oricha through her body, as the possessed oricha. At the same time, she presented the very materiality of her own body as offering.[33]

Milk of Amnesia/Leche de amnesia

I used to play a game in bed. About remembering. I would lie awake in my bed before going to sleep and remember. I'd remember the way to my best friend's house. I'd start at the front door of my house, cross the porch. Jump off three steps onto the sidewalk. I'd continue walking, crossing three streets, walking two blocks until I came to my best friend's house. I did this repeatedly, so I wouldn't forget. I would remember. But then one day, I forgot to remember. I don't know what happened... Now I can only walk to the third house. I've forgotten.

—Carmelita Tropicana

Like Mendieta in 1990, Alina Troyano/Carmelita Tropicana traveled to Cuba in August 1993. It was Troyano/Tropicana's first trip back to Cuba. Although I had met with Tropicana several times, our conversations and interactions until this trip had been purely professional. As a matter of fact, I knew just about everything there was to know about the performing Tropicana but hardly anything about Alina Troyano.

It was uncanny being in Havana together. This uncanniness was made even more awkward because memories and personal experiences are difficult to approach "professionally" while you are directly immersed in them, as was our case. Moreover, the very transnational/transcultural act of being there created a complex situation in which our relationship of scholar/investigator–performance artist seemed out of place in the then and there of Havana in August 1993. We talked about the oddity of feeling like tourists in what is supposed to be our own country. We commented on the incongruencies of contemporary life in Cuba. I even "translated" jokes and gestures for her, because I had arrived two weeks earlier than she had; I had thus been able to get a "head start" in the joyful and painful game of return.

One afternoon, as we were traveling from el Vedado to Machurrucutu, I told Alina that we were going to be very near where I thought she had lived. Do you remember your address? I asked her. She spat out "319 de la calle 8, entre quinta y tercera." Do you want to stop there, see if we can find it? She responded "¡Claro! But I'm not sure if I'm ready. It's all so quick!" I understood her doubts then, and now realize how lucky I was to have shared this experience with her, with Alina. As we approach her neighborhood, she can't stop the litany of "Yes, this looks familiar." We finally get close to Eighth Street, and she reminds me that it used to be a one-way street; we have to go around the block because it still is.

We finally arrive at the house and find that it is under construction. She jumps right out of the car, hurls herself into the house, and bolts upstairs, looking for her bedroom. I advise her to slow down, "Let's explain and ask if we can come in." But it is too late. She is already in the middle of an air-conditioned office. The house is now a construction company, a joint Italo-Cuban venture. She looks everywhere, takes a deep breath, and then proceeds to take pictures: the stairs, the bathroom with the same toilet and bidet, the door to her room, now an office. I offer to take pictures of her. "You never know," I say naively, "you might need them for a performance." These photographs are now part of Troyano/Tropicana's latest performance piece, *Milk of Amnesia/Leche de amnesia*. The personal visit to her house has now been transformed, like my narration/analysis, into something else. *Milk of Amneria/Leche de amnesia* is a one-woman show written and performed by Carmelita Tropicana. It has been performed as a work-in -progress at several places and premiered at P.S. 122 in November 1994. In it, Tropicana plays different characters, some of which we recognize as part of Tropicana's work. There is Carmelita herself; her male counterpart, Pingalito Betancourt; Columbus's horse, Arriero; and a new character, a little pig called Cochinito Mamón. The performance incorporates for the first time a more developed and more personal, autobiographical voice, which seems to be the voice of the artist/writer as opposed to the voice of Carmelita. This voice is literally a voice, because it generally appears as pre-recorded. The performance involves slides, video, a sound track of famous Cuban and Latin songs, and songs that Carmelita sings. The staging is minimal: the space, a microphone, and a small side table. Stage objects are also limited but excessive: a wonderful hat, a cigar, a yuca, a can of Goya beans, and a piñata in the shape of a pig.

The performance begins in a dark space with a female voice speaking in English with no trace of a Spanish accent. This voice narrates her process of deculturation using the image of milk as its marker. Although this female voice seems to speak perfect English, one of the first lines she delivers, "I was born *in* an island," already carries the traces of another language, betraying her bicultural identity. For her, cultural amnesia started precisely at the moment she began to enjoy the flavor of "American" things such as milk, "Grade A pasteurized, homogenized" (2), a flavor that little by little, has erased that of the sweet condensed milk associated with her Cuban childhood. At P.S. 122, when the lights came on, the whiteness of the milk whose flavor she had been able to incorporate also invaded visually the performing space: it was painted completely white and the artist wore a mostly white outfit.

This white space of assimilation as cultural amnesia functions as a blank space. However, blankness does not describe a not-written-upon as much as it locates a site for new, or over-inscriptions. The blank wall, like a screen, will be literally the site where slides will be projected, slides whose stories, Carmelita's stories, carry traces of preceding moments that alter the contemporaneous rendition. Carmelita's body, in a similar fashion, is that blank space as site of over-inscriptions. Like the Foucauldian body, Carmelita's body is the locus of a dissociated self, of a self in process of creation amid cultural alienation, of a self whose cultural and discursive creation lead to self-alienation. Blank, then, describes the tension between creation and alienation.

Throughout the performance, contrasts among different types of foods are used parodically to suggest Cuban-ness versus American-ness. But they are also transformed into markers of sexuality, lesbianism, concretely. The "homo" of milk, in fact, surfaces later as a "fruit." The voice of the artist narrates the following:

In high school, I was asked to write an essay on the American character. I thought of fruits. Americans were apples... Cubans were mangoes: juicy, real sweet, but messy... I stood in front of a mirror and thought, I should be more like an apple. A shadow appeared and whispered, mango stains never come off. I didn't write about fruits in my essay. I didn't want them thinking I wasn't normal. (7)

Compulsory homogenization into American-ness and compulsory heterosexuality are the subtext of this parodic redeployment of food. Tropicana's intersection of sexuality and nationality adds another "flavor" to the Cuban transcultural *ajiaco* ("stew"). As a matter of fact, the inclusion of "homo fruits" in Tropicana's performances, allows us to read them as a critical comment upon constructions of nationality, even transcultural ones, in which the element of sexuality is generally absent.

The personal narrative of the artist's cultural amnesia, initially staged through the sound track and in the dark, cedes a space to Carmelita's own amnesia. Within the "plot" of the performance, the artist tells us that Carmelita's amnesia is the product of an accident. The differences between Carmelita and the personal "I" that I have been referring to as the voice of the artist are presented to us early in the performance by this personal voice: "I couldn't stand in front of an audience, wear sequined gowns, tell jokes. But *she* could. She who was baptized in the fountain of America's most popular orange juice, in the name of Havana's legendary nightclub, the Tropicana, she could. She was a fruit and wasn't afraid to admit it. She was the past I'd left behind" (7). Most important, Carmelita always speaks with a heavy Cuban accent, whereas the artist's voice barely presents any Cuban trace.

The other characters enter the stage in order to help Carmelita recuperate her memory. The first one to appear is Pingalito Betancourt, the same bus driver of the M15 bus of *Memorias de la revolución/Memories of the Revolution*[34] As in *Memorias,* Pingalito's stylized and repetitive acts question different ways of signifying Latin(o/a) male and female. Through his/her verbal and body language, gestures, clothing, and movements, the performance dramatically unveils stereotypical signs of Latin(o) masculinity.[35] Pingalito's appearance also serves the purpose of demythifying "official" versions of history and literature. Thinking that Carmelita is, above all, 150% Cuban (3) and 150% an artist (4), s/he will borrow from those two histories to try to make her remember. S/he will make fun of markers of Cuban-ness present even in restaurant placemats, and of performance art itself: "I have here audiovisual aid number one, a placemat I pick up in Las Lilas restaurant of Miami titled 'Facts about Cuba' " (3). One of the facts that s/he reads out loud relates to the "official whitening" of Cuban history: "Three-fourths of all Cubans are white, of Spanish descent and a lot of these three-fourths have a very dark suntan all year round. When they ask me, Pingalito, and where is

Sin titulo, México, 1976

your grandmother?, I say, Mulata y a mucha honra. Dark and Proud" (4). In this scene, then, not only does s/he accurately correct official versions of our racial makeup but s/he proceeds to undermine biological definitions of race based on phenotypes.

As a matter of fact, the song played in the soundtrack that is used as a lead-in to Pingalito's entrance on stage is a famous mambo by Damaso Pérez Prado (b. 1922), Considered by many to be the "father of the mambo," Pérez Prado invented this new danceable musical rhythm, based on short melodic phrases, on which he superimposed syncopated Afro-Cuban rhythms that run parallel to a four by four measure. His orchestration was very similar to that of black North American orchestras, such as Jimmie Lunceford's. He began to play in Havana nightclubs in 1940, but his musical creations found little acceptance there, because they were considered to be too close to North American music and were impossible to play by the smaller Cuban orchestras of the time. He thus moved to Mexico in 1949, where the mambo became famous and where he made his fortune.[36]

Although the mambo is now considered to be one of the most typical Cuban rhythms—in Cuban culture, especially outside Cuba, it occupies the same position that the tango does in Argentina—its musical development and eventual commodification is typical of the processes of transculturation. Furthermore, the mambo, both as musical form and dance, is usually chosen as an example of the syncretic African presence in Cuban culture. It is this "Afro-Cuban-ness" of the mambo that the performance deploys. When Pingalito enters the stage walking to the rhythm and singing the tune and lyrics of Pérez Prado's mambo, the song becomes as emblematic a marker of Cuban-ness as his/her attire and body language. The song plays a double role in the performance. On the one hand, it is used to underscore the fact that Pingalito, like all Cubans, regardless of racial phenotype, is culturally connected to a hybridized African tradition. On the other hand, however, Pingalito's gestures, which accompany the song, present a critical comment on U.S. Cubans' redeployment of certain types of music as markers of Cuban-ness. Indeed, music and dance become performative markers of ethnic identity and are transformed by the performance into one of many repetitive acts that function as performative markers of Latino masculinity.[37]

When Carmelita is faced with Cuban foods given to her by her doctors, a similar transcultural cannibalization is at stake:

Then they tell me to eat the food they bring, because the French philosopher Proust ate one madeleine cookie, and all his childhood memories came rushing back to him.
[Picking up a can of goya beans]
Goy...Goya?
[Picking up a yuca]
Is this a yuca or a yuucka? Do I eat it or do I beat it? Oh, yuca, yucka, to be or not to be. But who, that is the question. (8)

In this scene, Carmelita obviously trivializes the European artistic tradition by "bringing down" to the mundane level of its Cartesian philosophical underpinning. Like Pérez Prado's music, which juxtaposes materials selected from "nativist" and "Western" sources, Tropicana incorporates Cuban and European sources, underscoring that both are part of her tradition. The can of beans is more than appropriate: what could be a better sign of contemporary Cuban-ness than a can of black beans whose label constantly reminds us of our Spanish colonial past—Goya—and our diasporic present—made in Miami?

Carmelita's creolization or indigenization of "to be or not to be" problematizes the Shakespearean existential conundrum and suggests that indeed, for the hybrid female subject, the question is much more complicated than to be or not be. Thus Carmelita and the artist embark upon their trip to Cuba in search of that "who" because, following the plot, neither Pingalito's nor the doctors' methods seem to have worked. As the lights dim, Carmelita narrates her first trip to the Miami airport. The transition to Carmelita's trip to Cuba is signaled in the performance by a pre-recorded song. This time, it is Carmen Miranda singing from the soundtrack of the film *Weekend in Havana:* "But you won't / No, you won't/ be the same anymore." And indeed, neither Carmelita nor the artist will be the same after this trip. Up to this moment in the performance, the audience has been able to distinguish Carmelita from the artist. If the two characters have been able to maintain a distance during the part of the performance that diegetically takes place in the United States, that distance is eliminated during the trip to Cuba once Carmelita's character and the personal voice of the artist get (con)fused. As Carmelita narrates her visit to her house, the slides show Troyano in her house in Havana. Whereas Carmelita is the one who visits the cemetery looking for ancestors; the general comment about the present-day situation in Cuba comes from the pre-recorded voice of the artist, without an accent. The character of Carmelita performs consistently a stereotypical version of feminine Cubanness or Latin(a)ness, in Cuba, however, the encounter with her "real" roots, or with that other construction of Cuban-ness, seems to cause a split in the subject, from which the more personal, directly autobiographical voice emerges. In other words, the encounter with and in Cuba functions as a primary scene in the Lukacsian sense, a scene that triggers the unfolding of both historical memory and its imaginative constructions.[38]

In *Milk of Amnesia/Leche de amnesia,* personal memories are associated with tastes, sights, and sounds. Although their trip to Cuba allows both Carmelita and the artist to recuperate their lost cultural memories, that recovery is also a discovery of the constructed and collective nature of memory itself, especially that of hybrid female subjects. When they get to the Cuban airport, for example, Carmelita says, "I see a field in the distance. Palm trees, two peasants, and an ox. It reminds me of Southeast Asia, Vietnam. I never been there. But who knows where memories come from: movies, books, magazines" (10). Indeed, throughout the performance, an amnesiac Carmelita borrows from other people's memories, what she playfully calls "a CUMAA Collective Unconscious Memory Appropriation Attack" (15).

It seems that what results from the "primary scene" is a series of double moves: the decoupling of the subject into a self/other (Carmelita and the artist) leads to a discovery of a different kind of subjectivity, one similar to what Trinh T. Minh-ha calls a "not you/like you." This affirmation of "I am (Cubana, Latina) like you" but different is tied, diegetically, to a recovery of a synthesizing memory. This recovery, in turn, is materialized performatively via the recoupling of different sensorial experiences through synesthesia: music triggers recollections of flavors, and sights trigger recollections of music. The best example of this recoupling comes toward the end of the performance, when we can no longer tell if it is the artist's voice or Carmelita who states, "These are *Star Trek* glasses. They form rainbows around everything you look at. Am I looking at Cuba from an American perspective? No es fácil. It's not easy to have clear vision. In seven days, I can get only sound bites" (22).

If, indeed, "all autobiographical memory is true" and it is up to the interpreter to decipher the purpose of its redeployment, I suggest that its redeployment here follows a clearly designed objective of tactical intervention: to initiate a dialogue between two contradictory histories and trajectories, the diasporic Cuban and the island Cuban. "No es fácil" ("It's not easy") proposes the link between the two. This phrase is repeated, as a leitmotif, many times in the performance. It is the phrase we heard most often during our stay in Cuba (1993), because Cubans on the island use it to refer to their present survival conditions. In the performance, however, Tropicana puts the phrase in the mouth of both islanders and diasporic Cubans. I read Carmelita's and Troyano's appropriation of "No es fácil" as an insinuation that, albeit the many differences, life is not easy for either the Cubans on the island or the diasporic Cubans. Most important, the performance connects this "No es fácil" with one of its causes, the U.S. embargo against Cuba. In fact, the performance ends with a prerecorded song by a Cuban musician from the island, which Carmelita also sings in English: "Todos por lo mismo, Everybody for the same thing" (23). She asks for the music in Spanish, saying, "Música maestra," and the tape begins to play Ferrer's song in Spanish. Carmelita then sings an English version, and the audience eventually sings along in both languages. Giving the last voice of the performance to Ferrer's song, Carmelita's "virtual duo" with Ferrer, and the audience singing with the two of them is a powerful last image. On the one hand, it underlines the desire and need of many Cubans, islanders and diasporic, for reunification. On the other hand, it establishes a direct correlation between the embargo and Cubans' necessities, both material and spiritual. The end of *Milk of Amnesia/Leche de amnesia* brings to the fore different voices in coalition—not only Cuban voices from both sides, but U.S. voices as well:

Todos por lo mismo;
entre las páginas del colonialismo
capitalistas, homosexuales, ateos,
espirituales y moralistas,
todos por lo mismo.
[Everybody for the same thing;
between the pages of colonialism

capitalists, homosexuals, atheists,
spiritualists and moralists,
everybody for the same thing.] (23)

Like Tropicana's tactical interventions, this last image of different voices in coalition, in both Spanish and English, also calls
for a redefinition of identity, especially national identity, along
more flexible and porous categories than that of self and other,
Western/hegemonic and "primitive"/subaltern, or, for that matter, Cuban/American and Cuban/Latino. Indeed, hybrid subjectivity constantly underlines a "flexibility of identity," as Chela
Sandoval calls it, which allows one to move beyond the category of otherness as an absolute difference from oneself. Constantly reaffirming a "not you" and "like you" gesture allows us
to locate points of "identity-in-difference," that is, points of identities in the present that allow us "to forge the needed solidari-
ties against repression and oppression."[39]

Mendieta's and Tropicana's performances stage the multiple
"in betweens" of hybrid subjectivity by means of different aesthetic approaches. In Mendieta's minimalist performances, as
ritualized dramatizations, what predominated was the use of the
physical presence of the body in relation to nature. Tropicana's
performances of excess, on the other hand, are subject to the
word, to narration and characterization in relation to a body
and a body of memories that know themselves to be a product
of that very discourse.

Whereas Mendieta's work is suspended, as John Perreault
states, "between the pain of exile and the transcendence of
ritual,"[40] Tropicana transforms that pain into ironic laughter
through the parody inherent in both lesbian and ethnic camp.
In spite of their different aesthetic conceptualizations, both artists open up a space for another type of self-representation, a
performative one that resists the objectification of female bodies. At the same time, their performances undermine the "natural" representation of gender in its ethnic intersection. Furthermore, both Mendieta and Tropicana enact in their performances
a ritual of recuperation of a split memory after exile. In their
recuperative attempt, they perform identity outside of essentialist paradigms. My reading suggests that this recuperative attempt
can become reality only if and when there is flexibility of identity in all of us involved. By keeping cultural similarities and

differences active at the same time, Mendieta's minimalist performances and Tropicana's ethnic and gender performances ar-
rest the ideological closure of anchoring culture within a stable
identity, in a specific geographical space and in a linear and
consecutive history. Most important, they propose that only when
we realize that all Cubans and Latinos/as are alike and not alike–
that Cuban identity, like Latino/a identity, is, indeed, identity-in-
difference–only then can we begin to forge a peaceful coexistence.

Notes

1. Biographical information about Ana Mendieta comes from Robert
Katz, *Naked By the Window: The Fatal Marriage of Carl Andre and Ana
Mendieta* (New York: The Atlantic Monthly Review Press, 1990);
Gerardo Mosquera, "Esculturas rupestres de Ana Mendieta," *Areito*
7.28 (1981): 54–56; Gerardo Mosquera, "La última silueta," *El caimán
barbudo* (February 1987): 23; Nereyda García and Brenda Miller, *Ana
Mendieta: Fuego de tierra* (video), 1988.
2. See Lillian Manzor-Coats, "Too Spik or Too Dyke: Carmelita
Tropicana," *Ollantay Theater Magazine* 2.1 (Winter/Spring 1994): 39–
55.
3. Personal communication with the artist. This story is also published
in Alisa Solomon, "The WOW Cafe," *The Drama Review* 29.1 (1985):
92–101.
4. See Alberto Sandoval Sánchez and David Román, "Caught in the
Web: AIDS and Allegory in *Kiss of the Spider Woman, the Musical*," unpublished manuscript.
5. A genealogy of Latino constructions by the Anglo cultural imaginary is being undertaken by Latino cultural critics. See Chon Noriega,
Chicanos and Film (New York: Garland Press. 1992); Chon Noriega, "El
Hilo Latino: Representation, Identity, National Culture,"*Jump Cut*
38(1993): 45–50; Ana López, John King, and Manuel Alvarado, *Medi-
ating Two Worlds: Cinematic Encounters in the Americas* (London: BFI.
1993); José Piedra, "His/Her Panics," *Dispositio* 16.41 (1991): 71–93;
David Román, "Teatro Viva! Latino Performance, Sexuality and
AIDS in Los Angeles," in *Lesbian and Gay Issues in Hispanic Literature*.
ed. Emilie Bergmann and Paul Julian Smith (New York and London:
Oxford University Press, forthcoming); Alberto Sandoval Sánchez,
"A Puerto Rican Reading of the 'America' in *West Side Story*," *Jump Cut*
39 (1994): 59–66; Alberto Sandoval Sánchez, "Staging AIDS: What's
Latino Got to Do with It? in *Negotiating Performance:Gender, Sexuality,*

and Theatricality in Latin/o America; ed. Diana Taylor (Durham: Duke University Press, 1993).

6. See Sandoval Sánchez and Román.

7. Respectively, Carmen Tafolla, *To Split a Human: Mitos, Machos y la Mujer Chicana* (San Antonio: Mexican American Cultural Center, 1985), 41; López, et al., 72; and Sandoval Sánchez's essay in this collection. Alfedro Villanueva-Collado has called the male counterpart of this mystification of the Other's sexual powers "The Mandingo Syndrome." See his "Emigration/Immigration: Going Home Where I Belong," in *Hispanic Immigrant Writers and the Question of Identity,* ed. Pedro Monge-Rafuls (New York: Ollantay Press, 1989), 42.

8. I know that this phrase, "Anglo cultural imaginary," is a loaded phrase that needs to be unpacked. But this is not the place to do it. This cultural imaginary, as many critics suggest, is a product of Hollywood's, Broadway's, and television's role as co-producers of cultural texts. As Ana López has analyzed: "Hollywood does not represent ethnics and minorities: it creates them and provides its audience with an experience of them. Rather than an investigation of the mimetic relationships, then, a critical reading of Hollywood's ethnographic discourse requires the analysis of the historical-political construction of self-'other' relations—the articulation of forms of difference, sexual and ethnic—as an inscription of, among other factors, Hollywood's power as ethnographer, creator and translator of 'otherness' " (68).

9. For the use of tactic as opposed to strategy, see Rey Chow, *Writing Diaspora* (Bloomington; Indiana University Press, 1993).

10. Katz, 9.

11. Mendieta was at the prime moment of her artistic career. Thus the first explanation/excuse offered by Andre, that the fall was a suicide, seems implausible to all those who knew Mendieta intimately, including the last two people who talked to her hours before her death: her sister and her best friend. The second reason offered by Andre was that the fall might have been an accident. This is also inconceivable to those who knew her well; Mendieta never got close to that window, because she was terrified of heights (see Katz *passim*).

12. Joyce Wadler, "A Death in Art," *New York,* (December 1985): 40.

13. Wadler, 41.

14. Judd Tully, "Andre Acquitted: Trial Kindles Sexual Politics in New York's Art World," *New Art Examiner* 4 (1988): 24.

15. Hoffinger, Andre's defense lawyer, tried to suggest through his questions that perhaps Mendieta had been the victim of a self-cast "voodoo spell," as he called it. During the trial, he mistakenly brought up the fact that Yemayá, a goddess that interested Mendieta, was "a deity that takes flight" (quoted in Katz, 354).

16. "Choices: Candela y Azúcar." *The Village Voice,* (February 1988): 34.

17. Robert Sandia, "Downtown Not Dead Yet," *Dance Magazine* (March 1991), 70.

18. "Carmelita aparenta jugar con los estereotipos Latinos, pero en realidad es con la cabeza de uno con quien está jugando. Es una terrorista cultural, una Carmen Miranda ataviada con frutas peligrosas." "Fiebre del trópico," *Más,* 1.4 (verano 1990): 14. Unless otherwise noted, all translations are my own.

19. López, et al., 74.

20. López, et al., 74.

21. Ana Mendieta, quoted in *Fuego de tierra.*

22. See Philip Auslander, *Presence and Resistance: Postmodernism and Cultural Politics in Contemporary American Performance* (Ann Arbor: University of Michigan Press, 1992); and Johannes Birringer, *Theatre, Theory, Postmodernism* (Bloomington: Indiana University Press, 1991).

23. Lois Camnitzer, *New Art of Cuba* (Austin: University of Texas Press, 1994), 91.

24. Kimberlé Crenshaw, "Whose Story Is It? Feminist and Antiracist Appropriations of Anita Hill," in *Race-ing Justice, Engendering Power: Essays on Anita Hill, Clarence Thomas, and the Construction of Social Reality,* ed. Toni Morrison (New York: Pantheon Books, 1992), 403. I borrow the term *conjunctural* from Elspeth Probyn, *Sexing the Self: Gendered Positions in Cultural Studies* (London and New York: Routledge, 1993).

25. As Rogoff states, "The transient status of the works…echoes other states of transience all linked to an earth which defines everything but cannot be adhered to in any way." Irit Rogoff, "In the empire of the Object–The Geographies of Ana Mendieta," unpublished manuscript, 1994, 27.

26. See Lillian Manzor-Coats, *Marginality Beyond Return;* unpublished book manuscript.

27. Mendieta, quoted in LACE, introduction.

28. Jorge Castellanos and Isabel Castellanos,. *Cultura Afrocubana 3: Las religiones y las lenguas* (Miami: Ediciones Universal, 1988), 239–40.

29. Quoted in Petra Barreras del Río, "Ana Mendieta: A Historical Overview," in *Ana Mendieta: A Retrospective* (New York: The New Museum of Contemporary Art, 1987), 29.

30. Mendieta called these performances transformations or ritualistic dramatizations. See Nancy Lynn Harris, "The Female Imagery of Mary Beth Edelson and Ana Mendieta," M.F.A. thesis, Louisiana State University, 1987, 46.

31. See Peter Frank, "The Human Figure: Present and/or Accounted For," in *Awards in the Visual Arts 4* (Winston-Salem, N.C.: Southeastern Center for Contemporary Art, 1985); Lalia Kahn, "Ana Mendieta," *Art New England* (June 1982): 7; Mosquera, 1987.

32. Castellanos y Castellanos. "Un contacto con los antepasados desaparecidos, con el mundo del 'más allá' y con los origenes míticos

de la secta," 238.

33. Not understanding how santería functions, Lucy Lippard intuitively sees her work as "an amulet against the evils of her internal tearing" in "Quite Contrary: Body, Nature, Ritual in Women's Art," *Chrysalis 2* (1977): 43.

34. Carmelita Tropicana and Uzi Parnés, *Memorias de la revolución/ Memories of the Revolution,* unpublished manuscript, 1987.

35. See Manzor-Coats, 1994.

36. Eventually, both Pérez Prado and the mambo made it to and in the United States, in much the same way that Gloria Estefan has made it on the contemporary pop charts. In 1955, Pérez Prado's orchestra was chosen the most popular orchestra in the United States, and RCA-Victor honored him with the golden record for "Cherry Pink and Apple Blossom Times," which broke a record that year, selling more than 1,800,000 copies. See Cristóbal Díaz Ayala, *Música Cubana: Del Areyto a la Nueva Trova,* (San Juan, P.R.: Editorial Cubanacán, 1981), 195.

37. This process is quite similar to what Elin Diamond elaborates on in her work as "gestic feminist criticism": "The spectator is enabled to see a sign system as a sign system—the appearance, words, gestures, ideas, attitudes, etc., that comprise the gender [and racial] lexicon become so many illusionistic trappings to be put on or shed at will." Elin Diamond, "Brechtian Theory/Feminist Theory," *The Drama Review* 32.1 (Spring), 82–94.

38. See Cristina Moreiras, "Resistencia autobiográfica en la España postfranquista," unpublished manuscript, 1994.

39. Chela Sandoval, "Feminism and Racism," in *Making Face, Making Soul/Haciendo Caras: Creative and Critical Perspectives by Women of Color,* ed. Gloria Anzaldúa (San Francisco: Aunt Lute, 1990). See also Norma Alarcón, "Chicana Feminism: In the Tracks of 'the' Native Woman," *Cultural Studies* Vol.4, No.3 (October 1990), 248–256.

40. John Perrault, "Earth and Fire: Mendieta's Body of Work," in *Ana Mendieta,* 14.

And She Wears It Well:
Feminist and Cultural Debates
in the Work of Astrid Hadad

Roselyn Constantino

In feminist criticism of the past two decades, the analysis of gender is frequently aligned with considerations of race, ethnicity, class, and, in many cases, national identity. In Latin America, however, recent cultural criticism questions the way in which we conceptualize and speak about these mistakenly assumed seamless categories.[1] In Mexico, the claim that Mexicans are a racially blind homogeneous group, unlike their violent, racist U.S. neighbors, has come back to haunt that society. The indigenous uprisings in Chiapas and Guerrero occurred in the precise moment in which the North American Free Trade Agreement was increasing the influx of foreign cultural products and influences; both events challenged and destabilized an already questionable national identity. *Pluralism* is a buzz word in Mexico that, along with *democratization,* is intended to indicate the (this time) honest effort to permit participation by all sectors of that heterogeneous society. The attainment of either pluralism or democracy is proving to be very painful. Thus the debate continues about the very structures and institutions of Mexican society and the nature of its culture and people as they move into the twenty-first century. In this essay, I posit that, despite lingering attitudes in some U.S. critical circles that no real theoretical debate occurs in Latin America, a re-examination of "identities" is indeed occurring on the Mexican "stage," as well as within intellectual and popular urban and rural discussions.[2] I also suggest a correspondence between certain Mexican women's and Latina/ Chicanas' choice of performance art with satirical ironic tones to express similar, although not identical, political and social criticism. In each case, an analysis of their works permits a formulation of a theoretical framework that contextualizes rather than appropriates these women's cultural production.

In Mexico, the work of actress and singer Astrid Hadad is an example of how these issues are aligned with an exploration of theatrical forms capable of articulating critical issues at the heart of Mexico's crisis. This essay considers the theatrical and artistic forms Hadad employs, examines one of her performances in Mexico City, and, with the goal of generating further discussion, poses questions that might frame the analysis of that performance within the context of contemporary debates on theater, feminist criticism, and Mexican sociocultural realities. I propose that, by way of Hadad's work, we can enter into a discussion of 1) the concept of "valid" forms of feminist art and criticism, especially in relation to Mexican women and Chicanas/Latinas; 2) how we, U.S. academics, might develop critical tools in order to analyze this art and situate it within the cultural panorama of Mexico, taking into consideration its reception as well as production; and 3) how this performance art fits into the panorama of a Mexico clamoring for democracy.

Hadad's works are motivated by a series of aesthetic and political considerations: the rejection of the bureaucracy, elitism, and inflexibility of worn-out forms and commercial interests that characterize much Mexican theater; the establishment of direct contact with the spectator; the resuscitation of traditional popular Mexican scenographic forms, such as review theater, cabaret, and teatro de carpa;[3] the representation of elements of popular culture shared by all Mexicans; the criticism of repressive systems of power; the highlighting of the ephemeral nature of real-life and artistic experiences; the search for language capable of articulating the complex reality of Mexico at the end of the millennium; and the recuperation of women artists for Mexican history and for a new generation of Mexican women. She refers to her work as "performance," and, as Antonio Prieto explains, this

differs from "theater" in that where theater is based on a text, a director, and repetition, performance is centered on the body, the actress, and the ephemeral. In theater, actors portray characters; in performance, the actor refers to herself. Theater represents; performance presents. Theater originates in the secular; performance moves toward ritual. Theater seeks to transcend; performance to transgress.[4]

Hadad's performance art creates an *espectáculo* (as both show and spectacle) that is not a simple imitation of imported models. In order to represent critical discourses and, at the same time, entertain, she incorporates elements from Mexican visual arts, music, and cinema, and action and gestures from popular culture. Other female artists in Mexico, often in collaboration with Hadad, also draw upon performance art in order to develop alternative artistic styles. Performance, according to Jesusa Rodríguez, is a *gabacho* [gringo] term that, nonetheless, is useful in describing forms and structures whose origins can be found in pre-Colombian society. Performance artist Guillermo Gómez-Peña notes that performance in Mexico departs from the spirit of involuntary actions and conduct seen within the popular urban culture, such as merolicos,[5] street-peddlers, fire-eaters, street theater, and so on: "It is a form that permits you to be an alburero [one who plays with language, using words and phrases often with implicit sexual connotations], to be subversive, humorous, witty, iconoclast, and myth-breaking."[6] Visual and performance artist Maris Bustamante suggests that Mexican performance also has antecedents in Mexico's art history with the estridentistas, who, during the first decades of this century, even more than the famous Mexican muralists, developed new attitudes toward life and art. Bustamante points out that European aesthetic forms, enriched by a ritualistic, festive, dramatic, ephemeral spirit particular to Latin America, give a contemporary meaning to the performances of today:

For me, performance is a way in which I can posit various ideas of how I see things, utilizing myself, my body, to communicate through action realized on stage. Concerns are translated constantly into forms, colors, spaces. An image is graphically displaced from the painting onto the body, artificially translating bodily experiences (like having sex, orgasms, and other life experiences) into images. Although performance has generated its own tradition in the U.S. and Europe and is already somewhat academic, it still provides an opportunity for rupture. Performance is a way to be subversive, to directly confront the spectator.[7]

Hadad borrows from Mexico's rich theatrical heritage (which, in official histories, tends to be reduced to theater of Western tradition): "My show has its roots in cabaret. I know that in the U.S., they call it performance. My style is syncretic, aesthetic, pathetic, and diuretic, which demonstrates, without shame, the attitudes of machismo, masochism, nihilism, and 'I-could-give-a-damn' inherent in all cultures."[8] Along with this "borrowing," possibilities for new modes of representation are created by the ruptures in form, the satirical and ironic tones of critical commentary of the content, and the distancing from the institutions that control theater production in Mexico—institutions that, Hadad, Bustamante, and Rodriguez[9] insist, depend upon hegemonic and masculinist programs of the government, cultural elites, and commercial interests. In Hadad's fast-paced, fragmented, nonlinear unveiling of traditional Mexican song, dress, dance, and political satire, the focus of work is the female body and its position and representation in these critical discourses.

The elements of the artist and political motivation of these women's work coincides with the production of certain Latina/Chicana counterparts, such as Coco Fusco, writer and critic of Cuban origin, who works, often in conjunction with Gómez-Peña, to break the stereotypes of Latina communities perpetuated by North American media and culture; Chicanas Elvira and Hortensia Colorado (Coatlique/Las Colorado), who have for years worked between and across the borders of performance art and theater, of racial and ethnic communities, in order to, as women suffering double oppression, transform their problematic into an artistic and spiritual search in collaboration with Latin American and U.S. Indian women; and Guadalupe García, who uses performance and video art to make visible that part of Mexican hybrid identity that many choose to ignore: the Mexican-American.'[10] In each case, as with Mexican women, these artists denounce arbitrary artistic, social, and cultural norms (particularly as they affect women) and, at the same time, celebrate what Gloria Anzaldúa refers to as "una conciencia mestiza." They underscore the need to open ideological, conceptual, and linguistic spaces in order to "work by way of the differences,"[11] but without falling into what Nestor García Canclini refers to as a nostalgia for "authentic" culture or sociocultural purity.[12]

Astrid Hadad: Performance, Feminism, and Cultural Politics

Hadad, of Lebanese parents, was born in the southern Mexican state of Quintana Roo (bordering Guatemala); thus, she is a member of several marginalized groups. She moved to Mexico City in 1980 and studied theater at the National Autonomous University. In 1984, she made her debut in Jesusa Rodríguez's production *Donna Giovanni.*[13] The show, in which almost all the actors were women, was not simply a feminist critique or classic theater, but rather, Jean Franco suggests, a celebration of the "libertine" in all of us—that is, of the naturalness of sexuality seen against society's deforming norms.[14] After this production, Hadad separated from Rodríguez to develop her own shows, in which she incorporated traditional ranchera and bolero music into political satire in the style of cabaret popular during the 1930s. *Nostalgia Arrabalera* and *Del Rancho a la Ciudad* were performed in what was then Rodríguez's Café-Bar El Cuervo, and *La Mujer del Golfo Apocalipsis* and La *Mujer Ladrina* in various cantinas in Mexico City. The artist then broadened her repertoire to include the "sketch" of review theater, a form popular from 1910 to 1940[15]—humorous sociopolitical criticism in which national and religious icons are represented, with the intention of recuperating the sexuality, sensuality, and human desires suppressed by the morality imposed by these institutions.

From this beginning emerged *Heavy Nopal (Ode to Lucha Reyes)*, *Letters to Dragoberta,* and *Faxes to Rumberta.* With the influence of the Caribbean culture found in Quintana Roo—the sensual dances and rhythms of rumba, salsa, and sones—in each piece the female body is both the vehicle of communication and the message. It is a body that continuously re-presents and constructs its gender; a body that, according to Hadad, is always the recipient of social signs of femininity.

For these productions, Astrid found inspiration in the pioneer of vernacular song in Mexico, Lucha Reyes.[16] Reyes (1904–1944) appeared on the Mexican musical scene in the 1930s; she introduced a bravía style of singing—a feminine interpretation of ranchera music.[17] "Feminine" here refers to Reyes's biological sex, not the gendered image of the submissive, negated, suffering Mexican woman. Star of French and Mexican opera and review theater, with more than one hundred recordings and many appearances in films, Reyes is compared to Billie Holiday, Edith Piaf, and Janis Joplin. According to Pablo Dueñas, the singer's form of expression emerged from the "female soldiers of the Mexican Revolution, prototypes of the tough people in the countryside, especially certain female characters that [Reyes] portrayed in cantinas."[18]

Reyes flaunted her deep, hoarse voice until it sounded as if it would tear. She moaned, she cried. It was a new style, and the public loved her, although critics could not accept her "lack" of refinement. Soon the "Mexican Diva symbolized and personified the temperamental, 'unpolished' woman that stood her ground against the macho Mexican boss-man."[19] She became the figure of the times: her plays on words and spicy jokes were popular, her "aggressive" appearance (as read by some), and her enormous capacity for affection symbolized a general feeling in Mexico, especially among Mexican women.[20] Friend and, according to some, lover of Frida Kahlo,[21] Reyes was tagged by author and cultural critic Salvador Novo as the representative of revolutionary Mexico:

Lucha Reyes erupted on the stage. She was a cry that gave cover to a collective sense of alleviation and defiance. If her life was marked by intensity, she took this to its ultimate consequences in public and in private. She practiced her sexuality freely, having affairs with one or the other sex.[22]

Considered by some a femme fatale, for others she personified a strong woman who takes responsibility for, and claims as her own, her sexuality, her economic well-being, her career, and her public and private identities. In a country where the citizens are criticized and criticize themselves for their often "sheepish acceptance of authority, their capacity for meekness and manageableness"[23]—a characteristic traced to Mexico's Hispanic and Roman Catholic roots—Reyes was and still offers a model of resistance for *both* women and men.

Hadad's "fatal attraction" (in her words) to Reyes's almost mythical figure and her incorporation of pieces of Reyes's life and work into her performance reflect a desire to recuperate female historical figures and elements of traditional Mexican culture. Similar to Chicanas' work with the figure of La Malinche (often referred to as the Mexican Eve), Hadad seeks to resignify and to situate these icons, myths, and real women within a new sociocultural history. I begin the examination of her efforts with observations from which emerged the questions that frame this study.

During the summer of 1993, I went to see Astrid's *Letters to Dragoberta* at the café/restaurant La Bodega, in Mexico City. Located in the Colonia Condesa, a historic, fashionable section of the city, it was obvious that the spectators in this small but packed dining room were from the middle-class and upper-middle class. The prices might explain that: sixty pesos (twenty dollars at that time) plus expensive food and drink—not a cheap night out, by Mexican standards. Astrid walks through the crowd, climbs onto the stage, and joins her two musicians, Los Tarzanes. What follows is a mixture of parodied artistic forms: visual art, dance, music, and theater of different genres. As in *Heavy Nopal* (1990) and *Faxes to Rumberta* (1994), Astrid is dressed in a nine-teenth-century-style green, full "peasant" skirt with a "feminine" white blouse with red trim—the colors of the Mexican flag. These colors are also visible in her glittered eye makeup and earrings. The folkloric image of the *china poblana* (a popular nineteenth-century image of women's dress in the province of Puebla) is completed with her hair arranged in two long braids and giant white lilies attached to her back, forming a type of crown over her head—as in the Diego Rivera painting of a young indigenous woman holding such flowers. Astrid dances and sings the well-known lyrics of a traditional song: "I am a virgin watering my flowers / and with the flowers, my identity."

On the one hand, Astrid's costumes are beautiful, many with historical value. On the other hand, the image created—in which objects of popular culture are represented and repeated, forming part, one might say, of Mexican "kitsch"—exemplifies, according to some cultural critics, the inscription of the indigenous and provincial as folkloric and exotic. The non-Western becomes synonymous with innocence, beauty, and nature. Such icons distance "ethnicity" from the reality of, for instance, the armed insurgents, who, in a centuries-old struggle in states such as Chiapas and Guerrero, are willing to die for land and dignity. The contradictions suggested by overlaying these images with humorous gestures, plays on words, and critical commentary implicit in the props and makeup create ironic and satirical tones that permit Astrid to recuperate and resignify these symbols to reflect the pluralism that marks Mexican culture. At the same time, she strikes a chord of the elusive ser mexicano, or Mexi-can-ness by, without falling into nostalgia, underscoring those sights, sounds, smells, traditions, and historical realities that do create a common bond within a shared geographic space.

Throughout the show, the actress continues to tour the Mexi-

(courtesy of Roselyn Constantino)

can cultural landscape. She sings songs of different styles and origins, including rancheras, boleros, corridos, pop music, Caribbean beats, and even some tunes from Broadway shows. Between the verses, Astrid narrates love letters, the kind written in the early part of the century by scribes in the Plaza Santo Domingo of Mexico City for lovers unable to read or write to sweethearts in the provinces. Tonight's letters are to Dragoberta, a young woman traveling and working around the country—breaking the norm for a woman in turn-of-the-century Mexico, the period indicated by the romantic language of the letters and by Astrid's costume. Her letters are parodies in which, while speaking about love and human relationships, she intertwines political commentary and current events. Dragoberta complains about the awful treatment to which she is subjected. The boyfriend's anger is revealed by his sarcastic remarks: "¿Oye, Dragoberta, why don't you just stay home, where you belong anyway?" His criticism is not unlike that levied upon Mexican women who are just beginning to enter previously restricted masculine spaces, although many of them meet with physical as well as verbal abuse.[24]

Laughter erupts as Hadad, acting the two parts, parodies rhetoric used by the Mexican power structures (the government and the Catholic Church) since the late nineteenth century as part of a strategy of nation-building, of constructing national identity. Highlighted in this rhetoric, which she both mocks and utilizes, is the appeal to "good" Mexicans inscribed upon the symbol of the Mexican flag and the image of the Virgin of Guadalupe, here clearly visible on her costume—a costume that was censored when Hadad appeared on national television, a medium with close ties to the ruling party for sixty-five years, the PRI.[25] The PRI has a legal monopoly on the colors of the flag—no other political party can use the red, white, and green in their logo, a fact that underscores the power of image that is so much a part of social control in that country. During the 1994 presidential elections, along with, and as a symbol of, the calls for election reform as part of the process of democratization, opposition political parties and the rebels in Chiapas demanded the "release" of the flag to all Mexicans.

The recognition of the "power of the image" is what has motivated Latina, Chicana, and female Mexican performance artists to select that medium to explore artistic and political concerns. Characterized by orality and openness, the histories of Hispanic American societies are filled with examples of a reverence for the visual representation—a reality upon which political, social, and economic elites have capitalized, in order to construct national identities as well as repress and control the masses in general and certain groups such as women, Indians, and homosexuals, in particular. In the sixteenth century, the cult of the Virgin of Guadalupe (a figure being recycled by a younger generation of Chicanas and Mexican women) caused fear in Church leaders when they realized the indigenous devotees believed in the miracle-performing powers of the painting of the mestiza Mexican Virgin, of her visual representation.[26] This devotion was taken advantage of by Church and government leaders as early as the seventeenth century: they added, at the feet of the Virgin, the eagle of the Mexican coat-of-arms. The figure of the Virgin, as well as of La Malinche and the goddesses Coatlicue and Tonantzin, became part of socially constructed gender and national identities. Women today are recycling these syncretic images (pre-Hispanic, Hispanic, and mestizo) and, in postmodern parodic tones coupled with feminist political will, converting them into new models, icons, and myths that represent real women's multiple identities in process. Due to the immediacy of, and the presence of the body in, performance, the spectator becomes a participant in the "trying on" of the new images.

Critic Rosa Beltrán comments on the complicity between Hadad and the spectator—a relationship that enhances solidarity among the various groups represented in the audience: "the wink of an eye in which she becomes the iconic referent of our national symbols as she interprets, to the letter, the songs to which we Mexicans usually cry with more pleasure."[27] Here the symbols are deconstructed and then resignified as Hadad juxtaposes the image of the "suffering Mexican who revels in the martyrdom evoked in the lyrics of the corridos and boleros that forged our nation"[28] and the image of Lucha Reyes—a figure representing other possibilities of being.

The solidarity that Hadad achieves has as a goal active social participation leading to transformation. Laughter becomes a release of the frustration Mexicans experience when they, as individuals, feel powerless to change systems operated by those

whose calls for "democracy" and "plurality" prove to be another exercise in public theatricality, a circus. As Diana Taylor
explains in *Theater of Crisis,* spectacle and theatricality have long
traditions in Latin American society, where art and politics cross
borders constantly.[29] Astrid forces to the foreground the connections among various discourses tossed around in the public spectacle, the most important of which is gender and ethnicity as
related to economics and power. She incorporates condoms,
basketballs, and musical instruments to evoke such diverse discussions as AIDS, the U.S. economic and cultural "imperialism" (which has intensified in Mexico since the signing of the
North American Free Trade Agreement), Mexico's painful steps
toward "democratization" of the authoritarian sociopolitical systems, and the appropriation of art forms by the intellectual and
artistic elite without a revalorization of their original context.
The seriousness of the issues, however, is cut by an almost circus atmosphere that seems to the observer to be a strategy to
cast important issues in such a manner as to make them ap-
proachable, to convert the overwhelming into collective resolve
and energy. For instance, the audience throws basketballs into
the hoop (a North American sport so popular that three Mexican magazines are dedicated to it). The ball is inscribed with the
name of a mayoral or presidential candidate; making a basket is
casting a vote. The spectators laugh at the reference to the mock-
ery the PRI makes of civil participation in supposedly democratic institutions. Here we see how the flexibility of performance
art creates a venue in which Hadad showcases the richness of
Mexican art and culture, while permitting collective "airing" of
aspects of social structures in need of change.

Her task is achieved, in part, through her use of parody that
Linda Hutcheon describes as postmodern: "a value-
problematizing, denaturalizing form of acknowledging the history (and through irony, the politics) of representations."[30]
Astrid's parody, satire, and irony encompass a full range of possibilities of intent that these styles and tones offer—at times re-
spectfully reinscribing the text parodied, at times deconstructing
the text in a mocking, critical tone. The text is "pinned down"
into the specific historic context that generates it, and the spectator engages in a process of decoding and interpretation that
underscores his or her complicity in the wide variety of social

and aesthetic practices being critically represented.

Hadad's work, although exploring theater as art, is politically and socially committed. She never attempts to mask the ideological premise of her work: on the contrary, she showcases it. She structures her performance around attacks on gender bias, political authoritarianism, feudal-style systems constructed upon ethnic groups and class distinctions, in general, and on female submission and male machismo in particular. Layers of clothing and props evoke the layers of meaning of seemingly innocent elements of popular culture that the Mexican audience obviously recognizes and responds to with enthusiastic laughter. The "discourses of power" are visually situated on a strong female body–a body whose sensuality Astrid emphasizes and takes pleasure in, although in Mexico, it is a body that all structures of society attempt to regulate. This control is cemented by what cultural critic Carlos Monsiváis refers to as Mexico's "Sacred Cows,"[31] none of whom escape Astrid's criticism: the Catholic Church and the pope, the president and other well-known politicians, and, of course, macho men and submissive women, some of whom compose tonight's audience.

At one point in the show, Astrid puts on a moustache as she speaks certain lines and, thus, acquires or appropriates "the power of the word" that dominates all official discourse in Mexico, be it religious, social, or political. The detachable moustache, in a pop-Freudian reading, metonymically represents the phallus and, in the Mexican context, evokes former President Salinas de Gortari, or the macho figure par excellence, Pancho Villa, or any other paternalistic figure of power, and thus visually represents the arbitrary and theatrical aspects of gender construction in her culture.

The attitude of Astrid toward her female body and her feminine self can be seen as a change from many of the representations of women on the Mexican stage. It varies from portrayals (still common) of the suffering, repressed female as victim, or from those in what she refers to as "sordid" strip-tease shows, where the naked woman's sexuality serves economic interest and male pleasure. Within a critique of institutionalized gender bias, Astrid derives pleasure from her sensuality, and evokes an eroticism seemingly created by and for her. Similar to the feminist criticism in Rosario Castellanos's play *The Eternal Feminine*

(courtesy of Roselyn Constantino)

(1972), Hadad underscores the individual's responsibility in her "victimization." She also presents identity, be it national or gender, as a space in which contradictions and idiosyncracies exist and are constantly being reformulated. In her work and her life, Astrid demands an open reading of that identity-in-process and urges others, women and men, to do the same:

I express the myriad contradictions which we are, all the variations on character and personality, moods and moments that define us and in which we exist. If there is a contradiction between the words of the songs I sing and what happens on stage, it is because we are that contradiction.[32]

In my mind, however, questions arise on how to analyze, from a feminist position, what Astrid presents on stage or the reactions of the audience. Is this feminist art? If not, why? It is a show that obviously entertains and affords intimate contact with audience members. The analysis becomes complicated the moment Astrid suddenly removes her blouse to reveal a red corset; that is, we see her in a corset with the china poblana skirt, which she eventually takes off, leaving her in sexy intimate apparel, obviously enjoying the sensuality of her performance. Much feminist film and theater criticism centers on the presence of the female body in performance and emphasizes the need to break the "male gaze" dominating all visual arts—a task that feminist critics Teresa de Lauretis, Laura Mulvey, Jill Dolan, and Linda Hutcheon insist is hindered by forms that have trained men and women to see indiscriminately and uncritically the female body as object. The spectator's self-conscious position is important in feminist aesthetic and social critique that move to avoid identification and attain critical distancing. Feminist artists attempt to escape what de Lauretis in *Alice Doesn't* refers to as the "male gaze." De Lauretis argues that women have historically remained the object of that gaze, not the subject, even when the gazer is a woman: "The woman is framed by the look of the camera as icon, or object of the gaze: an image made to be looked at by the spectator, whose look is relayed by the look of the male character(s). The latter not only controls the events and narrative action but is 'the bearer' of the look of the spectator."[33]

Film's formal mechanisms include the control of the viewer's gaze by controlling the dimensions of time and space, which,

(courtesy of Roselyn Constantino)

although different for a live, staged production, is approached in Astrid's work by the very small stage in a dining room that seats only about fifty spectators, and by the use of spotlights that illuminate only the performer's body (the rest of the stage and room are dark), both of which afford intimate contact with the audience. Through this controlled visual space, as Laura Mulvey posits, appeals are made to the "scopophilic instinct," the pleasure in looking at another person as an erotic object, which, in masculine works, highlights woman's to-be-looked-at-ness.[34] Desires and pleasure, however, are constructed within a range of signifying practices and, therefore, that "look" can be interrupted.[35] Therein, Hutcheon stresses, lies the revolutionary power of feminist representations that shake the spectator out of passive viewing. These norms, as human constructs, are authoritative only to those who have constructed or at least accepted them a priori.

Astrid moves toward disrupting that gaze and creating the possibility for the female body and desire to be recuperated from traditional readings. She makes spectators aware of their positions as voyeur, and of their complicit participation in the systems criticized. This is achieved, for example, by first seducing the spectators with the Latin rhythms (many are dancing in their seats) and then suddenly speeding the music's beat and her dancing to a comical, frantic speed and, at times, beating herself with her fists. These actions, metaphors for the inhumane rhythms of life in the megatropolis that is Mexico City, also comment on the representation of woman in Mexican song and film—a suffering woman who beats herself up by subscribing to the role that history designed for her—an image that Hadad re-presents and subverts on the stage. The actions express a defiant, contestatory, mocking stance toward the abyss between what society says she as a woman is and should be, and what she decides about herself as a woman. Alternating between sensual and hysterical gyrations, Astrid takes the audience from pleasure to sudden uneasiness and a denial of that pleasure.

Other details of the show, however, leave the feminist critic uneasy regarding just how resistant her work is. Along with questions of just how successful such art is at generating real transformational social action; judging from the obnoxious response of various males in this audience, for them, she is just another

(courtesy of Roselyn Constantino)

half-naked woman dancing for their pleasure.[36] Her goals are understood, perhaps, by the already "converted." Astrid admits that in early shows (often staged in cantinas in Mexico City), she frequently moved among and interacted with audience members. She no longer does, however, because, both in Mexico and abroad, she has been verbally and physically accosted by drunk, aggressive men (who feel free to grab her body) and by jealous wives.

Problematic also is the inclusion of elements of Mexican popular culture, such as traditional Latin American musical forms, that I refer to as "democratic": that is, all Mexicans, in the urban centers, in the provinces, from the working class to the economically well-off, sing and even cry with these songs. It is a phenomenon, in my opinion, without an equivalent in the United States. These songs, however, reveal Mexican machismo in the same manner that Mexican film did during its "Golden Age" of the 1940s and 1950s. Women are portrayed as either helpless victim or seductress–violated virgin or femme fatale. Mexicans–women included–sing these songs with emotional gusto. Why, then, would a self-declared feminist and lesbian revive a bastion of gender education essential to the construction of a mentality and society characterized by its machismo? Why revive a theatrical style–cabaret and review theater–in which women were viewed as props, as Enrique Alonso explains in *Las Divas en el teatro de revista mexicano:* "Beautiful women were fundamental. They added the erotic element and served as announcers of fashion, colors, hairdos, taking care of the teasing flirtations and sensuality of the works with their very skimpy costumes. All in all, their participation was extremely important."[37]

When asked about these aspects of her work–her use of the female body possibly reinscribing woman as object for male pleasure–Astrid noted that her position was challenged by some critics in the United States. When she performed in San Francisco in July 1994, harsh criticism was levied by feminists who questioned the possibility of a "feminist" performance when the performer flaunts her body–a marked body, according to them, with no chance of recuperation in existing systems of representation. Her reply: She demands, as a woman, her right to enjoy her body and sexuality, and offer them for enjoyment to others–men or women. She claims that women can enjoy other

(courtesy of Roselyn Constantino)

women, even if they are heterosexual (a position not well defined in recent feminist film and performance criticism). Astrid
maintains that the whole of her performance within its Mexican
context is what must be examined. She noted that the U.S. feminist position expressed in San Francisco is also a point of con-
tention for many Mexican feminists. Astrid insists that to re-
move the female body from the stage is only to deny access to it
by females; to attempt to force such choices upon a work in
order to be considered feminist is as authoritarian as the systems she attempts to dismantle. She argues that the history and
reality of women in Mexico—as slippery a category as "women"
is—are not the same as in the U.S. context and, therefore, feminist strategies will be different (PI).

How do we read Hadad's work and spectators' contradictory
responses? Is the reaction to her show a simple example of the
voyeurism and male gaze that resists rupture, simply recreating
and reinscribing the very systems it sets out to criticize? Do the
elements of popular culture, decontextualized to then be
recontextualized in the setting of La Bodega in the Colonia
Condesa of Mexico City, become Mexican kitsch—a bad imitation that, in the end, turns into folklore or commercializes popular Mexican culture without ever assigning it value as a "valid"
art form? Is Astrid's performance, in spite of her intentions, received by the audience as commercial entertainment empty of
the power to begin the process of social and political transformation?

I posit that part of the answer may be found in one of the
motivating forces behind Astrid's (and, similarly, other Chicana,
Latina, and Mexican women's) work—that of recycling and rein-
terpreting the very images, forms, and spaces that have constructed the categories of female, and, by extension, national
identity. The figure of the Diva in Mexican culture and the space
from which she emerged (cabaret, and review theater) historically have been considered "marginal" in national, social, and
artistic histories. However, as critics such as Carlos Monsiváis,
José Agustín, and Maris Bustamante have shown, these women
were instrumental in providing alternatives to the mainstream
images of women as far back as the emergence of modern Mexico
in the late nineteenth and early twentieth centuries, and models
for women and men in challenging and defying authority.

Monsiváis points out that, for themselves and their female audiences, as they existed in a man's world that excluded them, Divas created a space "by simultaneously using frantic movement and stillness of a statue-like body in a trance of hysteria, and a facial expression that was the equivalent of adultery and the loss of reason. They wore on the exterior, in order to learn their access to and the authenticity of, all passions ignored or suppressed."[38] Monsiváis suggests that the Divas, such as Celia Montalván, along with other notable (and, in some views, notorious) women, such as Lupe Marín, Tina Modotti, Frida Kahlo, Antonieta Rivas Mercado, Nahui Olin, Isela Vega, Lola Alvarez Bravo, and, later on, Chavela Vargas, demanded sexual and professional autonomy. They were models for women of all classes as they broke with convention and found spaces for behaviors and ways of being that previously had been inconceivable for women in Mexico—this by way of two determining forces: art and politics.[39] In many cases, the popularity of the cabarets provided one of the first and few escapes for poor women from the barrios who sought economic and personal freedom (although, to be sure not all were successful). They demonstrated that the spiritual is not the opposite of the corporal, but that the body, with its sensuality, sexuality, passions, and desires, is a sacred entity to be enjoyed by the woman to whom it belongs. It is not a coincidence that they are presently being revived, studied, and resituated in Mexican history—a departure point for new generations of Mexicans to construct identities in sync with their realities and times.

The questions raised here, as with the spaces and issues to which they refer, are not rhetorical or frivolous, as the 1995 economic and social crisis of Mexico make clear. Our work as critics requires the same kind of rethinking and reinterpretation that Hadad and other Latina, Chicana, and female Mexican artists are doing, in order to develop critical paradigms capable of reading art and artists within their particular context and historical moment. Perhaps the questions we ask will permit us to expand the field of inquiry to be more inclusive of the full range of issues at stake.

Notes

1. See, for instance, Les W. Field, "Who Are the Indians? Reconceptualizing Indigenous Identity, Resistance, and the Role of Social Science in Latin America," *Latin American Rererach Review* 29:3 (1994): 237–246.

2. Cultural critics Roger Bartra, Néstor G. Canclini, and William Rowe, among others, have written extensively on the success, or even the honesty, of these cultural projects. See Roger Bartra, *La jaula de la melancolía* (Mexico City: Grijalbo, 1987); Néstor G. Canclini, "Cultural Reconversión," trans. Holly Staver, in *On Edge:The Crisis of Contemporary Latin American Culture* ed. George Yúdice, Jean Franco, and Juan Flores (Minneapolis: University of Minnesota Press, 1992); and William Rowe and Vivian Schelling, *Memory and Modernity: Popular Culture in Latin America* (New York: Verso, 1991).

3. Literally, "theater under a tent"–itinerant theater popular in Mexico during the late nineteenth and early twentieth centuries. In the pre-mass media era, teatro de carpa featured "sketches" with political and social commentary that served to keep the populace, even in the remote areas of the country, informed of current events.

4. Antonio Prieto, "Más allá del límite: Teatro, performance y la experiencia chicana," unpublished manuscript, 1–2. All quotes in this essay, including those from texts and interviews in Spanish, are my translations.

5. Merolico is a familiar character in Mexican urban life, for which there is no good translation in English. The term refers to the wandering street peddler. who is as famous for his humorous oratory as for the wares being sold. Merolicos provide entertainment while they earn their living in the streets.

6. Quoted in Prieto, 5.

7. Personal interview. In this essay, PI refers to personal interviews conducted by me with the three artists–Astrid Hadad, Maris Bustamante, and Jesusa Rodríguez–during the summers of 1993 and 1994 in Mexico City.

8. Rosa Beltrán. "Entrevista con Astrid Hadad," *La jornada semanal,* (16 mayo 1993): 16–19.

9. Astrid Hadad (singer, and performance artist), Maris Bustamante (visual artist, performance artist, professor, and author), and Jesusa Rodríguez (actress, playwright, and entrepreneur) are important figures in the Mexican art/theater scene, not only for their creative innovations in their respective styles, but also because, as women, they work outside of mainstream commercial and government support systems. Female artist as businesswoman is a rare and admirable position within Mexican society. They also share a political and social commitment that motivates and structures their work.

10. Prieto, 14–17.

11. Prieto, 15.

12. Canclini, 40.

13. Jesusa Rodríguez is considered one of the prominent theater artists of the Mexican avant-garde of the past several decades. Often under the threat of official or unofficial censorship, Jesusa owns her own theater, La Capilla, and theater-bar, El Hábito, located in Mexico City. For an analysis of her work. see Diana Taylor, " 'High Aztec' or Performing Anthro Pop," *The Drama Review* 37:3 (1993): 142–152; Jesusa Rodríguez, personal interview, Mexico City, March, 1991; Jean Franco, "A Touch of Evil," *The Drama Review* 36:2 (1992): 48–55; and Kirsten Nigro, "Un revuelto de la historia, la memoria y el género," *Gestos* 9:17 (1994) 29–41.

14. Franco, 52.

15. Teatro de revista, or review theater, was popular during the end of the nineteenth and the first three decades of the twentieth century. It not only served as entertainment, but in a country as large as Mexico, due to illiteracy and lack of access to newspapers, review theater was a source of news and a venue for open criticism of the government or other figures of the times. See Francisco Escarcega Rodríguez, *El Teatro de Revista y la política nacional: 1910–1940*, Tesis de Licenciado en Literatura Dramática y Teatro (Mexico City: UNAM, 1988), 3–8.

16. In recent years, Reyes has captured the imagination of various Mexican female artists, who have attempted to revive her legendary strong personality and spirit as well as singing style. Astrid was one of the first on this project, writing a movie script that was then taken over by film director Arturo Ripstein. The result is the film *Reina de la noche* first screened in Mexico in August 1994, the anniversary of Reyes's death/suicide.

17 See Ernesto Márquez, "Lucha Reyes, a cincuenta años de su voz," *Tiempo libre* (21 julio 1994): 23.

18. Quoted in Luis Enrique Ramírez, "Derrumbe y partida final de Lucha Reyes," *La Jornada,* (17 julio 1994), 23.

19. Márquez, 23.

20. Raquel Peguero. "En cine, la Reyes sólo fue soldadera cantadora," *La Jornada* (19 julio 1994): 25.

21. Luis Enrique Ramírez, "Lucha Reyes: El vértigo de una voz," *La Jornada* (16 julio 1994): 21.

22. Quoted in Ramírez, 21.

23. Daniel Cazés, "Subestimar para saquearnos y volvernos a saquear," *La Jornada* (31 diciembre 1994): 9.

24. As I point out in my essay "Women and Democratic Change in Mexico," women who have organized into self-help or community action committees to fight for social justice, housing, and so on, often have encountered and overcome physical abuse from their partners.

Left-over attitudes of woman as property of man still influence the relations between the sexes in Mexico. See Roselyn Costantino, "Women's Urban Movements and Democratic Change in Mexico: No se hagan bolas," paper presented at Arizona State University, March 27, 1995.

25. When Astrid was interviewed in 1987 on national television, the camera crew, in order to censor the image of the Virgin of Guadalupe on her skirt, used special red lighting to block the image altogether.

26. See Francisco de la Maza. *El guadalupanismo mexicano* (Mexico City: Fondo de Cultura Económica, 1992 [1st ed. 1953]), 182–186.

27. Beltrán, 37.

28. Beltrán, 16.

29. See Diana Taylor, *Theater of Crisis: Drama and Politics in Latin America* (Lexington: The University Press of Kentucky, 1991).

30. Linda Hutcheon, *The Politics of Postmodernism* (New York: Routledge, 1989), 95.

31. See Carlos Monsiváis, *El amor perdido* (Mexico City: Ediciones Era, 1977).

32. Beltrán, 16.

33. Teresa de Lauretis. *Alice Doesn't: Feminism, Semiotics, and Cinema* (Bloomington: Indiana University Press. 1984), 138–139.

34. Laura Mulvey, *Visual and Other Pleasures* (Bloomington: Indiana University Press, 1989).

35. Mulvey, 11.

36. It is important to note that in performances in other venues with different spectators, the reception of her and her work is markedly different. For instance, in a tribute to Lucha Reyes, *Códigos secretos (Secret Codes),* presented at the Museo del Chopo in Mexico City (March 16, 1995), with an audience of mainly university students of limited means (they paid three pesos to get in), the response was overwhelming approval. From their reactions and comments, it was obvious that they understood the various levels of meaning encoded in all the languages of the stage and visual representation that Hadad incorporates.

37. Quoted in Pablo Duñas, *Las Divas en el teatro de revista mexicano* (Mexico City: Asociación Mexicana de Estudios Fonográficos, A.C., 1994), 9.

38. Carlos Monsiváis. *Escenas de pudor y liviandad* (Mexico City: Grijalbo, 1988). 27.

39. Monsiváis, 29.

Theater as Cultural Exchange: A Director's Perspective

Anita González-El Hilali

I am an advocate of theater in the Americas as cultural exchange, and I am a theater practitioner who is committed to finding cultural connections through Latin American performance. This essay is about empowering women theater artists who use their expertise to create performance works that speak to their own traditions, folklore, and politics. It is about my personal process as a director of multicultural performance works and my desire to see more theatrical events that promote the cultural exchange of performing artists and productions within the Americas.

More specifically, I want to focus on two projects that attempt to realize these goals; *Hymn to Demeter* and *Hola Oleada*. *Hymn to Demeter* premiered at the Tribeca Performing Arts Center/BMCC in New York City in 1993. *Hola Oleada* is scheduled to premiere at that same site in February 1996. In these productions, women artists from Mexico, Honduras, the United States, Puerto Rico, Trinidad, and Jamaica come together to recreate new stories of themselves through theater.

Hymn to Demeter is a retelling of the ancient Greek myth of the Divine Mother and child, using African-American and Mexican folklore. It is based on the Homeric poem "Hymn to Demeter" and incorporates regional songs and dances of the state of Veracruz. The production premiered in June 1993 and received funding from Fideicomiso, the Comisión México-Estados Unidos para el Intercambio Educativo y Cultural. It was developed and rehearsed in Xalapa, Mexico.

The second project, *Hola Oleada,* is a contemporary dance/theater work about immigrant Caribbean women "as they navigate the downs and ups of life in the shadow of the statue of liberty."[1] This work-in-progress uses Caribbean music and Garifuna funeral practices to show how women's maintenance of earth-based traditions in the urban United States helps to carry them through their daily struggles. Both productions focus upon women's issues of adaptation and change: the rite of passage from innocence to knowledge. Moreover, both projects use folklore to tell their stories.

As a director, I am interested in using women's traditional songs and dances in order to address contemporary concerns of both performers and audience. To do this requires an exchange of not only folklore but also history. There are many examples of the use of folkloric song and dance for nationalistic display and spectacle: the Ballet Folklórico of Mexico, Peni Negro, The Cuban Folkloric Ballet, and Tlenhuicani. Even within theatrical programs, traditional expressions are used for entertainment, ethnic color, and voyeuristic display. Shows such as *Once On This Island*, a Broadway musical extravaganza with a Caribbean theme, use folklore for ambience, that is, to create an idyllic, exotic tropical locale, and not to examine the real needs and societal beliefs behind cultural manifestations. In this musical, for example, a peasant woman rescues an aristocratic visitor who falls in love with her and then later leaves her to marry his pale-skinned fiancée. Although *Once on this Island* was based upon a folktale, the show portrayed the "black natives as happy, rhythmic, superstitious and simple."[2] This portrayal perhaps responds to playwrights' and audiences' fascination with racial difference. As Jim Moy suggests, "This fascination, though sometimes benign, has depended upon the process of fetishization."[3]

So where do we begin to construct new images of ourselves that resist fetishization while they speak to our everyday lives as we know them? Women such as Katherine Dunham in dance and Zora Neale Hurston in literature have used anthropological research as a tool for the development of artistic work that expresses women's perspectives. This can be done in the theater, too, as Ellen Donkin and Susan Clement suggest:

Because theater doesn't stop with the printed page, because plays are only a blueprint for production, the director moves into a position of enormous responsibility. How the production reads to an audience is her artistic and political responsibility. It is not possible to overemphasize the importance of her position. In the process of directing a play, she can completely upend the text, encourage her actors to develop subtexts the playwright never dreamed of, enlist her designers in the creation of a destabilizing visual counterpoint, or cast performers whose very presence throws the text into question.[4]

Within this context, *Hymn to Demeter* and *Hola Oleada* are experiments toward a new approach to women's folkloric theater. My objective was to use traditional cultural performance expressions to address contemporary issues, to incorporate "folkloric" songs and dances into theatrical works that would depict ethnic/cultural identity as an evolutionary, syncretic process. I wanted to feature performers who were well versed in their own cultural heritages and could place their folkloric expressions in dialogue with a modern/postmodem aesthetic.

Paul Gilroy, in his book *The Black Atlantic*, proposes a revised concept of ethnicity that embraces "the inescapability and legitimate value of mutation, hybridity, and intermixture en route to better theories of racism and of black political culture."[5] Gilroy's assertion is instrumental in rethinking the ways in which we construct identity categories. Tradition and modernity should not be set against each other as binaries: rather, modern performance works should strive to incorporate the multiplicity of identity categories through which we all function. If "authentic" cultural purity is a myth imposed upon disempowered people, and cultures are continuously metamorphisizing, then the reuse of traditions is a natural and necessary consequence of living and working in a culturally diverse world.

Afro-Latino performances feature selected cultural practices, such as capoeira, mambo, santería, and samba. Capoeira is an Afro-Brazilian martial art form characterized by circular kicking movements. Capoeira has been popularized in films such as *Only the Strong* [6] as a violent form of gang warfare and incorporated into contemporary modern dance company vocabulary as an ethnic novelty. Capoeira, however, originated with black Angolan slaves, who used the kicking movements to defend their maroon settlements.[7] Likewise, Brazilian samba dancing has been exploited for the showgirl connotations of the Rio de Janeiro carnival. The association of samba with fraternal solidarity organizations (cofradías) is largely ignored. Santería, a Yoruba-derived religion similar to Haitian voodun, has been selectively used on stage and in film to add an air of exotic mysticism to narratives or to ridicule the "superstitious" practices of Caribbean peoples.

These cultural manifestations are frequently decontextualized and reappropriated without acknowledgement of the traditions

(courtesy of Anita González-El-Hilali)

(courtesy of Anita González-El-Hilali)

and histories that have produced them. In many cases, isolated cultural elements become identifying markers to highlight the "otherness" of black culture. Afro-Latino performance expressions are thus constructed to exist outside of contemporary European-based performance practice. Artistic collaborations, where Caribbean artists are allowed to participate in the construction of their own images, are not often attempted on conventional stages. The *Hymn to Demeter* and *Hola Oleada* projects intend to open the door for this kind of dialogue through theater.

The *Hymn to Demeter* project began with the idea of identifying female archetypes and their transcultural translation. The classical Greek story tells how Demeter, the goddess of grain, earth, and fertility, lost her daughter Persephone to Hades, the lord of the underworld, who had stolen Persephone to be his wife in the land of the dead. Demeter searches the Earth for her daughter and, not finding her, causes all living plants to wither and die while she mourns. When she eventually finds her daughter, the child has eaten the food of the dead (six pomegranate seeds) and so can return to the land of the living for only six months of the year—thus the seasons were born.

The Homeric version of the myth attracted my collaborator, Kimberly Bush, and me, because it included minor female goddess figures and made reference to the Eleusinian mysteries. The story resonated for us as a tale of sexual awakening as well as death and regeneration.[8]

In May 1993, eight artists united in Xalapa to begin rehearsals. The Mexican performers came from the Ballet Folklórico de la Universidad Veracruzana and the Organización Teatral Universitaria de Veracruz (ORTEUV).[9] The American group was composed of four independent artists, including myself.[10] The script was a reductive version of the hymn, retaining the characters of Hecate, Helius, Hades, Demeter, Persephone, and Baubo. Each of these characters was archetypal: Moon, Sun, Death, Mother Earth, Virgin, and Courtesan. In the first meetings with the artists, cultural parallels were sought. What was a Mexican fertility symbol? (Corn.) An African mystery? (The oracle.) A Xalapan serenade? (The harp.)

The project collaborators intended to use signs characteristic of African-American and Totonac-Mexican culture in the theatrical restaging of the myth. Each scene was associated with a specific cultural phenomenon: Baubo with sexuality and the Congolese use of the hips; Demeter's mourning scene with the La Llorona myth of the woman who travels the world, lamenting the loss of her children; Hecate with the night oracle and the African seer who can look into the future.

In the mourning scene, for example, Demeter collapses after realizing that her daughter has been snatched by Hades. Baubo, the goddess of bawdy sexuality, decides to cheer her up with a sensuous phallic dance. Baubo writhes and undulates her hips as she slithers across the floor, causing Demeter to gasp and then laugh at her own repressed fecundity. Spurred on by the moon goddess, Demeter joins Baubo in a dance that celebrates women's active power over life and death. To the music of an African two-headed drum, the performers sing:

We are the singers, we sing for sustenance. We are the universal dancers, we are the great necromancers. Singing and dancing between life and death. Romancing the eater of breath O yayaO ye.[11]

Demeter becomes empowered through her interaction with the community of women and moves to the land of the dead to recover her daughter. The performers played with these universal images to tell a new story. What if the virgin (Persephone) was no longer a victim, but a willing adolescent waiting to express her budding sexuality? What if the mother's (Demeter's) fear was not of losing her daughter, but of releasing the fertility locked in every woman? The rehearsal process became an exploration of the power, sensuality, and joy that is embodied in women across all cultures.

The performers created a bilingual text and amplified this text with dances and gestures. Song became the unifying element that tied the cultures together. The cast composed and sang fifteen songs, based upon Jarocho, Caribbean, African, Son, and Fandango music. Language barriers within the rehearsal process were easily overcome. Those who could translate did so, and monolingual performers communicated with the hands, the body, and emotional gestures. Visual imagery enhanced the production. Visual designer Kimberly Bush spent two weeks painting large, colorful backdrops that unfurled to establish character and locale. When the production premiered in June 1993,

Eva Yaa Asantewaa of the *Village Voice* described the production as:

A vest-pocket carnival. This folkloric version of the Demeter/Persephone myth, saturated with Third World culture, features playful costumes and charming Mexican folk dancing. The work may feel casually constructed, but it soon becomes intoxicating, thanks largely to the music—a delicate, sensitive encounter of Mexicana, Africana, and sultry blues.[12]

Hola Oleada presented very different challenges. This theatrical project is being developed in the United States, with immigrant Caribbean women from different countries inventing a story about themselves. The performers work around a common concept and incorporate stories, songs, and customs from their specific cultures. The project theme is the struggle to assimilate or not—what to bring in the suitcase and what to leave behind. Here the cultural exchange takes place on a more local level; New York artists talk about society's use, misuse, and abuse of them. How do they cope with their illegal/legal status? How do they relate to other minority groups? How do they relate to other Latino groups? How can all of these feelings be expressed theatrically?

The title, *Hola Oleada,* refers to the new wave of immigrants in the urban United States. In a society based upon the myth of the melting pot, the latest arrival always gets the shaft. The presumed process of cultural assimilation may or may not occur: thus "four generations of Central American-Caribbean wimmin as they navigate the downs and ups of life in the shadow of the statue of liberty."[13]

Traditions and folklore exist in the world of *Hola Oleada.* How these beliefs are transformed and maintained becomes summarily important. Don't many of us have altars and recipes on scraps of paper to remind us of where we came from or where we might be going? Aren't there communities that Latinas find or establish when we go to the store, buy oranges on the street, or send an envio back home? The world of immigrant women, and, more important, the social perspective of these women is what is explored in this production.

One of the most effective scenes in early stagings of *Hola Oleada* was the symbolic burial of Rosa, the Trinidadian office worker. In this scene, women in an urban apartment setting remember

(courtesy of Anita González-El-Hilali)

(courtesy of Anita González-El-Hilali)

Rosa's life while singing about Caribbean food. The community of women wash the body of the deceased, cover it with a sheet, and begin to sing a Garifuna women's song of lament. The body is walked to an empty lot, where the punta, a hypnotic dance that emphasizes the hips, is performed. The punta is a fertility ritual dance associated with the Black Carib people of Honduras, Nicaragua, and Belize. Garifuna consultant Mimi Arriola Pérez assisted with the mounting of the celebratory death scene. The women finish the dance by placing a remembrance next to the body. Alternative Afro-Latino cultural aesthetics are incorporated into an urban scene of mourning.

A preliminary rehearsal period led to the mounting of three scenes. At the first meeting, ten women who had never met before remembered the details of their acculturation process. They started to talk about how they felt as immigrants in New York, what they remembered from back home, and how being from "there" affected the way that they lived their lives "here." What were their experiences in coping with children, language, identity, and race in a foreign environment? Did any of this affect their careers as dancers/actors? What would they say to a new immigrant from their own country about coping with life in the United States? Would they go back?

Everyone responded at once with a story, an expression of anger, or an assertion of identity:

My daughter said that she was American, but that I was
from someplace else.
They always typecast me according to how they think a Puerto Rican
woman should act.
I don't really speak Spanish, but I wish that I did.

As the director, I began to wrestle with how to shape these conflicting feelings into a cohesive whole.

Hola Oleada is still in development with a scheduled premiere in 1996. Cuban-American playwright Dolores Prida is now writing the script for the project. The performers and collaborators came together in January, 1995 to continue the process of molding the cultural exchanges into a cohesive musical theater production. Photos which accompany this article are from a preliminary version of the work that was mounted in June 1994.

In speaking of my directorial approach, it is important to mention that I am an African-American of Cuban descent, born and raised in the United States. My participation in the theater has always been as an outsider; my theatrical career has been about working in the nooks and crannies outside of the mainstream. Thus I feel a solidarity and cultural cohesion when working with Latinas on cultural projects that address issues of power and marginality.

At the same time, I am playing the middle woman. African-American theater groups have a long history in the United States and have made big strides in developing audiences and sponsorship for black productions. African-American women are still marginalized, but are beginning to publish and produce. Some female-run companies, such as the National Black Theater (Barbara Ann Teer), La MaMa E.T.C. (Ellen Stewart), and Jomandi Productions (Martha Jackson), have long production histories. Can the same be said of Latin American theater companies and Latina producers in the United States? I work with cultural exchange on this level as well: not only promoting but advocating for a stronger presence of Latin American and Latina women in the theater. My work stretches outside of the black theater circuit to try to embrace as many Latinas as possible; after all, there is a commonality of experience, and, in many cases, we are one and the same.

There is resistance within African-American theater institutions to the inclusion of Latinas in a field as competitive as theater, as there is a reluctance in Latin American and Latino theater institutions to embrace African aspects of Latino culture. The economics of survival in the United States have led to the fragmentation of what could be a unified community effort. Clearly, language differences can divide, but in urban environments, Latinas and African-American women live, work, and shop side by side. Although cultural mixing has always been acknowledged as a reality of life in the Americas, discussion has only just begun about the tensions and the commonalities that exist among African, Indian, and Mestizo American populations.

Hola Oleada is being commissioned by the Tribeca Performing Arts Center of New York in collaboration with the Nexus Arts Center of Atlanta. This project has sparked certain management and sponsorship concerns, which are indicative of the issues at stake in productions involving transcultural exchanges. For ex-

ample, administrators have been having trouble finding coop-
erative Latino institutions with a large enough fiscal base to co-
commission or coproduce this project. Questions are being raised
about the difference between Latino culture and African diaspora
culture. Incredibly, many North Americans are unaware of an
African presence in Latin America. The African-American
struggle often is equated with the civil rights movement and dis-
associated from a larger struggle for the political rights of people
of color throughout the Americas. In the United States, there
have been efforts, such as Jesse Jackson's Rainbow Coalition, to
promote unified political struggles across ethnic boundaries, but
artistic ventures involving cultural connections are less frequently
explored. Should the syncretic nature of Latin American performance be addressed by arts institutions? Does this
problematize the jobs of already overburdened arts administrators, who might find it easier to sell to clearly defined market
groups than to campaign for a product that acknowledges the
syncretic nature of performance in the Americas?

Needless to say, cultural exchange projects are expensive to
mount and produce. U.S. theater depends upon corporate or
government sponsorship for artistic projects, and funding institutions tend to have local, rather than global, interests. If a
project is multinational in scope, sponsorship becomes even more
complicated because of international airfares, immigration and
visa regulations, and translation costs.

Even a local project such as *Hola Oleada,* which integrates diverse communities, can become administratively challenging due
to political divisions within arts communities. Although partnerships are becoming more common, institutions have generally operated as isolated entities who work with their own spe-
cialized target groups. Latino theaters may work with a clientele
that is not likely to interact with experimental theater groups,
feminist theater venues, or African-American performance
spaces.

There are also aesthetic considerations. Experimental venues
may perceive folklore as something outside of postmodern aesthetics; feminist venues may reject what might be seen as an
"essentialism" integral to some African-American and Latin
American religious and gender beliefs. As with most activist efforts, fragmentation rather than cooperation is the tendency.

Ultimately, a cultural exchange project may be much more difficult to produce and market than a local performance project that expresses a unified cultural worldview and reaches a predetermined target group. I would like to see an international network of theatrical institutions collaborating with Latina producers, directors, and performers. Also, we need spaces where individual artists can go to teach, give workshops, and mount productions; and we need places where production companies can find supportive audiences and forums for the testing of innovative scripts and other cultural perspectives. These places may not yet exist; but if just a few institutions are willing to work this way and are able to devote the time and energy necessary to develop this type of work, then I will be taking a step toward reaching my goal.

Author's Note

This paper was presented at the conference "Un escenario propio," University of Cincinnati, October 1994.

Notes

1. Title and subtitle were written by Hattie Gossett in 1994.
2. William A. Henry III, "Back to Giddy Simplicity" *Time* 136, November 12, 1990: 88.
3. James S. Moy, *Marginal Sights: Staging the Chinese in America* (Iowa City: University of Iowa Press, 1993).
4. *Upstaging Big Daddy: Directing Theater as if Gender and Race Matter,* ed. Ellen Donkin and Susan Clement (Ann Arbor: University of Michigan Press, 1993).
5. Paul Gilroy, *The Black Atlantic: Modernity and Double Consciousness* (Cambridge: Harvard University Press, 1993).
6. *Only the Strong.* A film by Sheldon Lettich, 1993. Twentieth Century Fox in association with Freestone Pictures and Davis Films.
7. Almeida, Bira, *Capoeira: A Brazilian Art Form—History, Philosophy, and Practice* (Berkeley: North Atlantic Books, 1986).
8. For more information on female iconography in the Homeric hymn see *The Homeric 'Hymn to Demeter': Translation, Commentary and Interpretive Essays* edited by Helen P. Foley, (Princeton: Princeton University Press, 1994).
9. Sr. Miguel Velez is the Director of the "Balet Folclórico de la

Universidad Veracruzana." Sr. Manuel Montoro directs the "Organizacion Teatral de la Universidad Veracruzana."

10. Tiye Giraud, Yekk Music, and Kimberly Bush.

11. Music and lyrics by Tiye Giraud, 1992.

12. Asantewaa, Eva Yaa, "Hot as Hades," *Village Voice.* August 3, 1993: 93.

13. Hattie Gossett, 1994.

Contributors

Elia Arce is a performance artist, writer, director, and filmmaker. She was raised in Costa Rica and has been living in the United States since 1984. She studied film at New York University and graduated from the School of Film and Television at the University of California, Los Angeles. She worked with the Bread and Puppet Theater and codirected and performed with the Los Angeles Poverty Department (LAPD) during the group's first five years. She has performed at Highways, the Institute of Contemporary Art in London, and the X-Teresa Arte Alternativo in Mexico City. She has been an artist-in-residence at the Banff Center for the Performing Arts and the recipient of a J. Paul Getty Foundation Individual Artist Fellowship (1993), and a Rockefeller Multi-Arts Production Grant (1994), which facilitated the production and touring of *Stretching My Skin Until It Rips Whole*. She was coproducer of *Clima Natal: Traces and Voices from Central America*, a traveling exhibition of three contemporary Costa Rican painters, which opened at the Carpenter Center at Harvard University and then traveled throughout California.

Alicia Arrizón was born and raised in the borderlands of Arizona and Sonora, Mexico. During her undergraduate years, she was a member of Teatro Ensemble de Arizona. In 1984, she was one of the founders of Belicias S.A., a multicultural theater company that continues its residence at Arizona State University. In graduate school, at Stanford University, she was one of the founders of Teatro Xicana/o, a student theater company. Currently she is Associate Professor at the University of California, Riverside. Her areas of teaching are literary and cultural studies. Her academic work deals with the intersections of feminism, theater, performance, and Latina identity. Her book, *Latina Performance: Traversing the Stage* is forthcoming with Indiana University Press.

Roselyn Constantino has been an Assistant Professor of Spanish at Pennsylvania State University, Altoona since 1992, when she received her Ph.D. from Arizona State University. Most of her research is dedicated to Mexico: Mexican women and women writers, women in/on the Mexican stage, feminism in the theater and performance of Mexican women writers, and popular culture and literary criticism in Mexico. She is presently on a Helena Rubenstein Faculty Fellowship, completing her manuscript on contemporary Mexican women and women's theater and performance. Her most recently published articles have appeared in *Literal, Hispania,* and *Latin American Theater Review* among others.

Migdalia Cruz is a published playwright who was born and raised in the Bronx and now lives in New Canaan, Connecticut. Her work has been produced in London, Montreal, New York, Chicago, and other cities in the United States. She has written more than twenty plays, musicals, and operas. She has received commissions from several theaters and institutions, including Playwrights Horizons, INTAR, the Cornerstone Theatre, the American Music Theatre Festival, the Ballet Hispanico, Arena Stage, and, currently, the Latino Chicago Theatre Company. Her plays have been produced by these institutions and also by the Houston Grand Opera, En-Garde Arts, Teatro Misión, NYSF's Festival Latino, Intersections for the Arts/LATA, DUO, Theatre X, and others. Cruz is the recipient of National Endowment for the Arts and McKnight fellowships, and a Connecticut Commission for the Arts grant, and was a 1991 finalist for the Susan Smith Blackburn Prize. She was nurtured by Fornes's playwriting workshop at INTAR. She is a member of New Dramatists, the New York Playwrights' lab, and is a PEW/TCG national artist-in-residence at the Classic Stage Company. Cruz is an artistic associate of the Latino Chicago Theatre Company, which in 1995 produced a full season of her work.

Dyan Garza has exhibited her art since 1980 using watercolor, oil, pen, ink and pencil, focusing on sensual shapes. This figurative subject matter has been created in murals and set designs for one-woman theatrical shows. She is currently merging her poetry with illustrations and creating children's books that speak to the heart. In creating the book cover, "Latinas on Stage" (17 x 24, watercolor, gauche and pencil), Garza represents some of the performance artists from this book, choosing brilliant colors and a sensual line to bring them all together on stage.

Laura Esparza is a theater director, writer, administrator, and performance artist whose work reflects her interests in Latino and women's theater. She is one of only two directors to hold an M.F.A. in directing and Latino theater from the University of California, San Diego. As founding director of Teatro Misión at the Mission Cultural Center in San Francisco, she forged the first Latino theater center in the United States, with year-round main-stage and children's performances by Bay Area Latino theaters. In 1995, she toured the United States as one of four directors chosen nationwide to receive the prestigious Theatre Communications Group/National Endowment for the Arts Directors' Fellowship, working with productions by Peter Sellars, Anne Bogart, Ralph Lee, and Theatre de la Jeune Lune. Following the fellowship, she joined the Group Theater in Seattle as Associate Artistic Director/Education Director. She has been the Artistic Director of Sister Stage Theatre in Bellingham, Washington, and the coordinator for the Multicultural Theatre Festival at The Group Theatre. Recent directing credits include *When el Cucui Walks,* by Roy Conboy, at the Guadalupe Cultural Center in San Antonio; *Miriam's Flowers,* by Migdalia Cruz at Intersection for the Arts in San Francisco; Lorca's *Yerma* at the UCSD/La Jolla Playhouse; and *Harvest Moon* and *Roosters* at The Group Theatre. She is presently writing two performance pieces on La China Poblana and sexual harassment among Chicanos.

Yolanda Flores is a native of Bakersfield, California. She earned her undergraduate degree, with majors in history and Spanish, at the University of California, Berkeley; her M.A. from the University of Chicago; and her Ph.D. from Cornell University. Her dissertation, "The Drama of Gender: Feminist Theatre by Women of the Americas," is an interdisciplinary comparative study of contemporary Latina playwrights from Brazil, Argentina, Mexico, and United States Latinas. Since her undergraduate experience, Flores has consistently built alliances with other women of color. She is the Northeast representative of Mujeres Activas en Letras y Cambio Social.

Anita González-El Hilali is a Ph.D. candidate at the University of Wisconsin-Madison and a scholar in residence at Beloit College. Her works, directing and choreographic, have been presented in theaters and performance spaces in the United States, Mexico, and Central America. Her work *Totem* was recently featured in the Rebekah Films documentary *Conjure Women* (1995), sponsored by the Corporation for Public Broadcasting. A 1992 production, *Sueño nuevo,* was created and directed for Teatro la Fragua of Honduras and continues to tour throughout Central America. In 1993, González-El Hilali choreographed a lecture demonstration about Latin American dance for Ballet Hispánico of New York. *Hola Oleada* is her newest theatrical work and premiered in February 1996. She has received numerous academic and professional grants, including two Senior Scholar Fulbright Awards, one in 1987 to research dance, film, and video in Mexico, and one in 1992 to teach directing and acting at the University of Honduras. González-El Hilali continues to direct and choreograph under the name Bandana Women and to write about Latin American and African-American performance traditions.

Michelle Habell-Pallan is an Assistant Professor of American Ethnic Studies at the University of Washington in Seattle. She was an active member of the Women of Color in Conflict and Collaboration Research Cluster at the University of California, Santa Cruz. Recently she was awarded the University of California Presidents Postdoctoral Fellowship (1997–1998) and is completing her manuscript on chicana/o and Latina/o performance culture.

Ellie Hernández is a writer and doctoral student in English literature at the University of California, Berkeley. Her work centers around theoretical and cultural issues in literary forms and community interests and gay/lesbian theory. Currently, she is examining the relationship between U.S. minorities and postcolonial issues in the United States. She is a former actress, who studied theater at Texas A & I University; she toured Mexico with the Bilingual Theater Company during the early 1980s.

Tiffany Ana López is Assistant Professor of English at the University of California, Riverside. She did her graduate work at the University of California at Santa Barbara in the departments of English and Women's Studies; also she was an affiliate of the

Chicana/o Studies Department. She edited *Growing Up Chicana/o* (William Morrow & Co., 1993). She was a U.S. Latina Dissertation Fellow at Dartmouth College in 1994, where she completed her dissertation: "Comunidad y más: Representations of the Body as Cultural Critique in U.S. Latina Drama."

Michelle Macau is a freelance theater director, teacher, and administrator. As a director and teacher, she has worked at Carnegie-Mellon University, the La Salle School of Drama in Singapore, the Los Angeles Theater Center, and the University of California, Riverside. At the New York Shakespeare Festival, she administered the Shakespeare on Broadway Project, under the direction of Estelle Parsons. She has worked on original plays by writers Lynne Alvarez, Ariel Dorfman, Bruce Graham, Lisa Loomer, Carlos Morton, Susan Rubin, Steve Swartz, and JoanneT. Waters.

Lillian Manzor is Associate Professor of Spanish and Comparative Literature at the University of Miami. She has published widely on Latina/o and Caribbean cultural studies in journals such as *Gestos, The Drama Review, La Ma Teodora* and *Ollantay Theater Magazine.* She is completing a book manuscript on U.S. Cuban culture entitled *Marginality Beyond Return: Gender, Racial and Linguistic Politics in U.S. Cuban Performances.*

Maria Teresa Marrero is a Cubana raised in California. She holds a Ph.D. from the University of California, Irvine. Currently, she is an Assistant Professor at the University of North Texas. Besides critical essays published in *Negotiating Performance: Gender, Sexuality, and Theatricality in Latin/o America* (Duke University Press, 1994), *Ollantay: Theater Magazine, Gestos,* and *LATR,* she has also published narrative fiction in *The Michigan Quarterly Review* and *Linden Lane Magazine.*

Cherríe Moraga is the coeditor of the landmark collection, *This Bridge Called My Back,* and the author of *The Last Generation* and *Loving in the War Years.* She is a playwright whose work has been nationally produced.

Monica Palacios is a Chicana lesbian writer/performer who has three one-woman shows; *Latin Lezbo Comic; Confessions: A Sexplosion of Tentalizing Tales;* and *Greetings from a Queer Señorita.* She was awarded a fellowship from the Latino Theatre Initiative at the Mark Taper Forum in Los Angeles to develop her play, *Clock.* She has taught writing and performing classes at UCLA; Pomona College; The University of Texas, San Antonio; University of Massachusetts, Amherst; and UC Berkeley. Her performances and publications continue to be studied in college curriculums throughout the country. Palacios is featured in many anthologies such as *Living Chicana Theory; A Funny Time To Be Gay; Latina: Women's Voices from the Borderlands; Chicana Lesbians: The Girls Our Mothers Warned Us About.* She has been producing art shows and poetry readings such as the highly acclaimed *Chicks and Salsa* with VIVA (a Lesbian and Gay Latino Artists Organization), and is one of VIVA's Board of Directors. Currently, she is teaching playwriting at Los Angeles High School District through the Audrey Skirball Kenis Theatre Projects.

Liz Ramírez, Ph.D, has taught at the University of Texas at Austin, the University of Arizona, and Harvard University. Ramírez has published a book, *Footlights Across the Border: A History of Spanish Language Professional Theatre* (1990), and numerous articles and reviews on Chicana/ Chicano/ Latina/ Latino theater. Founder of the Chicano Program at California State University, Sacramento, Ramírez is currently an Assistant Professor and graduate coordinator in the Theatre Arts Department and Director of Ethnic Studies at the University of Oregon. She also works professionally as a dramaturg and is Vice President of the Literary Managers and Dramaturgs Associations.

Alberto Sandoval Sánchez is Associate Professor of Spanish at Mount Holyoke College. He received his Ph.D. in 1983 from the University of Minnesota. He is both a creative writer and a cultural critic. His bilingual book of poetry, *New York Backstage/ Nueva York Tras Bastidores,* was published in Chile. In 1993, Mount Holyoke College produced his theatrical piece *Side Effects,* based on his personal experiences with AIDS. He has just edited a special issue on U.S. Latino theater and AIDS for *Ollantay: Theater Magazine.* He has published numerous articles on U.S. Latino theater, Latin American colonial theater and identity, Spanish baroque theater, Puerto Rican migration, and images of Latinos in film. He is currently working on two books: *José, Can You See?: Essays on Theatrical and Cultural Representations of Latinos* and *Stages of Life: Latinas in Teatro* (in collaboration with Nancy Saporta Sternbach from Smith College).

Caridad Svich is a playwright of Cuban, Croatian, Argentine, and Spanish descent. She was born in Philadelphia and now lives in Los Angeles. Svich holds an M.F.A. in theater playwriting from the University of California, San Diego. She is listed in *Who's Who among Hispanic Americans,* and is a member of the Dramatist Guild, the Women's Project of New York, and PEN Center USA. Her credits include her play *Alchemy of Desire/Dead-Man's Blues* (winner of the 1994 Rosenthal New Play Prize) at the Cincinnati Playhouse in the Park and as part of the New Plays by American Writers Reading Festival at the Royal Court Theatre in London. Other productions: *but there are fires* at The Women's Project of New York, and *Any Place But Here,* circulated byTCG's Plays-in-Progress, and produced at INTAR and Latino Chicago Theatre. Her play *Gleaning/ Rebusca* is featured in a collection of Hispanic women's plays entitled *Shattering the Myth* (Houston: Arte Público Press, 1992). Svich is the recipient of a California Arts Council Fellowship in Playwriting, and has held a residency in dramaturgy at the La Jolla Playhouse. She was also playwright-in-residency at INTAR Hispanic American Art Center in New York for four years (where she trained with Maria Irene Fornes), and has completed TCG -supported residencies at the Goodman Theater and the Steppenwoff Theater in Chicago. Her work has also been developed at South Coast Repertory's Hispanic Playwrights Project, the Playwrights' Center in Minneapolis, and The Audrey Skirball-Kenis Theater in Los Angeles, among others.

Carmelita Tropicana, baptized in the name of one of the U.S. most popular brands of orange juice and of Havana's legendary night club, is a Cuban American writer/performance artist who has been performing since 1984 and has presented her work nationally and internationally. Tropicana has written plays with Uzi Parnes and Ela Troyano, and coauthored with Troyano the screenplay for award-winning film *Carmelita Tropicana: Your Kunst*

Is Your Waffen (1993). The New York Foundation for the Arts awarded her two fellowships, one for screenwriting/ playwriting (1991) and one for performance art (1987). Currently she is working on a play about Sor Juana Inés de la Cruz.

Antonia Villaseñor is a native of Los Angeles. She is a Ph.D. candidate in history at the Claremont Graduate School in Southern California. In addition to her academic pursuits, Villaseñor is a photographer, documenting queer activists of color. She is a member of the board of directors of VIVA, a Latino/a, Los Angeles-based gay and lesbian arts organization.

Marguerite R. Waller chairs the Women's Studies Department and teaches in the English Department and the Film and Visual culture Program at the University of California, Riverside. She has been a member of Las Comadres, a collective group of women's art-making. Her current interests include new feminisms evolving in militarized situations (including the U.S. Mexico border), constructions of space and time in non-Hollywood films, and shooting and editing her own videos. She has published extensively on Italian cinema and Renaissance European literature.